THE BEGINNINGS OF ISLAMIC LAW

The Beginnings of Islamic Law is a major and innovative contribution to our understanding of the historical unfolding of Islamic law. Scrutinizing its historical contexts, the book proposes that Islamic law is a continuous intermingling of innovation and tradition. Salaymeh challenges the embedded assumptions in conventional Islamic legal historiography by developing a critical approach to the study of both Islamic and Jewish legal history. Through case studies of the treatment of war prisoners, circumcision, and wife-initiated divorce, she examines how Muslim jurists incorporated and transformed "Near Eastern" legal traditions. She also demonstrates how socio-political and historical situations shaped the everyday practice of law, legal education, and the organization of the legal profession in the late antique and medieval eras. The book highlights the unending process of legal change that is inherent to all legal traditions. Aimed at scholars and students interested in Islamic history, Islamic law, and the relationship between Jewish and Islamic legal traditions, this book's interdisciplinary approach provides accessible explanations and translations of complex materials and ideas.

LENA SALAYMEH is Associate Professor (Senior Lecturer) of Law at Tel Aviv University. A prolific author and frequent public speaker, she is currently writing on the secularization of Islamic law and the role of materiality in Islamic legal history.

THE BEGINNINGS OF ISLAMIC LAW

Late Antique Islamicate Legal Traditions

LENA SALAYMEH

CAMBRIDGE
UNIVERSITY PRESS

CAMBRIDGE
UNIVERSITY PRESS

University Printing House, Cambridge CB2 8BS, United Kingdom

One Liberty Plaza, 20th Floor, New York, NY 10006, USA

477 Williamstown Road, Port Melbourne, VIC 3207, Australia

314-321, 3rd Floor, Plot 3, Splendor Forum, Jasola District Centre, New Delhi-110025, India

79 Anson Road, #06-04/06, Singapore 079906

Cambridge University Press is part of the University of Cambridge.

It furthers the University's mission by disseminating knowledge in the pursuit of education, learning and research at the highest international levels of excellence.

www.cambridge.org
Information on this title: www.cambridge.org/9781107589711

First published 2016
First paperback edition 2018

A catalogue record for this publication is available from the British Library

Library of Congress Cataloging in Publication data
Names: Salaymeh, Lena, author.
Title: The beginnings of Islamic law : late antique Islamicate legal traditions / Lena Salaymeh.
Description: Cambridge [UK] : Cambridge University Press, 2016. |
Includes bibliographical references and index.
Identifiers: LCCN 2016026401 | ISBN 9781107133020 (hardback : alk. paper)
Subjects: LCSH: Islamic law — History. | International law (Islamic law) — History.
Classification: LCC KBP55 .S25 2016 | DDC 340.5/9—dc23
LC record available at https://lccn.loc.gov/2016026401

ISBN 978-1-107-13302-0 Hardback
ISBN 978-1-107-58971-1 Paperback

for amjad,
whose absence is painfully ever-present
and whose ephemeral presence was my supreme
lesson in the essence of being

Contents

Acknowledgments *page* xi
Note on the text xiii

Introduction: Genealogies of Islamic Law 1
Contours 2
Conventional Historiography's Limitations: Developmentalism and Essentialism 3
Countering Developmental and Essentialist Approaches 6
Beyond Contextualization 11
Synopsis 15
Remarks 18
Visualization 20

1 Legal-historical Beginnings – Outlining Late Antique Islamic Law 21
Metaphors for Historical Theory: Origins/Conception 21
Positivism and Linearity: Source-criticism 23
Documentary Sources for Late Antique Islamic Historiography 24
Narrative-historical Sources for Late Antique Islamic Historiography 28
Source-criticism's General Rules 30
Politics and Ideology: Textual Criticism and Subaltern Critique 35
Alternatives: Late Antique Beginnings and Historical Sources 39
Implications and Applications 41

2 Legal Historiography – a Case Study in International Law 43
Prisoners of War in Islamic History: The Prophetic Period 47
Late Antique Qur'ānic Exegesis 53
Late Antique Islamic Law (up to 800 CE) 58
Medieval Exegesis 61
Representative Medieval Jurists (*c.* 800–1400 CE) 67
Silent Authority and Precedents of Professional Jurists 68
Qur'ān and Precedents in "Professional" Islamic Legal Discourse 70
A Presumed Precedent: A Historical "Execution" of War Prisoners? 74
Slippage: The Complexity of Legal-historical Categorization 75
Another Possibility 80
Conclusion 82

3 Legal-historical Hybridity – Tracing Islam in its Islamicate Context 84
Metaphors for Historical Theory: Borrowing/Parentage 85
Aryan Birth Father 87
Semitic Birth Father 88
Aryan/Semitic "Origins" 89
Positivism and Linearity: Comparative Philology 90
Politics and Ideology: Authenticity, Ethnicity, and "Religion" 93
An Aryan/Secular Methodology 98
Alternatives: Hybrid Law in Islamicate Societies 100

4 Legal Custom – a Case Study in Ritual Law 105
Ritual Comparisons 106
Ritual Meaning 108
Ritual Genealogy: Late Antique Circumcision 108
Ancient and Arabian Circumcision 109
Near Eastern Circumcision: Biblical, Rabbinic, and Christian 110
Islamicizing Circumcision 114

Beyond Abraham: Ritualizing Customary Practice 120
Legalizing an Islamic Ritual 123
Ritual Precedent 124
Ritual Obligation or Recommendation? 126
Ritual Performance 128
Ritual Conversion 130
Ritual Implications 132
Gender of Ritual 133
A Ritual of "Conclusion" 134

5 Legal Historicizing: Moments in Macro-histories 136
Metaphors for Historical Theory: Maturity/Formative 137
Linearity: From Progress and Decline to Orthodoxy 139
Orthodox Stories 142
Politics and Ideology: Scholarly Orthopraxy 145
Alternatives: Contingent Historical Moments 146
Moments in Islamic Legal History 147
Moments in Islamicate Legal History 157
Implications and Applications 161

6 Legal Comparisons – a Case Study in Family Law 163
Defining Wife-initiated Divorce 164
A Judaic Chronology of Wife-initiated Divorce 165
Rabbinic (70–620 CE) 165
Geonic Era (620–1050 CE) 168
Era of the Rishonim (1050–1400 CE) 170
An Islamic Chronology of Wife-initiated Divorce 172
Legal Circles (610–800 CE) 172
Professionalization of Legal Schools (800–1000 CE) 175
Consolidation (1000–1200 CE) and Technochratization (1200–1400 CE) 178
Disenchanting the Orthodox Narratives 179
Reevaluating Causal Influence 181
Giving Voice to the Geonim 185
Which Context? 186

An Interwoven Narrative of Wife-initiated Divorce 188
Antiquity and Late Antiquity (up to 800 CE) 188
Medieval Era (800–1400 CE) 191
Speculating on the Interwoven Narrative 194
Conclusion 196

Conclusion 197
Legal Orthodoxy and Islamic Jurisprudence 200
Legal Historiography and Sources 202
Legal Culture and Islamicate Society 203
Legal Moments and Periodization 204
Structure 205
Subtexts 206
Further Directions 206

Works Cited 208
Index 235

Acknowledgments

Ira Lapidus has been my mentor in the truest sense; he taught me how to be a historian of Islam, guided me through many professional obstacles, and offered consistently reliable advice. His encouragement and input were instrumental in the writing of this book, which he read with meticulous care several times. In addition to his generosity and kindness, I shall be forever grateful that he urged me to clarify my ideas and focus on accessibility in writing.

Rhiannon Graybill has been my writing partner and feminist ally for many years; her support and feedback on this book have been invaluable. I can only hope that our future collaborations will be as fruitful and rewarding as our past ones.

What modest involvement I have in Jewish studies, I owe to the many, many years of teaching, support, and encouragement from both Chava and Daniel Boyarin. In the cocoon they created for me, there was nothing at all controversial or problematic about thinking through and questioning the relationships between Jewish and Islamic legal traditions. I am deeply grateful for their nurturing.

I am very grateful to my mother and sister for keeping me connected to reality and for always finding ways to make me laugh. I thank my friends for their willingness to listen, their always helpful advice, and their support: Kfir Cohen, Heather Ferguson, Jonathan Freeman, Bluma Goldstein, Muʿtaz al-Khaṭīb, Sarah Levin, David Moshfegh, Amr Osman, Nima Rabiee, Zvi Septimus, and Esther and Yaacov Yadgar.

Much gratitude is owed to Laurent Mayali for providing me with the privilege of being the Robbins Postdoctoral Fellow. Learning about his path's obstacles helped me endure my struggles; his loyalty and support sustained me through difficult times. I thank Chris Tomlins for welcoming me into his community of legal historians, discussing legal historiography with me, and being an always reliable source of advice. I thank Maria Mavroudi for teaching in words and in example the importance of perseverance and endurance. I thank Wael Hallaq for exemplifying how to think differently about Islamic legal studies, as well as for being my teacher and supporter. I thank Mark Bevir for showing me how to be a critical historian and for answering all my questions over the years – even the ones I asked him in the gym. I thank David Powers for his meticulous reading of most of this book and his very helpful suggestions and comments; I sincerely appreciate his generosity. I am grateful for the gift of support and encouragement from many scholars, many of whom may not be aware of my appreciation: Khaled Abou El Fadl, Gil Anidjar, Hocine Benkheira, George Bisharat, Ritu Birla, Mark Cohen, Lahcen Daaïf, Chris Desan, Mohammad Fadel, Duncan Kennedy, Bruce Mann, Michelle McKinley, William Ian Miller, Jim Whitman, and David Wilkins.

Contradictions and conflicts became inevitable when I began this research path and no part of my journey has been uncomplicated. I thank my colleagues at Tel Aviv Law for creating an improbable, albeit convoluted, sanctuary for me: my move had meanings that I continue to battle and implications that battle me. Shai Lavi first imagined the possibility of shielding my scholarship from the academic politics of silencing and sabatoging; I am deeply grateful for his profound friendship and productive partnership. For their support and collegiality amidst injustice and oppression, I thank Gadi Algazi, Binyamin Blum, Julie Cooper, Khaled Furani, Ron Harris, Michael Karayanni, Assaf Likhovski, Esti Micenmacher, and Yossi Schwarz.

And, most of all, I thank Amjad for insisting that I promise him that I would never give up and would never let anyone stop me. Because they did try. I encountered many obstacles, but this book is here. And this is merely a beginning.

Note on the text

Chapter 2 is a revised version of a previously published article, Lena Salaymeh, "Early Islamic legal-historical precedents: prisoners of war," *Law and History Review* (2008): 521–44, © Cambridge University Press 2008, reproduced with permission. Parts of Chapters 3 and 4 appeared in modified form in "'Comparing' Jewish and Islamic legal traditions: between disciplinarity and critical historical jurisprudence," *Critical Analysis of Law, New Historical Jurisprudence* 2:1 (2015): 153–72. Chapter 5 includes revised passages reprinted, with permission from Elsevier, from "Islamic law" in *The International Encyclopedia of Social and Behavioral Sciences*, edited by James D. Wright, Oxford: Elsevier, 2015, 746–53. Chapter 6 is a revised version of another previously published article, "Every law tells a story: orthodox divorce in Jewish and Islamic legal histories," *UC Irvine Law Review* 4:1 (2014): 19–63. Every effort has been made to secure necessary permissions to reproduce copyright material in this work, though in some cases it has proved impossible to trace copyright holders. If any omissions are brought to our notice, we will be happy to include appropriate acknowledgments on reprint or in a subsequent edition.

Parts of this book began as a dissertation that was funded by a Javits Fellowship, as well as the Al-Falah Program and the Sultan Program at the Center for Middle Eastern Studies (UC Berkeley). The writing and revising of this book were supported by a Robbins Postdoctoral Fellowship (UC Berkeley School of Law).

Various parts of this book were presented at many conferences and as invited lectures at several universities; it was truly a privilege to have so many hosts, interlocutors, and audiences. Thank you for listening.

Introduction: Genealogies of Islamic Law

What does it mean to encounter Islamic law from the perspective of the society that began elaborating it? With the establishment of a Muslim community in late antique Arabia, Islamic law began as a simultaneously revolutionary and customary normative tradition.[1] The Prophet's preaching in Mecca disturbed the social, political, and economic order in which he had been raised. That very same preaching claimed historical and divine legitimacy by continuing customary practices. This interplay between innovation and tradition had lasting echoes in Islamic jurisprudence. Generations of Muslim legal actors, historians, and leaders who succeeded the Prophet interpreted scripture and precedents in ways that simultaneously renewed and perpetuated legal traditions. They created a dialect of Islamic law; this book is an exercise in listening to its discourses.

To hear Islamic law's beginnings, I fine-tuned my instruments. Immersing myself in the world of jurists, I absorbed Islamic law's operational logics. To comprehend Islamic law more fully as one dialect of the language of law, I explored other legal traditions and observed a common legal grammar. Through the lens of jurisprudence, I observed expressions of Islamic law that did not conform to scholarly depictions, to public perceptions, or to my own assumptions. The language of jurisprudence revealed law's rootedness in historically situated societies. Because law and history are intertwined, this book attends to them separately and in conjunction. To address the interchange between law and history, I have designed an alternating two-part structure in this book, with odd-numbered chapters focusing on historiography and even-numbered chapters focusing on historical jurisprudence.

[1] The temporal classification of late antiquity (as well as medieval) will be discussed below.

Contours

Defining law is an elusive endeavor. Yet, as challenging as it may be, it is necessary to begin with a definition because conventional Islamic legal historiography focuses on what makes Islamic law *Islamic*, rather than what makes it *law*. In this book, I define law as a system of interacting norms and practices.[2] Law encompasses both non-state law and institutionalized state law. (My use of the term "state" refers to a political system of governance and not a modern nation-state.[3]) Law, as Dirk Heirbaut has observed, "is not a fixed body of norms, but an interpretative praxis, in which a community constantly justifies its own legal decisions."[4] I differentiate between a legal tradition (roughly, jurisprudence and legal doctrines) and a legal system (a system of legal rules supported by an enforcement mechanism).[5] Written documents, official courts, professional judges, professional jurists, and states are not necessary for the operation of law. Correspondingly, individuals who functioned as judges or jurists will be identified as such, even if they were not specialized as judges or jurists.[6]

Since law exists wherever communities engage a legal-interpretive praxis, Islamic law began when a Muslim community began. Thus, I define "Islamic law" as the diverse legal traditions that have been and continue to be produced with the objective of being part of the Islamic movement.[7] As a result, the subject of this book is not only "Islamic law" but also Islamic societies, their institutions, and their social and legal

[2] On defining law broadly, see Brian Z. Tamanaha. "Understanding legal pluralism: past to present, local to global." *Sydney Law Review* 30:3 (2008): 375–511; William Twining, *General jurisprudence: understanding law from a global perspective*, Law in context (Cambridge: Cambridge University Press, 2009); William Twining, "Normative and legal pluralism: a global perspective." *Duke Journal of Comparative & International Law* 20:3 (2010): 473–518.

[3] I define "state" based on the work of Bevir and Rhodes, who describe "the state as a series of contingent and unstable cultural practices, which in turn consist of the political activity of specific human agents." Mark Bevir and R. A. W. Rhodes, *The state as cultural practice* (Oxford: Oxford University Press, 2010), 1.

[4] Dirk Heirbaut, "An unknown treasure for historians of early medieval Europe: the debate of German legal historians on the nature of medieval law." In *Zeitschrift des Max-Planck-Instituts für europäische Rechtsgeschichte*, ed. by Thomas Duve (Frankfurt am Main: Vittorio Klostermann GmbH, 2010), 89.

[5] On legal traditions, see H. Patrick Glenn, *Legal traditions of the world: sustainable diversity in law* (Oxford; New York: Oxford University Press, 2007), xxvii.

[6] I do not use problematic developmental terminology – such as "proto-judges" – to describe individuals or aspects of law prior to the institutionalization of Islamic legal schools. For instance, the Prophet's Companions were not only pious figures, but also teachers and practitioners of law.

[7] The Islamic movement should be understood broadly as group action in the name of Islam; this movement began when the Prophet began seeking followers.

practices. Similarly, I do not focus on "sources" of Islamic law (such as the Qurʾān), but rather on legal traditions. The term "Islamic law" can be misleading because in actuality Islamic law is generated by multiple groups and institutions (legal polycentricity) and non-Islamic legal traditions coexist with Islamic ones (legal pluralism).[8] (Notably, I prefer to use "Islamic," the adjectival form of Islam, although the demands of clarity and grace result in some use of the term as a noun.[9])

Conventional Historiography's Limitations: Developmentalism and Essentialism

To uncover Islamic legal history, we have to immerse ourselves in an Islamic legal past without assuming that that past inescapably leads to an Islamic legal present. Contemporary conceptualizations of Islamic legal history are often historically inaccurate because they do not fully appreciate that Islamic law could have been very different – it could have been something else entirely. The objective of this book is to sketch what that something else might have been. I apply a genealogical-historical approach in order to elucidate that historical processes comprise, as Mark Bevir describes, "a series of contingent even accidental appropriations, modifications, and transformations from the old to the new."[10] Because the past does not lead inevitably to the present, this book highlights the problematic implications of terms and concepts that are embedded in developmental – or determinist, or progressive, or unilinear – historiographies. I advocate adopting a non-developmental (such as radical historicist) approach to historiography in order to refine understandings of Islamic legal history.[11]

8 Reza Banakar. "Power, culture and method in comparative law." *International Journal of Law in Context* 5:1 (2009): 69–85 at 82 ("the diversity of sources and forms of law within the same social space (legal pluralism) or within the same legal system (legal polycentricity)."). On legal pluralism generally, see Sally Engle Merry. "Legal pluralism." *Law & Society Review* 22:5 (1988): 869–96.

9 I avoid ascribing agency to Islam because, as Robinson has exhorted, "let us abandon 'Islam' as a term of historical explanation." Chase F. Robinson, "Reconstructing early Islam: truth and consequences," in *Method and theory in the study of Islamic origins*, ed. by Herbert Berg (Leiden: Brill, 2003), 101–35 at 134.

10 Mark Bevir. "What is genealogy?" *Journal of the Philosophy of History* 2:3 (2008): 263–75 at 267.

11 Whereas dominant historicist approaches in Islamic studies are developmental in orientation, this book implements radical historicism as defined by Bevir: "when other people believe that certain social norms or ways of life are natural or inevitable, radical historicists denaturalize these norms and ways of life by suggesting that they arose out of contingent historical contests." *Ibid.*, 271. Radical historicism is inspired by Nietzsche and Foucault. See Friedrich Wilhelm Nietzsche, *The use and abuse of history* (New York: Liberal Arts Press, 1957); Michel Foucault, "Nietzsche, genealogy, history." In *The Foucault reader*, ed. and trans. by Paul Rabinow (New York: Pantheon, 1984) 76–100.

My critical approach is necessary because much conventional Islamic legal historiography imagines Islamic law as having an "origin" and as developing in a linear (or evolutionary) trajectory. (The scholarship briefly reviewed in this book is representative of the prevailing historiographic discourse in the field.[12] More recent scholarship indicates productive changes, but the "origins" paradigm critiqued here remains influential and dominant.) I outline these common developmental conceptions in the odd-numbered chapters, which focus on a set of scholarly terms and ideas that I identify as "origins"-terminology. "Origins" is both explicit and implicit in the rhetoric of Islamic legal studies. Marc Bloch critiqued the "obsession with origins" for having two problematic implications: denoting a total causal explanation and conveying (or concealing) value judgments.[13] Bloch's observation resonates in "origins"-oriented historiography of Islamic law. Developmental terms (such as "formative" and "classical") distort Islamic legal history in myriad ways. In this book, I will focus on how "origins"-related terminology in conventional Islamic legal historiography (in the West) frames three distinct issues: (1) when Islamic law began; (2) which pre-Islamic laws were integrated into Islamic law; and (3) when Islamic legal orthodoxy became dominant. This "origins"-terminology (and its developmental misunderstandings) is misleading because it implies that these three issues are equivalent to Islamic law's (1) conception, (2) parentage, and (3) maturation.[14] By highlighting the interconnections between "origins"-terminology and these anthropomorphic metaphors, I reveal how a developmental framework both organizes and constrains much Islamic legal historiography. Notably, a mere alteration of terminology (such as from "origins" to beginnings) would not be sufficient to ameliorate the underlying conceptual problems in conventional historiography: terms reflect methods and methods determine substantive knowledge.

Scholarly identifications of Islamic law's (metaphorical) date of birth, place of birth, parentage, or maturity also reflect a misunderstanding of "Islam." Conventional definitions of Islam (mis)identify it as having

[12] For an overview, see Knut S. Vikør, "The origins of the sharia." In *The Ashgate research companion to Islamic law*, ed. by Rudolph Peters and P. J. Bearman (Farnham: Ashgate, 2014), 13–26.

[13] Marc Bloch, *The historian's craft* (New York: Knopf, 1953), 29–31.

[14] These anthropomorphic metaphors are both explicit and implicit in conventional Islamic legal historiography. I engage these metaphors because they are not only inherent in language, but they also reveal meanings in ways that are not always easily perceptible. On how metaphors shape our conceptual understandings, see George Lakoff and Mark Johnson, *Metaphors we live by* (Chicago, IL: University of Chicago Press, 1980).

an essence; correspondingly, Islamic law is also perceived as having an essence.[15] These conventional definitions assume that in order for law to be Islamic, it must have specific attributes. Contrary to such essentialist presumptions, however, what makes law Islamic is that it is generated as part of the Islamic movement and not that it has particular attributes.[16] An important goal of this book is to de-essentialize Islamic law by presenting its contingency, its multivalence, and its legal-hermeneutic centrifuges. Each of the three case studies (in the even-numbered chapters) in this book exposes how a particular area of law is shaped by legal hermeneutics and by socio-political conditions in distinct ways. These chapters display multiple expressions of Islamic law and thereby challenge essentialist assumptions.

Essentialist thinking often mistakenly correlates Islamic law's essence with "orthodoxy." I use the term "orthodoxy" to delineate normative aspects of Islamic traditions that are reinforced through a network of power. More specifically, legal orthodoxy implies the existence of a hierarchical legal institution or group (not necessarily empowered by a state) that can label norms or practices as deviant and can punish – through social pressure or otherwise – deviance. I recognize the problems with using the term "orthodoxy," but do so in the absence of an adequate alternative.[17] As Talal Asad explains, "orthodoxy is not a mere body of opinion but a distinctive relationship – a relationship of power. Wherever Muslims have the power to regulate, uphold, require, or adjust *correct* practices, and to condemn, exclude, undermine, or replace *incorrect* ones, there is the domain of orthodoxy."[18] (Notably, "Islamic orthodoxy" is not equivalent to Sunnism, just as "Jewish orthodoxy" is not equivalent to rabbinic Judaism.[19] Because orthodoxy is itself a shifting relational category, the dichotomy between orthodoxy and heresy exists even within normative

[15] Essentialism is the assumption that an entity has necessary qualities or characteristics. Philosophical debates about essentialism have a long history, as evident in Aristotle's *Metaphysics*. As Foucault observed, "he who listens to history finds that things have no pre-existing essence." Foucault, "Nietzsche, genealogy, history," 78.

[16] Essentialism is problematic because, by discounting variability and historical change, it is reductionist. Philosophical critiques of essentialism vary widely; key philosophers who critiqued essentialism include Marx, Hegel, Sartre, and Kierkegaard.

[17] M. Brett Wilson. "The failure of nomenclature: the concept of 'orthodoxy' in the study of Islam." *Comparative Islamic Studies* 3:2 (2007): 169–94.

[18] Talal Asad, *The idea of an anthropology of Islam* (Washington, DC: Center for Contemporary Arab Studies, Georgetown University, 1986), 15.

[19] See A. Kevin Reinhart, "On Sunni Sectarianism*," in *Living Islamic history: studies in honour of Professor Carole Hillenbrand*, ed. by Yasir Suleiman (Edinburgh: Edinburgh University Press, 2010), 209–25.

categories, such as Sunnism or rabbinic Judaism.) At any given historical moment, Islamic law – like all legal systems – was shaped by a struggle for legal-political authority. It is important to recognize these dynamics because medieval Islamic legal orthodoxy is ordinarily, but incorrectly, identified as the essence of Islamic law. Yet minority and extinct legal opinions provide important evidence of diversity and heterodoxy – particularly in late antiquity – that negate the assumption that orthodoxy is the essence of Islamic law.[20] With the aim of decoupling essence and orthodoxy, each case study (in the even-numbered chapters) examines an Islamic legal beginning in order to highlight how particular legal perspectives became orthodox over time.[21]

Countering Developmental and Essentialist Approaches

A crucial objective of this book is to challenge essentialist and orthodox assumptions about Islamic law. These twin objectives are realized by strategically situating Islamic law within diverse contexts. By "context," I refer to three overlapping notions: temporal (late antique and medieval), geographic (the "Near East"), and intellectual (pagan, Jewish, and Christian intertextuality). I acknowledge, as Gabrielle Spiegel succinctly explains, that "historical contexts do not exist in themselves; they must be defined, and in that sense, constructed, by the historian before the interpretive work of producing meaning, of interpreting the past, can begin."[22] Although I recognize its potential pitfalls, historical contextualization is a crucial deconstructive tool that needs to be exercised in Islamic legal studies in order to lay the groundwork for more productive scholarship.[23] Notwithstanding the vulnerabilities of contextualism, I do not collapse

[20] I delineate the late antique Islamic period as from the beginning of Islam to approximately 800 CE. This period is commonly described by scholars as "early Islam." I will address my alternative periodization throughout this book.

[21] This historical-anthropological approach to Islamic legal beginnings is evident in the work of Mohammed Hocine Benkheira, "Jouir sans enfanter? Concubines, filiation et coït interrompu au debut de l'Islam." *Der Islam* 90:2 (2013): 245–305; Mohammed Hocine Benkheira, "Un libre peut-il épouser une esclave? Esquisse d'histoire d'un débat, des origines à al-Shāfiʿī (m.204/820)." *Der Islam* 84:2 (2008): 246–355; Lahcen Daaïf. "Le prix du sang (*diya*) au premier siècle de l'islam." *Hypothèses* 1:10 (2007): 329–42.

[22] Gabrielle M. Spiegel, *The past as text: the theory and practice of medieval historiography* (Baltimore, MD: Johns Hopkins University Press, 1997), xix.

[23] On reconciling postfoundationalism with historicist contextualization, see Mark Bevir. "How to be an intentionalist." *History and Theory* 41:2 (2002): 166–75. Benjamin critiqued historicism in Walter Benjamin, "Theses on the philosophy of history." In *Illuminations*, ed. by Hannah Arendt (New York: Schocken Books, 2007), 253–64.

Islamic law into its contexts, nor do I claim that the meaning of Islamic law depends entirely on contextual circumstances.[24] While this book is a work of socio-legal history (i.e., it fuses the approaches and sources of social and intellectual history), it does not present Islamic law as merely contingent, indeterminate, or plural.[25] Instead, contextualism instigates a process of reassessing how to narrate Islamic legal historiography and why. Historical contextualization simultaneously demonstrates that Islamic law did not develop in a unilinear fashion and that attributes conventionally identified as essential to Islamic law (such as legal orthodoxy) are the result of contingent or accidental historical events.

Temporal contextualization. I situate the beginnings of Islamic law in its temporal context by using the terms "late antique Islamic" and "Islamic late antiquity."[26] With the objective of respecting the unique chronology and dynamics of Islamic history, much scholarship employs a periodization of Islam that is wholly based on events internal to Islamic history, without reference to other global historical periods. For instance, many scholars continue to accept a problematic periodization that differentiates between "late antiquity" and "early Islam."[27] However, late antiquity persisted into the eighth and even ninth centuries.[28] "Islamic late antiquity" refers roughly to the period from the beginning of Islamic history to the end of the eighth century CE. I also use the term 'Islamic late antiquity'

[24] Chris Tomlins elaborates this critique of historicist contextualism in much of his writing. See especially Christopher Tomlins, "Historicism and materiality in legal theory." In *Law, theory and history: new essays on a neglected dialogue*, ed. by Maksymilian Del Mar and Michael Lobban (Oxford: Hart Publishing, 2016).

[25] Tomlins critiques historicism and contextualization for producing contingency, indeterminacy, and plurality. Christopher Tomlins, "What is left of the law and society paradigm after critique? Revisiting Gordon's 'Critical Legal Histories'." *Law & Social Inquiry* 37:1 (2012): 155–66.

[26] In doing so, I follow Thomas Sizgorich, "Narrative and community in Islamic late antiquity." *Past & Present* 185:1 (2004): 9–42; and *Violence and belief in late antiquity: militant devotion in Christianity and Islam* (Philadelphia, PA: University of Pennsylvania Press, 2008).

[27] This is evident in scholarship that distinguishes between the late antique context and the rise of Islam. See Chase F. Robinson (ed.), *The formation of the Islamic world, sixth to eleventh centuries*, The new Cambridge history of Islam vol. I (Cambridge: Cambridge University Press, 2011). Similarly, al-Azmeh's recent book does not recognize late antique Islam as a category in and of itself and relies instead on the term "Paleo-Islam." Aziz A. Al-Azmeh, *The emergence of Islam in late antiquity: Allah and his people* (Cambridge: Cambridge University Press, 2014). In addition, some scholars employ an "origins" approach by identifying Islam "as a child of Late Antiquity." Robert G. Hoyland, "Early Islam as a late antique religion." In *The Oxford handbook of late antiquity*, ed. by Scott Fitzgerald Johnson (Oxford; New York: Oxford University Press, 2012), 1053–77 at 1069.

[28] The integration of Islamic history within late antique studies was initiated by Peter Brown and continued by scholars such as Thomas Sizgorich. See Peter R. L. Brown, *The world of late antiquity: from Marcus Aurelius to Muhammad*, Library of European civilization (London: Thames and Hudson, 1971); and *The world of late antiquity: AD 150–750* (New York: W.W. Norton, 1989). See also Sizgorich, "Narrative and community in Islamic late antiquity."

to describe a period of Islamic legal heterodoxy that preceded the consolidation and dominance of orthodox Islamic legal schools.[29] The emerging scholarly trend of accepting the period of late antiquity as relevant for framing Islamic history leads, in turn, to accepting its corollary, the medieval era. "Medieval" refers roughly to the period from the beginning of the ninth century to the fifteenth century CE. To emphasize the distinctiveness of post-late antique legal authorities, I use both "medieval" and "professional" to describe jurists affiliated with orthodox legal schools. (The term "professional" refers to a broad and protracted process of professionalization and specialization of Muslim legal authorities.)

In this book, "late antique" and "medieval" represent blocks of time that link Islamic history to both regional and global dynamics.[30] Although I make use of these global historical classifications, I do so without relying on common assumptions about the substantive or Eurocentric content of these periods.[31] The minimization of "medieval Islamic history" as a salient category inadvertently informs the prejudicial (and incorrectly evolutionary) idea that because Islam was not part of the medieval era, it has not yet entered modernity. This is evident in contemporary propaganda that characterizes Islamic law as a "medieval" legal system. To be clear, I am not arguing against a periodization of Islamic history that focuses on internal dynamics, but rather against the exclusive use of such a periodization. In Chapter 5, I present both an internal and regional periodization.

Geographic contextualization. As noted, Islamic law is "Islamic" because it is generated by an interpretive process anchored in Islamic sources (broadly defined). Nevertheless, Islamic law is also more than simply "Islamic" because it assimilated and generated diverse "Near Eastern" legal traditions. Therefore, I use the term "Islamicate" to refer to the heterogeneous contexts in which Islamic law existed.[32] Marshall Hodgson defined

[29] I have used the terms "late antique Islam" and "Islamic late antiquity" in numerous previous publications.

[30] Richard Maxwell Eaton, *Islamic history as global history*, Essays on Global and Comparative History (Washington, DC: American Historical Association, 1990); Marshall G. S. Hodgson, *Rethinking world history: essays on Europe, Islam, and world history*, ed. by Edmund Burke (Cambridge; New York: Cambridge University Press, 1993).

[31] On the complexities of global (or world) history periodization, see Jerry H. Bentley, "Cross-cultural interaction and periodization in world history." *The American Historical Review* 101:3 (1996): 749–70; William A. Green, "Periodizing world history." *History and Theory* 34:2 (1995): 99–111. Despite the limitations of periodization, I rely upon it as a framework for explaining historical changes. For a recent questioning of periodization, see Jacques Le Goff, *Must we divide history into periods?* Trans. by M. B. DeBevoise (New York: Columbia University Press, 2015).

[32] The term Islamicate only applies to regions under Islamic empires; for pre-Islamic history, I refer to the "Near East."

"Islamicate" as referring "not directly to the religion, Islam, itself, but to the social and cultural complex historically associated with Islam and the Muslims, both among Muslims themselves and even when found among non-Muslims."[33] The category of Islamicate is a heuristic tool that enriches our understanding of Islamic legal history by recognizing that Islamic law, from its beginning, structured relationships between and among Muslims and non-Muslims. The result was Islamicate legal syncretism.[34]

The geographical focus of this book is Southwestern Asia, commonly identified as the "Near East." The "Near East" is a problematic political (specifically, British colonial) category lacking an apparent geographic boundary. I would prefer to use the more geographically descriptive (and less geopolitically constructed) term Southwest Asia. (I also appreciate Garth Fowden's suggestions of "Eurasian hinge."[35]) Toward the end of the late antique period (i.e., approximately 800 CE), the Islamic empire encompassed much of modern-day Spain, the northern parts of Africa, the Levant, the Arabian peninsula, Mesopotamia, Persia, and parts of South and Central Asia. In this book, I concentrate on Southwestern Asia (rather than North Africa or Central Asia). While geographical specification – at the micro-level of local communities – is a worthy intellectual endeavor, it is not my objective.[36] I rely on a flexible correlation between sources and their geographic location because the geographic reach of both literary and documentary sources does not neatly correspond to their place of production or discovery. Historical texts simultaneously reflect their local contexts and broader regional trends. For instance, although much of the surviving Arabic papyri have been recovered in Egypt, the authors and subjects of these documents are not limited to Egypt.[37] Instead of reconstructing local practices or localizing historical sources, this book embraces a wide-ranging view of Islamic legal history.

[33] Marshall G. S. Hodgson, *The venture of Islam: conscience and history in a world civilization*, vol. I (Chicago, IL: University of Chicago Press, 1974), 59.

[34] Laurent Mayali. "Introduction. De la raison à la foi: l'entrée du droit en religion." *Revue de l'histoire des religions* 4 (2011): 475–82 at 482.

[35] Garth Fowden, *Before and after Muḥammad: the first millennium refocused* (Princeton, NJ: Princeton University Press, 2014).

[36] An outstanding model for geographic specificity of late antique Islamic materials is Mohammed Hocine Benkheira. "L'impuissance sexuelle, motif légal de rupture du lien matrimonial." *Islamic Law and Society* 21:1–2 (2014): 1–48.

[37] On the geographic range of Arabic papyri, see Lennart Sundelin, "Introduction: papyrology and the study of early Islamic Egypt." In *Papyrology and the history of early Islamic Egypt*, ed. by Petra Sijpesteijn and Lennart Sundelin (Leiden; Boston, MA: Brill, 2004), 1–19 at 7, n. 20.

Intellectual contextualization. Although contextualization guides us to the notion of Islamicate, it should not be understood as directing us toward comparison. Indeed, this book is a critique of conventional comparison – both implicit and explicit – because it obscures Islamic legal historiography. It is commonplace for Islamic legal historiography to describe and to evaluate Islamic law in *comparison* to modern Western law (a secular legal archetype) or to rabbinic Jewish law (a "religious" legal archetype). Both comparisons impose interpretations and assumptions about Islamic law that are incongruent with historical evidence and laden with problematic value judgments.

Most scholarly comparisons with modern Western law are made implicitly. These comparisons are evident in the way Islamic law is described in modern discourse, both academic and popular. The very identification of Islamic law as a "religious" legal system marks it as non-secular and often implies that it is not rational and is not generated through formal processes. By way of example, the Weberian myth of "Kadijustiz" (*sic*) caricatures Islamic law as an irrational, arbitrary legal system, the antithesis of liberal and predictable, modern (secular) law.[38] While generations of scholars have refuted the Weberian stereotype, the underlying dichotomization of modern Western law and Islamic law remains germane to scholarship (and public discourse). Comparisons between medieval Islamic jurisprudence and modern Western law are incongruent and thereby reinforce stereotypes about Islamic law's illiberality, violence, or rigidity. In contemporary discourse, the dominant trope about Islamic law is that it is "different" – different from modern, secular law. This is one reason why the othering of Islamic law should be resisted, as I have argued elsewhere.[39]

Although the Islamic versus modern/Western comparative framework is relevant to my portrayal of Islamic law in this book, a complementary modality may be more pertinent: "comparing" Islamic law and Jewish law. Standard scholarly comparisons of Jewish and Islamic legal traditions perceive them as "similar." This characterization is, undoubtedly, a plausible one since these legal traditions produced legal literature that appears analogous: canonical legal texts in Islamic and Jewish traditions resemble each other in significant ways; moreover, much of Islamic and Jewish legal

[38] Max Weber, *Economy and society: an outline of interpretive sociology* (Berkeley, CA: University of California Press, 1978), 2: 976–8 (discussing "kadijustice").

[39] Lena Salaymeh, "The politics of inaccuracy and a case for 'Islamic law,'" *The Immanent Frame* (July 7, 2011), http://blogs.ssrc.org/tif/2011/07/07/the-politics-of-inaccuracy-and-a-case-for-islamic-law; and "Commodifying 'Islamic law' in the U.S. legal academy." *Journal of Legal Education* 63:4 (May 2014): 640–6.

literature differs considerably from Christian legal literature (and in similar ways). However, these perceived similarities are not the consequence of Islam and Judaism being "essentially similar," but rather of their shared socio-political space (the "Near East") and time (medieval era). Here again, contextualization deters essentialization.

The prevalent tendency to compare Islamic and Jewish legal traditions, moreover, is a manifestation of the modern religio-secular dichotomy: because Jewish and Islamic legal traditions are perceived as "religious," they are frequently grouped together or compared to each other. This grouping places both traditions in a position subordinate to secularism (or Western Christianity, since Eastern Christianity should not be collapsed into Western Christianity). That is, Jewish and Islamic legal traditions are "othered" by (Western) Christianity in similar ways. Not surprisingly, comparisons between Islamic law and Christian law are less frequent than comparisons between Islamic law and Jewish law.

Thus, Jewish and Islamic legal traditions have unique historical and contemporary relationships. By emphasizing the relationship between historiography and history, I highlight the exceptional relationship between Islamic and Jewish legal traditions in two ways: (a) historiographically, by exploring how and why modern scholars have emphasized that Islamic law "borrowed" from Jewish law and (b) historically, by showing how Islamic and Jewish legal traditions overlapped through dialectical interchange, shared customary traditions, and shared contexts. As I pursue these enquiries, I push back against the conventional view that law is the "essence" of both Islam and Judaism.

Beyond Contextualization

I utilize several modes of contextualization in this book strategically, in order to lay the groundwork for a deeper understanding of Islamic legal history.[40] In my work, contextualizing Islamic law is a preliminary move toward critical historical jurisprudence.[41] Critical historical jurisprudence, as practiced here, begins with questioning dominant disciplinary

[40] Sewell justifies historical contextualization by asserting that "We cannot know what an act or an utterance means and what its consequences might be without knowing what the semantics, the technologies, the convention – in brief, the logics – that characterize the world in which the action takes place." William H. Sewell Jr., *Logics of history: social theory and social transformation*, Chicago Studies in Practices of Meaning (Chicago, IL; London: University of Chicago Press, 2005), 10.

[41] Lena Salaymeh. "'Comparing' Jewish and Islamic legal traditions: between disciplinarity and critical historical jurisprudence." *Critical Analysis of Law, New Historical Jurisprudence* 2:1 (2015): 153–72.

methodologies, recognizing ideology in scholarly production, and identifying the limits of modern terms and concepts. These critical techniques minimize both anachronistic and problematic distortions of Islamic law, revealing that Islamic jurisprudence – like any jurisprudential system – is always in a dialogical relationship with contemporaneous and predecessor legal traditions. The logic of Islamic law simultaneously recycles and innovates Islamic traditions within a dynamic normative space. This logic is evident in each of the even-numbered chapters, which explore the intersections of precedent, scripture, and social transformation in Islamic legal history.

One reason why problematic philosophies of history continue to shape scholarship is that they are intertwined with modern disciplinary methods – especially positivist ones.[42] The odd-numbered chapters demonstrate the relationship between philosophy of history and method by correlating each anthropomorphic metaphor (conception, parentage, and maturation) with a particular problem in each of three disciplinary methods: textual criticism, comparative philology, and linear, developmental history. I argue that while these methods may not be acknowledged explicitly, they – much like anthropomorphic metaphors – reflect nearly imperceptible dynamics in Islamic legal studies. These disciplinary methods force historical evidence into linear and narrow frameworks that are incongruent with the historical situations of Islamic law. I pay particular attention to interrelated political and ideological resistances by examining the intersections of ahistoricism, power, and ideology.[43] (Notably, it is beyond the scope of this book to survey the wide-ranging academic gaps or emphases within the discipline of Islamic legal studies.[44]) Thus, by elucidating how

[42] By "positivist methods," I refer specifically to post-Enlightenment academic approaches that viewed methodological rules as generating "factual" knowledge. See Theodor W. Adorno, *The positivist dispute in German sociology*, trans. by Glyn Adey and David Frisby (London: Heinemann, 1976), xii.

[43] These investigations are necessary because, as Hallaq observed, "the legal history of the first three centuries of Islam has yet to be written and must, in the process, abandon the archaic assumptions that have dominated Orientalism so far." Wael B. Hallaq, "The quest for origins or doctrine? Islamic legal studies as colonialist discourse." *UCLA Journal of Islamic and Near Eastern Law* 2:1 (2002–2003): 1–31 at 30.

[44] For broad analyses of Islamic legal studies scholarship, see Salaymeh, "Commodifying 'Islamic law' "; and "Propaganda, politics, and profiteering: Islamic law in the contemporary U.S.," *Jadaliyya* (2014), www.jadaliyya.com/pages/index/19408/propaganda-politics-and-profiteering_islamic-law-i. See also Hallaq, "The quest for origins or doctrine?"; John Strawson, "Encountering Islamic law," *Critical Legal Conference held in New College* (1993), www.witness-pioneer.org/vil/Articles/shariah/jsrps.html and "Islamic law and English texts." *Law and Critique* VI:1 (1995): 21–38. Also Lama Abu-Odeh, "The politics of (mis)recognition: Islamic law pedagogy in American academia." *The American Journal of Comparative Law* 52:4 (2004): 789–824; Jane F. Collier, "Intertwined histories: Islamic law and Western imperialism." *Law & Society Review* 28:2 (1994): 395–408; Enid

methodology bleeds into abstract ways of thinking in scholarship, the odd-numbered chapters of this book strive toward a socio-anthropological analysis of contemporary Islamic legal studies in the West.

The "West" plays a powerful role in the contemporary and international production of knowledge about Islamic law.[45] Following Asad, my usage of the term "Western" does not imply "that there is an integrated Western culture, or a fixed Western identity, or a single Western way of thinking, but that a singular collective identity defines itself in terms of a unique historicity in contrast to all others, a historicity that shifts from place to place."[46] I use the "West" to refer to a broad but ambiguous geographic space in which many people self-identify as the inventors and protagonists of modernity. As a result, I draw upon postcolonial theory to analyze dominant and conventional approaches to Islamic studies in the West, while recognizing that these approaches have disseminated globally.[47] A crucial component of resisting Western frameworks is resisting the modern category of religion.[48] As Robinson has observed, "'religion' was conceptualized as a sphere of human action and belief that was distinct from other human activities (e.g. political movements or economic production), endowed with its own evolution (origins being given particular emphasis), and made a transcendent object through history."[49] As the case studies in this book demonstrate, this modern, Western construction of "religion" is incongruent with the historical realities of Islamic law. Too often, invoking the relationship between Islamic studies and the West is perceived as "politicizing" scholarship, but scholarship is always and already politicized. Because debates about Orientalism have been so contentious in recent years, it must be emphasized that the critiques in this book are not based on the *identity* of Western scholars, but rather on their positions of power. Indeed, regardless of their identity, non-Western scholars (both inside and outside the West) can and do espouse Orientalist positions. Identity politics is not relevant, but ideology and politics are.[50]

Hill, "Comparative and historical study of modern Middle Eastern law." *American Journal of Comparative Law* 26:2 (1978): 279–304.

45 Salaymeh, "The politics of inaccuracy"; and "Commodifying 'Islamic law.'"

46 Talal Asad, *Genealogies of religion* (Baltimore, MD: Johns Hopkins University Press, 1993), 18–19.

47 On the relevance of postcolonial theory to medieval studies, see Bruce W. Holsinger, "Medieval studies, postcolonial studies, and the genealogies of critique." *Speculum* 77:4 (2002): 1195–227.

48 Asad, *Genealogies*, 1 ("while religion is integral to modern Western history, there are dangers in employing it as a normalizing concept when translating Islamic traditions.").

49 Robinson, "Reconstructing early Islam," 105.

50 Indeed, contemporary Western scholars – both non-Muslim and Muslim – of Islamic studies often impose identity categories or employ identity politics in ways that have severely limiting effects on scholarship in Islamic studies. Salaymeh, "Propaganda, politics, and profiteering."

By attending to how modern Western disciplinary practices and modern Western ideologies shape conventional Islamic legal historiography, we open up the possibility of radically redefining Islamic law. However, what tools should we use to define Islamic law? Claude Lévi-Strauss famously noted that the "error of traditional anthropology, like that of traditional linguistics, was to consider the terms, and not the relations between the terms."[51] While my own work is not structuralist in its orientation, this observation resonates with the challenge of understanding Islam's beginnings. An error similar to the one Lévi-Strauss identified occurs when we demarcate late antique Islam/Muslim in isolation from late antique Judaism/Jew (or Christianity/Christian, or paganism/pagan). To avoid this shortcoming, I examine competing and coexisting legal systems in late antiquity. In the late antique setting, Roman/Byzantine, Eastern Christian, and Sasanian legal practices contributed greatly to Near Eastern legal culture.[52] Since Near Eastern legal systems deserve more comprehensive and deeper study than can be offered in this book, I have chosen to focus on Jewish law, for the reasons enumerated above. At the same time, I would note my own skepticism toward the interest in exhaustively comparing Near Eastern legal systems because this too often leads to a borrowing/influence paradigm. As the case studies in this book indicate, questions about Islamic legal history directed my research toward Jewish legal opinions. I did not begin with the objective of comparison for the sake of comparison.

Critical historical jurisprudence exposes Islamic law as operating much like other legal traditions: scriptural/canonical texts and historical precedents act as centrifugal forces in the normative space of law. In the case study on prisoners of war (Chapter 2), I examine how jurists interpreted and reinterpreted historical and exegetical sources in an intertextual process that shaped and expanded Islamic law until an orthodox perspective

[51] Claude Lévi-Strauss, *Structural anthropology*, trans. by Claire Jacobson and Brooke Schoepf (New York: Basic Books, 1963), 46.

[52] Following Crone, I use the term "Roman provincial law" in recognition of the hybrid Roman and customary practices that were likely prevalent in the Near East prior to the Arab/Muslim conquests. Patricia Crone, *Roman, provincial and Islamic law: the origins of the Islamic patronate* (Cambridge: Cambridge University Press, 2002). Recently, scholars have begun to explore Eastern Christian and Islamic legal interactions and I hope that this book will provide a helpful complement for future research in this growing field. On Eastern Christian law in the Islamicate world, see Uriel I. Simonsohn, *A common justice: the legal allegiances of Christians and Jews under early Islam*, Divinations: Rereading Late Ancient Religion (Philadelphia, PA: University of Pennsylvania Press, 2011); Lev E. Weitz, "Syriac Christians in the medieval Islamic world: law, family, and society, " PhD dissertation, Princeton University, 2013.

transformed historiography through law. In the case study on circumcision (Chapter 4), I identify the shifting and varied ways in which Muslim jurists and exegetes delineated circumcision as *Islamic* in dialogue with regional customary practices (including Arabian monotheism, Judaism, and Christianity). In the case study on wife-initiated divorce (Chapter 6), I track parallel changes in Jewish and Islamic legal histories in an effort to present an Islamicate legal history that accounts for the contextual factors that resulted in both legal systems limiting a woman's divorce options. In each of these case studies, I begin with a precise legal question and follow a labyrinthine path through hybridity and heterodoxy to observe the inseparability of law and history and the dialogical connection between Islamic and non-Islamic legal traditions.

These case studies establish that specific areas of Jewish and Islamic law relate to each other in distinct ways because of the dissimilar legal sources and circumstances that generate those areas of law. In the first case study (Chapter 2) on prisoners of war, the relationship between Islamic and Jewish legal ideas seems distant because the international law of these two systems is quite distinct. Because Jewish law was not tied to a state, in either the late antique or medieval eras, rabbinic jurisprudence did not scrutinize the treatment of war prisoners systematically. By contrast, the matter was of direct and immediate relevance to Islamic states, thereby necessitating juristic exploration. In the second case study (Chapter 4) on circumcision, the relationship between Islamic and Jewish legal systems seems close because the ritual laws of these legal systems are presumed to be similar. However, circumcision's status within Islamic law is ambiguous in comparison to the clear commandment of circumcision in Jewish law. Indeed, there are noticeable differences in how late antique Muslims and Jews viewed circumcision. Finally, in the third case study (Chapter 6) on wife-initiated divorce, parallel changes in women's divorce options among Muslims and eastern Jews point to a broader Islamicate setting for the dominance of legal orthodoxy. Each case study reveals a discrete relationship among Islamic, Jewish, and other Near Eastern legal systems.

Synopsis

As may already be evident, this book engages critical theory in an effort to deconstruct Islamic legal historiography and to reconstruct Islamic legal history. My approach is not simply "postmodern," an antiquated label that is sometimes used pejoratively to dismiss scholarship. Instead, I engage in a postfoundationalist understanding of history that rejects the positivist methodologies of modernism and the nihilistic relativism of post-modernism. A postfoundational understanding of historical objectivity rejects the positivist notion that particular methodologies generate Truth; instead, postfoundationalism pursues heuristics that generate historical truth.[53] Bevir explains, "postfoundationalism challenges modernist theory with its focus on facts and its methodological ambitions. Historical theory need not be about devising rigorous methods to secure facts. In addition, postfoundationalism challenges postmodern theory with its focus on the study of the literary and aesthetic features of historical writing."[54] Although historiography is an interpretive project that does not produce Truth (or Facts), it is based on rigorous historical-textual studies. Each chapter in this book fuses precise theoretical insights with close examinations of sources.

In Chapter 1, I offer a postfoundationalist understanding of late antique Islamic sources, advocating that they be read critically and in conjunction. When scholars of Islamic studies describe their sources as "problematic," they are often implicitly comparing those sources to modern state archives or evaluating them as biased because they are "religious." The characterization of late antique and medieval Islamic sources as problematic (or unreliable or inauthentic) is fundamentally dubious because it is based on a presumption that other (usually modern) sources are less problematic (or more reliable or more authentic). Consequently, I understand the diversity of sources and their forms of composition and transmission as *advantages*, rather than disadvantages. Indeed, the challenge for scholars of Islamic studies is not to resolve "problems" in the sources, but to avoid a hegemonic narrative of Islamic exceptionalism: the dehistoricization of Islamic sources cannot be disentangled from the dehistoricization of Islam.

In Chapter 2, I use a variety of historical and legal sources (*sīrah, maghāzī, muṣannafāt, masānīd*) to reconstruct the treatment of prisoners of war during the Prophetic era (610–632 CE) in Medina and in the decades immediately afterward. I argue that both historical narratives and late antique juristic opinions indicate that it was likely impermissible to execute prisoners of war, a position that differs from medieval Islamic juristic rulings that generally permitted the execution of war prisoners. A key legal-historical event that underlies the jurisprudence on war

[53] See Mark Bevir, "Objectivity in history." *History and Theory* 33:3 (1994): 328–44.

[54] Mark Bevir, "Why historical distance is not a problem." *History and Theory* 50:4 (December 2011): 24–37 at 33.

prisoners is the treatment of three Jewish tribes in Medina. I demonstrate that, in their treatment of this crucial legal-historical event, medieval Muslim jurists may have recategorized the event as relevant to war prisoners, while also fusing pre-Islamic traditions and modifying the historical evidence to create historical bases for their legal opinions.

In Chapter 3, I investigate non-linear relationships in Islamic law's historical context in order to highlight the syncretism in Islamic law. The project of seeking to identify Islamic law's "origins" in Roman, Jewish, or other legal systems is ideologically motivated and intellectually ineffective. To clarify the relational focus of this book, I introduce some critical assessments of previous scholarship that "compares" Jewish and Islamic law and argue for more critical, contextualized, and systematic approaches. Reflecting the methodology of comparative philology, common presumptions of linear derivation are based on mistaken assumptions about the "purity" of identity and of law. Islamic and eastern Jewish legal systems did not "borrow" from each other, but rather occupied the same socio-historical space and, in some cases, responded similarly to a shared context. The shared Islamicate context – rather than "essential" features of Islamic or Jewish jurisprudence – clarifies whatever resemblances there may be between the two legal systems.

Chapter 4 elucidates the impossibility of measuring Jewish (or other) "influences" on Islamic law. Relying on a variety of Islamic and non-Islamic sources, I show that male circumcision in late antiquity was a ritual and an identity marker with dissimilar values in Jewish, Christian, and Islamic legal practices. Muslim scholars interpreted Abrahamic precedents and Islamic scripture to explain circumcision as necessary for ritual purity. Some Muslim jurists feared that performing circumcision at the same time as Jews would confuse Jewish and Muslim identities. In this case study, I explore the Islamicate pastiche that occurred as Islamic law assimilated the Near Eastern customary practice of male circumcision.

Chapter 5 illustrates what makes Islamic and Jewish legal systems "Islamicate," part of the same larger intellectual and social environment. First, I outline a periodization of Islamic legal history with attention to the overall changes in legal education, jurists, and the judiciary. Second, I sketch a periodization of Islamicate legal history to highlight the nearly parallel and gradual shift from heterodoxy to orthodoxy in Jewish and Islamic legal history. I argue that both Jewish and Islamic legal systems formulated a legal orthodoxy during roughly the same period, in roughly the same space, and the same socio-political context. Legal orthodoxy shaped the everyday practice of law, legal education, and the organization of the legal profession. I intentionally do not include a fully synthesized narrative of Islamic legal history in these periodizations; instead, I point to how an Islamicate legal history can illuminate subtle aspects of how Muslim jurists integrated and transformed Near Eastern legal traditions while adapting to broad socio-political and economic changes.

Chapter 6 presents two chronologies of legal changes related to wife-initiated divorce in Jewish and Islamic legal history, using a wide array of legal texts and documentary evidence. Interweaving these two narratives of wife-initiated divorce, I argue for a historicized, contextual understanding of law by demonstrating that the changes in each legal system were part of a regional, socio-political process of juridical professionalization. I demonstrate that the characterization of a particular Geonic decree related to wife-initiated divorce as an "innovation" caused by Islamic "influence" is historically inaccurate; this characterization reflects a broad struggle for legal authority. In both legal systems, divorce – in jurisprudential texts and legal practice – was transformed from contract dissolution to contractual breach. I suggest that these changes were the result of contingent socio-political contexts of imperial expansion, the professionalization of jurists, and the elaboration of urban market structures.

Remarks

Because many of the approaches implemented in this book are not common in Islamic legal studies, some readers may perceive this book as being about something other than Islamic law. This is due in part to the field being dominated by the disciplines of "Near Eastern studies" and "religious studies," rather than history or law. (The disciplinary distance between historians and classicists is roughly the same as that between historians and Near Eastern studies scholars.[55]) My objective is to challenge readers from every disciplinary background to rethink their presumptions about Islamic law. Interdisciplinary studies do not dilute scholarship: by integrating legal theory, critical theory, and Jewish sources, I seek to complement, rather than subtract, from the contributions of this book to Islamic studies.[56] The study of Islamic and Jewish legal traditions in

[55] On these disciplinary distinctions, see Elizabeth A. Clark, *History, theory, text: historians and the linguistic turn* (Cambridge, MA: Harvard University Press, 2004), 166.

[56] Or, more appropriately than interdisciplinary, this book is "infradisciplinary" because the study of law predates modern disciplines. See Mariana Valverde. "Between a rock and a hard place: legal studies beyond both disciplinarity and interdisciplinarity." *Critical Analysis of Law* 1:1 (2014): 51–62.

conjunction is appropriate because of their shared temporal, geographic, and social spaces – not for any political or polemical reasons.

I present extensive theoretical and methodological discussions in the odd-numbered chapters. These chapters address many common reactions to my scholarship by illuminating sometimes imperceptible or subconscious dimensions of conventional Islamic studies. I recognize that some of these problems return to debates long past in many fields.[57] I also recognize that some of the theoretical and methodological discussions in this book will be foreign to some scholars of Islamic studies. I have sought to clarify and to simplify these topics, which are elaborated primarily in the odd-numbered chapters. In the particular field of Islamic studies, this book advocates neither source criticism nor source revisionism. Instead, it offers an alternative to this common bifurcation by merging social theory with deep engagement of historical texts.

We stand on the shoulders of giants. However, recognizing limitations in the paradigms of our precursors or colleagues is not an act of disrespect or a rejection of their contributions. It is a necessary and fundamental part of the scholarly process. It is especially important for scholarship of the late antique Islamic era because this period remains relatively isolated from late antique studies. Furthermore, critique is important for the field of Islamic studies because it is a hierarchically insular field, dominated by the pursuit of technical knowledge. More importantly, as I highlight in the odd-numbered chapters of this book, the field is intensely politicized in ways that are difficult for both insiders and outsiders to ascertain.

A few final notes: Throughout this book, I use the term "the Prophet" to refer to Muḥammad. I do this for the sake of clarity because Muḥammad is a common name. In addition, all dates in this book are of the Common Era (CE) – unless otherwise indicated – because the Common Era is accessible for my readers and situates Islamic history within broader historical discussions. Usage of the Common Era should not be understood as a promotion of the Gregorian calendar or a dismissal of the Islamic (*hijrī*) calendar. Whenever possible, I have identified the author of a primary source by including death date and location (alternately using the historical or modern name of the location). Locations are not necessarily the place where an author was born, or where he died, but rather where he was intellectually active; in addition, I often use general and broad regional terms, rather than naming specific cities, even when that information is

[57] For a broad discussion, see Gabrielle M. Spiegel, *Practicing history: new directions in historical writing after the linguistic turn* (New York: Routledge, 2005).

readily available, because the reader is likely more familiar with the region than the city. All translations from original sources are my own unless otherwise indicated; I have consulted original sources even when I have cited translations or secondary sources discussing original sources. I refer to English translations as part of a strategic effort to introduce non-specialist readers to these important sources. For citations to the Qur'ān, I have relied upon and modified Yūsuf ʿAlī's translation.[58]

Visualization

The images that introduce each chapter represent distinct foci.[59] These images were inspired by a tradition I learned from Maria Mavroudi, who, in turn, learned it from her teacher, Ihor Ševčenko:

> the one [historian] can be likened to the brightly-colored butterfly flitting about over a flowerbed, the other, to the crawling caterpillar whose worm's eye view covers the expanse of a single cabbage leaf. The simile of butterfly and caterpillar is useful, since it suggests that a relationship may exist between the vivid historian and the technical historian.[60]

The distinct perspectives of different forms of historical inquiry are conveyed in this book by the placement of geometric images at the beginning of each chapter. Each successive image depicts an additional layer of geometric shapes, correlating to each chapter's topical focus (from one legal system, to a few legal systems, to a legal culture) and use of sources (from concentrated explorations to broad engagement). Each odd-numbered chapter adds a contour image (representing abstract and theoretical issues of Islamic historiography) and each even-numbered chapter adds a shaded image (representing substantive engagement with Islamic legal history). These visual depictions illustrate how historiographic frameworks (contours) circumscribe historical writing (shaded images). Most importantly, I deploy these images as heuristic devices to structure meaning by capturing the intentionality behind the myriad choices made in this book.

58 *The Holy Qur-ān*, trans. by ʿAbdāllah Yūsuf ʿAlī (Medina: King Fahd Holy Qur-ān Printing Complex, 1989–1990).

59 I thank Sarah Levin for her superb graphic design advice on these images.

60 Ihor Ševčenko. "Two varieties of historical writing." *History and Theory* 8:3 (1969): 332–45 at 332.

CHAPTER 1

Legal-historical Beginnings – Outlining Late Antique Islamic Law

Law and history are inseparable. Law relies on and constructs historical precedents. Law exists in and transforms historical moments. And law is a window into history. Like any window, it frames and colors the landscape, providing an imperfect view of a historical scene that is barely recoverable.

The historical landscapes of Islamic law are detectable in a variety of sources. In interpreting those sources, however, it is crucial to avoid imposing essentializations of Islamic law. Thus, in this chapter, I focus on illustrating the relationship between historiographic methods for studying Islamic law and essentialism of Islamic law. Conventional scholarship applies "origins"-methods and imposes "origins"-constructions of Islamic law. Much conventional scholarship seeks to identify a temporal and geographic "origin" of Islamic law by dating Islamic legal sources, typically by using source-criticism. (The emphasis on "original" sources is an extension of nineteenth century, modern "scientific" history, which effectively defined historiography as source-criticism.[1]) This chapter illustrates the connection between two insights: Islamic law does not have an "origin," but rather a beginning; historical sources do not contain Truth, but rather historical truth.

Metaphors for Historical Theory: Origins/Conception

Conventional Islamic legal historiography essentializes Islamic law by seeking to identify the historical "origins" of its "essential" features. A non-essentialist

[1] C. Lorenz, "History: theories and methods." In *International Encyclopedia of the Social & Behavioral Sciences*, ed. by Neil J. Smelser and Paul B. Baltes (Oxford: Pergamon, 2001), 6869–76 at 6871.

understanding of Islamic law recognizes that Islamic law simply changes over time and, therefore, Islamic law has a beginning, but not an origin. The common essentialization of Islamic law is most evident in the frequent use of the term "origins" in the titles of influential works that explore Islamic law's beginnings.[2] (Indeed, the field of Islamic legal studies is saturated with references to "origins."[3]) In Islamic legal historiography, "origins" often conveys a sense of "conception" or "birth" as scholars seek to date a teleological starting point for an Islamic law ideal-type. "Origins" insinuates a history that is not only teleological, but also metaphorically anthropomorphized through a developmental (i.e. linear) historical progression: from conception (indicated in the term "origins"), to childhood (the terms "early" or "formative"), to maturity (the term "classical"). (The latter two anthropomorphic metaphors are further explored in Chapters 3 and 5.) This misconception is also perpetuated in the labeling of the period from the seventh through ninth centuries CE as "early Islam." These conventional terms imply linear development of an essentialized subject that passes from an earlier to a more developed phase.[4] Instead of anthropomorphizing and essentializing periods, I use "Islamic beginnings" and "Islamic late antiquity." The intertwined notions of "origins" and "conception/birth" anthropomorphize Islamic law in ways that limit our understandings of Islamic legal history.

A pioneer of "origins"-oriented studies of Islamic law was Joseph Schacht (d. 1969), one of the most influential twentieth-century scholars of Islamic law. He claimed that "[d]uring the greater part of the first century Islamic law, in the technical meaning of the term, did not as yet exist."[5] For Schacht, "the starting-point of Muhammadan jurisprudence lies in the practice of the late Umaiyad [*sic*] period,"[6] approximately

[2] See Joseph Schacht, *The origins of Muhammadan jurisprudence* (Oxford: Clarendon Press, 1950); Majid Khadduri and Liebesny Herbert J. (eds.), *Origin and development of Islamic law* (Washington, DC: Middle East Institute, 1955); Harald Motzki, *The origins of Islamic jurisprudence: Meccan fiqh before the classical schools* [Die Anfange der islamischen Jurisprudenz: Ihr Entwicklung in Mekka bis zur Mitte des 2./8. Jahrhunderts (1991)], trans. by Marion H. Katz, Islamic history and civilization. Studies and texts, vol. XLI (Leiden; Boston, MA: Brill, 2002); Yasin Dutton, *The origins of Islamic law: the Qur'an, the Muwaṭṭa' and Madinan 'amal*, Culture and civilization in the Middle East (Surrey, UK: Curzon, 1999); Crone, *Roman, provincial and Islamic law*; Wael B. Hallaq, *The origins and evolution of Islamic law* (Cambridge: Cambridge University Press, 2005).

[3] An *Index Islamicus* database search (without date restrictions) for "Islamic law" and "origins" yielded 129 results, whereas a search for "Islamic law" and "beginnings" yielded 20 results; "Islamic law" and "late antiquity" yielded only 2 results. (Database search last accessed June 29, 2014.)

[4] As Said asserted, "whereas an *origin* centrally dominates what derives from it, the beginning (especially the modern beginning) encourages nonlinear development." Edward Said, *Beginnings: intention and method* (New York: Columbia University Press, 1985), 373, emphasis added.

[5] Joseph Schacht, *An introduction to Islamic law* (London: Oxford University Press, 1964), 19.

[6] Schacht, *The origins*, 1.

100 AH (after *hijrah*), or 718 CE.[7] After Schacht, succeeding generations of scholars have sought to offer alternative – usually earlier – dates for the "origins" of Islamic law, expressed as conception or birth (explicitly or implicitly). Goitein (d. 1985) identified Islamic law's birth as five years before the Prophet's death (i.e. 627 CE).[8] Crone, one of the most influential contemporary scholars in Islamic studies, remarked that Islamic law evolved "from *embryonic* beginnings to classical shapes."[9] Motzki argued that Schacht dated Islamic jurisprudence too late and suggested 25–50 *hijrī*, or 645–670 CE.[10] Dutton isolated the earliest record of Islamic law in a mid-eighth century text.[11] And Hallaq dated "the *embryonic* formation of the [legal] schools" to "sometime during the last decades of the seventh century."[12] The prevalence of the term "origins" and the metaphors of gestation are interrelated and dispersed throughout Islamic legal studies.[13] Regardless of the precise terminology, the emphasis on dating Islamic law is essentialist; it generates a linear understanding of Islamic legal history and neglects Islamic law's embeddedness in distinct contexts. As emphasized in the introduction, it is crucial to recognize that a legal tradition is not born, it does not mature, and it does not die – it merely begins and changes.

Positivism and Linearity: Source-criticism

In this section, I suggest that Islamic studies scholarship concentrates on searching for "origins" because the field is focused on the source-critical

[7] Schacht alleged that "the traditions from the Prophet do not form, together with the Koran, the original basis of Muhammadan law, but an innovation begun at a time when some of its foundations already existed." *Ibid.*, 40.

[8] Shelomo Dov Goitein, "The birth-hour of Muslim law?" *The Muslim World* 50:1 (1960): 23–9 at 27.

[9] Crone, *Roman*, 26, emphasis added.

[10] Motzki stated that "[t]he beginnings of a law that was Islamic in the true sense of the word and of theoretical occupation with it are placed too late by a good half to three quarters of a century." Motzki, *The origins*, 296.

[11] The *Muwaṭṭa'*, composed by Mālik ibn Anas (d. 179/795; Arabia) and dated to *c.* 150/767, is a book of local practice (*'amal*), which, according to Dutton, is "not only our earliest formulation of Islamic law, but also our earliest record of that law as a lived reality rather than the theoretical construct of later scholars." Dutton, *The origins of Islamic law*, 4.

[12] Wael B. Hallaq, *An introduction to Islamic law* (Cambridge; New York: Cambridge University Press, 2009), 35, emphasis added.

[13] For example, El Shamsy pinpoints the "*birth* of classical Islamic law" to the eighth and ninth centuries CE. Ahmed El Shamsy, *The canonization of Islamic law: a social and intellectual history* (New York: Cambridge University Press, 2013), i, emphasis added.

objective of identifying a "reliable" historical text.[14] Source-criticism consists of "the techniques by which the temporal and spatial *origins* of the sources are established as well as their authenticity."[15] Many contemporary scholarly positions (in Western Islamic studies) apply some form of source-criticism to Islamic sources. In turn, the essentialized caricature of Islamic law is treated as an object that can be dated – much like material or narrative-historical sources. Nineteenth-century European scholars delineated source-critical techniques, which remain commonplace and widespread; still, these techniques need to be reassessed because they were intended to make historiography a "pure science."[16] Traditional source-critical rules contribute to a positivist orientation that is presumed either to generate Truth or to be the only valid means of creating historical truth. Likewise, the general assumptions ingrained in scholarly discourse are directed toward discovering an imagined "original" Islam, rather than in exploring historical beginnings. By exploring how conventional scholarship assesses both documentary and non-documentary sources, we can begin to examine the many ways in which source-critical methods limit our engagement with late antique Islamic history.

Documentary Sources for Late Antique Islamic Historiography

Since conventional source-criticism viewed primary sources as the only reliable historical sources, many scholars perceived documentary sources as "original" sources.[17] Consequently, it is not uncommon for Islamic studies scholars to suggest that the "origins" of Islamic law can only be ascertained through documentary sources. This poses a challenge because relatively few documentary or material sources survive from the late antique Islamic period.[18] Besides Qur'ān fragments, the oldest surviving Arabic papyrus

[14] For example, Motzki states that "[i]f this study can contribute to bringing back the debate on the *origins* of Islamic jurisprudence and early traditions in general to a more 'philological' level of interpreting the texts – 'philological' does not necessarily mean 'uncritical' or 'essentialist' – then it will have fulfilled its purpose." Motzki, *The origins*, xvii, emphasis added.

[15] Lorenz, "History: theories and methods," 6871, emphasis added.

[16] On source-criticism in modern historiography, see Martha C. Howell and Walter Prevenier, *From reliable sources: an introduction to historical methods* (Ithaca, NY: Cornell University Press, 2001), 60, 88.

[17] Documentary sources have also received increased scholarly attention in Islamic studies. See Alexander T. Schubert and Petra Sijpesteijn (eds.), *Documents and the history of the early Islamic world*, Islamic history and civilization (Leiden: Brill, 2015); Andreas Kaplony, Daniel Potthast, and Cornelia Römer (eds.), *From Bāwīṭ to Marw: documents from the medieval Muslim world*, Islamic history and civilization, vol. CXII (Leiden: Brill, 2015).

[18] A list of late antique material sources (not all of which are Islamic) is provided in Al-Azmeh, *The emergence of Islam*, 531–3. Since paper became predominant in the Near East only at the end of the

is dated to 643 CE and, like other late antique Arabic papyri, is bilingual because it includes Greek terms.[19] Government and private institutions maintained documentary archives under the Umayyad empire (661–750 CE), if not earlier.[20] There is evidence that the earliest Islamic state relied on written documentation, which suggests that writing may have had a much stronger role to play in the beginning of Islamic history than commonly presumed.[21] However, few documents survive because papyri and other material sources were reused, deteriorated due to environmental conditions, or were destroyed under various circumstances; in addition, it appears that documentary information was recorded in narrative-historical sources with awareness that documents would not be preserved.[22]

In addition to the randomness of preservation and the scarcity of late antique or medieval archives, colonialism and theft have greatly affected the survival of documentary materials. Since the eighteenth and nineteenth centuries, if not earlier, European travelers have been stealing (or purchasing) Near Eastern artifacts[23] – sometimes claiming that theft was necessary to protect artifacts from "native" neglect. In addition, during some European excavations in Egypt and elsewhere, "it often happened that when later documents were found in the course of excavation, they were simply discarded by collectors who were really only interested in classical period texts."[24] Consequently, thousands of Arabic (as well as

tenth century, I focus on papyri. W. Matt Malczycki, "The papyrus industry in the early Islamic era." *Journal of the Economic and Social History of the Orient* 54:2 (2011): 185–202 at 197; Sundelin, "Introduction," 16.

19 Adolf Grohmann and Raif Georges Khoury, *Chrestomathie de papyrologie arabe: documents relatifs à la vie privée, sociale et administrative dans les premiers siècles islamiques* (Leiden; New York: E.J. Brill, 1993), 7. I do not deal with Qur'ān manuscripts in this section. See Keith E. Small, *Textual criticism and Qur'ān manuscripts* (Lanham, MD: Lexington Books, 2011).

20 The ʿAbbāsid empire likely continued and expanded upon Umayyad practices. On ʿAbbāsid archives, see Maaike van Berkel. "Reconstructing archival practices in Abbasid Baghdad." *Journal of Abbasid Studies* 1:1 (2014): 7–22. But see the discussion of archival practices in Michael Chamberlain, *Knowledge and social practice in medieval Damascus, 1190–1350*, Cambridge Studies in Islamic Civilization (Cambridge: Cambridge University Press, 1994), Introduction.

21 Robin notes that "[c]ette réforme de l'écriture arabe pendant les premières décennies de l'Islam prouve que le premier État musulman (avant la sortie d'Arabie) n'a pas d'aversion pour l'écriture, mais, bien au contraire, en fait un usage constant." Julien Christian Robin, "La réforme de l'écriture arabe à l'époque du califat médinois." *Mélanges de l'Université Saint-Joseph* 59 (2006): 319–64 at 351. Schoeler notes that "The practice of depositing official documents and other important texts in special places (temples, archives and libraries) was widespread in classical antiquity, both in Orient and Occident." Gregor Schoeler, "Writing and publishing: on the use and function of writing in the first centuries of Islam." *Arabica* 44:3 (July 1997): 423–35 at 425.

22 Chase F. Robinson, *Islamic historiography* (Cambridge; New York: Cambridge University Press, 2003), 146–7.

23 Sundelin, "Introduction," 2 ("European travelers to Egypt had been bringing home scraps of ancient texts on papyrus for centuries").

24 *Ibid.*

Byzantine Greek and Coptic) documents were destroyed.[25] Multiple foreign interventions in the Near East have contributed to the global scattering of late antique (and medieval) Arabic documentary sources and archives (or collections).[26] Not surprisingly, the very discipline of Arabic papyrology is dominated by Western scholars.[27]

We cannot know how much documentary material has been lost – or continues to be destroyed as the result of occupations, civil wars, and other forms of political violence. It is not surprising then that so few Arabic papyri survive from the seventh through ninth centuries.[28] (In addition, many thousands of surviving Arabic papyri have not been edited or published; the public availability of these documents could alter our current understanding of late antique Islamic archives.[29]) Furthermore, we must recognize that (a) documentary sources may be preferable, but are not incumbent for historical inquiry; (b) documentary sources have limited reliability because they are not unambiguously factual; (c) preservation of documentary sources is so arbitrary that historiography based on these sources is as speculative as historiography based on narrative or other sources. The dearth of documentary sources does not, in and of itself, eliminate the possibility of exploring late antique Islamic historiography, but it has discouraged some Islamicists. Crone, for instance, applies a common source-critical assumption by stating, "Very much indeed must have happened in the period from about 620 to 820, that is in the period for which our documentation is poor. Our chances of being able to reconstruct the *origins* of Islamic law with any degree of certainty are accordingly somewhat limited."[30] Crone's claim illustrates the correlation between the notion of "original" sources and Islamic law's "origins."

Crone's statement also presumes that documentary sources are more reliable than other sources and thereby generate more historical certainty; I am skeptical of both presumptions. Recent scholarship on Arabic papyri typically portrays these documents as close to infallible, capable of

[25] *Ibid.*
[26] *Ibid.*, 5.
[27] This point is mentioned in Geoffrey Khan, *Bills, letters, and deeds: Arabic papyri of the 7th to 11th centuries*, Nasser D. Khalili Collection of Islamic Art (New York: Nour Foundation in association with Azimuth Editions and Oxford University, 1993), 12–13.
[28] Geoffrey Khan, "An Arabic legal document from the Umayyad period." *Journal of the Royal Asiatic Society* 4:3 (1994): 357–68 at 357.
[29] Sundelin cites Yusuf Raghib's estimate of more than 150,000 documents (including 46,300 papyri and 36,335 papers in Vienna); only a small number of these documents have been edited. Sundelin, "Introduction," 4.
[30] Crone, *Roman*, 26, emphasis added.

verifying historical sources or of resolving conflicts in them. While I recognize that most papyrologists today do not subscribe to "pure documentary empiricism," there is still a common empiricist/positivist assumption in the field.[31] For example, Khan claimed that Arabic papyri provide "first-hand, unmediated evidence."[32] Similarly, Frantz-Murphy asserted that documentary sources provide "unbiased, contemporary testimony written by and for the local population, reflecting actual day-to-day practices and circumstances."[33] While these are not uncommon or unreasonable assumptions, documentary sources are produced by individuals who are comparably as subjective as those who compose narrative-historical sources.

I propose that we understand the relationship between documentary and narrative-historical sources as a complementary one: these two genres offer layers of historical evidence.[34] Documentary and narrative-historical sources are not mutually exclusive categories: documentary evidence has been identified within narrative-historical texts and narrative-historical texts have been (re)constructed from documentary sources.[35] (This is why some scholars have sought to recreate documentary archives from narrative-historical sources.[36]) The general presumption that needs to

[31] Roger S. Bagnall, *Reading papyri, writing ancient history* (London; New York: Routledge, 1995), 2.

[32] Geoffrey Khan, *Arabic papyri: selected material from the Khalili collection*, Nasser D. Khalili Collection of Islamic Art (London; New York: Nour Foundation in association with Azimuth Editions and Oxford University Press, 1992), 24.

[33] Gladys Frantz-Murphy, "Arabic Papyrology and Middle Eastern Studies." *Middle East Studies Association Bulletin* 19:1 (1985): 34–48 at 35. See also Sundelin, "Introduction," 8.

[34] In the specific example discussed by Frantz-Murphy and Sundelin, Qurra ibn Sharīk (early eighth century) can be simultaneously both a "tyrant" (as described in narrative-historical sources) and "a careful administrator" (as suggested by documentary sources) because individuals are multidimensional. Consequently, each source uniquely contributes to our knowledge of the past. Frantz-Murphy, "Arabic Papyrology and Middle Eastern Studies," 36. Sundelin, "Introduction," 8.

[35] For examples, see: Raif Georges Khoury, "Papyruskunde." In *Grundriss der Arabischen Philologie* (Wiesbaden: L. Reichert, 1983), 252–70. Wadād al-Qāḍī. "A documentary report on Umayyad stipends registers (*dīwān al-ʿaṭāʾ*) in Abū Zurʿa's *Tārīkh*." *Quaderni di studi arabi* 4 (2009): 7–44; "An Umayyad papyrus in al-Kindī's *Kitāb al-Quḍāt*?" *Der Islam* 84:2 (December 2008): 200–45; "The names of estates in state registers before and after the arabization of the 'dīwāns'." In *Umayyad legacies: medieval memories from Syria to Spain*, ed. by Antoine Borrut and Paul M. Cobb (Leiden: Brill, 2010), 643–59; and "The salaries of judges in early Islam: the evidence of the documentary and literary sources." *Journal of Near Eastern Studies* 68:1 (2009): 9–30; Andrew Marsham. "The pact (*amāna*) between Muʿāwiya ibn Abī Sufyān and ʿAmr ibn al-ʿĀṣ (656 or 658 CE): 'documents' and the Islamic historical tradition." *Journal of Semitic Studies* 57:1 (2012): 69–96.

[36] Muhammad Hamidullah, *Majmūʿat al-wathāʾiq al-siyāsīyah lil-ʿahd al-nabawī wa-al-khilāfah al-rāshidah* (Beirut: Dār al-Irshād, 1969); Muḥammad Māhir Ḥamādah, *al-Wathāʾiq al-siyāsīyah wa-al-idārīyah al-ʿāʾidah li al-ʿaṣr al-umawī: 40–132 H/661–750 M* (Beirut: Muʾassasat al-Risālah, 1974); and *al-Wathāʾiq al-siyāsīyah wa-al-idārīyah al-ʿāʾidah li al-jazīrah al-ʿarabīyah khilāla al-ʿuṣūr al-islāmīyah al-mutatābiʿah: min al-ʿaṣr al-umawī ilá al-fatḥ al-ʿuthmānī li-bilād al-shām wa-miṣr wa-al-jazīrah al-ʿarabīyah 40h-922h = 661m-1516m* (Beirut: Muʾassasat al-Risālah, 1987).

be resisted is that documentary sources contain "original" (or True) historical evidence and that other sources contain unreliable information.[37] Parallel to this, we must reject the not uncommon notion that documentary sources report "original" Islamic law and narrative-historical sources report "unreliable" Islamic law because this way of thinking is a misapplication of source-criticism. Documentary and narrative-historical sources provide different kinds of historical evidence, with the former providing information about daily life that is largely unseen in narrative-historical sources.[38] Numismatics, for example, informs primarily political and economic history.[39] While some late antique documentary sources can provide the basis for a micro-study of local communities (especially in Egypt[40]), such studies would be thematically limited. To pursue late antique Islamic historiography, it is essential to combine both documentary and non-documentary sources.

Narrative-historical Sources for Late Antique Islamic Historiography

I define a non-documentary, late antique Islamic historical source as any source that discusses or reports information about the late antique Islamic period, without considering that the source must survive from the late antique period or that the author or compiler must have lived during late antiquity. Late antique historical sources include biography (*sīrah*), campaigns (*maghāzī)*, compilations of tradition-reports (*muṣannafāt* and *sunan*), exegesis (*tafsīr*), and canonical collections of tradition reports. For the most part, the information contained within these overlapping genres are reported as *aḥadīth* (singular, *ḥadīth*), which means that they are oral history reports on the statements or acts of the Prophet, his Companions, or their Successors.[41] (Whenever possible, I use the term "tradition-report" in lieu of *ḥadīth*.) Throughout the late antique Muslim world, oral

[37] Or, in other words, we should heed Dominick LaCapra's warnings against the "archival fetish." Dominick LaCapra, *History & criticism* (Ithaca, NY: Cornell University Press, 1985), 92.

[38] Sundelin, "Introduction," 9.

[39] Stefan Heidemann, "Numismatics." In *The formation of the Islamic world, sixth to eleventh centuries*, ed. by Chase F. Robinson (Cambridge: Cambridge University Press, 2011), 648–53.

[40] See, for example, Maged S. A. Mikhail, "An orientation to the sources and study of early Islamic Egypt (641–868 ce)." *History Compass* 8:8 (2010): 929–50.

[41] Late antique Islamic narrative-historical sources are comprised, primarily, of traditions: *aḥadīth* (singular, *ḥadīth*) are reports of what the Prophet said, did, or approved; *khabar* can refer to traditions of the Prophet, Companions, or Successors; *āthār* (singular, *athar*) are usually traditions from Companions or Successors, but can also refer to Prophetic traditions. For the sake of clarification, *sunnah* is a normative custom of the Prophet or late antique Muslim community.

transmission was often supplemented by writing as part of an expansive process that intertwined oral and written forms of learning and communication.[42] Although materials for writing were readily available and used for specific purposes (primarily for government administration and correspondence), most late antique narrative-historical sources were produced in oral form and transmitted orally for several generations before being transcribed in their surviving textual forms approximately a century after the events. But this does not reflect a simple "aversion" to writing. Indeed, orality appears, at least in some cases, to have been an intentional choice.[43] Orality was normative in late antiquity, arguably because it is a relatively egalitarian form of knowledge transmission, which may have suited the Islamic movement.[44] In effect, late antique Muslim societies maintained oral archives in which they preserved historical reports. Too often, scholars treat institutional (particularly state) archives as authoritative, without acknowledging the elite and subjective nature of those archives.[45] We need to reconsider our assumptions about the nature and significance of institutional archives.[46] And we need to recognize non-institutional archives; it is important to acknowledge that oral transmission is an archival practice.

The evaluation of narrative-historical sources is the subject of intense controversies in Islamic studies and beyond. Indeed, no student of Islamic history can escape the conundrum of debates surrounding these sources. Robinson aptly observed, "it is a measure of just how conservative the professional study of Islamic history remains that the noisiest controversy of the last 25 years concerns the reliability of our written sources, rather than the models according to which we are to understand and use them."[47] In this book, I attempt to provide such a model. I am not interested in "resolving" these intractable debates or in admonishing my colleagues with opposing views/methods.

[42] Gregor Schoeler, *The oral and the written in early Islam*, ed. by James E. Montgomery, trans. by Uwe Vagelpohl, Routledge Studies in Middle Eastern Literatures (London and New York: Routledge, 2006), 41–7.

[43] Michael Cook, "The opponents of the writing of tradition in early Islam." *Arabica* XLIV (1997): 437–530.

[44] On egalitarianism in late antique Islamic history, see Louise Marlow, *Hierarchy and egalitarianism in Islamic thought* (New York: Cambridge University Press, 1997).

[45] On the elitism of state archives, see Ranajit Guha, *Elementary aspects of peasant insurgency in colonial India* (Delhi: Oxford, 1983), 14–15.

[46] See Jacques Derrida and Eric Prenowitz. "Archive fever: a Freudian impression." *Diacritics* 25:2 (1995): 9–63.

[47] Robinson, "Reconstructing early Islam," 115. See also Chase F. Robinson, *Empire and elites after the Muslim conquest: the transformation of northern Mesopotamia* (New York: Cambridge University Press, 2000).

Source-criticism's General Rules

As previously noted, many of the general principles of source-criticism operate as a search for an "original" historical source. As a result, a great deal of scholarship places too much epistemological value on the notion of "origins." My critique of the dominant ways in which documentary and historical sources are valued and used in Islamic studies is a critique of positivism more generally.[48] The continued predominance of positivist orientations is not merely a neutral matter of the field's resistance to non-positivist methods. Many late antique Islamic sources are historical, but not in the *modern* sense of the term.[49] Thus, "origins"-oriented methodologies (such as source-criticism) impose an understanding of history that is incongruent with late antique Islamic sources – sources that reflect an "antihistorical consciousness."[50] There is a mismatch between the nature of these sources (in a non-judgmental sense) and the methods applied to study them in modern scholarship; this mismatch corresponds to the divergence between source-criticism and historiography. When a scholar makes a claim about the supposed unreliability of late antique Islamic sources, she assumes a philosophical position about the nature of truth and imposes a modern understanding of historiography.[51] Indeed, any evaluation of a society's historiography must be culture-specific because there are no universal rules for what constitutes valid historical writing. The dichotomy between literary and historical writing is a modern one that likely would not have been recognized in the late antique and medieval periods.[52] Consequently, modern methodologies of source-criticism constitute "a procedure that subordinates these narratives to the rules of evidence and to the secular, linear calendar that the writing of

[48] On this critique, see Adorno, *The positivist dispute in German sociology*.

[49] For a brief and accessible overview of modern historiography, see G. G. Iggers, "Historiography and historical thought: modern history (since the eighteenth century)." In *International Encyclopedia of the Social & Behavioral Sciences*, ed. by Neil J. Smelser and Paul B. Baltes (Oxford: Pergamon, 2001), 6798–804.

[50] Dipesh Chakrabarty, "Postcoloniality and the artifice of history." In *A subaltern studies reader, 1986–1995*, ed. by Ranajit Guha (Minneapolis, MN: University of Minnesota Press, 1997), 263–93.

[51] Clark notes that "A central issue distinguishing ancient from modern historiography concerns the assessment of truth claims." Clark, *History, theory, text*, 167. This is because modern historiography was primarily positivist, meaning that it seeks to determine "the Truth."

[52] On the modern (particularly Western) distinction between literary and historical writing, see *Ibid.*, 166–7. Robinson expressly notes the absence of this distinction in medieval Islamic historical sources. Robinson, *Islamic historiography*, 84. Similarly, Gafni implies that "Christian historiography" differs from "rabbinic historiography" in its fundamental understandings of the past. Isaiah Gafni, "Rabbinic historiography and representations of the past." In *The Cambridge companion to the Talmud and rabbinic literature*, ed. by Charlotte Elisheva Fonrobert and Martin S. Jaffee (Cambridge; New York: Cambridge University Press, 2007), 295–312 at 307.

'history' must follow."[53] Source-critical methodologies do not merely organize or classify Islamic sources; they construct them in new ways.[54]

The variety of positions on interpreting Islamic narrative-historical sources are too numerous and intricate to be surveyed here.[55] In this section, I will briefly address some common suppositions about the authenticity, reliability, and historical meaning of late antique and medieval Islamic narrative-historical sources. In doing so, I intend to suggest that we can bridge the gap between oral and written sources by recognizing the multi-layered nature of late antique and medieval Islamic archives. I posit that source-critical techniques analyze historical sources, but these techniques do not provide guidelines for writing historiography.

Many specialists in the field of Islamic studies presume that the oral beginnings of late antique Islamic sources render these sources historically unreliable.[56] However, oral transmission – as the primary archival form – is not necessarily less reliable than written transmission, in light of scribal errors, problems of textual preservation and transmission, and scribal agency. Schoeler observes, "it is as easy to falsify material in writing as it is in oral transmission!"[57] The oral transmission of these sources, coupled with their redaction or recording in written form at least a century after the events transpired, leads to allegations that all the sources for late antique Islamic history are unreliable – or deeply suspect.[58]

[53] Chakrabarty, "Postcoloniality and the artifice of history," 285.

[54] As Asad has explained in an analogous context, "statistics has been not merely a mode of *representing* a new kind of social life but also of *constructing* it." Talal Asad. "Ethnographic representation, statistics and modern power." *Social Research* 61:1 (1994): 55–88 at 70.

[55] For different perspectives on Islamic historiography, see 'Abd al-'Azīz al-Dūrī, *The rise of historical writing among the Arabs*, ed. by Charles Issawi and Bernard Lewis, trans. by Lawrence I. Conrad, Modern classics in Near Eastern Studies (Princeton, NJ: Princeton University Press, 1983). Fred M. Donner, *Narratives of Islamic origins*, Studies in Late Antiquity and Early Islam 14 (Princeton, NJ: The Darwin Press, 1998). See also Robert G. Hoyland, "History, fiction and authorship in the first centuries of Islam." In *Writing and Representation in Medieval Islam: Muslim horizons*, ed. by Julia Bray, Routledge Studies in Middle Eastern Literatures (London and New York: Routledge, 2006), 16–46.

[56] For a relevant discussion, see James E. Montgomery's introduction in Schoeler, *The oral and the written*, 13. Vansina counters assumptions about the unreliability of oral sources, noting that "oral tradition is not necessarily untrustworthy as a historical source, but, on the contrary, merits a certain amount of credence within certain limits." Jan Vansina, *Oral tradition: a study in historical methodology*, trans. by H. M. Wright (Chicago, IL: Aldine Pub. Co., 1965, c1961), 1.

[57] Schoeler, *The oral and the written*, 41.

[58] Donner's view in this regard is typical: "as any serious student of Islamic *origins* will know, these literary sources pose various problems as evidence for Islamic *origins*. First of all, there is the fact that they are not contemporary sources; sometimes they were written many centuries after the events they describe. It is obvious that reconstructing Islamic *origins* on the basis of such literary materials violates the first law of the historian, which is to use contemporary sources whenever possible." Donner, *Narratives*, 4, emphasis added.

Sources that were not written contemporaneously with historical events are not fundamentally ahistorical for several reasons. First, contemporaneous sources are not inherently more reliable than later sources; there is no general rule that can be applied to all sources or that can guarantee the reliability of a particular kind of source. Second, not all written sources should be categorized as "later" because the narratives transcribed in them were initially composed orally and transmitted contemporaneously as part of both a narrative-historical and a living legal tradition.[59] For instance, some narratives about the Prophetic and Caliphal past were actively used as precedents for legal decisions and were preserved not simply in narrative-historical form, but also socio-legal practice. (I take up this overlap between historical events and legal practice in greater detail throughout the subsequent chapters of this book.) Third, later written sources are based on both oral sources and contemporaneous written texts that are no longer extant. In other words, contemporaneous documentary sources that did not survive may be embedded within later written texts. Fourth, the dismissal of later historical sources often serves to elevate documentary sources, creating a false dichotomy between those sources and engendering false trust in documentary sources.[60] Finally, we know about vast periods of history from a wide variety of areas exclusively through the accounts of non-contemporary sources; if we rejected these sources or falsified them, it would be impossible to write historiographies of these periods and places.

Another repeated criticism of late antique Islamic sources is that they cannot be factual because they are inconsistent, as manifested in variant narratives of the same historical event.[61] This criticism is based on the incorrect premise that consistency is a necessary precondition for the reliability of historical sources. But individuals experience, interpret, and relate facts differently. For example, variations in the testimonies of several

[59] For a discussion of orality in Islamic historiography, see Schoeler, *The oral and the written*.

[60] For example, Sundelin claims, "[i]n comparison with literary sources which were usually written long after the events they purport to describe, the papyri and these other documentary materials offer an immediate and relatively unmediated window through which to view the early development of an Islamic society." Sundelin, "Introduction," 7.

[61] Donner provides a succinct description of this argument: "The skeptical approach derives plausibility from years of source-critical and tradition-critical research that has conclusively demonstrated the existence in Islamic tradition of a heavy overlay of pious legend and the influence of manipulations, distortions, and fabrications of all kinds. This tampering with the tradition makes it unclear where the kernel of historical 'truth' may lie, and gives the skeptics the opening to claim that there is no historical kernel at all, only successive layers of repeatedly reshaped and redacted material." Donner, *Narratives*, 25.

witnesses to a crime are normative and do not preclude the admissibility of the testimony. The expectation that only one consistent narrative is factual is a manifestation of a positivist orientation that presumes only one Truth. Or, as Mohammed Bamyeh notes, "With some effort at listening to the interplay of ideational and discursive configurations reverberating through the classical story of Islam, almost all 'contradictions' uncovered by revisionist historians can be shown to be contradictions solely in modern logic and modality of reading."[62] The processes used in transmitting, transcribing, and compiling late antique Islamic sources inevitably resulted in dissimilarities, but these variations do not mean that the sources are unreliable.[63] There are slippages and ambiguities in all historical sources, but, as I explore in the next chapter, these aspects can be productive sites of historical inquiry. Muslim historians, transmitters, or compilers did not modify the "truth" only in order to serve their interests or the interests of their patrons; they also understood history differently from each other. Moreover, Muslim historians of late antiquity were not a homogenous group. The myriad political and theological debates that animated late antique Muslim societies suggest that moments of consensus among Muslim historians are unlikely to be mere fabrications.[64] Historians can build upon both the unanimity and the divergences evident in our diverse textual evidence.[65]

Two default modes of engaging narrative-historical sources dominate the field of Islamic studies: one presumes that the available sources are false and looks for snippets of factuality, while the other presumes that

[62] Mohammed A. Bamyeh, *The social origins of Islam: mind, economy, discourse* (Minneapolis, MN: University of Minnesota Press, 1999), viii.

[63] Schoeler provides a comprehensive and thorough discussion of variant traditions. Schoeler, *The oral and the written*, 33.

[64] Tucker explains that "consensus on historiographic beliefs in uncoerced, heterogeneous, and sufficiently large groups of historians is indicative of knowledge of history." Aviezer Tucker, *Our Knowledge of the Past* (Cambridge: Cambridge Unviersity Press, 2004), 23. Similarly, Gil observed, "I find the general corpus of traditions – as preserved in the Arab sources – to be essentially genuine. I am well aware of the trend among some distinguished scholars, which is now in vogue to consider most traditions regarding the period of the Prophet to be mere inventions dating from later periods, a kind of typological construction. It is clear that there was some embellishment by later generations, often encouraged by rulers for propaganda purposes ... traditionalists were aware of such interests, which often conflicted with each other, and it is easy for us to detect them; basically, however, the facts we do have could not have been invented, and there is a fair amount of unanimity in the way they are presented." Moshe Gil, "The earliest waqf foundations." In *Related worlds: studies in Jewish and Arab ancient and early medieval history* (Aldershot; Burlington, VT: Ashgate, 2004), Ch. IX at 125.

[65] Donner contends that "consensus exists because events actually did happen in the way described by our sources, and were so well known in the early community that all groups were required to accept the basic 'script' of events." Donner, *Narratives*, 289.

they are true and searches for snippets of inaccuracy. This binary is unproductive for multiple reasons. Most Islamic narrative-historical sources convey the testimony of several historical actors; the veracity of all these sources cannot be negated based on problems (or fabrications) in some of the reports.[66] Moreover, there is no hierarchical organization that appears to have altered Islamic sources to conform to a particular historical vision – in late antiquity or the medieval era.[67] It is not uncommon for scholars to claim that late antique Islamic sources reveal more about their compilers (or "authors") than historical "facts."[68] But this skepticism is applicable to all historical sources (including contemporaneous ones) and does not justify a complete dismissal of a source's historical value. Moreover, all sources – including material and archival sources – are subjective because human actors (all of whom are subjective) interpret them. Those who maintain archives of documentary sources and those who compose documentary sources are as ideologically invested as those who compose, redact, or transmit oral sources. In other words, subjectivity does not negate historical reliability.

In recent years, some scholars have relinquished attempts to use late antique Islamic sources for historiographical purposes and chosen instead to explore the fictional or narrative dimensions of these texts.[69] This

[66] As Motzki astutely noted, "The possibility that *isnāds* and biographies were fabricated does not allow one to conclude that they really were fabricated. This must be positively proven first. The proof that some *isnāds* or some information contained in biographies of tradents were really fabricated does not necessarily mean that most of them or even all of them were." Harald Motzki, "The question of the authenticity of Muslim traditions reconsidered: a review article." In *Method and theory in the study of Islamic origins*, ed. by Herbert Berg (Leiden: Brill, 2003), 211–58 at 245.

[67] Donner noted, "It is noteworthy that in a century of close work on Islamic *origins*, during which a vast number of new sources of every variety have been recovered from manuscripts and published, the new debates or opinion groups that have come to light appear to be not so much ones that reveal dangerous opinions suppressed by the 'authorities,' but marginal positions that simply died out for lack of sufficient interest to sustain them in the community." Donner, *Narratives*, 28–9, emphasis added. See also, al-Dūrī, *The rise of historical writing*.

[68] Referring to narratives about the beginning of Islamic history, Donner claims "We might liken these accounts collectively to a mirror, in which the authors of the second and third centuries looked to see Islam's *origins*, but saw reflected mainly themselves – their own understandings of how those *origins* 'must have been,' based on the conditions and ideals of their own age." Donner, *Narratives*, 284, emphasis added. This view is also implemented in Suleiman Ali Mourad, *Early Islam between myth and history: al-Ḥasan al-Baṣrī (d. 110H/728CE) and the formation of his legacy in classical Islamic scholarship*, Islamic Philosophy, Theology and Science. Texts and Studies, 62 (Leiden; Boston, MA: Brill, 2006). See also Tayeb El-Hibri, *Reinterpreting Islamic historiography: Harun al-Rashid and the narrative of the `Abbasid caliphate* (New York: Cambridge University Press, 1999); and *Parable and politics in early Islamic history: the Rashidun caliphs* (New York: Columbia University Press, 2010).

[69] For instance, Rubin states, "The question 'what really happened' in Muḥammad's times is not the one asked in this book, which instead is concerned with the manner in which the texts tell the story of Muḥammad's life, and is aimed to discover how the various evolving versions of this story

narrative approach to the sources purportedly reflects the postmodern linguistic turn. While this approach contributes to literary scholarship, it minimizes the historicity of these texts. Any assumption of a dichotomy between facts and narratives is misguided because facts are always narrativized (or embedded in narratives).[70] To relegate narrative-historical sources to an *exclusively* literary analysis is a disservice to historiography. Like all historical sources, late antique Islamic texts are neither purely fictional nor purely factual. Because oral sources are comparable to written sources or to documentary evidence, verifying historical probability always involves a comparison of all the available historical evidence. As Vansina explains, "The comparative method is the one which enables the historian to arrive at an overall estimate of the relative reliability of the various testimonies."[71] While most scholars in Islamic studies rely on the available sources, they do so while interpolating numerous caveats about their reliability, authenticity, or validity. These caveats are based on rigid understandings of conventional source-criticism. As Spiegel has asserted, "ultimately, medieval textuality grants us (mediated) access to the past."[72] As for medieval sources, so too for late antique sources: historians should question why we mediate our sources in the way we do. In pondering this question, I want to point out the power dynamics that underlie methodological discussions. While the aforementioned critiques of late antique Islamic sources are common in the field and presented as neutral or empirically based, there are deeper historical and ideological consequences for how these sources are evaluated.

Politics and Ideology: Textual Criticism and Subaltern Critique

In an attempt to forge a middle path between rejection and acceptance, some scholars have developed a variety of techniques for establishing the historical validity of late antique Islamic sources; this is most evident in

tell us about the image of the Prophet as perceived by the believers among whom these texts were created and circulated." Uri Rubin, *The eye of the beholder: the life of Muḥammad as viewed by the early Muslims: a textual analysis*, Studies in late antiquity and early Islam, 5 (Princeton, NJ: Darwin Press, 1995), 1.

70 Postfoundationalists do not consider historical distance (i.e., the presumed gap between facts and narratives) to be a problem. Bevir explains, "All knowledge – including natural science as well as history – involves a kind of theoretical or literary construction of the facts." Bevir, "Why historical distance is not a problem," 32.

71 Vansina, *Oral tradition*, 114.

72 Spiegel, *The past as text*, xviii.

ḥadīth studies. One of the more dominant and respected contemporary methodologies for analyzing Islamic narrative-historical sources is dating tradition-reports (*aḥadīth*). Dating tradition-reports has become a significant objective of many Islamic law scholars, most likely because they view the identification of an "original" source as necessary for discovering Islamic law's "origins."[73] Many scholars apply a modified version of one form of source-criticism: textual criticism. Textual criticism is an influential source-critical method that was traditionally concerned with uncovering an "original" text (*Urtext*); while textual criticism is not necessarily positivist, it commonly is.[74] Responding to this trend, Hallaq argued that "[t]o search for the 'origins' of Islamic law in the long process of *hadīth* evolution – as some prominent modern scholars have done – is therefore to miss the point altogether."[75] This is because the dominance of traditional textual criticism leads some Islamicists to pursue the equivalent of a "critical edition" of Islamic history, which has three significant effects: (1) it ignores multiple "editions" (or beginnings); (2) it imposes the notion of an individual author; (3) it imposes a date that is associated with the author (rather than the text, broadly conceived). Ironically, literary and bibliographic scholars have reconsidered the utility of the "critical edition" because it erases, rather than recovers, the "original text."[76] Much like the "rules" for textual criticism/editing, rigid methodological rules do not recover/reconstruct "original" tradition-reports, but rather create a construct that is identified as an "original" source.

Motzki and others have advocated for their persuasive methodology of *isnād-cum-matn* (i.e., chain of transmission and text) analysis.[77] Motzki argue that late antique Islamic sources are not "trustworthy" because they "originated in subsequent centuries" and are "based on earlier oral and/

[73] See, for example, Mohammed Shahab Ahmed, "The Satanic verses incident in the memory of the early Muslim community: an analysis of the early *riwāyahs* and their *isnāds*." Dissertation, Princeton University, 1999.

[74] Traditional textual criticism is the scholarly pursuit of a critical edition of a historical text in order to "recreate" a lost "original" text. See Sebastiano Timpanaro and Glenn W. Most, *The genesis of Lachmann's method* (Chicago, IL: University of Chicago Press, 2005). The practice of textual criticism has been the subject of vigorous debates and has changed considerably in recent years; for an overview, see G. Thomas Tanselle, *Textual criticism since Greg: a chronicle, 1950–2000* (Charlottesville, VA: The Bibliographical Society of The University of Virginia, 2005).

[75] Hallaq, *The origins*, 200.

[76] For a discussion of the ambiguities and shifts in meaning of "original text," see Epp Eldon Jay. "The multivalence of the term 'original text' in New Testament textual criticism." *The Harvard Theological Review* 92:3 (1999): 245–81.

[77] Harald Motzki. "Theme issue: methods of dating early legal traditions: introduction." *Islamic Law and Society* 19:1–2 (2012): 1–10 at 3.

or written sources."[78] Consequently, he presents a methodology for dating tradition-reports that resembles the scholarly interest in "dating" the birth of Islamic law. His approach entails analyzing the text (*matn*), chain of transmission (*isnād*), and biographical information about the transmitters of tradition-reports in order to identify the "originator" of the report.[79] This then allows a scholar to date the report to that "originator" – rather than accepting the tradition-report's reported date. In other words, if a report narrates an event that took place during the Prophet's life, it would be dated to the "originator" (who may not have lived until decades after the Prophet's death). This "originator" is sometimes identified as the "author" of the tradition,[80] reflecting a modern interest in delineating a text's authority through an authorial figure.[81] In other words, this dating methodology *constructs* an author by identifying the first "verified" transmitter. The communal process by which late antique Islamic historical sources were compiled is disconcerting to modern scholars who are more trusting of individual or institutional authors. Notably, one implication for this interest in individual authorship is reflected in contemporary Islamic legal historiography's focus on one jurist, al-Shāfiʿī (d. 820; Arabia/Egypt), as the "author" of orthodox Islamic jurisprudence.[82] This "great man" approach to Islamic legal history has been critiqued.[83] By contrast, in this book, I resist both examining a tradition-report's chain of transmission and overemphasizing "great jurists."

In addition to identifying an author, modern dating methods assemble sources to fit into a linear paradigm. It is common for contemporary scholarship dealing with tradition-reports to include visual representations of the chain of transmission; these images represent the sources in

78 *Ibid.*, 1.

79 This methodology is briefly described in *Ibid.*, 2–3. It is more fully elaborated in Motzki's other work; see Harald Motzki, Nicolet Boekhoff-van der Voort, and Sean W. Anthony, *Analysing Muslim traditions: studies in legal, exegetical and maghāzī ḥadīth* (Leiden; Boston, MA: Brill, 2010). It is also applied in Pavel Pavlovich, *The formation of the Islamic understanding of kalāla in the second century AH (718–816 CE): between scripture and canon* (Boston, MA; Leiden: Brill, 2016).

80 By way of example, see Nicolet Boekhoff-van der Voort, "The *kitāb al-maghāzī* of ʿAbd al-Razzāq b. Hammām al-Ṣanʿānī: searching for earlier source-material." In *The transmission and dynamics of the textual sources of Islam: essays in honour of Harald Motzki*, ed. by Harald Motzki *et al.* (Leiden; Boston, MA: Brill, 2011), 27–47 at 42.

81 I am not arguing that the author is dead (à la Barthes and Foucault), but rather that the interest in identifying an individual author is incongruent with late antique Islamic sources. Relatedly, I am not denying authorial intentions, but rather complicating the modern construct of "an author" as applied to these sources.

82 Schacht was a major proponent of this theory; see Schacht, *The origins*.

83 See Wael B. Hallaq. "Was al-Shafiʿi the Master Architect of Islamic Jurisprudence?" *International Journal of Middle East Studies* 25:4 (1993): 587–605.

vertical linearity, implying an evolutionary progression of the report from one transmitter to another. This hierarchical, linear framework implicitly shapes the scholar's task as a search for one "origin/truth" and it reflects the imposition of textual critical methodologies in modern *ḥadīth* criticism. Yet tradition-reports are historical narratives that do not neatly correspond to manuscript variants (the focus of textual criticism). Both documentary and narrative-historical sources are texts; reading these texts cannot be limited to their "technical" dimensions (of dating, authorship, or transmission), but also must include their substantive dimensions. When scholars convert late antique Islamic sources into empiricist forms (by dating and quantifying them), they erase some of the historiographic, literary, and oral dimensions of these sources. I am not arguing that the entire enterprise of textual criticism is flawed or that scholars should not create visual representations (i.e., visual chain of transmission trees) of tradition-reports. I am merely pointing out that searching for an "original" text/author is intimately related to searching for an "original" Islam.

The seemingly neutral methodological choices of source-criticism have broad, limiting implications for knowledge production; methodological choices have political and ideological consequences that are not easily discernable. This becomes apparent when we contrast modern source-criticism (and textual criticism) with the internal heuristics applied by late antique and medieval Muslim scholars. The forms of historical criticism deployed by medieval Muslim scholars clearly differed from those of modern scholars.[84] We have extensive evidence that medieval Muslim historians employed a variety of techniques to evaluate the reliability and authenticity of oral reports.[85] Much like Motzki's *isnād-cum-matn* analysis, medieval Muslim scholars analyzed both the text of reports and the chain of transmission.[86] Moreover, the medieval Muslim scholars who compiled and redacted tradition-reports created an archive. While the heuristics and archival practices of late antique and medieval Muslims differed from

[84] For an evaluation of "the criticism of traditions as practised by the Muhammadan scholars" as "inadequate," see Schacht, *The origins*, 4.

[85] For historical works, see Muslim ibn Hajjāj al-Qushayrī (d. 875), *al-Tamyīz*, ed. Ṣāliḥ ibn Aḥmad ibn Thābit Dayyān (Ṣan'ā': Maktabat al-Imām al-Albānī, 2009); Abū Bakr Aḥmad ibn 'Alī al-Khaṭīb al-Baghdādī (d. 1071; Iraq), *Kitāb al-kifāyah fī 'ilm al-riwāyah* (Cairo: Dār al-Kutub al-Ḥadīthah, 1972); 'Uthmān ibn 'Abd al-Raḥmān Ibn al-Ṣalāḥ al-Shahrazūrī (d. 1245), *Muqaddamat Ibn al-Ṣalāḥ fī 'ulūm al-ḥadīth* (Damascus: Dār al-Ḥikmah, 1972). See also Ṣubḥī Ṣāliḥ, *'Ulūm al ḥadīth, wa-muṣṭalaḥuhu: 'arḍ wa-dirāsah*, 2nd edn. (Damascus: University of Damascus Press, 1963).

[86] Mu'taz al-Khaṭīb, *Raddu al-ḥadīth min jihat al-matn: dirāsah fī manāhij al-muḥaddithīn wa al-uṣūlīyīn* (Beirut: Arab Network for Research and Publishing, 2011).

those of modern scholars, they are just as subjective and imperfect. When modern scholars dismiss the products of traditional Islamic *ḥadīth* science, they effectively dismantle the oral–written archive of late antique and medieval Muslim scholars. In other words, because modern methodologies identify Islamic historical sources (particularly tradition-reports) as myth and folklore, rather than history, they task themselves with creating new, modern archives that effectively "subalternize" the sources. By this I mean a double subalternizing effect: (1) the subaltern narrator of the tradition-report is subjected to a linear, textual critical analysis that "modernizes" his or her speech; (2) the subaltern, medieval Muslim historian is erased by the application of source-critical methods.[87] The reasons for doing so are political, not methodological; debates about "methodologies" cannot be isolated from their ideological subtexts. Indeed, many scholars in the field of Islamic studies treat their methodologies as orthodoxies. Because these methodologies are hegemonic, resistors are silenced in much the same ways that the sources themselves are silenced.

Alternatives: Late Antique Beginnings and Historical Sources

I follow historians who view their craft as presenting theories about the past by critically using all the available historical evidence. Thus, I resist the search for "origins," as manifested in both the prevailing philosophy of history and the conventional methodologies of contemporary Islamic studies. It is worth repeating that I do not reject this scholarship entirely. Similarly, I do not consider all late antique Islamic sources to convey Truth, but rather the potential for historical truth, which is discerned through close textual analysis with cultural, critical interpretative work.[88] I concur with other scholars who advocate that scrutinizing the entire Islamic historiographical tradition, along with links to non-Islamic sources, is the ideal means of pursuing late antique Islamic historiography. Our task is to investigate how to interpret our sources critically. To do so, we cannot focus solely on the linguistic codes of our sources; instead, we must integrate a historical understanding of social codes. Reading diverse

[87] I recognize that subalternity generally refers to a class of non-elite historical actors; while late antique or medieval Muslim historians may have been relatively "elite," I use the term to draw a comparison as to how modern historical methods silence these historical sources.

[88] This balancing objective is shared by other scholars in fields with similar debates about sources. For example, see Geoffrey Herman, *A prince without a kingdom: the Exilarch in the Sasanian era* (Tübingen: Mohr Siebeck, 2012), 17.

sources must occur in conjunction with an engagement of their historical contexts.

This book's three case studies (the even-numbered chapters) share some important commonalities in their approach to primary sources. Each case study integrates insights from several genres of Islamic historical sources and juxtaposes them with historical evidence from other "Near Eastern" communities. This book mines late antique Islamic sources for evidence of oral traditions.[89] Chapters 2 and 4 rely on a similar set of textual sources. I explore biographical texts (*sīrah* and *maghāzī)* for information about Prophetic-era legal practices. Pre-canonical collections of traditions (*muṣannafāt* and *sunan*) provide evidence of historical practices that sometimes were not included in canonical texts.[90] Specifically, I rely on two of the earliest surviving compilations of reports (*muṣannafāt*) by al-Ṣanʿānī (d. 827; Yemen) and Ibn Abī Shaybah (d. 849; Iraq). For historical information about the mid-seventh to mid-eighth centuries, I focus on these sources because they are less entangled in particular juristic outcomes than other collections. That is, unlike some of their contemporaries and successors, these two scholars were more focused on compiling tradition-reports than on substantiating particular legal opinions through tradition-reports.[91] Both Chapters 2 and 4 make extensive use of exegetical works; I focus on differentiating between late antique exegetes – including Ibn ʿAbbās (d. 687; Arabia), Mujāhid ibn Jabr (d. *c.* 720; Arabia), and Muqātil ibn Sulaymān al-Balkhī (d. 767; Iraq) – and their foremost medieval successor, al-Ṭabarī (d. 923; Iraq). I examine these sources for information about how historical interpretive communities might have understood particular Qurʾānic verses with legal consequences. In addition, the legal opinions of late antique Muslim jurists who implemented law prior to the consolidation of legal schools are collected from multiple sources; likewise, the legal norms of pre-Islamic communities are introduced to

89 Underlying the aggrandizement of written legal texts and corresponding diminishment of the oral tradition is a clear scholarly bias: "Classic legal theory has a pejorative view of orally based law, which is defined negatively in relation to written law. In our view this approach bears all the hallmarks of evolutionism, and should not be spared criticism." Norbert Rouland, *Legal anthropology*, trans. by Philippe G. Planel (Stanford, CA: Stanford University Press, 1994), 170.

90 In some cases, I offer possible explanations for discrepancies between pre-canonical and canonical texts. However, because the process of canonization is complex and difficult to trace, I will not elaborate this point. See ʿAbd al-Majīd Maḥmūd ʿAbd al-Majīd, *al-Ittijāhāt al-fiqhīyah ʿinda aṣḥāb al-ḥadīth fī al-qarn al-thālith al-hijrī* (Cairo: Maktabat al-Khānjī, 1979).

91 See *Ibid.* On the historical value of these sources, see Harald Motzki. "The *muṣannaf* of ʿAbd al-Razzāq al-Ṣanʿānī as a source of authentic *aḥādīth* of the first century A.H." *Journal of Near Eastern Studies* 50:1 (1991): 1–21; and *Ḥadīth: origins and developments* (Aldershot; Burlington, VT: Ashgate/Variorum, 2004).

suggest the complexity of intertextuality in the late antique Near East. These chapters illustrate the overlaps of juristic and historical texts.

The case study in Chapter 6 takes a larger and broader approach to sources. I use a multitude of Judaic and Islamic legal texts dating from the third through fourteenth centuries to create two chronologies of legal changes in Judaic and Islamic legal history related to wife-initiated divorce. In particular, I emphasize the rabbinic reception of a seventh-century Geonic decree about wife-initiated divorce by examining Judaic legal texts dating from the eighth through fourteenth centuries and their Islamicate context. I then offer an alternative understanding of this Geonic decree by examining Near Eastern legal precedents. Alongside papyrological evidence, I interweave legal evidence from several regional legal systems.

Implications and Applications

The common focus on "origins" in Islamic legal historiography essentializes Islamic law (and Islam in general) in two ways: by anthropomorphizing it (as an animate object) and by objectifying it (as a material object). The anthropomorphizing of Islamic law is apparent in scholarship that seeks to identify its "birthdate"; correspondingly, the objectification of Islamic law is evident in scholarship that seeks to identify the (birth)date of its *sources*. "Origins"-oriented historiography parallels the dominance of conventional source-critical methods that seek to identify "original" historical sources. In particular, outdated textual critical searches for an "original" text (*Urtext*) shapes Islamic legal studies. These "origins" methodologies frame historiography as a positivist search for Truth. By correlating the prevalent philosophy of history with evaluations of historical sources in conventional Islamic legal historiography, I have illustrated the overlapping influences of anthropomorphic and of positivist thinking in Islamic studies.

The case study in the next chapter offers a non-linear, contextualized narrative of late antique Islamic legal history that parallels my non-positivist, multi-layered approach to historical sources. In it, I rely on multiple genres (biography, historiography, exegesis, and law) to compose a historical narrative that is critical without being needlessly fixated on problematic assumptions about the reliability or authenticity of sources. Reading the available sources closely and comprehensively introduces new or underappreciated insights. As the next chapter illustrates, the available historical sources indicate that a late antique legal opinion prohibiting the execution of war prisoners is consistent with the history of battles waged by the Prophet. By scrutinizing a variety of historical sources, I illustrate that, over time, Muslim jurists interpreted the Qur'ān and key events in Islamic history in different ways. In doing so, I recognize that this process is normative to all societies and does not reflect a unique weakness in Islamic historical sources.

CHAPTER 2

Legal Historiography – a Case Study in International Law

Law defines violence, law provokes violence, and law legitimates violence. Yet the possibility that law may limit violence in warfare is an enduring question.[1] While debates about the laws of warfare often focus on protecting civilian life, the treatment of enemy combatants is a no less significant measure of war's brutality and of law's role in it. In this chapter, I will investigate law's violence as it pertains to a matter of international law: the treatment of prisoners of war. This chapter will contrast late antique (beginning of Islam to 800 CE) and medieval (after 800 CE) legal debates about the treatment of war prisoners by juxtaposing a range of historical sources. In relying upon these sources, I apply the insights of Chapter 1, in which I asserted that there is a connection between a historical (rather than essentialist) understanding of Islamic law's beginnings and a historical (rather than a source-critical) approach to late antique Islamic sources. Correspondingly, in this chapter, I scrutinize a variety of historical sources to reconstruct an Islamic legal beginning on the treatment of war prisoners that would otherwise be indiscernible.

I demonstrate that historical interpretation is an integral component of legal hermeneutics and that it can generate juristic disagreement. By tracking the shift from prohibition to permissibility of executing prisoners

[1] Law's potential to limit violence in warfare animated the Boalt-UNLV Symposium on *Law, War, and History* in February 2007; I thank Harry Scheiber and David Tanenhaus for their invitation to deliver an earlier version of this chapter at that symposium. I thank Ira Lapidus, David Lieberman, Hossein Modarressi, and the anonymous reviewer of *Law and History Review* for their comments and suggestions on a previous version of this chapter. I thank Rhiannon Graybill, Maria Mavroudi, and Amr Osman for their comments on a revised version.

of war between the late antique and medieval periods, I expose the connections between changing legal opinions and changing interpretations of Islamic legal history. In late antiquity, the majority of Muslim jurists (or legal traditionists) prohibited executing prisoners of war. The authority of these late antique jurists was based on their reputation, popularity, or, in some cases, their appointments as judges. In the medieval era, with the establishment of legal orthodoxy, the authority of jurists came to be interlinked with the authority of an orthodox legal school and was applied by courts. In this period, prohibition of execution became a minority opinion, attested in the Imāmī Shīʿī school[2] and in the dissenting perspective of the Ḥanafī school.[3] By contrast, the majority opinion during the medieval period was to permit prisoner execution.

For our purposes, "prisoner of war" refers to combatants captured during or immediately after warfare. In the context of seventh-century Arabia, "combatants" generally means males above the age of puberty and capable of engaging in warfare.[4] I do not address the question of when warfare ends, but undeniably this temporal issue was relevant to the delineation of who constitutes the enemy. That is, if war is ongoing – and not limited to a particular battlefield for a specific time – then "prisoner of war" is a less stable category. In turn, the porousness of "war prisoner" likely obfuscated the distinction between combatant and enemy. In addition, the frequency of warfare is difficult to measure, but likely also relevant to delineating the category of "prisoner of war." It is possible that as the medieval Islamic empires continued to expand, Muslims found themselves in constant states of warfare and orthodox jurists took for granted that the enemy could always be killed rather than imprisoned. However, empirically determining this possibility is beyond the scope of this chapter. Instead, I will focus on tracking the discursive shifts in exegesis, historiography, and law about prisoners of war.

I will explore a few questions in order to highlight the ambiguous, overlapping roles of historians and jurists as they construct (legal) histories:

[2] al-Ḥasan ibn Yūsuf Ibn al-Muṭahhar al-Ḥillī (d. 1325; Iraq), *Tadhkirat al-fuqahāʾ*, 20 vols. (Qum: Muʾassasat Āl al-Bayt li-Iḥyāʾ al-Turāth, 1993/1994), 9: 154–55 (Imāmī Shīʿī: if a combatant is imprisoned after combat ends, he may not be executed and the Imām decides between freeing, ransoming, or enslaving).

[3] Muḥammad ibn Aḥmad al-Sarakhsī (d. eleventh century; Transoxania) and Muḥammad ibn al-Ḥasan al-Shaybānī (d. 804/5; Iraq), *Sharḥ al-siyar al-kabīr*, ed. by Ṣalāḥ al-Dīn Munajjid, 5 vols. (Cairo: Maʿhad al-Makhṭūṭāt bi-Jāmiʿat al-Duwal al-ʿArabīyah, 1971/1972), 3:1024 (Ḥanafī jurists al-Ḥasan bin Zīyād and Ḥammād bin Abī Sulaymān opposed prisoner execution).

[4] The normative Islamic legal opinion is that non-combatants may not be killed. Non-combatants are generally defined as children, women, the elderly, the sick (physically or mentally), and the disabled.

(1) Do historical narratives about the battles that occurred during the Prophet's lifetime illustrate his legal practice concerning the treatment of prisoners of war?
(2) How did late antique exegetes gloss specific Qur'ānic verses in light of relevant historical events?
(3) After the Prophet's death, how did late antique Muslim jurists adjudicate the treatment of war prisoners?
(4) What legal reasoning did key Muslim jurists of the medieval period apply in permitting the execution of war prisoners?
(5) What can explain the discrepancy between the chronologically earlier opinion (prohibiting prisoner execution) and the later, more dominant legal opinion (permitting prisoner execution)?

Asking and answering these questions will illustrate the complicated, dynamic process by which legal normativity changes despite juristic claims of *following* tradition.

My focus is on late antique historiography and on the legal reasoning articulated by generations of Muslim scholars in an array of legal and historical texts, rather than on reconstruction of normative war practices that may have influenced legal opinions.[5] I will occasionally refer to contemporaneous war situations, but I avoid fully exploring them because historical sources report an inconsistent variety of practices.[6] Historical evidence cannot verify if late antique wars differed from medieval wars in such a way as to affect the prohibition on war prisoner execution. Similarly, socio-economic consequences to the legal ruling on war prisoner execution cannot be easily measured or historically reconstructed; keeping

[5] Khaled Abou El Fadl suggests that the prohibition of prisoner execution disappeared from Islamic legal history because it was "inconsistent with the war practices of the age." Khaled Abou El Fadl. "The rules of killing at war: an inquiry into classical sources." *The Muslim World* 89:2 (April 1999): 144–57 at 153. For a brief overview of Islamic legal opinions on prisoners of war, see Abū Ja'far Muḥammad ibn Jarīr al-Ṭabarī (d. 923; Iraq), *Kitāb al-jihād wa-kitāb al-jizyah wa-aḥkām al-muḥāribīn min kitāb ikhtilāf al-fuqahā'*, ed. by Joseph Schacht (Leiden: Brill, 1933), 141–6.

[6] For instance, the *Life* of Theodota of Amid (d. 698) reports collecting ransom money from church attendees (living under Islamic rule) for the purpose of ransoming captives (presumably held by the Byzantines). See MS Jerusalem (St Mark's, Syrian Orthodox Patriarchate) 199, fol. 557b (an eighteenth-century Arabic translation of a Syriac vita originally composed in the early eighth century). Writing in the twelfth century, the Patriarch of Antioch, Michael the Syrian, reported that Muslims both killed and freed war prisoners throughout the eighth century CE. See Michael I. Patriarch of Antioch (d. 1199; Syria), *Chronique de Michel le Syrien: patriarche jacobite d'Antioche (1166–1199)*, trans. by Jean Baptiste Chabot, 4 vols. (Paris: Ernest Leroux, 1899–1910), 2:479, 501, 26 and 3:1–2. (I thank Jack Tannous for these references.) See also Youval Rotman, *Les esclaves et l'esclavage: de la Méditerranée antique à la Méditerranée médiévale: VIe-XIe siècles* (Paris: Belles lettres, 2004), 56–62, 68–75.

prisoners of war alive (rather than executing them) likely burdened an army's movement and resources (by generating additional needs for provisions) and burdened the local population near the battlefield. While I recognize the significance of facts on the ground, in this chapter my primary objective is to scrutinize the internal dynamics of *legal* reasoning. Thus, historical analysis of each individual jurist's possible contextual influences is beyond the scope of this chapter. Moreover, I contend that the majority opinion pertaining to prisoner of war execution shifted from prohibition to permissibility not because of changes in normative war practices, but rather changes in how jurists interpreted historical narratives. By combining biographical, exegetical, historical, and legal sources, I demarcate that a significant shift in the majority juristic opinion regarding prisoner execution (from prohibition to permissibility) likely occurred in conjunction with a change in the juristic understanding of key historical events and Qur'ānic verses.

It should be noted that I will not deal with the granting of safe conduct (*amān*) in this chapter because it is not directly relevant to the questions addressed here. The granting of safe conduct occurs when a Muslim gives a non-Muslim an assurance of safety from being hurt by Muslims. However, it appears to have been infrequent for these assurances to be given during battles.[7] Specifically, juristic discussions suggest primarily non-warfare circumstances for granting safe conduct.[8] Moreover, late antique jurists who did mention safe-conduct on the battlefield implied that the context of war alters normative procedures. For example, the fourth caliph and first Shīʿī Imām, ʿAlī ibn Abī Ṭālib (d. 661; Arabia) declared that a political leader could choose whether to honor the granting of safe conduct to a combatant who has laid down his weapons.[9] Similarly, the late antique jurist Sufyān al-Thawrī (d. 778; Kūfah) declared that a prisoner of war may not be granted safe conduct.[10] Analyzing the juristic reasons

[7] On the political uses of safe conduct, see Mathieu Tillier. "Le cadi et le sauf-conduit (*amān*): les enjeux juridiques de la diplomatie dans l'Orient abbasside." *Islamic Law and Society* 19:3 (2012): 201–21; Andrew Marsham and Chase Robinson. "The safe-conduct for the Abbasid ʿAbd Allāh b. ʿAlī (d. 764)." *Bulletin of the School of Oriental and African Studies, University of London* 70:2 (2007): 247–81.

[8] See, for example, the discussion of safe conduct as it pertains to traders, potential converts, and others in ʿAlī ibn Abī Bakr al-Marghīnānī (d. 1197; Farghāna), *Al-Hidāyah = the Guidance: a translation of al-Hidāyah fī sharḥ Bidāyat al-mubtadī, a classical manual of Ḥanafī law*, trans. by Imran Ahsan Khan Nyazee (Bristol: Amal Press, 2006), 325–8.

[9] Muḥammad Rawwās Qalʿah'jī, *Mawsūʿat fiqh ʿAlī ibn Abī Ṭālib*, Fī sabīl mawsūʿah fiqhīyah jāmiʿah; Silsilat mawsūʿat fiqh al-salaf, 4 (Damascus: Dār al-Fikr, 1983), 118.

[10] Muḥammad Rawwās Qalʿah'jī, *Mawsūʿat fiqh Sufyān al-Thawrī*, Fī sabīl mawsūʿah fiqhīyah jāmiʿah; Silsilat mawsūʿat fiqh al-salaf, 10 (Beirut: Dār al-Nafā'is, 1990), 157.

for limiting or halting the granting of safe conduct on a battlefield would require more thorough investigation than this chapter can sustain. Thus, in this chapter, I assume that the category of prisoners is not related to safe conduct.

Prisoners of War in Islamic History: The Prophetic Period

Since the actions and legal pronouncements of the Prophet are authoritative in orthodox Islamic legal theory, it is necessary to begin by reconstructing the battles during his life.[11] My objective is to trace historical narratives about prisoners in Islamic sources that would later form the basis for jurisprudential reasoning. Therefore, the focus of the following pages is on reconstructing internal Muslim histories. For the purposes of this chapter, I base all references to historical battles on histories related by Muslim historians.

Since there were no battles during the first decade of the Muslim community's existence, I investigate battles that occurred between 622 CE (the year of the *hijrah*, or migration to Medina) and 632 CE (the year of the Prophet's death). I will distinguish between raids and actual battles involving a military confrontation of two sides; only those events in which two armies appear to have challenged each other will be categorized as battles.[12] In part, I achieve this goal by differentiating between conflicts motivated primarily by politics (i.e., battles) and by economics (i.e., raids).[13] Similarly, the sources do not clearly delineate between combatants killed during battle and prisoner-combatants killed in captivity, but I delineate this distinction from details in the narratives. (As noted, the conduct of warfare is beyond the scope of this chapter.) The main sources for the following

[11] Motzki noted that "already in the first/seventh century people consciously resorted to the Qur'ān and to rulings of the Prophet as sources of the law, if not as extensively as in later times." Motzki, *The origins*, 295.

[12] I intentionally modify the lists of battles reported in canonical sources, such as Muḥammad Ibn Sa'd (d. *c.* 845; Iraq), *Kitāb al-ṭabaqāt al-kabīr*, trans. by S. Moinul Haq, assisted by H. K. Ghazanfar, 2 vols. (Karachi: Pakistan Historical Society, 1967), 2:2. See also Muḥammad Ibn Isḥāq (d. 767; Iraq) and 'Abd al-Malik Ibn Hishām (d. 833; Egypt), *The life of Muḥammad: a translation of Isḥāq's Sīrat rasūl Allāh*, trans. by Alfred Guillaume (Karachi: Oxford University Press, 1955, 2004), 659–60; Muslim ibn Hajjāj al-Qushayrī (d. 875; Khurāsān), *Ṣaḥiḥ Muslim; being traditions of the sayings and doings of the prophet Muhammad as narrated by his companions and compiled under the title al-Jāmi'-uṣ-ṣaḥīh, by Imām Muslim*, trans. by 'Abdul Ḥamīd Ṣiddīqī, 4 vols. (Lahore: Sh. Muhammad Ashraf 1971–75), 3:1004–5, nn. 4462–70.

[13] This is because raids or "*Ghazw* had always been an important component of the Bedouin economy of survival." Bamyeh, *The social origins of Islam*, 42. Thus, this differentiation between a raid and a battle is fashioned from indications in the sources; admittedly, the distinctions are ambiguous.

historical reconstruction of late antique Islamic warfare are the eighth-century biography by Ibn Isḥāq (d. 767; Iraq) and several collections of tradition-reports (primarily late-eighth- and early-ninth-century texts).[14] These sources are not exhaustive but they represent conventional historical knowledge among Muslims in the late antique and medieval eras.

The first battle waged by the late antique Muslim community was at Badr in 624 CE/2 AH; a Muslim army of approximately 300 soldiers confronted the Quraysh army of nearly 1,000. (The Quraysh were the powerful pagan Arabs who had mistreated the Prophet and his followers in Mecca for approximately thirteen years.) Combat began with a traditional three-on-three challenge; the three Muslims defeated the three Qurashīs. Open combat then began, but only lasted a few hours before most of the Qurashī army fled. Nearly 70 Qurashīs were killed in battle and a similar number were taken captive.

On the issue of the handling of the majority of Badr prisoners, the historical sources are relatively consistent and transparent: they report that the Badr prisoners were ransomed.[15] It appears that the Prophet considered the possibility of executing the prisoners and rejected it. But there may have been communal discomfort with his rejection of execution, which would explain why there are narratives suggesting that the Prophet could have chosen to execute the prisoners. Rather than interpreting the Prophet's rejection of execution as a prohibition of execution, some Muslims interpreted the issue as a matter of choice. For example, a widely disseminated tradition-report claims that the Prophet consulted two of his Companions (Abū Bakr and ʿUmar, the first two men who succeeded him as caliphs) on the situation of the prisoners; the former recommended ransoming and the latter recommended execution.[16] Similarly, a tradition-report claims

[14] On biographical literature, see Harald Motzki (ed.), *The biography of Muḥammad: the issue of the sources*, Islamic history and civilization. Studies and texts, vol. XXXII (Leiden; Boston, MA: Brill, 2000).

[15] Muḥammad ibn Muslim al-Zuhrī (d. 742; Syria), *al-Maghāzī al-nabawīyah*, ed. by Suhayl Zakkār (Damascus: Dār al-Fikr, 1981), 65–6; Maʿmar Ibn Rāshid (d. 770; Baṣrah) and ʿAbd al-Razzāq ibn Hammām al-Ḥimyarī al-Ṣanʿānī (d. 827; Yemen), *The expeditions: an early biography of Muḥammad*, trans. by Sean W. Anthony (New York; London: New York University Press, 2014), 58–9; ʿAbd al-Razzāq ibn Hammām al-Ḥimyarī al-Ṣanʿānī (d. 827; Yemen), *Muṣannaf fī al-ḥadīth*, ed. Ayman Naṣr Azharī, 12 vols. (Beirut: Manshūrāt Muḥammad ʿAlī Bayḍūn, Dār al-Kutub al-ʿIlmīyah, 2000), 5:141, 144, 240. (On the historical value of this source, see Motzki, "The muṣannaf of ʿAbd al-Razzāq al-Ṣanʿānī.")

[16] In another version, the Prophet consulted the community, which chose ransoming. ʿAbd Allāh ibn Muḥammad Ibn Abī Shaybah (d. 849; Iraq), *Muṣannaf fī al-aḥādīth wa-al-āthār*, ed. by Saʿīd Laḥḥām, 9 vols. (Beirut: Dār al-Fikr, 1989), 7:673 and 8:474–5. See also Abū Jaʿfar Muḥammad ibn Jarīr al-Ṭabarī (d. 923; Iraq), *Tafsīr al-Ṭabarī: jāmiʿ al-bayān ʿan taʾwīl āy al-qurʾān*, ed. by ʿAbd Allāh ibn ʿAbd al-Muḥsin Turkī, 26 vols. (Riyadh: Dār ʿĀlam al-Kutub, 2003), 11:273–5.

that the angel Gabriel offered the Prophet the option of killing the Badr prisoners.[17] According to other reports, two Qurashī prisoners – both of whom had tormented the Prophet when he was in Mecca – were executed: al-Naḍr bin al-Ḥārith and ʿUqbah b. Abī Muʿayṭ.[18] As for al-Naḍr, who had vehemently opposed the Prophet in Mecca, it is not possible to determine whether the Prophet ordered or approved his killing, which may have occurred during battle.[19] As for ʿUqbah, who had humiliated the Prophet in Mecca by placing a camel's fetus on his back while he was prostrated in prayer,[20] reportedly, he was seen "lying slain in the battlefield."[21] This account directly contradicts a different report that claims ʿUqbah was executed.[22] These contradictory reports call into question the executions themselves – or, at least, the timing (i.e., during or after battle). Indeed, both individuals are listed as Qurashī losses, not prisoners, at Badr – possibly implying that they were killed during battle.[23] Moreover, it is unclear if these executions were exceptional – for example, if these two individuals were killed in retaliation for a particular crime in accordance with tribal custom. To delineate the status of this event as specific or general, we must analyze the treatment of other Badr prisoners and also prisoners from other battles.

Every historical source incorporates the interpretations of its author. By reading a variety of sources against each other, however, we can trace inconsistencies and scrutinize how Muslim jurists dealt with these inconsistencies. In this case, the two purported prisoner executions at Badr contradict not only the reported Prophetic decision against execution, but also many other accounts of how war prisoners at Badr were treated. The Prophet "divided the prisoners amongst his companions and said, 'Treat them well.' "[24] Ibn Isḥāq cites one of the prisoners as recounting that "when they ate their morning and evening meals they gave me the bread and ate the dates themselves in accordance with the orders that the apostle

17 ʿAbd al-Razzāq ibn Hammām al-Ḥimyarī al-Ṣanʿānī (d. 827; Yemen), *Mukhtaṣar al-muṣannaf*, 4 vols. (Beirut: Dār al-Jīl, 1997), 2:291.

18 al-Ṣanʿānī, *Muṣannaf*, 5:140–1, 250. Ibn Abī Shaybah, *Muṣannaf*, 8:477. Ibn Rāshid, *The expeditions*, 58–9.

19 Ch. Pellat, "al-Naḍr b. al-Ḥāri<u>th</u> b. ʿAlḳama b. Kalada b. ʿAbd Manāf b. ʿAbd al-Dār b. Ḳuṣayy." In *Encyclopaedia of Islam*, ed. by P. Bearman *et al.* (Leiden; Boston, MA: Brill, 2007).

20 Ibn Abī Shaybah, *Muṣannaf*, 8:441; al-Qushayrī, *Ṣaḥiḥ Muslim*, 3:986–87, nn. 4421–22.

21 Ibn Abī Shaybah, *Muṣannaf*, 8:441. al-Qushayrī, *Ṣaḥiḥ Muslim*, 3:987, no. 4424.

22 Moreover, tradition-reports identify ʿAlī ibn Abī Ṭālib (d. 661; Arabia) as the executioner; ʿAlī, who would later become the fourth caliph and the first Shīʿī Imām, is credited in the Imāmī Shīʿī school as having prohibited execution of war prisoners.

23 Ibn Isḥāq and Ibn Hishām, *The life*, 337.

24 *Ibid.*, 309.

had given about us. If anyone had a morsel of bread he gave it to me."[25] It is also reported that the Prophet was unable to sleep because a Badr prisoner (reportedly Ibn ʿAbbās) was bound too tightly; he relaxed once the prisoner's bindings were loosened.[26] These narratives imply that the Badr prisoners of war were fed and clothed before being set free – some without and others with a ransom. Ibn Isḥāq reports the situation of a poor prisoner (and poet) who requested to be set free; the Prophet granted his request on condition that he would not fight against the community again.[27] While these historical narratives romanticize the Prophet's pious behavior, they also suggest that most prisoners from the battle of Badr were not executed and were specifically protected by the Prophet's command and practice. (Indeed, the motif of a prophet protecting captives from execution, as well as feeding and freeing them, echoes the biblical story of Elisha (2 Kings 6:20–24).[28] The biblical text describes the Israelites as treating their Judahite captives well (2 Chronicles 28:12–15).) When the narratives about the majority of Badr prisoners being treated well are compared with the conflicting narratives about two prisoner executions, it becomes more difficult to determine a lucid historical precedent for legal purposes. The significance of these contradictory and vague narratives is in their interpretation by later generations of Muslims – especially jurists.[29] Scrutinizing narratives from late antique Muslim historiography about subsequent battles may illuminate a historical pattern.

The second major Muslim battle was at Uḥud in 625 CE/3 AH. The Quraysh of Mecca, angered by the preceding year's defeat at Badr, fortified their army and returned to battle the Muslim army. Interestingly, the third caliph, ʿUmar ibn al-Khaṭṭāb, is reported to have claimed that after the Prophet consulted and rejected his advice at Badr (see above), prisoners were executed at Uḥud rather than ransomed.[30] Contradicting this reported claim, historical works do not indicate that any prisoners of war were taken.[31] The next battle, which occurred in 627 CE/5 AH, is

[25] *Ibid.*

[26] al-Zuhrī, *al-Maghāzī*, 66; Ibn Rāshid, *The expeditions*, 58–9; al-Ṣanʿānī, *Muṣannaf*, 5:240.

[27] Ibn Isḥāq and Ibn Hishām, *The life*, 318. (Incidentally, this poet reportedly did help Quraysh in their next battle, Uḥud, against the Muslim community.)

[28] *The new Oxford annotated Bible with Apocrypha: new revised standard version*, ed. by Michael David Coogan *et al.*, 4th edn. (New York: Oxford University Press, 2010), 543.

[29] For an example of how a jurist interpreted these events, see ʿAbd al-Salām ibn Saʿīd al-Saḥnūn (d. 854; Tunisia) *et al.*, *al-Mudawwanah al-kubrá li-Imām Mālik ibn Anas al-Aṣbaḥī*, ed. by ʿĪsá ibn Masʿad Zawāwī, 5 vols. (Beirut: Dār al-Kutub al-ʿIlmīyah, 1994), 1:502–3.

[30] Ibn Abī Shaybah, *Muṣannaf*, 8:475.

[31] Ibn Isḥāq and Ibn Hishām, *The life*, 387–89; Ibn Rāshid, *The expeditions*, 76–81. Other sources suggest one prisoner (the poet from the battle of Badr) was executed, but this may have occurred

known as the Battle of the Trench because the Muslim community dug a defensive trench around a critical part of the city of Medina. The battle was a prolonged siege: the confederation of troops led by the Quraysh could not cross the ditch and after three weeks of besieging the city of Medina, cold, sandstorm weather sent them fleeing. There are no reports of prisoners being taken.[32] The next battle was also a prolonged siege – this time at Khaybar in 628 CE/6 AH; no prisoners are reported to have been taken captive.[33] In 629 CE/7 AH, the Prophet sent numerous letters to diplomatic figures in and near the Arabian Peninsula. Northern Arab tribes under Byzantine protection reportedly killed his emissaries. Consequently, a Muslim army marched northward to Mu'tah to confront a large Byzantine army; the Muslim army was defeated and no Byzantine prisoners appear to have been taken.[34] The Battle of Ḥunayn took place in 630 CE/8 AH. Women, children, and, apparently, combatants were taken as captives, but they were all released without ransom.[35] While there are some reports of additional events that may be classified as battles, they are not relevant here because they did not result in prisoners of war.[36]

In compiling this brief sketch of Prophetic battles, I have relied primarily upon late antique Islamic historical sources. My categorization of these battles differs from some historical and contemporary sources.[37] In large part, this is because, as previously mentioned, I differentiate between battles and expeditions or raids.[38] The Prophet's battles, all of which occurred

during battle or as a result of his violating a prior agreement with the Prophet (not to fight against the Muslim community). This discrepancy needs further investigation, beyond the scope of this chapter.

[32] Ibn Isḥāq and Ibn Hishām, *The life*, 459–60.

[33] al-Zuhrī, *al-Maghāzī*, 84–5; Ibn Rāshid, *The expeditions*, 90–1. A few non-combatant captives may have been taken as booty, but no "soldiers" were captured. Ibn Isḥāq and Ibn Hishām, *The life*, 511, 514–16.

[34] Ibn Isḥāq and Ibn Hishām, *The life*, 535. See also of David Stephan Powers, *Muḥammad is not the father of any of your men: the making of the last prophet* (Philadelphia, PA: University of Pennsylvania Press, 2009), Ch. 5.

[35] al-Zuhrī, *al-Maghāzī*, 94. Ibn Isḥāq and Ibn Hishām, *The life*, 570, 576; Ibn Rāshid, *The expeditions*, 104–9; Muḥammad ibn Ismā'īl al-Bukhārī (d. 870; Khurāsān), *Ṣaḥīḥ al-Bukhārī = The translation of the meanings of Ṣaḥiḥ al-Bukhārī, Arabic–English* [Jami' al-sahih], trans. by Muhammad Muhsin Khan, 9 vols. (Medina: Dar al-Fikr, 1981), 4:235.

[36] For example, al-Wāqidī reports that the Prophet sent Usāmah bin Zayd bin Ḥārithah to the people of Ubná and massacred them; the report is not widely disseminated. More importantly, he does not appear to have taken any war prisoners. Muḥammad ibn 'Umar al-Wāqidī (d. 822; Medina/Iraq), *Kitāb al-maghāzī*, ed. by Marsden Jones (Beirut: 'Ālam al-Kutub, 2006).

[37] See, for example, 'Abd al-Salām bin al-Ḥasan Adghīrī, *Ḥukm al-asrá fī al-islām wa-muqāranatuhu bī al-qānūn al-dawlī al-'āmm* (Rabat: Maktabat al-Ma'ārif, 1985), 89–117. But see Ra'ūf Shalabī, *al-Jihād fī sabīl allāh: majālatuhu wa-wasā'iluhu wa-āhdāfuhu* (Cairo: Dār al-Turāth al-'Arabī, 1974), 106–7.

[38] See footnote 12.

during the last decade of his life, offer us only two clear situations in which he dealt with combatant prisoners of war – Badr and Ḥunayn. At Badr, most prisoners were ransomed, in accord with tribal custom. At Ḥunayn, the prisoners were set free without ransom. In all the battles following Badr, no prisoners appear to have been executed. This series of events would be logical if the post-Badr directive of treating a prisoner precluded the prerogative of execution and was implemented in subsequent battles. Viewed in light of narratives from all the battles during the Prophet's lifetime, the overall treatment of prisoners of war at Badr more likely suggests the impermissibility of poor treatment (including killing).

Other historical narratives about the Prophet's practices corroborate this interpretation (against the permissibility of prisoner execution) of the imperfect historical record. For instance, the Prophet ordered that someone be set free when he was captured during a raid.[39] Another tradition-report explicitly suggests that not executing prisoners is divinely approved (or ordained).[40] Similarly, in his detailed history of raids, al-Wāqidī (d. 822; Medina/Iraq) relates that during the raid of Nakhlah a prisoner was taken and (the future second caliph) ʿUmar ibn al-Khaṭṭāb (d. 644; Arabia) wanted to kill him, but the Prophet prohibited it.[41] The evidence relating to these specific raids further implies that the Prophet's normative practice was not to execute captives. There is an additional, potentially corroborating narrative about an expedition, which differs from both a battle and a raid because no fighting is involved or expected. The Prophet sent Khālid ibn al-Walīd (d. 642; Arabia/Syria) to the Jadhīma tribe near Mecca in order to invite them to submit (to Islam) and reportedly instructed him (and his entourage) not to fight.[42] Khālid ibn al-Walīd asked the tribesmen to relinquish their arms and seems to have assured them that they would not be hurt; but then he restrained them and killed some of them. The Prophet vigorously condemned Khālid's act and sent ʿAlī ibn Abī Ṭālib to the tribe to compensate them for the wrongful deaths of their tribesmen; the sources describe the incident as a pagan act that was the subject of significant scrutiny.[43] While the men in this incident

[39] The individual was Thumāma. See al-Qushayrī, *Ṣaḥiḥ Muslim*, 3:962–3, n. 4361.

[40] The report narrates that "eighty persons from the inhabitants of Mecca swooped down upon the Messenger of Allah (may peace be upon him) from the mountain of Tanʿīm. They were armed and wanted to attack the Holy Prophet (may peace be upon him) and his Companions unawares. He (the Holy Prophet) captured them but spared their lives. So, God, the Exalted and Glorious, revealed the verses: 'It is He Who restrained your hands from them and their hands from you in the valley of Mecca after He had given you a victory over them.'" *Ibid.*, 3:1001, n. 4452.

[41] al-Wāqidī, *Kitāb al-maghāzī*, 48.

[42] Ibn Isḥāq and Ibn Hishām, *The life*, 561.

[43] *Ibid.*, 562.

were not war prisoners, the narrative indicates that *potential* combatants who surrender should not be killed.

While historical sources attribute piety to the Prophet's practice of protecting prisoners, it may have also been motivated by an economic interest in benefiting from ransoming.[44] That execution of war prisoners was an economically poor choice (in comparison to ransoming or enslavement) is unmistakable. Indeed, ransoming prisoners was a profitable enterprise that benefited these struggling tribal communities. Because war prisoners could offer slave labor and specialized skills or knowledge, there were practical reasons to prohibit their execution.[45] Although there was a clear incentive *not* to execute war prisoners, there appears to be little evidence for why prisoners *should* be executed (other than retaliation/revenge against particular individuals). To answer the first question, *Do historical narratives about the battles that occurred during the Prophet's lifetime represent his legal practice concerning treatment of prisoners of war?*: the strongest conjecture based on the available historical evidence suggests that the Prophet's legal practice was not to kill prisoners of war.[46] It must be noted, however, that there are no reports of the Prophet explicitly prohibiting execution of prisoners of war.

Late Antique Qur'ānic Exegesis

Biographical and historical texts were compiled and redacted in late antiquity alongside an overlapping genre: exegesis.[47] Late antique exegetes implicitly produced legal opinions because their interpretations of verses had significant legal consequences. In determining the legal implications of a verse, scholars often attempted to reconstruct the historical events related to the verse. In this section, I will explore key Qur'ānic verses pertaining to war prisoners, with particular attention to how these verses can (or cannot) be reconciled with the historical materials presented above. I will outline the exegesis of important late antique figures, including Ibn

[44] Indeed, exegetes attributed this economic motivation to the Prophet. See footnote 94.

[45] Many medieval Islamic sources report that some prisoners of war were released on condition of teaching a certain number of Muslims to read. Muhammad Hamidullah, *Muslim conduct of state: being a treatise on Siyar* (Malaysia: Islamic Book Trust, 2012), 233.

[46] For a contemporary text echoing this interpretation, see ʿAbd al-Wāḥīd Muḥammad Fār, *Asrá al-ḥarb: dirāsah fiqhīyah wa-taṭbīqīyah fī niṭāq al-qānūn al-duwalī al-ʿāmm wa-al-sharīʿah al-islāmīyah* (Cairo: ʿĀlam al-Kutub, 1975), 192.

[47] On exegetical texts, see Andrew Rippin. "Al-Zuhrī, *Naskh al-Qur'ān* and the problem of early *Tafsīr* texts." *Bulletin of the School of Oriental and African Studies, University of London* 47:1 (1984): 22–43.

ʿAbbās (d. 687; Arabia), Mujāhid ibn Jabr (d. *c.* 720; Arabia), and Muqātil ibn Sulaymān al-Balkhī (d. 767; Iraq).[48]

Qur'ān 8:67 states, "It is not fitting for a prophet to have prisoners of war until he has thoroughly subdued (*yuthkhina*) the land. You seek the temporal goods of this world; but God is concerned with the hereafter." There are two interrelated interpretations of this verse associated with Ibn ʿAbbās. The first interpretation is that Ibn ʿAbbās identified this verse as having been revealed after Badr. He explained the key term (*yuthkhina*) as meaning overcoming the enemy in fighting (*qitāl*); Ibn ʿAbbās also suggested that Muslims at that battle were more interested in collecting ransom for prisoners than in fighting and that this verse was an exhortation to combat.[49] This first interpretation implies that prisoners of war should be taken only after a military victory through combat has been established. Ibn ʿAbbās' second interpretation comes from a source that is considered less reliable; this second commentary claims that Q 8:67 was revealed at Badr when Muslims were weak and it was later supplemented by Q 47:4 (see below); accordingly, the two verses provide Muslims with three options for dealing with war prisoners: killing, enslaving, and ransoming.[50] Notably, this second interpretation does not include freeing war prisoners, which is mentioned in Q 47:4. (If Ibn ʿAbbās' personal experiences were relevant to his exegesis, the second interpretation seems unlikely: he himself reported being imprisoned at the battle of Badr and ransoming himself; surely he would have been aware that permitting prisoner execution would more likely result in reciprocation.[51])

Echoing the reference to Q 47:4 in Ibn ʿAbbās' second interpretation, Mujāhid claims that Q 8:67 allows two possibilities for dealing with war prisoners – ransoming or freeing; despite this explanation, he defines the key verb (*yuthkhina*) as killing (*qatl*).[52] Mujāhid's interpretation of this

[48] On Ibn Abbās, see Herbert Berg. "The *isnād* and the production of cultural memory: Ibn Abbās as a case study." *Numen* 58:2 (2011): 259–83; I. E. Jaffer. "The asānid of Ibn ʿAbbās in the tafsīr of Al-Ṭabarī and Ibn Kathīr." *Journal for Semitics* 16:2 (2007): 449–70.

[49] Muḥammad ibn Yaʿqūb al-Fīrūzābādī (d. 1414/5; Iran), *Tanwīr al-miqbās min tafsīr Ibn ʿAbbās* (Beirut: Dār al-Kutub al-ʿIlmīyah, 1980), 151; and *Tafsīr Ibn ʿAbbās*, trans. by Mokrane Guezzou (Louisville, KY; [Amman, Jordan]: Fons Vitae; Royal Aal al-Bayt Institute for Islamic Thought, 2008), 225.

[50] ʿAlī ibn Abī Ṭalḥah (d. 760/1), *Ṣaḥīfat ʿalī ibn abī ṭalḥah: ʿan ibn ʿabbās fī tafsīr al-qurʾān al-karīm*, ed. by Rāshid ʿAbd al-Munʿim al-Rajjāl (Cairo: Maktabat al-Sunnah, 1991), 256. Also cited in Muḥammad Rawwās Qalʿahʾjī, *Mawsūʿat fiqh ʿAbd Allāh ibn ʿAbbās*, Fī sabīl mawsūʿah fiqhīyah jāmiʿah; Silsilat mawsūʿat fiqh al-salaf (Beirut: Dār al-Nafāʾis, 1996), 121.

[51] Ṭalḥah, *Ṣaḥīfat ʿAlī ʿan Ibn ʿAbbās*, 257.

[52] Mujāhid Ibn Jabr (d. *c.* 720; Arabia), *Tafsīr al-Imām Mujāhid ibn Jabr: al-mutawaffā sanat 102 H*, ed. by Muḥammad ʿAbd al-Salām Abū al-Nīl (Cairo: Dār al-Fikr al-Islāmī al-Ḥadīthah, 1989), 358.

verse is illogical because if "subduing" means "killing," then there would be no prisoners of war because dead combatants cannot be ransomed or freed. Mujāhid's interpretation of this verse would be logical if the key verb means fighting (*qitāl*) – as Ibn ʿAbbās suggests – instead of killing (*qatl*); the orthographic difference between the terms is one long vowel and it is entirely possible that it was caused by a transmission (oral or scribal) error.[53] In comparison, Muqātil explains the first clause of the verse ("it is not fitting for a prophet") as meaning before the Prophet Muḥammad, such that the Prophet was permitted to have prisoners; Muqātil identifies this verse as being revealed after Badr and does not specify the meaning of the key verb (*yuthkhina*).[54]

How can we reconcile the historical events outlined above with Q 8:67 and its commentaries? As previously noted, there were only war prisoners at Badr and Ḥunayn and after those battles they were ransomed and freed, respectively. If this verse were occasioned by Badr, then it would not be a prohibition against having war prisoners because the Prophet did have prisoners afterward (at Ḥunayn). Likewise, the key verb (*yuthkhina*) is unlikely to mean killing because there is no indication that the Prophet killed all the war prisoners at subsequent battles. Indeed, historical texts refer to Muslim armies *overcoming* the enemy army without killing all the combatants.[55] Thus, Ibn ʿAbbās' first commentary on this verse is most congruent with the historical materials: the verse chastises Muslims for collecting prisoners to ransom instead of fighting. To clarify further how late antique exegetes understood this verse, we need to examine Q 47:4.

Qur'ān 47:4 states, "Therefore, when you meet the unbelievers, smite at their necks; At length, when you have thoroughly subdued them (*athkhantumūhum*), bind a bond firmly (on them): thereafter (is the time for) either generosity (grace) or ransom." (The key verb, *athkhantumūhum*, in this verse is from the same root as the key verb, *yuthkhina*, in Q 8:67.) Here again, two divergent interpretations of this verse are associated with Ibn ʿAbbās. The first interpretation explains the key verb (*athkhantumūhum*) as overcoming and imprisoning, at which point the prisoner may be freed or ransomed.[56] (This interpretation is consistent

[53] A similar reading of Q 47:4 is suggested in al-Ṭabarī, *Tafsīr*, 21:190. As I explained in Chapter 1, I am skeptical of the methodology of textual criticism and I therefore do not claim that this suggested reading recovers the "original" text.

[54] Muqātil ibn Sulaymān al-Balkhī (d. 767; Iraq), *Tafsīr Muqātil ibn Sulaymān: 80–150 hijrīyah*, ed. by ʿAbd Allāh Maḥmūd Shiḥātah, 5 vols. (Cairo: al-Hay'ah al-Miṣrīyah al-ʿĀmmah lil-Kitāb, 1979), 2:125.

[55] As David Powers pointed out to me, a possible exception is the raid on Ubná. But see footnote 36.

[56] al-Fīrūzābādī, *Tanwīr*, 427; al-Fīrūzābādī, *Tafsīr Ibn ʿAbbās*, 678.

with how Ibn ʿAbbās explained the key verb in Q 8:67.) Yet the second (and less credible) interpretation claims that Ibn ʿAbbās understood this verse as providing four options: killing, enslaving, ransoming, and freeing.[57] By contrast, Mujāhid explained the key verb (*athkhantumūhum*) as meaning submission (*islām*).[58] Muqātil glossed Q 47:4 as instructing Muslims, after *fighting*, to overcome and imprison the enemy, who should then be freed or ransomed. Thus, if we set aside the second interpretation attributed to Ibn ʿAbbās, these late antique exegetes seem to agree in reading this verse as a rather lucid instruction that war prisoners should be ransomed or freed after fighting. Yet, here again, the relative clarity of one verse (Q 47:4) was obscured by the commentary on another verse.

Qur'ān 9:5 states, "But when the forbidden months are past, then *kill* the polytheists wherever you find them, *and* seize them (take them captive), beleaguer them, and use against them every stratagem (of war)." Curiously, Q 9:5 instructs Muslims both to kill the polytheists in battle and to take them as captives, without clarifying if these are two equal options. This verse need not provide a direct legal command, but it is important to investigate what legal consequences jurists derived from it. I want to suggest two readings that may clarify the legal implications of this verse: first, the term "kill" may be an orthographic error (again) because the insertion of one long vowel would render this term "fighting," which renders the verse more coherent (i.e., fight the polytheists and take them captive). Second, the conjunction "and" could mean "or" because the same word in Arabic has both meanings; the verse would then be an exhortation to kill/fight *or* to seize combatants. These readings might clarify the legal implications of this verse.

The exegesis of Q 9:5 reflects the potential confusion of "killing and then seizing." Ibn ʿAbbās specified that the verb "to kill" refers only to polytheists with whom treaties have expired and he explains the rest of Q 9:5 as referring to the capture of war prisoners.[59] A divergent second transmission attributed to Ibn ʿAbbās glosses this verse as meaning that Arab polytheists should be killed unless they submit (i.e., enter *islām*).[60]

57 Ṭalḥah, *Ṣaḥīfat ʿAlī ʿan Ibn ʿAbbās*, 453.

58 Mujāhid, *Tafsīr al-Imām Mujāhid*, 604. I translate *islām* as submission and not conversion. I have done so because submission is a legal category that entails a group's acceptance of Muslim political authority and it is not equivalent to conversion (as it is understood in the modern discourse of religion). See Lena Salaymeh, "Taxing citizens: socio-legal constructions of late antique Muslim identity." *Islamic Law and Society* 23:4 (2016), 1–35.

59 al-Fīrūzābādī, *Tanwīr*, 153; al-Fīrūzābādī, *Tafsīr Ibn ʿAbbās*, 229.

60 Ṭalḥah, *Ṣaḥīfat ʿAlī ʿan Ibn ʿAbbās*, 259.

Mujāhid claimed that the Companions of the Prophet expressed a consensus that Q 9:5 superseded Q 47:4, thereby providing a Muslim leader with the options of execution, ransom, freeing, or enslaving prisoners of war.[61] He asserted that Arab polytheists must either submit (*islām*) or be killed and should not be ransomed or freed; however, paradoxically, this same tradition-report then claims that if war prisoners are taken, they may be killed, freed, or ransomed.[62] Muqātil replicates this interpretation.[63] Muqātil asserted that killing and overcoming must continue until polytheism is removed from Arabia and this requirement eliminates the possibility of ransoming or freeing war prisoners.[64] Muqātil interpreted Q 9:5 as referring to the imprisonment of enemy combatants and as superseding other verses on warfare.[65] I suspect that the second reading I suggested – that the conjunction means "or" instead of "and" – would clarify their exegesis as recognizing that it was permissible for enemy combatants to be killed on the battlefield *or* to be taken captive.

Undeniably, the exegesis of these three verses is too succinct to offer an unambiguous portrayal. The brevity of the reported commentaries is further confounded by the ambiguity of the relationship between these verses. While difficult to ascertain definitively, attempts to order the Qurʾān chronologically suggest that Q 8:67 was revealed prior to Q 47:4, which was revealed prior to Q 9:5.[66] Thus, I presented these verses in what may be their chronological order. Can we historicize these verses in terms of their chronology? I propose a historical reading of these verses based on the above-mentioned summary of Muslim battles. The criticism of the Muslim community in Q 8:67 appears to be that war should not be a primarily profitable enterprise; that is, the verse instructs believers to battle for spiritual reasons, rather than economic incentives. At the battle of Badr (the subject of Q 8:67), all the prisoners were ransomed.

[61] al-Ṣanʿānī, *Muṣannaf*, 5:143–4; Ibn Abī Shaybah, *Muṣannaf*, 7:672. I use the term "supersede" rather than "abrogate" to differentiate between late antique and medieval practices. I will discuss abrogation below; see footnotes 87–9.

[62] al-Ṣanʿānī, *Mukhtaṣar al-muṣannaf*, 2:291–2; Qalʿahʾjī, *ʿAbd Allāh ibn ʿAbbās*, 121–2.

[63] Notably, both Mujāhid and Muqātil interpret Q 47:4 to mean that the option of having war prisoners (who might then be freed or ransomed) is only permissible if the enemy are not polytheists. That is, according to their interpretation, Q 9:5 dictates how to deal with polytheist enemies (i.e., killing them if they do not submit). While it is not entirely clear, Mujāhid and Muqātil might have asserted that non-polytheist prisoners may only be freed or ransomed, as required by Q 47:4.

[64] Muqātil, *Tafsīr Muqātil*, 4:44.

[65] *Ibid.*, 2:157.

[66] Theodor Nöldeke, *Tārīkh al-Qurʾān [Geschichte des Qorans]*, ed. by Friedrich Schwally, Gotthelf Bergstrasser, and Otto Pretzl, trans. by Georges Tamer (Beirut: Konrad Adenauer Foundation, 2004), xxxvi.

Subsequently, prisoners were freed at Ḥunayn, which is why verse Q 47:4 rules that prisoners of war may only be pardoned or ransomed.[67] In addition, Q 9:5 is a general exhortation to fight that does not preclude the taking of war prisoners. Viewing Q 9:5 in harmony with Q 47:4's instruction that war prisoners should be freed or ransomed is consistent with the strongest historical evidence: after Badr, the Prophet freed all the captives from the battle of Ḥunayn (the only other identifiable battle that resulted in prisoners).[68] It is not possible to know if late antique Muslims scholars relied on a chronology of the Qur'ān. Still, this historicization of these Qur'ānic verses may explain the legal opinions of some jurists. Did late antique Muslim jurists understand these three verses within the historical narrative I have (re)constructed? In the next section, I attempt to answer this question.

Late Antique Islamic Law (up to 800 CE)

Both the historical narratives presented in the first section and the exegetical materials presented in the second section were components of the (legal) education of jurists. In this section, I survey how late antique jurists contended with the precedential value of the historical evidence and the legal-interpretive weight of the exegesis. Compilations of tradition-reports and medieval juristic texts record the opinions of late antique jurists.[69] These sources report juristic opinions directly following the Prophet's death. The Prophet's Companions often acted as legal authorities and the majority of them appear to have prohibited prisoner execution.[70] (One important exception: As the exegetical section above illustrated, there are conflicting reports about the legal opinion of Ibn

[67] For an example of this legal argument, see Shalabī, *al-Jihād fī sabīl allāh*, 104–5.

[68] This historical interpretation is evident in some contemporary texts, which suggest that executions of war prisoners were the consequences of prior crimes unrelated to prisoner status. See 'Ulyān's chapter on "Prisoners of war in Islam" in Muḥyī Hilāl al-Sarḥān, *Asrá al-ḥarb fī al-islām wa-al-qānūn al-dawlī* (Baghdad: al-Jumhūrīyah al-'Irāqīyah, Wizārat al-Awqāf wa-al-Shu'ūn al-Dīnīyah, Majallat al-Risālah al-Islāmīyah, 1986), 39–51. See also Shalabī, *al-Jihād fī sabīl allāh*, 104–7.

[69] As the citations in this section indicate, the legal opinions of the Prophet's Companions, Successors, Followers, and the famous late antique legal authorities who led legal circles and networks are reported in late antique texts (*sunan* and *muṣannafāt*), as well as jurisprudential texts (up to the fourteenth century). I have also relied on Muḥammad Rawwās Qal'ah'jī's contemporary compilations of the legal opinions of prominent jurists of the first Islamic century; his work is based on extensive research in late antique and medieval Islamic texts.

[70] Concerning prohibition of prisoner execution, Ibn Rushd mentions that: "al-Ḥasan ibn Muḥammad al-Tamīmī reported that there is a consensus of the Companions on this issue." Abū al-Walīd Ibn Rushd (d. 1198; Andalusia/Maghreb), *Bidāyat al-mujtahid wa-nihāyat al-muqtaṣid* ed.by Mājid al-Ḥamawī, 4 vols. (Beirut: Dār Ibn Ḥazm, 1995), 2:738.

ʿAbbās.[71] One tradition-report claims that he ruled against killing war prisoners and another claims that he permitted killing or ransoming.[72]) Yet late antique jurists played minimal political roles and, in contrast to them, the Prophet's immediate political successors do not appear to have definitively prohibited war-prisoner execution. The first caliph, Abū Bakr (d. 634; Arabia) asserted that polytheist prisoners must be killed, but it is unclear what his position would have been for non-polytheist prisoners.[73] There are conflicting reports on the practice of the second caliph, ʿUmar ibn al-Khaṭṭāb (d. 644; Arabia).[74] The third caliph, ʿUthmān ibn ʿAffān (d. 656; Arabia) may have recognized killing, ransoming, freeing, and enslaving as options.[75] The fourth caliph and first Shīʿī Imām, ʿAlī ibn Abī Ṭālib (d. 661; Arabia) prohibited killing prisoners of war, limiting options to freeing, ransoming, or enslaving; he reportedly did not kill his own war prisoner.[76] There are conflicting traditions attributed to the second caliph's son, ʿAbd Allāh ibn ʿUmar (d. 693; Arabia): reportedly, he both prohibited prisoner execution and claimed that Q 9:5 (kill and seize the enemy) abrogated Q 47:4 (grace or ransom), resulting in execution of war prisoners as a legal option.[77]

After the generation of Companions, some Muslim legal authorities and jurists prohibited prisoner execution: Saʿīd bin Jubayr (d. 714; Iraq), al-Ḥasan al-Baṣrī (d. 728; Iraq), and ʿAṭāʾ bin Abī Rabāḥ (d. 732/3; Mecca).[78]

[71] On problems of attribtion to Ibn ʿAbbās, see the two chapters by Rippin in Andrew Rippin, *The Qurʾan: formative interpretation*, Formation of the classical Islamic world, vol. XXV (Brookfield, VT: Ashgate, 1999).

[72] Qalʿahʾjī, *ʿAbd Allāh ibn ʿAbbās*, 121–2.

[73] Muḥammad Rawwās Qalʿahʾjī, *Mawsūʿat fiqh Abū Bakr al-Ṣiddīq*, Fī sabīl mawsūʿah fiqhīyah jāmiʿah, 1; Silsilat mawsūʿat fiqh al-salaf (Damascus: Dār al-Fikr, 1983), 39. al-Ṭabarī, *Tafsīr*, 21:184; Abī ʿAbd Allāh Muḥammad ibn Aḥmad al-Anṣārī al-Qurṭubī (d. 1273; Cordoba), *al-Jāmiʿ li-aḥkām al-qurʾān*, 20 vols. (Beirut: Dār Iḥyāʾ al-Turāth al-ʿArabī, 2002), 16:227.

[74] al-Awzāʿī reports conflicting practices (killing or ransoming/enslaving prisoners). ʿAbd al-Raḥmān ibn ʿAmr al-Awzāʿī (d. 774; Syria), *Sunan al-Awzāʿī: aḥādīth wa-āthār wa-fatāwá*, ed. by Marwān Muḥammad al-Shaʿʿār (Beirut: Dār al-Nafāʾis, 1993), 403. al-Ṭabarī, *Tafsīr*, 21:186.

[75] Muḥammad Rawwās Qalʿahʾjī, *Mawsūʿat fiqh ʿUthmān ibn ʿAffān*, Min al-turāth al-Islāmī, al-kitāb 32 (Mecca: Jāmiʿat Umm al-Qurá, Kullīyat al-Sharīʿah wa-al-Dirāsāt al-Islāmīyah, Markaz al-Baḥth al-ʿIlmī wa-Iḥyāʾ al-Turāth al-Islāmī, 1983), 58–9.

[76] Muḥammad ibn al-Ḥasan al-Ḥurr al-ʿĀmilī (d. 1693; Lebanon), *Wasāʾil al-Shīʿah ilá taḥṣīl masāʾil al-sharīʿah*, ed. by ʿAbd al-Raḥīm Rabbānī, Muḥammad Rāzī, and Abū al-Ḥasan Shaʿrānī, 7 vols. (Tehran: Maktabat al-Islāmīyah, 1956), 6:53–4.

[77] Muḥammad Rawwās Qalʿahʾjī, *Mawsūʿat fiqh ʿAbd Allāh ibn ʿUmar: ʿaṣruhu wa-ḥayātuh*, Fī sabīl mawsūʿah fiqhīyah jāmiʿah, 7 (Beirut: Dār al-Nafāʾis, 1986), 118–19.

[78] Reported in: al-Ṭabarī, *Tafsīr*, 21:186; Aḥmad ibn Muḥammad al-Naḥḥās (d. 950; Egypt), *al-Nāsikh wa-al-mansūkh fī al-qurʾān al-karīm*, ed. by Muḥammad ibn ʿAli Udfuwī (Egypt: al-Maktabah al-ʿAllāmīyah, 1938), 165–6, 221; Muwaffaq al-Dīn ʿAbd Allāh ibn Aḥmad Ibn Qudāmah al-Maqdīsī (d. 1223; Syria), *al-Mughnī*, ed. by ʿAbd Allāh ibn ʿAbd al-Muḥsin Turkī and ʿAbd al-Fattāḥ Muḥammad Ḥulw, 16 vols. (Imbābah, Cairo: Hajr, 1986), 13:45 (Ḥanbalī); Ibn

These legal authorities/jurists adjudicated prior to the emergence of professional schools of law.[79] They (and others) are reported to have cited the consensus of the Prophet's Companions, the historical practice of the Prophet, and a verse of the Qur'ān (47:4) as limiting the options for dealing with prisoners of war to freeing or ransoming.[80] Specifically, al-Ḥasan al-Baṣrī prohibited prisoner execution based on Q 47:4 and asserted that prisoners may only be ransomed or freed.[81] (al-Ṭabarī referred to Ḥasan al-Baṣrī's prohibition of prisoner execution and indicated that it was based on a report that ʿAbdallāh ibn ʿUmar, son of the second caliph, refused to execute a prisoner in accordance with Q 47:4.[82]) These late antique Muslim jurists probably found no discrepancy between Q 47:4 and the practice of the Prophet, with which they were likely intimately familiar. Prohibiting prisoner execution may not have been limited only to legal authorities: the Umayyad caliph ʿUmar ibn ʿAbd al-ʿAzīz (d. 720; Arabia/Syria) is reported to have prohibited prisoner execution and to have freed war prisoners who agreed to pay the poll tax.[83] (There is, however, a report that he executed one prisoner under peculiar circumstances, but he did not kill any other war prisoner during his reign.[84])

The opinion against prisoner execution was not, however, unanimous. There was a minority opinion among late antique jurists – including Ibrāhīm al-Nakhaʿī (d. 717; Kūfah) and Sufyān al-Thawrī – that permitted prisoner execution as one of several options available to a Muslim leader.[85] Unfortunately, the reasoning relied upon by these jurists in declaring this legal opinion is not reported in the sources. The legal reasoning of late antique jurists was rarely recorded and, even if it had been, jurists did not always engage issues of precedent.[86] It is possible, however, that these

al-Muṭahhar al-Ḥillī, *Tadhkirat al-fuqahā'*, 9:156 (Imāmī Shīʿī). But see the opposite opinion attributed to Saʿīd bin Jubayr in al-Qurṭubī, *al-Jāmiʿ*, 16:227–8.

79 On late antique scholars and jurists, see Steven C. Judd, *Religious scholars and the Umayyads: piety-minded supporters of the Marwanid Caliphate* (London; New York: Routledge, 2014).

80 Ibn Abī Shaybah, *Muṣannaf*, 7:671, 73–4. Also cited in Ibn Qudāmah, *al-Mughnī*, 13:45 (Ḥanbalī); Ibn al-Muṭahhar al-Ḥillī, *Tadhkirat al-fuqahā'*, 9:156 (Imāmī Shīʿī).

81 Muḥammad Rawwās Qalʿah'jī, *Mawsūʿat fiqh al-Ḥasan al-Baṣrī*, 2 vols., Fī sabīl mawsūʿah fiqhīyah jāmiʿah, 9 (Beirut: Dār al-Nafā'is, 1989), 1:127–8.

82 See Qalʿah'jī, *ʿAbd Allāh ibn ʿUmar*, 118.

83 Muḥammad Rawwās Qalʿah'jī, *Mawsūʿat fiqh ʿUmar ibn ʿAbd al-ʿAzīz*, Fī sabīl mawsūʿah fiqhīyah jāmiʿah; Silsilat mawsūʿat fiqh al-salaf (Kuwait: Jāmiʿat al-Kuwayt, 2001), 114–15.

84 This particular prisoner is reported to have killed many Muslims in battle in intensely violent ways. *Ibid.*; al-Ṭabarī, *Tafsīr*, 21:186.

85 Muḥammad Rawwās Qalʿah'jī, *Mawsūʿat fiqh Ibrāhīm al-Nakhaʿī*, 2 vols., Fī sabīl mawsūʿah fiqhīyah jāmiʿah, 8 (Beirut: Dār al-Nafā'is, 1986), 1:282; Qalʿah'jī, *Sufyān al-Thawrī*, 156.

86 Rationalists (*ahl al-rā'y*) were less likely than traditionists (*ahl al-ḥadīth*) to refer to Prophetic precedents. But this was less relevant after the first century of Islamic history. See Wael B. Hallaq, *Sharīʿa: theory, practice, transformations* (Cambridge: Cambridge University Press, 2009), 55–60.

opinions correspond – perhaps directly – to the variations in the historical narratives about the treatment of prisoners of war in the Prophetic era or to variations in Qur'ānic exegesis. Moreover, while it is difficult to determine how many other late antique jurists permitted prisoner execution, it appears to have been the dissenting perspective. It is clear then that the prohibition of prisoner execution was an attested legal opinion supported by major jurists of the late antique period. I emphasize this because medieval, orthodox Muslim jurists legitimated their jurisprudence by claiming continuity and preservation of the legal practices of their predecessors. If most late antique jurists who lived closest in time to the Prophet prohibited it, how would later generations of jurists regulate prisoner of war execution?

Medieval Exegesis

To understand how medieval jurists would rule on prisoner of war execution, we must return to exegesis in order to investigate any shifts in how specific verses were glossed between the late antique and medieval eras. In this section, I will revisit the three verses outlined above, focusing on how medieval exegetes understood them and elaborated their legal implications. Undoubtedly, as indicated in the section on late antique exegesis, there was confusion and inconsistency in the exegesis of verses pertaining to war prisoners. Exegetes sought to clarify this confusion through the doctrine of abrogation; abrogation determines the legal significance of a verse by comparing it to another verse, usually revealed chronologically later.[87] The merging of historiography and law is particularly evident in the doctrine of abrogation because it relies on identifying a historical context and a chronology for the Qur'ān.

[87] On abrogation, see ʿAbd al-Mutaʿāl Muḥammad Jabrī, *Nāsikh wa-al-mansūkh bayna al-ithbāt–wa-al-nafy* (Cairo: Maktabat Wahbah, 1987); Muḥammad Wafā, *Aḥkām al-naskh fī al-sharīʿah al-islāmīyah* (Cairo: M. Wafa, 1984). See also Louay Fatoohi, *Abrogation in the Quran and Islamic law: a critical study of the concept of "naskh" and its impact* (New York: Routledge, 2012), 12–31; John Burton, *The sources of Islamic law: Islamic theories of abrogation* (Edinburgh: Edinburgh University Press, 1990); David S. Powers. "On the abrogation of the bequest verses." *Arabica* 29:3 (1982): 246–95; Koby Yosef. "Between al-Zuhrī (d. 124/742) and Qatāda (d. 118/736): two early treatises on abrogation in the Qur'ān." *Jerusalem Studies in Arabic and Islam* 42:1 (2015): 73–128; David S. Powers, "The exegetical genre *nāsikh al-Qur'ān wa mansūkhuhu*." In *Approaches to the history of the interpretation of the Qur'ān*, ed. by Andrew Rippin (Oxford; New York: Clarendon Press; Oxford University Press, 1988), 117–38.

The concept of abrogation was initially used to refer to verses that were removed from the Qurʾānic corpus.[88] In late antiquity, exegetes understood some verses as general and others as particular; by the medieval era, however, orthodox Sunnīs developed a doctrine of abrogation intended to harmonize the legal commands in the Qurʾān, with the result that the meaning of the term "abrogation" (*naskh*) changed.[89] (In light of this historical trajectory in the meaning of abrogation, the section above on late antique exegesis did not use the term "abrogation" even when the Arabic sources used the term *naskh*.) It is possible that medieval exegetes assumed that their late antique predecessors had the same understanding of abrogation; specifically, Mujāhid and Muqātil are reported to have claimed that Q 9:5 abrogated Q 47:4, but it is unlikely that they understood abrogation in the same way as their medieval successors understood it.[90] Regardless of the terminology, the doctrine of abrogation probably was not orthodox in late antiquity. While historicization and chronology were matters of interest to late antique scholars, medieval exegetes emphasized the chronology of Qurʾānic verses in order to determine which verses were abrogated.[91] There were multiple interpretations of chronology and it is difficult to determine a specific jurist's perspective. The historical reading of late antique exegesis that I offered above is implicitly shaped by Imāmī Shīʿī jurisprudence, which rejects abrogation of Qurʾānic verses and thereby rejects prisoner of war execution as an option.[92]

In this section, I will examine a few canonical (or orthodox) medieval exegetical texts with legal implications. I will summarize the exegetical commentaries of al-Ṭabarī (d. 923; Iraq), a jurist, historian, and exegete who both contributed to and reflected orthodox legal opinions. I will supplement al-Ṭabarī with references, when available, to three medieval exegetical works: al-Naḥḥās' (d. 950; Egypt) *al-Nāsikh wa-al-mansūkh* (the abrogated and abrogating), al-Wāḥidī's (d. 1075/6; Nishapur) *Asbāb*

[88] Modarressi explains that "[t]he concept of abrogation of the revelation (*naskh al-Qurʾān*) apparently referred originally to those parts that were not included by the Prophet in the scripture." Hossein Modarressi. "Early debates on the integrity of the Qurʾān: a brief survey." *Studia Islamica* 77 (1993): 5–39 at 7.

[89] al-Shāṭibī discusses the distinctions in how late antique and medieval scholars understood abrogation. Ibrāhīm ibn Mūsá al-Shāṭibī (d. 1388; Granada), *al-Muwāfaqāt fī uṣūl al-aḥkām*, ed. by Muḥammad al-Khiḍr Ḥusayn al-Tūnisī, 4 vols. (Beirut: Dār al-Fikr, 1922), 3:65. (I thank Islam Dayeh for this reference.)

[90] For example, al-Qurṭubī, *al-Jāmiʿ*, 8:73.

[91] An important work on chronology is Jalāl al-Dīn ʿAbd al-Raḥmān ibn Abī Bakr al-Suyūṭī (d. 1505; Egypt), *al-Itqān fī ʿulūm al-qurʾān*, ed. by Muḥammad Abū al-Faḍl Ibrāhīm, 2nd edn. (Tehran: Manshūrāt al-Raḍī, 1984).

[92] Ibn al-Muṭahhar al-Ḥillī, *Tadhkirat al-fuqahāʾ*, 9:158 (Imāmī Shīʿī).

al-nuzūl (occasions for revelation) and al-Qurṭubī's (d. 1273; Cordoba) *Aḥkām al-qur'ān* (Qur'ānic legal rulings). The aim of this summary is to demonstrate that medieval commentaries begin with certain assumptions that differ from those of their late antique predecessors.

Qur'ān 8:67 declares, "It is not fitting for a prophet to have prisoners of war until he has thoroughly subdued (*yuthkhina*) the land. You seek the temporal goods of this world; but God is concerned with the hereafter." al-Ṭabarī lucidly explains this verse as indicating that the Prophet would have done better to kill, rather than to ransom, the prisoners at the battle of Badr.[93] He explains Q 8:67 as an admonishment of the Muslim community for trying to profit from war prisoners (by ransoming them), rather than killing them. al-Ṭabarī defines the key verb (*yuthkhina*) in this verse as overwhelming the enemy through killing.[94] (Other medieval exegetes interpreted this verse similarly.[95]) The first authority that he cites to support his reading is the second interpretation attributed to Ibn 'Abbās,[96] according to which this verse was abrogated by Q 47:4 and provides the options of killing, enslaving, or ransoming (but not freeing).[97] He also cites Mujāhid to define the key verb (*yuthkhina*) as "killing" (*qatl*).[98] al-Ṭabarī does not engage the historical evidence, late antique exegetical ambiguities (including a conflicting tradition-report from Ibn 'Abbās), or the opinions of late antique jurists. Instead, he simply presents his interpretive reasoning as an established legal matter.

Naḥḥās identifies Q 8:67 as an injunction against having war prisoners and states that Q 47:4 abrogated it, leaving Muslims with the options of killing, enslaving, or ransoming.[99] Wāḥidī explains the occasion of the verse as being a response to the Prophet's solicitation of advice from Abū Bakr and 'Umar on how to deal with the Badr prisoners; he claims that this verse was a response to the Prophet's error in judgment.[100] Qurṭubī

[93] al-Ṭabarī, *Tafsīr*, 11:271.

[94] *Ibid.*

[95] Maḥmūd ibn 'Umar al-Zamakhsharī (d. 1144; Khwārazm), *al-Kashshāf 'an ḥaqā'iq al-tanzīl wa-'uyūn al-aqāwīl fī wujūh al-ta'wīl*, ed. by 'Alī ibn Muḥammad al-Sayyid al-Sharīf Jurjānī, Aḥmad ibn Muḥammad Ibn al-Munayyir, and al-Ḥamawī Muḥibb al-Dīn Muḥammad ibn Abī Bakr, 4 vols. (Cairo: al-Bābī al-Ḥalabī, 1966), 2:168. See also 'Abd Allāh ibn 'Umar al-Bayḍāwī (d. 1286; Shīrāz), *Anwār al-tanzīl wa-asrār al-tā'wīl. Beidhawii Commentarius in Coranum: ex codd. Parisiensibus, Dresdensibus et Lipsiensibus*, ed. by Heinrich Leberecht Fleischer, 2 vols. (Lipsiae: Sumptibus F.C.G. Vogelii, 1846–1848), 1:374.

[96] Ṭalḥah, *Ṣaḥīfat 'Alī 'an Ibn 'Abbās*, 256.

[97] al-Ṭabarī, *Tafsīr*, 11:272.

[98] *Ibid.*

[99] al-Naḥḥās, *al-Nāsikh*, 158.

[100] Abū al-Ḥasan 'Alī al-Wāḥidī (d. 1075/6; Nishapur) and Hibat Allāh Ibn Salāmah (d. 1019), *Asbāb al-nuzūl* (Egypt: Maṭba'at Hindīyah, 1897), 178–80.

follows suit and cites the same narrative about the Prophet soliciting advice from Abū Bakr and ʿUmar.[101] Citing Mujāhid, Qurṭubī defines the key verb (*yuthkhina*) as widespread killing, although he also acknowledges that the term could potentially mean "overcoming."[102] Qurṭubī mentions a tradition-report that did not appear in late antique texts: at Badr, the Prophet *offered* the Muslim community the options of killing or ransoming; this narrative functions as a historicized license to execute war prisoners and seems crafted to respond to the critique that execution is not an option.[103] In addition, Qurṭubī claims that the "executions" of al-Naḍr and ʿUqbah were precedents.[104]

Qur'ān 47:4 states, "Therefore, when you meet the unbelievers, smite at their necks; At length, when you have thoroughly subdued them (*athkhantumūhum*), bind a bond firmly (on them): thereafter (is the time for) either generosity (grace) or ransom." al-Ṭabarī expounds on Q 47:4 as an instruction to tie the bonds of a prisoner of war tightly lest he escape and cause harm.[105] He also delineates a controversy about Q 47:4 that is evident in juristic texts: some scholars held that the verse is a valid, unabrogated rule (thereby prohibiting prisoner execution), while other scholars held that the verse was abrogated by Q 9:5 or Q 8:57.[106] He recognizes that there are jurists who consider this verse unabrogated and thereby rule that prisoners may only be freed or ransomed.[107] al-Ṭabarī expresses his opinion that verse Q 47:4 is not abrogated and is an unexpired legal command; but he claims that Q 9:5 is chronologically earlier than Q 47:4 and therefore offers a Muslim leader the additional option of executing war prisoners. al-Ṭabarī alleges that it was the practice of the Prophet to kill some war prisoners and not others.[108] The only two historical precedents he cites for the execution of war prisoners is ʿUqbah at Badr and the Qurayẓah clan (discussed below).[109] That al-Ṭabarī assumes these two incidents to be precedents is interesting for two reasons: first, it is unclear if ʿUqbah was a war prisoner or simply died on the battlefield, as discussed above. Second, since Qurayẓah was a Jewish clan, the general permission to kill polytheists in Q 9:5 would be inapplicable.

[101] al-Qurṭubī, *al-Jāmiʿ*, 8:46–7.
[102] *Ibid.*, 8:48.
[103] *Ibid.*
[104] *Ibid.*, 8:49.
[105] al-Ṭabarī, *Tafsīr*, 21:183.
[106] *Ibid.*
[107] *Ibid.*, 21:185.
[108] *Ibid.*, 21:187.
[109] *Ibid.*

Naḥḥās identifies five positions on Q 47:4 (that are later elaborated by Qurṭubī): (1) it is abrogated by Q 9:5; (2) it refers to all polytheists and is abrogated; (3) it is the abrogating verse and it is impermissible to execute a prisoner of war because only ransoming or freeing are permitted; (4) taking prisoners is permissible only after extensive fighting and killing, and the (Muslim) leader has the option of choosing between killing or ransoming; (5) it is not abrogated or abrogating and the leader has the option of treating prisoners however he chooses.[110] He cites as precedents the executions of Abū ʿAzzah (at Uḥud) and ʿUqbah (at Badr).[111] Qurṭubī defines the key verb (*athkhantumūhum*) as "having killed many" and observes that this same verb occurs in Q 8:67.[112]

Echoing Naḥḥās, Qurṭubī identifies five positions on the status of this verse:[113] (1) it is abrogated by Q 9:5, 8:57, or 9:36, according to several Kufan scholars, on the authority of Ibn ʿAbbās; (2) it is abrogated by Q 9:5 because polytheists must be killed unless they pay the poll tax, according to Mujāhid and Abū Ḥanīfah (d. 767; Iraq), among others; (3) it abrogates Q 9:5 and precludes execution, leaving the options of freeing, ransoming, or enslaving; (4) it applies only after "killing" and does not preclude execution – an opinion that is attributed to Saʿīd bin Jubayr (who is reported in other texts to have opposed execution); (5) it provides a political leader with the option of freeing or ransoming, but does not prohibit execution – an opinion that is attributed to Ibn ʿAbbās (the second interpretation cited above), as well as some late antique jurists (ʿAbd Allāh ibn ʿUmar, al-Ḥasan al-Baṣrī, and ʿAṭāʾ bin Abī Rabāḥ), whom other sources cite as being opposed to execution. Qurṭubī claims that since the Prophet exercised several options for dealing with war prisoners, Muslim leaders may do likewise; he cites the executions of ʿUqbah and al-Naḍr (at Badr) as Prophetic precedents legitimating the option of execution.[114]

Qurʾān 9:5 states, "But when the forbidden months are past, then *kill* the polytheists wherever you find them, *and* seize them (take them captive), beleaguer them, and use against them every stratagem (of war)." Ṭabarī explains this verse as commanding killing and imprisoning and he does not seem to perceive any inconsistency in this command.[115] Naḥḥās identifies three opinions on this verse: (1) that it was abrogated by Q 47:4,

110 al-Naḥḥās, *al-Nāsikh*, 220–1.
111 *Ibid.*, 220.
112 al-Qurṭubī, *al-Jāmiʿ*, 16:226.
113 *Ibid.*, 16:227–8.
114 *Ibid.*, 16:228.
115 al-Ṭabarī, *Tafsīr*, 11:343.

such that only freeing or ransoming are legal options; (2) that it is unabrogated (i.e., remains effective) and abrogates Q 47:4, such that polytheists may only be killed, not freed or ransomed, unless they submit; (3) that both verses are valid and provide the options of killing, ransoming, or freeing.[116] Naḥḥās treats the "executions" of al-Naḍr and ʿUqbah as Prophetic precedents.[117] Qurṭubī comments that "kill the polytheists" is qualified by the condition of their agreeing to pay the poll tax and by the prohibition against killing women, children, monks, and other protected groups.[118] Acknowledging the debate over the status of this verse as abrogated or abrogating, Qurṭubī declares that both Q 47:4 and Q 9:5 are legally valid verses that give Muslims the options enumerated in both verses – killing, ransoming, and freeing.[119] Many exegetes identified this verse as the "sword verse," which abrogated many other verses about negotiation, peace, and avoiding warfare. It is problematic that verse Q 9:5 was identified as a general and overriding rule for warfare because this verse likely refers to polytheists who had violated a treaty agreement and, therefore, its relevance to warfare is questionable.[120] Indeed, the conflation of treaty violations with all forms of warfare is reflected in references to the Qurayẓah incident, to be addressed below.

Since both al-Ṭabarī and Qurṭubī mention the possibility that Q 8:57 – a verse not previously discussed – abrogated Q 47:4, I will briefly summarize both the late antique and medieval exegesis of the verse. **Qur'ān 8:57** states, "If you overcome them in war, disperse them, and those who follow them, so that they may remember." Ibn ʿAbbās explains this verse as referring to prisoners and their transportation, but he implies that the occasion of the verse's revelation was an incident involving the Qurayẓah clan.[121] Mujāhid ibn Jabr does not fully explain this particular verse, but he mentions Qurayẓah in discussing the verses before and after Q 8:57.[122] According to Muqātil, this verse refers to prisoners taken during warfare and does not mention killing.[123] These three late antique exegetes do not have lucid or extensive commentaries on this verse. al-Ṭabarī explains this

[116] al-Naḥḥās, *al-Nāsikh*, 165–6.
[117] *Ibid.*, 166.
[118] al-Qurṭubī, *al-Jāmiʿ*, 8:72.
[119] *Ibid.*, 8:73.
[120] Muḥammad Yūsuf Mūsá, *Tārīkh al-fiqh al-Islāmī*, 2nd edn., 3 vols. (Cairo: Dār al-Maʿrifah, 1964–1966), 2:513–4 (discussing Q 9:5 as an abrogating verse of Q 47:4).
[121] al-Fīrūzābādī, *Tanwīr*, 151.
[122] Mujāhid, *Tafsīr al-Imām Mujāhid*, 357.
[123] Muqātil, *Tafsīr Muqātil*, 2:122.

verse as referring to the imprisonment of Qurayẓah for breaking their truce agreement.[124]

The medieval exegesis of the verses presented in this section indicates that it was in the medieval period that the doctrine of abrogation became established, with significant legal implications. By abrogating the verse (Q 47:4) that served as the basis for the late antique opinion against executing prisoners of war, medieval jurists established the option of execution as authoritative. Importantly, they pointed to Prophetic precedents (al-Naḍr, ʿUqbah, and the Qurayẓah clan) without engaging the historical evidence or fully explicating the majority late antique opinion against execution. In this way, these medieval exegetes established an orthodox narrative of Islamic law that legitimated prisoner of war execution. Indeed, these medieval exegetes might have assumed that there was a precedent for executing war prisoners and then determined the abrogation status of the verses accordingly.

Representative Medieval Jurists (*c.* 800–1400 CE)

Medieval jurists formed a majority opinion that accepted execution of prisoners of war.[125] These professional Muslim jurists authored their own individual legal texts or their students recorded their legal opinions; in addition, the genre of juristic disagreement (i.e., texts that record differences of opinion among jurists) further illuminates and substantiates juristic debates about the permissibility of executing prisoners of war. In this section, I briefly summarize the legal opinions of a few mainstream and prominent Muslim jurists. These legal opinions represent several centuries and four major Sunnī legal schools (Ḥanafī, Mālikī, Shāfiʿī, and Ḥanbalī).[126] The aim of this intentionally ahistorical and limited presentation is to identify trends and assumptions in orthodox legal discourse and to demonstrate that Prophetic precedent was not a significant factor in medieval Islamic legal reasoning. Professional jurists who permitted prisoner execution assumed various conditions that led to Q 8:67 being

[124] al-Ṭabarī, *Tafsīr*, 11:236.

[125] There was no consensus on the treatment of war prisoners, as documented by Ibn Ḥazm. ʿAlī ibn Aḥmad Ibn Ḥazm (d. 1064; Andalusia), *Marātib al-ijmāʿ fī al-ʿibādāt wa-al-muʿāmalat wa-al-ʿitiqādāt* (Beirut: Dār al-Kutub al-ʿIlmīyah, 1970), 114 (Ẓāhirī: jurists disagree about treatment of war prisoners in terms of killing, ransoming, and freeing).

[126] Sunnī legal schools differ in many respects, but these differences are not pertinent to this study. The Imāmī Shīʿī school is a minority legal school and it prohibits prisoner execution. See footnote 2.

viewed as general (and, sometimes, Q 47:4 as specific). Rather than being exhaustive or authoritative, the following section outlines the discursive framework in which jurists treated the question of prisoners of war. I have selected a few influential texts that are representative of a larger body of legal texts and that allow us to focus on the salient modes of legal reasoning in the medieval era. The legal schools represented in this selection share a basic formula for deriving Islamic legal rulings: the highest authority is the Qur'ān and the secondary authority is the Prophet's statements or deeds. It is of particular interest how jurists grappled with the historical record, given that the narratives cited in the preceding section were integral to their (legal) education. In other words, how did jurists reconcile all of the divergent historical narratives they inherited (presented in the first two sections)?

Silent Authority and Precedents of Professional Jurists

One of the earliest extant Islamic juristic texts that discusses prisoners of war is the *Siyar* of Shaybānī (d. 805; Iraq), a Ḥanafī Iraqi jurist. Shaybānī recorded the teachings of Abū Ḥanīfah (d. 767; Iraq) on the authority of Shaybānī's teacher, Abū Yūsuf (d. 768; Iraq), a prominent figure in the Ḥanafī school; thus, the substance of Shaybānī's text dates to the life of Abū Ḥanīfah (about fifty years earlier). Abū Ḥanīfah reportedly stated, "The Imām is entitled to a choice between taking them to the territory of Islam to be divided and killing them ... [The Imām] should examine the situation and decide whatever he deems to be advantageous to the Muslims."[127] Although this text is terse, it is noteworthy that Abū Ḥanīfah does not appear to have referred to any precedents or legal authority – or his student does not report the basis of his legal reasoning. The legal question and response are presented succinctly and simply.[128] Notably, Abū Ḥanīfah was a near contemporary of the three late antique legal authorities who opposed prisoner execution.[129] Since he was likely aware of their opinion on prisoner execution, it is noteworthy that he did not attempt to refute their reasoning.

[127] Muḥammad ibn al-Ḥasan al-Shaybānī (d. 804/5; Iraq), *The Islamic law of nations: Shaybānī's Siyar*, trans. by Majid Khadduri (Baltimore, MD: Johns Hopkins Press, 1966), 100 (Ḥanafī).

[128] This succinctness is also evident in a twelfth-century Ḥanafī legal compendium; see Abū Bakr ibn Mas'ūd Kāsānī (d. 1189; Syria), *Badā'i' al-ṣanā'i' fī tartīb al-sharā'i'*, ed. by Aḥmad Mukhtār 'Uthmān, 10 vols. (Cairo: Zakarīyā 'Alī Yūsuf, 1968), 9:4307. A minority Ḥanafī opinion prohibits prisoner execution (see footnote 2).

[129] See footnote 78.

Al-Qayrawānī (d. 996; Tunisia), a Mālikī jurist, declared, "It is not wrong to kill a non-Arab unbelieving prisoner, but no one is to be killed after being given a guarantee of safety (*amān*), and treaties with the enemy are not to be violated."[130] Like Abū Ḥanīfah, al-Qayrawānī seemed unconcerned with historical precedents or legal authority for this particular issue.[131] Following his Mālikī predecessor, Ibn ʿAbd al-Barr (d. 1071; Cordoba) succinctly identifies a Muslim leader's options to deal with prisoners of war: killing, freeing, ransoming, or enslaving.[132]

al-Nawawī (d. 1277; Syria), a Shāfiʿī jurist, asserted that a Muslim leader may kill, ransom, or enslave a prisoner of war based on the needs of society, but without citing the Qurʾān or historical precedents.[133] By contrast, his Imāmī Shīʿī contemporary, Jaʿfar ibn al-Ḥasan Muḥaqqiq al-Ḥillī (d. 1277; Iraq), noted that prisoners who are captured during warfare may not be killed and that the Imam may choose between freeing, ransoming, or enslaving war prisoners.[134] The Ḥanbalī jurist Ibn Taymiyyah (d. 1328; Syria) also declared that a ruler has four options for dealing with prisoners. He asserted, "This is the opinion of the majority of the jurists, as

[130] ʿAbd Allāh ibn ʿAbd al-Raḥmān Ibn Abī Zayd al-Qayrawānī (d. 996; Tunisia), *The Rísâla: treatise on Mâlikî law of ʿAbdallâh Ibn-Abî-Zayd Al-Qayrawânî (922–996): an annotated translation*, trans. by Joseph Kenny (Minna: Islamic Education Trust, 1992), 107. See also ʿAbd Allāh ibn ʿAbd al-Raḥmān Ibn Abī Zayd al-Qayrawānī, *al-Risālah al-fiqhīyah* (Beirut: Dār al-Gharb al-Islāmī, 1986), 189 (Mālikī: it is permissible to kill prisoner combatants). al-Qayrawānī likely presumed that believing (i.e., Muslim) prisoners may not be killed. This may be a reference to *bughāh*, Muslims who resist government authority. See Abou El Fadl, "The rules of killing at war," 146.

[131] In al-Qayrawānī's time, a non-Arab non-believing prisoner could have been Byzantine. To give an example of contemporary war practices, Byzantine Emperor Nikephoros II Phocas (d. 969) advised his soldiers on prisoner execution in his military treatise: "Mais s'il arrive qu'ils soient poursuivis par l'ennemi, les cavaliers devront aller rejoindre les quarante autres restés sur place, mettre à mort ou envoyer en avant les prisonniers qu'ils auront faits, s'en aller au plus vite et gagner l'endroit bien défendu." Byzantine Emperor Nikēphoros II Phōkas (d. 969), *Le Traité Sur la Guérilla de l'Empereur Nicéphore Phocas (963–969)*, trans. by Gilbert and Haralambie Mihăescu Dagron, Le monde Byzantin (Paris: Editions du Centre National de la Recherche Scientifique, 1986), 74. This implies that the Byzantines likely accepted or practiced prisoner execution in cases in which the army was retreating and these prisoners were slowing them down. It is unclear if this practice had any effect on their Muslim neighbors.

[132] Yūsuf ibn ʿAbd Allāh Ibn ʿAbd al-Barr (d. 1070; Andalusia), *Kitāb al-kāfī fī fiqh ahl al-Madīnah al-Mālikī*, ed. by Muḥammad Muḥammad Aḥīd Wuld Mādīk Mūrītānī, 2 vols. (Riyadh: Maktabat al-Riyāḍ al-Ḥadīthah, 1980), 1:467 (Mālikī).

[133] Abū Zakarīyā Muḥyī al-Dīn ibn Sharaf al-Nawawī (d. 1277; Syria), *Rawḍat al-ṭālibīn*, ed. by ʿĀdil Aḥmad ʿAbd al-Mawjūd, ʿAlī Muḥammad Muʿawwaḍ, and Jalāl al-Dīn ʿAbd al-Raḥmān ibn Abī Bakr al-Suyūṭī (d. 1505), 8 vols. (Beirut: Dār al-Kutub al-ʿIlmīyah, 1992), 7:450–1 (Shāfiʿī). See also Abū Zakarīyā Muḥyī al-Dīn ibn Sharaf al-Nawawī (d. 1277; Syria) *et al.*, *al-Majmūʿ, sharḥ al-Muhadhdhab*, ed. Zakarīyā ʿAlī Yūsuf, 18 vols. (Cairo: Maṭbaʿat al-ʿĀṣimah, 1966–69), 17:102 (Shāfiʿī).

[134] Jaʿfar ibn al-Ḥasan al-Muḥaqqiq al-Ḥillī (d. 1277; Iraq), *Mukhtaṣar al-nāfiʿ fī fiqh al-imāmīyah* (Tehran: Asadī, 1967), 137 (Imāmī Shīʿī).

they have concluded from the Book and the Sunna; though some jurists consider the liberation of such a captive as well as the ransom in return for his liberty as abrogated."[135] The permissibility of executing war prisoners was so obvious to Ibn Taymiyyah that he simply pointed to the Qur'ān and Prophetic practice, without any elucidation. For these distinguished jurists, representing each of the four orthodox Sunnī schools of law, Qur'ān and history were either irrelevant or provided so obvious an authority/precedent that it did not need to be explained. Since these legal texts are part of a broader discursive milieu – in which the Qur'ān, exegesis, tradition-reports, and historical precedents were intimately familiar – it is possible that this disregard for authority or precedent is only striking to a present-day reader. Still, it is remarkable that neither historical events, nor late antique exegesis, nor the opinions of late antique jurists were engaged. Precedents and late antique juristic opinions were less influential to medieval Muslim jurists than might be assumed based on contemporary understandings of orthodox Islamic jurisprudence.

Qur'ān and Precedents in "Professional" Islamic Legal Discourse

While some jurists omitted discussion of legal authority or precedents, others cited and explained specific Qur'ānic verses and historical events to support the permissibility of prisoner execution. Māwardī (d. 1058; Iraq), a Shāfi'ī jurist, listed the same four options delineated above (execution, enslavement, ransoming, and release).[136] Māwardī offered an obscure (and inconsistent) interpretation of Q 47:4 by implying that bonds should be tied around executed soldiers.[137] He failed to explain how executed prisoners could be freed or ransomed (as the verse demands). In relying on this verse to support prisoner execution, he provided no precedents of the Prophet (or his Companions) executing war prisoners. By contrast,

[135] These four options are freeing, ransoming, enslaving, or killing. Aḥmad ibn 'Abd al-Ḥalīm Ibn Taymīyah (d. 1328; Syria), *Ibn Taimiyya on public and private law in Islam; or, Public policy in Islamic jurisprudence* [al-Siyasah al-shar'iyah fi islah al-ra'i wa-al-ra'iyah], trans. by Omar A. Farrukh (Beirut: Khayats 1966), 142, citation omitted (Ḥanbalī).

[136] 'Alī ibn Muḥammad al-Māwardī (d. 1058; Iraq), *The ordinances of government* [Al-ahkām al-sulṭāniyya w'al-wilāyāt al-dīniyya], trans. by Wafaa H. Wahba, The great books of Islamic civilization (Reading: Garnet, 1996), 54 (Shāfi'ī). See also footnote 127. See also his Shāfi'ī successor, Abū Isḥāq Ibrāhīm ibn 'Alī ibn Yūsuf Fīrūzābādī al-Shīrāzī (d. 1083; Iran), *al-Muhadhdhab fī fiqh al-imām al-shāfi'ī*, 2 vols. (Cairo: Sharikat Maktabat wa-Maṭba'at Muṣṭafá al-Thānī al-Ḥalabī wa-Awlādahu bi-Miṣr, 1959), 2:236 (Shāfi'ī: Imām may choose to kill, enslave, ransom, or free male combatants (i.e., not minors) as he deems appropriate).

[137] al-Māwardī, *Ordinances*, 54.

Māwardī mentioned examples of grace and ransom from the biography of the Prophet and the history of the late antique Muslim community.[138] By citing incidents from the Prophet's practice that legitimize only some of the legal options he lists, Māwardī demonstrated that precedent was not crucial to his legal reasoning. Indeed, Māwardī's uneven discussion of prisoner of war execution appears outcome determinative because it was based on a nonsensical interpretation of a Qur'ānic verse and on selective references to Prophetic precedents.

To support his ruling further, Māwardī adduced a narrative alleging that the Prophet disapproved of ransoming. He cited the aforementioned report concerning the Prophet's consultation with Abū Bakr and 'Umar at Badr and then used it to interpret Q 8:67 as a condemnation of ransoming and a reproach of the Prophet for ransoming the Badr prisoners.[139] Māwardī declared, "After this verse was revealed, God's Messenger, God bless him and grant him peace, said, 'Had God decreed our punishment in this verse, 'Umar, you would have been the only one to escape it.'"[140] This is a peculiar report to use as a precedent because it is negative evidence, suggesting that the Prophet made a mistake by *not* executing prisoners of war. Nevertheless, if the Prophet did err in his judgment, where is the explanation of his error or the advice to his followers on the proper course of action? More importantly, other versions of this story do not cite the Prophet as approving 'Umar's earlier suggestion to execute prisoners.[141] Māwardī uses this specific historical narrative to legitimate prisoner execution – without providing an actual historical example of prisoner execution.[142]

Like Māwardī, Ibn Rushd (d. 1198; Andalusia/Maghreb) combed the Qur'ān for evidence concerning the execution of war prisoners.[143] This Mālikī jurist and philosopher asserted that the juristic disagreement results from inconsistences between Prophetic acts and the meaning of

[138] *Ibid.*, 54–5.

[139] See footnote 16.

[140] al-Māwardī, *Ordinances*, 50–1.

[141] See footnote 16. See also al-Qushayrī, *Ṣaḥīḥ Muslim*, 3:962, n. 4360.

[142] Living under the Būyids (r. 934–1055 CE), Māwardī was unlikely to have been influenced by ongoing battles with non-Muslims, since the Būyids were involved in conquering Muslim territories. Could Māwardī's juristic opinion on prisoners of war have been a polemical dispute with the Būyid Shī'ī jurists around him? It is difficult to identify the contextual background of this jurist's legal reasoning.

[143] Ibn Rushd was born during the Almohad rebellions, received protection from Ya'qūb al-Manṣūr (an Almohad Amīr, r. 1184–1199 CE), and, toward the end of his life, witnessed Almohad victories over the Portuguese (in 1191) and the Castilians (in 1195). Ongoing battles with Christian armies may have motivated Ibn Rushd to assume the permissibility of prisoner of war execution.

the Qur'ān.[144] Ibn Rushd explained Q 47:4 as limiting a Muslim leader to "only pardon or take ransom."[145] Yet, like Māwardī, Ibn Rushd claimed that Q 8:67 implies that execution is better than ransoming (exemplified by the mistake made at Badr) and that the Prophet's acts relating to treatment of prisoners were inconsistent.[146] What is curious about Ibn Rushd's interpretation of Q 8:67 is that he defined the key verb (*yuthkhina*) as "to kill" whereas he interpreted a different form of the same verb (*athkhantumūhum*) in Q 47:4 as meaning "to overcome" or "to subdue." This verb (*th-kh-n*) can mean to slaughter, to subdue, or even to apply oneself energetically; it is peculiar that within one discussion of these two verses, Ibn Rushd defined the same verb inconsistently. He asserted that the status of this verse as abrogated or not is the crux of the legal controversy.[147] He claimed that those who argue that prisoner execution is not permissible hold that Q 47:4 abrogated the acts of the Prophet. (A few Muslim scholars suggested the possibility of Prophetic acts abrogating the Qur'ān.[148]) But, as indicated above, many of Ibn Rushd's late antique predecessors did not perceive any conflict between Q 47:4 and the Prophet's acts.[149] Thus, he presumed that the medieval minority opinion (prohibiting prisoner execution) relied on the same understanding of historical events as his own (i.e., that the Prophet executed war prisoners), rather than an alternative version.

al-Rāfiʿī (d. 1226; Iran), a Shāfiʿī jurist, claimed that the Prophet himself exercised all four options, with the precedent of execution coming from the executions of al-Naḍr and ʿUqbah at Badr, as well as of Abū ʿAzzah al-Jumaḥī at Uḥud.[150] He asserted that a leader must determine

[144] Abū al-Walīd Ibn Rushd (d. 1198; Andalusia/Maghreb), *The Distinguished Jurist's Primer: a translation of Bidāyat al-mujtahid wa-nihāyat al-muqtaṣid* ed. by Muhammad Abdul Rauf, trans. by Imran Khan Nyazee, 2 vols. (Reading: Garnet Publishing, 1994), 1:456 (Mālikī).

[145] *Ibid.*

[146] *Ibid.*

[147] *Ibid.*, 1:457 (Mālikī).

[148] See Fatoohi, *Abrogation.*

[149] "Those who maintained that the verse, which is specific about the matter of captives (prohibiting execution), has abrogated the acts of the Prophet, said that the captive is not to be executed. Those who maintained that the verse neither mentions captives nor is its purpose the final disposal of the question of what is to be done to the captives, and that the act of the Prophet (God's peace and blessings be upon him) is an addition to what is in the verse, when they take into account the censure of the failure to execute the captives said that the execution of the captives is permitted." Ibn Rushd, *Distinguished Jurist's Primer*, 1:457 (Mālikī).

[150] ʿAbd al-Karīm ibn Muḥammad al-Rāfiʿī (d. 1226; Iran), *al-ʿAzīz sharḥ al-wajīz: al-maʿrūf bi-al-sharḥ al-kabīr*, ed. by ʿAlī Muḥammad Muʿawwaḍ and ʿĀdil Aḥmad ʿAbd al-Mawjūd, 14 vols. (Beirut: Dār al-Kutub al-ʿIlmīyah, 1997), 11:410. His Shāfiʿī predecessor cites three executions at Badr, one at Uḥud, and one in Mecca. al-Shīrāzī, *al-Muhadhdhab*, 2:237 (Shāfiʿī: offering historical examples of the Prophet executing prisoner combatants).

which of the four options is best for the community. He maintained that Q 8:67 and Q 47:4 are context specific: Q 47:4 demanded either the freeing or ransoming of prisoners because the community was strong at that time, whereas Q 8:67 recommended execution of prisoners (in his interpretation) because the community was weak.[151] While al-Rāfiʿī refers to a change in circumstances, he does not elaborate on the relevant historical details.

This brief presentation of the legal reasoning of some major jurists of the tenth through thirteenth centuries has demonstrated an unsystematic use of Qurʾānic authority and inconsistent references to tradition-reports and historical precedents. This variety, which reflects the legal polycentricity that pervades Islamic legal traditions, also suggests that precedent (i.e. Prophetic practice as preserved in historical sources) is less instrumental to the reasoning of Muslim jurists than might be presumed. While Prophetic practice may be characterized as inconclusive, all these jurists approached the issue of war prisoners with little concern for expressly justifying the legal opinions they advocated with clear legal-historical precedents. None of the jurists cited here referenced the tradition-report in which the Prophet commanded that prisoners of war be treated well. Most jurists simply discussed the legal status of prisoners of war without reconciling their judgments with the historical narratives about most war prisoners being ransomed or freed.[152]

A possible explanation for these diverse references to precedent is that these juristic opinions were outcome determinative or utilitarian; this would be yet another example of jurists using legal rhetoric to arrive at a desired result. Or perhaps the majority of jurists were legitimating "executive authority" by asserting that a ruler has a multitude of options or by expressing their individual opinions without regard for precedent/authority. Be that as it may, these explanations are too simplistic and too cynical because these jurists probably perceived their legal rulings to be legitimate. While the socio-political objectives of jurists certainly influenced their understandings of the Qurʾān and Prophetic practice, in the course of debating other jurists or teaching their students, jurists must have had to defend their opinions by substantiating them. Why did they

[151] al-Rāfiʿī, *al-ʿAzīz*, 11:410. His Shāfiʿī predecessor offered the same rationalization for a presumed "confusion" in the Qurʾānic verses. al-Shīrāzī, *al-Muhadhdhab*, 2:237 (Shāfiʿī: when Muslims were weak, they ransomed their prisoners; when they became strong, they executed them).

[152] This corresponds to Abou El Fadl's observations about "a selective and creative process by which the jurists construct and negotiate certain values." Abou El Fadl, "The rules of killing at war," 149, citation omitted.

not defend their legal opinion on the permissibility of war prisoner execution with exhaustive references to Prophetic precedents or refutations of late antique juristic opinions?

Despite their abstract commitment to implementing authentically *Islamic* rulings, most of these jurists seem unconcerned with explicitly identifying and examining historical precedents from the lifetime of the Prophet. One reason for this phenomenon is that the jurists assumed the familiarity of the audience (likely other jurists or law students) with the text and exegesis of the Qurʾān, the biography of the Prophet, and late antique Islamic history. Even those jurists who did cite legal-historical authority seemed to perceive executing a war prisoner as historically normative in some way; Māwardī, Ibn Rushd, and al-Rāfiʿī selectively referred to Prophetic precedents that legitimated their interpretations of the Qurʾān. I contend that this presumption of normativity arises from two interrelated genres: exegesis and historiography. This outline of medieval juristic perspectives illustrates that jurists did not rigorously scrutinize historical materials to establish a definitive legal-historical precedent. Instead, by engaging the language of the Qurʾān (and not historical-legal precedents), the jurists were able to avoid an important legal-historical question: if the Qurʾān stipulates that prisoners of war should be executed, when and how did the Prophet implement this command after Badr?

A Presumed Precedent: A Historical "Execution" of War Prisoners?

Medieval Qurʾānic exegetes relied on a historiographically based presumption – one that may be unarticulated – about a verse's context. Jurists who permitted prisoner of war execution may have abbreviated the explanations of their legal reasoning precisely because canonical sources offered a well-known scriptural and precedential justification for their legal opinions. In the Islamic juristic tradition, Qurʾānic exegesis and historiography are intertwined and integral to Islamic legal reasoning. (Specifically, in al-Ṭabarī's *Tafsīr*, a jurist may have located a post-Badr example of prisoner execution.) I will briefly present two examples of juristic texts that appear to rely on, or to concur with, the historical interpretation embedded in medieval exegetical texts. This intricate intertextuality also exposes the mutually influential relationships between historical narratives, exegesis, and legal opinions.

The Ḥanafī jurist al-Sarakhsī (d. 1090; Transoxania) mentioned the majority view of four options and then the minority opinion (within his legal school) against prisoner execution.[153] He explained that dissenting

[153] The four options are freeing, enslaving, ransoming, or killing.

jurists (al-Ḥasan [al-Baṣrī] and Ḥammād bin Abī Sulaymān) relied on a narrative according to which the son of the Caliph 'Umar refused to execute a prisoner of war; these dissenting jurists considered this to be a binding precedent.[154] Echoing al-Ṭabarī, Sarakhsī claimed to have historical evidence for the permissibility of execution after imprisonment in the Badr executions (al-Naḍr and 'Uqbah) and the story of the Qurayẓah clan.[155]

Similarly, Ibn Qudāmah (d. 1223; Syria), a Ḥanbalī jurist, advocated the same four options that the majority of jurists permitted. He noted that the dissenting opinions of three late antique jurists (Sa'īd bin Jubayr, al-Ḥasan al-Baṣrī, and 'Aṭā' bin Abī Rabāḥ) were based on the ransoming of Badr prisoners as a precedent and on Q 47:4 as limiting the options for dealing with war prisoners to the two (ransoming and grace) mentioned in the verse.[156] Ibn Qudāmah substantiated his legal opinion with allusions to two executions at Badr (al-Naḍr and 'Uqbah), the killing of the poet (Abū 'Azzah) at Uḥud, and the execution of the Qurayẓah clan.[157] The ambiguity of these historical precedents was discussed above (in the first section) – except for the story of the Qurayẓah clan. Both Sarakhsī and Ibn Qudāmah accept the abrogation of a key verse (Q 47:4) based on a historiographical identification of a weighty precedent: the Prophet executed prisoners of war after Badr. But does the Qurayẓah incident offer a post-Badr precedent for prisoner execution?

Slippage: The Complexity of Legal-historical Categorization

Many (if not most) jurists who permitted prisoner execution probably believed that the Prophet did execute prisoners of war. Yet it is odd that two isolated and specific prisoner executions at Badr or one execution at Uḥud would be sufficient to validate such a significant opinion. As confirmed by al-Ṭabarī and some juristic texts, another incident was selectively cited as a historical precedent for prisoner execution.[158] Some exegetes, tradition-report compilers, and jurists categorized (perhaps

[154] al-Sarakhsī and al-Shaybānī, *Sharḥ*, 3:1024 (Ḥanafī).
[155] *Ibid.*, 3:1025 (Ḥanafī).
[156] Ibn Qudāmah, *al-Mughnī*, 13:45 (Ḥanbalī).
[157] Muwaffaq al-Dīn 'Abd Allāh ibn Aḥmad Ibn Qudāmah al-Maqdīsī (d. 1223; Syria), *al-Mughnī*, ed. by 'Abd Allāh ibn 'Abd al-Muḥsin Turkī and 'Abd al-Fattāḥ Muḥammad Ḥulw, 2nd edn., 15 vols. (Cairo: Hajr, 1992), 13:46 (Ḥanbalī).
[158] By way of example, Mālik cites the execution of 'Uqbah and "seventy prisoners" in reference to the Qurayẓah clan. Saḥnūn, *al-Mudawwanah*, 1:502–3 (Mālikī).

inaccurately?) an incident involving the Qurayẓah clan as one of warfare, rather than breach of treaty or treason.[159] Medieval exegetes who viewed Q 9:5 (on treaty violations by polytheists) as abrogating Q 47:4 (on warfare) reinforced a conflation of warfare and treaty violation by decontextualizing these two verses from their respective historical contexts.[160]

The Qurayẓah clan was arguably the most powerful of the more than twelve Jewish Arab tribes in Medina.[161] When the Muslim community settled in Medina, the Prophet entered into some kind of treaty agreement (likely based on tribal legal custom) with this Jewish Arab tribe as well as with others.[162] Several years later, it was suspected and alleged that the Qurayẓah clan had collaborated with the enemy during the Battle of the Trench – thereby breaching the treaty agreement between the groups. After the battle, a Muslim army besieged their fortress. The Qurayẓah clan surrendered and Saʿd bin Muʿādh (chief of a clan allied with them) was appointed arbitrator; the tribe may have specifically chosen Saʿd to be arbitrator instead of the Prophet.[163] Saʿd reportedly declared that the tribe had committed treason and he imposed a common legal norm by ordering the execution of the combatants (i.e., men beyond puberty) and the enslavement of the women and children. The ruling may have been an application of tribal law or Biblical law. As a case in point, there are reports that Jewish law (whatever that meant in seventh-century Arabia) was applied

159 For a historical depiction of these events, see Abū Jaʿfar Muḥammad ibn Jarīr al-Ṭabarī (d. 923; Iraq), *The victory of Islam*, trans. by Michael Fishbein, *The history of al-Ṭabarī, VIII* (Albany, NY: State University of New York Press, 1997), 27–41. Tradition-reports concerning the Qurayẓah clan were placed in the book of warfare of later tradition-report collections. See al-Qushayrī, *Ṣaḥīḥ Muslim*, 3:966, nn. 4368–71. But al-Shāfiʿī classifies this incident under treaty violation. See footnote 168.

160 The focus of what follows is not moral evaluation (since contemporary morality is not superior to this history), but how and why a historical incident is interpreted by successive generations in certain ways. This event is not entirely verifiable and its non-occurrence has been argued. For opposing interpretations of this narrative (as fictional or factual), see W. N. Arafat, "New Light on the Story of Banū Qurayẓa and the Jews of Medina." *Journal of the Royal Asiatic Society of Great Britain and Ireland* 108:2 (1976); M. J. Kister, "The massacre of the Banū Qurayẓa: a re-examination of a tradition." *Jerusalem Studies in Arabic and Islam* 8 (1986): 61–96. On the problematic motif of "Muḥammad and the Jews," see Rizwi S. Faizer, "Muhammad and the Medinan Jews: a comparison of the texts of Ibn Ishaq's *Kitāb sīrat rasūl Allāh* with al-Waqidi's *Kitāb al-maghāzī*." *International Journal of Middle East Studies* 28:4 (1996): 463–89.

161 See Michael Lecker, "Wāqidī's account on the status of the Jews of Medina: a study of a combined report." *Journal of Near Eastern Studies* 54 (1995): 15–32.

162 See Michael Lecker, *The "Constitution of Medina": Muḥammad's First Legal Document*, Studies in Late Antiquity and Early Islam 23 (Princeton, NJ: The Darwin Press, 2004), 48. The smaller, more numerous Jewish Arab tribes appear to have been party to the so-called Constitution, whereas the three largest and more powerful tribes entered into separate agreements.

163 al-Zuhrī, *al-Maghāzī*, 81–2; Ibn Rāshid, *The expeditions*, 86–7.

in judgment against Jewish adulterers.[164] Even if Muslim jurists viewed this event as an Islamic legal precedent, how did it relate to war prisoners?

Late antique Islamic historiography was generally structured around the recording of battles; the very genre of historiography is closely associated with warfare.[165] (Yet, ironically, an empirical analysis of this genre indicates that only a small percentage of raids or battles resulted in loss of life or actual combat; while the genre is described as "raids" (*maghāzī*), most of the recorded events are expeditions.) Since the Qurayẓah trial immediately followed the Battle of the Trench, historical sources likewise place it directly after descriptions of the battle, which was actually a siege – no combat took place. This may explain why readers (historically and contemporaneously) interpret the Qurayẓah trial as part of the battle. This is, of course, an interesting case of the structure of a historical narrative having substantive (legal) implications. Likewise, there are contradictory references to the Prophet approving or implementing the order; thus characterizing it as an application of Islamic law is questionable.[166] The presumption that this incident is an implementation of "Islamic law" ignores the treaty agreement, third-party involvement, trial-like circumstances, indefinite legal application (tribal, Jewish, or Islamic?), and lack of combat that distinguish a battle and prevent it from having clear precedential value.[167] I am not interested in answering the historical question of what happened to the Banū Qurayẓah. Instead, I am interested in what makes this incident an *Islamic* legal precedent for Muslim jurists.

Islamic legal literature reflects the ambiguity of this event's precedential value. The late antique majority opinions and medieval dissenting opinions cited at the beginning of this chapter may attest to a period in Islamic history when this event was *not* understood as corresponding to prisoners of war. Indeed, even the medieval majority opinions that permitted prisoner execution attest to the inexplicit and ambiguous precedential value of this incident. Juristic references to this incident fall under discussions of both non-aggression treaties and general ordinances for warfare. For example, al-Shāfiʿī (d. 820; Arabia/Egypt) cites the incident

164 For the most often-cited example of Jewish law being applied to the Jewish community in Medina, see al-Bukhārī, *Ṣaḥīḥ al-Bukhārī*, 8:550 (no. 825).

165 On the relationship between biographical literature and expedition literature, see Josef Horovitz and Lawrence I. Conrad (eds.), *The earliest biographies of the Prophet and their authors* (Princeton, NJ: The Darwin Press, 2002), 4.

166 The incident is described as the judgment of Saʿd in al-Ṣanʿānī, *Muṣannaf*, 5:280. See also differing attributions of the judgment to God or Saʿd in Ibn Abī Shaybah, *Muṣannaf*, 8:503.

167 By way of example, Muqātil describes the Banū Qurayẓah incident as one in which a mediator found the tribe guilty of treason. Muqātil, *Tafsīr Muqātil*, 2:108–9.

under treaty violation and does not clearly characterize Qurayẓah as war prisoners.[168] Some jurists likely differentiated between war prisoners and captured traitors. Of all the juristic texts examined for this chapter, only two explicitly cite Qurayẓah as a precedent for prisoner execution and both are post-tenth-century legal texts – meaning both are chronologically later than al-Ṭabarī's *Tafsīr*. Sarakhsī claimed that the Qurayẓah incident is the precedent for permissibility of execution.[169] A century later, Ibn Qudāmah observed that narratives about Qurayẓah and two Badr executions "were disseminated and well-known."[170] More thorough and comprehensive legal-textual searches would be necessary in order to establish that the Qurayẓah incident became a precedent in the medieval era. It is certainly remarkable that numerous earlier jurists and contemporaries of Sarakhsī and Ibn Qudāmah did not cite the incident as a precedent. Whether stated or implied, if some jurists presumed that the Qurayẓah incident was a precedent for executing war prisoners, then their reasoning neglects both the historical circumstances and other historical precedents. Many jurists avoided or neglected reconciling all the historical narratives pertaining to actual prisoners of war in their legal analysis. Some of these jurists may have perceived the Qurayẓah incident as the presumptive basis for the normativity of prisoner execution.

It is possible that medieval Muslim scholars characterized an internal dispute with one of the Jewish Arab tribes as a war because they conceptualized Jewish Arab tribes as clearly distinguishable from pagan Arabs and Muslim Arabs – a dichotomy (between Jewish and Muslim) that is not historically attested in the seventh century (and beyond).[171] Indeed, the overwhelming evidence of intermarriage[172] and integration,[173] as

[168] Muḥammad ibn Idrīs al-Shāfiʿī (d. 820; Arabia/Egypt), *al-Umm*, ed. by Ismāʿīl ibn Yaḥyá Muzanī (d. 878). Reprint of the edn. published in Cairo, 1321 (1903/4), 7 vols., Kitāb al-Shaʿb (Cairo: Dār al-Shaʿb, 1968), 4:107.

[169] al-Sarakhsī and al-Shaybānī, *Sharḥ*, 3:1025.

[170] Muwaffaq al-Dīn ʿAbd Allāh ibn Aḥmad Ibn Qudāmah al-Maqdisī (d. 1223; Syria), *al-ʿUmdah fī al-fiqh al-Ḥanbalī*, ed. by al-Hawwārī and Anwar Zahrāʾ (Damascus: al-Dār al-Muttaḥidah lil-Ṭibāʿah wa-al-Nashr, 1990), 46.

[171] I disagree with Donner's claim that "the Believers may have adopted a distinct confessional identity as Muslims only in the second half of the first century AH." Donner, *Narratives*, 99, fn 1. But see Amikam Elad. "Community of believers of 'holy men' and 'saints' or community of Muslims? The rise and development of early Muslim historiography." *Journal of Semitic Studies* 47:2 (2002): 241–308.

[172] Michael Lecker, "A note on early marriage links between Qurashīs and Jewish women." *Jerusalem Studies in Arabic and Islam* 10: (1987): 17–39.

[173] Lecker notes that "fosterage was probably the social institute that facilitated the absorption of Arab children by Jewish clans." Michael Lecker, "ʿAmr ibn Ḥāzm al-Anṣārī and Qurʾān 2, 256: 'No compulsion is there in religion'." *Oriens* 35 (1996): 57–64 at 63. See also Michael Lecker,

well as of socio-political contracts, indicates that Jewish Arab tribes were an integral component of Medinan society. Most historiographical works about this event reify the confessional identity of the tribe, thereby ignoring the salient historical fact that there were no apparent conflicts between the late antique Muslim community and the majority of Jewish Arab tribes in Medina and that there may have been economic undercurrents to the strained relationship with the Qurayẓah clan. Economically powerful in Medina, some Qurayẓah members had served as tax collectors for the Sasanians; the Prophet appears to have undertaken some redistribution of property that may have antagonized them.[174] It is probable that at least some late antique jurists (and possibly the Prophet's Companions) did not share the same historiographical understanding of this incident as medieval jurists did; this difference in historical understanding may correlate to the differences of opinion on the legality of executing prisoners of war.

Medieval Muslim jurists either could not conceptualize the complex hybridity of Jewish-Muslim-Arab identity or chose not to accept it. The prolonged existence of Jewish-Christians is a comparable historical case that further substantiates the likelihood of fluid confessional identity during this period.[175] Most contemporary historians, unfortunately, have continued to disregard the complex nature of historical identity by projecting modern identity categories onto this historical period. The exegesis and historiography of medieval jurists signals that they assumed unambiguous confessional identities, manifested in violent hostilities between groups. The reality of late antique Arabia was more complex than the emplotted narrative of the Qurayẓah incident composed by medieval Muslim scholars. Their late antique predecessors attest to divergent historiographic and legal opinions.

"Zayd b. Thābit, 'a Jew with two sidelocks': Judaism and literacy in pre-Islamic Medina (Yathrib)." *Journal of Near Eastern Studies* 56 (1997): 259–73.

174 Mahmood Ibrahim, *Merchant capital and Islam* (Austin, TX: University of Texas Press, 1990), 180.

175 Daniel Boyarin noted, "In suggesting that Judaism and Christianity were not separate entities until very late in late antiquity, I am, accordingly, not claiming that it is impossible to discern separate social groups that are in an important sense Christian/not-Jewish or Jewish/not-Christian from fairly early on (by which I mean the mid-second century)." Daniel Boyarin, *Border lines: the partition of Judaeo-Christianity*, Divinations: Rereading Late Ancient Religion (Philadelphia, PA: University of Pennsylvania Press, 2004), 21. Similarly, I recognize that in the beginning of Islamic history there were groups that could be identified as Muslim/not-Jewish, but the "fuzziness of the borders" that Boyarin discusses is relevant to understanding how Muslim identity changed in late antiquity.

Another Possibility

Thus far, I have focused on textual continuities and discontinuities of late antique and medieval Muslim scholars, with particular attention to history, exegesis, and jurisprudence. However, normativity cannot be located exclusively in Islamic texts or in Muslim historical figures. Wars against non-Islamic empires, for example, may have shaped (even subconsciously) how jurists viewed the legal status of prisoners of war. A more thorough analysis of socio-political contexts, which is beyond the scope of this chapter, would likely be inconclusive. Prisoner exchange was common between the Byzantine and Islamic empires between the eighth and tenth centuries,[176] but actual war practices varied across time and region. Jurists were concerned not only with overcoming their political adversaries: they asserted that they were following Islamic tradition, or what they supposed was Islamic tradition. I am not here making a claim about internally-motivated legal reasoning as "good faith" and externally-motivated legally reasoning as "bad faith." Instead, I want to emphasize that all jurists are equally motivated by factors that are both internal and external to their formal jurisprudential methodology. Although I have concentrated on precedents, exegesis, and legal reasoning specific to the Muslim community, there is more to consider.

Generally, the Prophet and late antique Muslim jurists acted in harmony with the prevailing socio-legal norms of the region.[177] It appears that pre-Islamic tribal custom was to ransom prisoners of war, but not to execute them. By comparison, Roman law assumed the enslavement of war prisoners, which was widely practiced.[178] By contrast, a significant Near Eastern, pre-Islamic legal norm that explicitly advocated prisoner execution is found in Biblical law. Deuteronomy 20:13 states, "And when the Lord your God delivers it into your hand, you shall put all its males to the sword."[179] Rabbis throughout the antique and late antique eras

[176] Rotman, *Les esclaves et l'esclavage*, 56–62, 68–75.

[177] Coulson asserts, "In short, the Qur'ānic regulations modify in certain particulars rather than supplant entirely the existing customary law." Noel J. Coulson, *A history of Islamic law* (Edinburgh: Edinburgh University Press, 1964), 15.

[178] See references to the enslavement of prisoners of war in *The Digest of Justinian* trans. by Alan Watson, revised English-language edn., 2 vols. (Philadelphia, PA: University of Pennsylvania Press, 1998), 1:1.5.4.2 and 2:49.15. See also *The Institutes of Justinian: text, translation, and commentary*, trans. by Joseph Anthony Charles Thomas (Amsterdam; New York: North-Holland Pub. Co.; American Elsevier Pub. Co., 1975), I.3, p. 14.

[179] *NRSV Bible*. The verse's indifference to the category of non-combatant males is echoed in Ibn Ḥazm's ruling that all male enemies – combatant or non-combatant – may be killed. ʿAlī ibn

interpreted this verse as referring to an optional war, which they differentiated from obligatory wars (in which all inhabitants would be killed).[180] Rabbinic Jewish traditions constituted part of the normativity of the medieval Islamic world. Indeed, Qurṭubī cites a unique version of the tradition-report about the Prophet consulting Abū Bakr and ʿUmar on how to handle the Badr prisoners of war: his version suggests that Abū Bakr's opinion is consistent with that of Abraham and Jesus (*ʿĪsá*), whereas ʿUmar's opinion is consistent with that of Noah and Moses.[181] This is an interesting tradition-report because Abraham and Jesus are authority figures for Arabian monotheists and Christians, respectively, while Noah and Moses are authority figures for Jews. Since Qurṭubī's exegesis validates ʿUmar's permission of prisoner execution, he implicitly accepts the "Jewish" practice.

It is possible that the normativity of prisoner execution is a remnant of the biblical tradition, which itself is indicative of ancient Near Eastern customary practices.[182] Of course, no Muslim jurist cited the Torah as precedent for prisoner of war execution and there is an insufficient evidentiary basis for making such a claim.[183] Because legal interpretive communities are fluid, the normalcy of prisoner execution within Near Eastern customs might have been integrated subtly into Islamic traditions. My point is that there may have been a deep-rooted customary practice legitimating prisoner execution that is unrelated to the Qurʾān, or the practice of the Prophet and his Companions, or normative Islamic legal methodology. After all, these communities (Muslim, Jewish, Christian) were not easily distinguishable in late antiquity. What was normative to a Muslim jurist was not grounded in a "purely" Islamic tradition and this may explain the juristic tendency to read the historical record as permitting, even prescribing, prisoner execution. Moreover, the possibility that the Bible and its history of interpretation can shed light on late antique Muslim

Aḥmad Ibn Ḥazm (d. 1064; Andalusia), *al-Muḥallā*, ed. by Ḥasan Zaydān Ṭulbah, 12 vols. (Cairo: Maktabat al-Jumhūriyah al-ʿArabīyah, 1967–1971), 7:345 (Ẓāhirī).

180 See the eighth chapter of Sōṭah in the Mishnah, Tosefta, Palestinian Talmud, and Babylonian Talmud, discussing optional and obligatory wars.

181 al-Qurṭubī, *al-Jāmiʿ*, 8:47.

182 As I explain in Chapters 3 and 4, "borrowing" is an inaccurate way of characterizing the complicated transformation of these hybrid communities.

183 On the acceptability of non-abrogated, pre-Islamic laws (such as Biblical law) as a source of Islamic jurisprudence, see ʿAbd al-Raḥmān ibn ʿAbd Allāh Darwīsh, *al-Sharāʾiʿ al-sābiqah wa-madá ḥujjīyatihā fī al-sharīʿah al-islāmīyah* (Saudi Arabia: ʿA. al-R. b. ʿA. A. al-Darwīsh, 1989); Anwar Shuʿayb ʿAbd al-Salām, *Sharʿ man qablanā: māhīyatuhu wa-ḥujjīyatuhu wa-nashʾatuhu wa-ḍawābiṭuhu wa-taṭbīqātuh* (Kuwait: Lajnat al-Taʾlīf wa-al-Taʿrīb wa-al-Nashr, 2005).

communities is an important illustration that Islamicate culture needs to be appreciated in any historical investigation of Islamic law.

Conclusion

Historiography, exegesis, and jurisprudence are overlapping yet distinct genres. Within each of these genres, there are distinctions between late antique and medieval sources. The historical summary, late antique exegesis, prohibition of execution by most late antique jurists, and historical reconstruction of a key event, may all be harmonized by rejecting the notion that Q 47:4 was abrogated. In other words, the disparate historical evidence (biographical, legal, and exegetical) suggests that Q 47:4 limits treatment of prisoners of war to freeing or ransoming, which was the Prophet's practice, as reflected in the opinion of many late antique jurists. The medieval, orthodox perspective that Q 47:4 was abrogated may have been prompted by genuine contentions, by assuming a particular historiography, by utilitarian objectives, or by adherence to a (legal or social) tradition. I contend that all these factors played a role in constructing what medieval jurists believed to be normative.

In this chapter, I have focused on the "internal" dynamics of changing Islamic legal consciousness and consequently I have avoided fully engaging the influence of actual, contemporaneous practice on legal hermeneutics. During the medieval period, jurists relied on the interpretation of historical texts and of the Qur'ān. In the case of prisoners of war, the majority of these professional jurists arrived at interpretations that seem inconsistent – or at least unconcerned – with some historical evidence or with some of the opinions of earlier jurists. I situated the Qurayẓah incident within a broader framework of Islamic history; many late antique jurists and a minority of medieval jurists (Imāmī Shīʿī and Ḥanafī) who prohibited prisoner execution shared this historical understanding.[184] It is unclear what the majority (professional or contemporary) Islamic legal opinion on prisoner execution would be if late antique Muslim historians had clearly distinguished between the Battle of the Trench and the Qurayẓah incident. Nor can we determine what the prevailing legal opinion would be if professional jurists had applied more precision in their analysis of historical precedents and Qur'ānic verses. The legal reasoning of jurists does not simply arise from the methodology they purport

[184] For a contemporary presentation of this legal interpretation, see Shalabī, *al-Jihād fī sabīl allāh*, 101–7.

to apply or from presumed utilitarian objectives. Interpretations of and assumptions about legal texts and precedents – rooted in complex, multi-layered traditions – intermingle to produce juristic opinions. Variations in Islamic historiography and exegesis both generate and reflect juristic disagreement.

Precedent may be used to support contradictory rulings; jurists are subjective and may make outcome-determinative decisions; jurists are not skilled historians and employ historiography in problematic ways. I have attempted to deepen these observations: most medieval, orthodox jurists began with a genuine presumption that executing prisoners of war is a viable option. In citing the Qur'ān or tradition-reports (*aḥadīth*), most medieval jurists instinctively understood these sources as sanctioning prisoner execution, despite the late antique differences of opinion. Executing war prisoners may have been a normative or long-standing practice that was not weakened by late antique Islamic perspectives that likely prohibited it. My objective has been to scrutinize the juristic discourse, rather than pass judgment on the legitimacy of this perspective. The intertextual process of creating precedents, as depicted in this chapter, is not unique to the Islamic legal tradition. For legal historians, this case study is a complicated inquiry into how historians construct histories, how jurists interpret those constructions, and how those created legal-historical precedents are used in legal traditions. This chapter has demonstrated the significance of intertexual legal-historical analysis by demarcating how orthodox jurists interpreted the permissibility of prisoner of war execution as a historical truth.

In this chapter, I briefly presented how some late antique Muslims engaged with Jews, how some medieval Muslims perceived that interaction, and how Biblical law reflects regional norms that may have been integrated in Islamic law. The next chapter delves more deeply into the relationship between Jews and Muslims, and Jewish law and Islamic law.

CHAPTER 3

Legal-historical Hybridity – Tracing Islam in its Islamicate Context

How should we understand the relationship between Islamic law and precursor legal systems in the Near East? This question is at the heart of the Islamic law "origins" debate. It is by no means a simple question because answering it – or attempting to answer it – necessitates rigorous methodological examination. As I discussed in the Introduction, this question must begin with a clear definition of what *law* is. And as I discussed in Chapter 1, this question necessitates a hybrid and historical understanding of Islam's beginnings in order to define properly the meaning of *Islamic*. Having interrogated the meanings of *law* and *Islamic*, we can begin to examine the relationship between pre-Islamic and Islamic legal traditions. Islamic law was, from its beginning, a composite legal system, mixing laws, customs, and norms from a multitude of traditions. While this mixing is acknowledged in orthodox Islamic sources, elaborating historical Muslim perspectives on Islamic legal beginnings is beyond the scope of this chapter.[1] In Chapter 1, I demonstrated how a model of textual criticism dominates studies of Islamic law's beginnings by searching for an "internal original" text. This same model corresponds to the dominant one used in the field to search for Islamic law's "external origins" in pre-/non-Islamic traditions. As I will elaborate in this chapter, the prevalent

[1] How late antique and medieval Muslim scholars viewed the relationship between Islamic law and pre-Islamic legal traditions is the subject of my ongoing and future research. Some scholars explored pre-Islamic divine laws as a source of Islamic law; some scholars noted the ways in which Islamic law overruled pre-Islamic, pagan tribal laws; other scholars claimed that Islamic law was revolutionary, new, and authentically Islamic. Critiquing these views is beyond the objectives of this book.

ways of conceptualizing Islamic law's relationship to other legal systems are clouded by modern identity categories.

Metaphors for Historical Theory: Borrowing/Parentage

A significant anthropomorphic effect of origins-oriented historiography is manifest in scholarship that identifies Islamic law's birthplace (geographic location) or its parentage (i.e., ethnic DNA).[2] Schacht identified the "problem of origins and the problem of foreign elements,"[3] which continues to impact scholarship today.[4] Schacht located Islamic jurisprudence's "origins" in Iraq.[5] (Likewise, Jokisch specified that Islamic law was "born" in Baghdad.[6]) Crone rejected an Arabian locus of Islamic law's "origins" in favor of the Fertile Crescent.[7] By contrast (and often responding to Schacht), many scholars identify the "birthplace" of Islamic law in the Arabian Peninsula or the Near East,[8] while others characterize it more specifically as in Mecca[9] or in Medina.[10] The purpose of identifying a

[2] See, for example, Goitein, "The birth-hour of Muslim law?" I recognize that some pre-modern Muslim scholars engaged with "origins" ideas or identified a "birthplace" for Islamic law, but critiquing this literature is beyond my objectives in this chapter.

[3] Joseph Schacht, "Foreign elements in ancient Islamic law." *Journal of Comparative Legislation and International Law* 32:3/4 (1950): 9–17 at 10.

[4] Maghen notes that "[m]any scholars influenced by Schacht have also supported and extended the 'massive importation' postulate. The disclaimers of these authors – coupled as they are with confident declarations regarding the large amount of borrowing that 'must' have taken place – make for frustrating reading." Ze'ev Maghen, "Dead tradition: Joseph Schacht and the origins of 'popular practice'." *Islamic Law and Society* 10:3 (2003): 276–347 at 294.

[5] Schacht claimed, "The evidence available to us now shows that Muhammadan legal science started in Iraq about A.H. 100." Schacht, "Foreign elements," 13.

[6] Jokisch echoes Schacht: "it is here [Baghdad], in the bosom of humanism, and not in Kūfa, Madīna or anywhere else, that Islamic law was *born*." Benjamin Jokisch, *Islamic imperial law: Harun Al-Rashid's codification project*, ed. by Lawrence I. Conrad, Studien zur Geschichte und Kultur des islamischen Orients (Berlin; New York: Walter de Gruyter, 2007), 20, emphasis added.

[7] Crone and Silverstein assert that "the key transmitters of *originally* ancient Near Eastern culture will prove to be the inhabitants of the Fertile Crescent, now assisted by the Arabian tradition and now without it, but not usually the Arabians on their own." Patricia Crone and Adam Silverstein, "The ancient Near East and Islam: the case of lot-casting." *Journal of Semitic Studies* 55:2 (2010): 423–50 at 450, emphasis added.

[8] "Arabia has provided an equally, if not more, convincing source for much of the law that Islam came to adopt." Hallaq, *The origins*, 4. Hallaq also argued that "Islamic law is a creature of the legal culture of the Near East, especially those forms of it that the Arabs of the south and the north lived and experienced between the fifth and seventh centuries AD." Hallaq, *Sharīʿa*, 13.

[9] Motzki "limit[s] the scope for such an influence, temporally, to the end of the first/seventh century (including pre-Islamic times) and, spatially, to the Arabian Peninsula." Motzki, *The origins*, xv. See also Harald Motzki, "The role of non-Arab converts in the development of early Islamic law." *Islamic law and society* 6:3 (1999): 293–317.

[10] Dutton concludes that "Madinan *ʿamal* as depicted in the *Muwaṭṭa'* represents a continuous development of the 'practice' of Islam from its initial *origin* in the Qur'an, *via* the *sunna* of the

birthplace is not, however, in determining location, but rather in ascertaining lineage. This is why Schacht asserted that Iraq "account[s] for the existence of concepts and maxims of Roman jurisprudence in early Islamic legal science, and the regular occurrence of parallels in Talmudic law."[11] Schacht further claimed that "Islamic law was created by Islam, but the raw material out of which it was formed was to a great extent non-Islamic."[12] This debate about Islamic law's "birthplace" implies that where Islamic law was "born" is indicative of its cultural or ethnic identity.

Scholarly searches for Islamic law's birth or parentage echo the discourse of comparative philology, a discipline that dominated the academies in the West during the nineteenth and early twentieth centuries.[13] Nineteenth-century European comparative philology, like other disciplines in that era, was particularly focused on "origins."[14] Comparative philology articulated its "origins" orientation through the concept of *Ursprache*, which sought to identify an "original" Indo-European (Aryan) or Semitic language.[15] Comparative philologists created tree models (*Stammbaum*) to depict language evolution. I contend that scholarship continues to conceptualize the relationships between Islamic and other legal systems as embedded within a linear framework that is structured like a proto-Semitic family tree; consequently, scholars focus on identifying the derivative relationship between "older" Semitic laws and Islamic law. "Borrowing" and "influence" are two prevalent terms in Islamic studies that insinuate a comparative philological method.

Prophet as its first expositor." Dutton, *The origins of Islamic law*, 180, emphasis added. See also Dutton's introduction in Mālik Ibn Anas (d. 795; Arabia) and Muḥammad ibn Muḥammad Rāʿī (d. 1449), *Original Islam: Mālik and the madhhab of Madina*, trans. by Yasin Dutton (London; New York: Routledge, 2007).

[11] Schacht, "Foreign elements," 13.

[12] Joseph Schacht, "Pre-Islamic background and early development of jurisprudence," in *Origin and development of Islamic law*, ed. by Majid Khadduri and Herbert J. Liebesny (Washington, DC: Middle East Institute, 1955), 28.

[13] See Salaymeh, "'Comparing' Jewish and Islamic legal traditions."

[14] Olender observes, "Long confined to the realm of theology, controversies over origins – of language, religion, society, and civilization – spilled over into secular discourse and kindled countless disputes as the human sciences began to flourish in the nineteenth century." Maurice Olender, *The languages of Paradise: race, religion, and philology in the nineteenth century* [Les langues du paradis], trans. by Arthur Goldhammer (Cambridge, MA: Harvard University Press, 1992), 19. I am not, however, claiming that comparative Semitic linguistics is a modern invention; for a historical example, see Judah Ibn Quraysh (d. tenth century; North Africa), *Risalat al-ḥakīm*, ed. by J. J. L. Bargès and Baer ben Alexander Goldberg (Lutetiae Parisiorum: B. Duprat, D. Maisonneuve, 1857).

[15] As Tuska Benes has noted, "comparative philology epitomized the nineteenth-century German quest for origins." Tuska Benes, *In Babel's shadow: language, philology, and the nation in nineteenth-century Germany* (Detroit, MI: Wayne State University Press, 2008), 10.

As a result of comparative philology's impact, it became commonplace to identify the equivalent of a "language family" to which Islamic law belongs by suggesting either an Aryan or Semitic "origin." As I will elaborate, much scholarship continues to be oriented toward tracing Islamic law's "origins" in a linear model that fuses ethnic, racial, and religious classifications. Scholarly inquiries into "origins" or "borrowing" are like Islamic law's paternity tests: is the father Roman (Aryan) or Jewish (Semitic)? While the notion of Aryan law seems outdated and irrelevant to contemporary scholars, the basic assumptions underlying a distinction between Aryan and Semite continue to inform the production of scholarship. Contemporary historiographic practices perpetuate the Aryan/Semite dichotomy, but using different vocabulary. Indeed, merely replacing the term "borrowing" with some other term (such as "adaptation") would not resolve the underlying problematic assumptions about identity and authenticity that continue to animate scholarship on Islamic legal history.

Aryan Birth Father

The "Aryan origins" of Islamic law are alternately identified as Christian, Roman, or Persian (notably, these classifications are not equivalent). In his contribution to a *Festschrift* for Theodor Nöldeke (d. 1930), Crawford Toy (d. 1919), professor of Hebrew and Oriental languages at Harvard, claimed, "Undoubtedly the Koran contains non-Semitic elements, derived from Christianity and Persia."[16] In his entry on *fiqh* for the *Encyclopaedia of Islam*, Goldziher (d. 1921) asserted that *fiqh* is "like the *jurisprudentia* of the Romans"[17] and alleged "the thoroughgoing adoption of Roman law by the jurists of Islām."[18] Schacht declared, "many prominent features of Islamic civilization, notwithstanding *a deceptive Arab appearance*, turn out to be *borrowings* from the Hellenistic and the Iranian world."[19] In addition, Schacht claimed, "that legal concepts and principles, including even fundamental ideas of legal science, entered Muhammadan law from outside,

[16] Crawford H. Toy, "The Semitic conception of absolute law." In *Orientalische Studien Theodor Nöldeke zum siebzigsten Geburtstag (2. März 1906) gewidmet von Freunden und Schülern und in Ihrem Auftrag herausgegeben von Carl Bezold. Mit dem Bildnis Th. Nöldeke's, einer Tafel und zwölf Abbildungen*, ed. by Carl Bezold (Gieszen: A. Töpelmann, 1906), 797–804 at 801.

[17] Ignaz Goldziher (d. 1921), "Fiḳh," in *The Encyclopaedia of Islam: a dictionary of the geography, ethnography and biography of the Muhammadan peoples*, ed. by M. Th. Houtsma *et al.* (Leiden; London: E.J. Brill; Luzac & Co., 1913), 101–5 at 101.

[18] *Ibid.*, 102.

[19] Schacht, "Foreign elements," 10, emphasis added.

in particular from Roman law."[20] In other words, Schacht claimed that Islamic law "borrowed" from Aryan law – and, perhaps to a lesser extent, from other Semitic legal systems. Coulson (d. 1986) alleged that "[o]ver the whole of the Umayyad period standards and norms of foreign law (Sasanian Persian as well as Roman law) gradually infiltrated into legal practice, so that Muslim jurisprudence in the mid-eighth century could take them for granted when conscious knowledge of their *origin* had been lost."[21] A more recent allegation that Muslims "borrowed" from Aryan law comes from Jokisch, who declared that "most of the Sharīʿa experts gave preference to Roman law, classical or post classical, and secondly to Jewish law."[22] These scholars share an interest in identifying Islamic law's non-Semitic "origins."

Semitic Birth Father

Some scholars seek to identify Islamic law's Semitic "origins," which are primarily associated with Jewish law. Within Western scholarly traditions, Jewish law has traditionally been viewed as the principal source of "influence" on Islamic law; most comparative studies of Jewish and Islamic law focus on this issue.[23] By referring to Islamic law's "Jewish origins" or "Jewish borrowings," scholars tacitly place Islamic law in a lineage relationship with Jewish law. Vesey-Fitzgerald claimed, "Any influence which Roman law may have had on Islamic jurisprudence was not by the channels of direct or conscious *borrowing* and may for our present purpose be ruled out. But the case was otherwise with Rabbinical law."[24] Similarly, Crone argued that "[t]he *a priori* case for a Roman and/or provincial component in Umayyad law is thus very strong" but "arguments for Roman influence can probably never be as decisive as those for Jewish *origins*."[25] Perhaps reflecting a notion of "proto-Semitic" culture, Crone viewed

[20] *Ibid.*, 17.

[21] Coulson, *A history*, 28, emphasis added.

[22] Jokisch, *Islamic imperial law*, 75.

[23] Libson notes that "Liebesny, Fitzgerald, Snouck Hurgronje, and Brunschvig, took Judaism as their point of departure in their quest for outside influences on Islam … modern scholarship largely agrees that Judaism influenced Islamic law or contributed to its consolidation; different authors, however, dispute the measure of that influence and its depth." Gideon Libson, *Jewish and Islamic law: a comparative study of custom during the Geonic period*, Harvard series in Islamic law, 1 (Cambridge, MA: Islamic Legal Studies Program, Harvard Law School, 2003), 4.

[24] Seymour Gonne Vesey-FitzGerald, "Nature and sources of the sharīʿa." In *Origin and development of Islamic law*, ed. by Majid Khadduri and Herbert J. Liebesny (Washington, DC: Middle East Institute, 1955), 85–112 at 89, emphasis added.

[25] Crone, *Roman*, 16.

Aramaic culture (i.e., the shared culture of Christians, Jews, and pagans in the Near East) as Islam's "origins."[26] Similarly, Wegner claimed that exegetical principles in Islamic jurisprudence were derived from Talmudic principles.[27] Moreover, Wegner used philology to legitimate her theory of Islamic borrowing from Judaism; she alleged that the term Qurʾān is an example of borrowing.[28] All of these scholarly identifications of Islamic law's "Jewish origins" function as an identification of Islamic law's parentage. By implicitly assuming that Islam is "Semitic," much scholarship stresses Islam's "Semitic origins" in Jewish law.

Aryan/Semitic "Origins"

In effect, many scholars treat Islamic law as the "illegitimate" child of an "Arab" mother and either an Aryan or a Semitic father – depending on whether a scholar understands Islamic law as purely Semitic or hybrid Aryan/Semitic. (The genders in this "illegitimate" child metaphor are intentional.[29]) Bloch warned of the "danger of confusing ancestry with explanation" in origins-oriented historiography.[30] The notion of illegitimacy – and its inherent connection to birth metaphors – is reflected in Schacht's claim that "concepts and maxims *originating* from Roman and Byzantine law, from the Canon law of the Eastern Churches, from Talmudic and Rabbinic law, and from Sasanian law, *infiltrated* into the *nascent* religious law of Islam during its period of *incubation*, to appear in the doctrines of the second century A.H."[31] In response, some scholars wrote articles specifically contesting the Orientalist presumption of excessive "foreign" influences on Islamic law.[32] Noting the prevalence of Schachtian ideas about "origins" and foreign influences, Maghen concluded that "the hasty assignment of entire realms of Islamic

[26] Crone and Silverstein claimed that "a great deal of Islamic culture is Aramaic culture, brought into Islam in the form in which it had developed under Greek and Persian rule, to develop in new directions thereafter." Crone and Silverstein, "The ancient Near East and Islam," 448–9.

[27] Judith Romney Wegner, "Islamic and Talmudic jurisprudence: the four roots of Islamic law and their Talmudic counterparts." *The American Journal of Legal History* 26:1 (1982): 25–71 at 48 (citing Schacht and Hurgronje).

[28] *Ibid.*, 32 ("*qaraʾa* is not a native root in South Semitic (Arabic) but was 'borrowed' from North Semitic (Hebrew or Aramaic) because of earlier development of literacy among the northern Semites.").

[29] See Anne McClintock, *Imperial leather: race, gender, and sexuality in the colonial contest* (New York: Routledge, 1995).

[30] Bloch, *The historian's craft*, 32.

[31] Schacht, *An introduction*, 21, emphasis added. See also Schacht, "Pre-Islamic background," 35.

[32] See Wael B. Hallaq. "Review: The use and abuse of evidence: the questions of provincial and Roman influences on early Islamic law." *Journal of the American Oriental Society* 110:1 (1990): 79–90;

law – including their methodologies and minutiae – to wholesale importation, or even just to significant foreign influence, is often a misguided and misleading enterprise."[33] Many scholarly critiques largely operate within the same "origins" paradigm by suggesting "native" Muslim influence, rather than rejecting the entire framework of borrowing/influence. The problem with this scholarly debate is not that it misidentifies the source of "borrowing," but that it even accepts the possibility of "borrowing." I maintain that, too often, Islam is conceptualized as an ethnic category, which leads to inquiries about its ethnic DNA. The endeavor of "origins"-oriented historiography confuses ethnic identity (Arab) and a socio-political movement (Islam), suggesting an inability to distinguish between "Islam" and "Arab." While these categories obviously overlapped considerably during the late antique period, they are analytically distinct.

Positivism and Linearity: Comparative Philology

Comparative philology was a positivist discipline that celebrated European ascendency through linear causality. As Olender has demonstrated, nineteenth-century philological studies shaped later understandings of history in the West, as well as many ideologies (including anti-Semitism).[34] Comparative philological studies overlapped with comparative religion. For instance, Ernest Renan (d. 1892) merged the two disciplines, claiming that Semites created religions.[35] (Not coincidentally, in his discussion of the "origins obsession," Bloch cited Renan as relying on the term and concept of origins, which was typical of Renan's era.[36]) According to Renan, Aryans were the only people who understood liberty and simultaneously believed in a strong state and in individual freedom.[37] By contrast, the political life of Semites was marked by theocracy, anarchy, and despotism.[38] (I hope that my readers hear the echoes of these ideas

Motzki, "The role of non-Arab converts." It is not my objective here to evaluate the substantive assertions made by either Hallaq or Motzki in these two articles.

33 Ze'ev Maghen. "First blood: purity, edibility, and the independence of Islamic jurisprudence." *Der Islam* 81:1 (2004): 49– 95 at 95.

34 Olender, *The languages of Paradise*.

35 Renan claimed, "[l]a race sémitique, en particulier, ayant marquée sa trace dans l'histoire par des creations religieuses." Ernest Renan, *Histoire générale et système comparé des langues sémitiques* (Paris: Calmann Levy, 1928), 441.

36 Bloch, *The historian's craft*, 29.

37 Ernest Renan, *De la part des peuples Sémitiques dans l'histoire de la civilisation: discours d'ouverture du cours de langues Hébraïque, Chaldaïque et Syriaque, au Collége de France* (Paris: M. Lévy Frères, 1862), 14, 28.

38 *Ibid.*, 16.

in contemporary discussions.) I suspect that Renan's understanding of Semites extended to their legal systems, such that "Semitic law" would be the legal system that facilitated religion, theocracy, and despotism, while limiting liberty, strong states, and individuality.[39] While modern scholarship repudiates (or is even unaware of) Renan's legacy, it has left an indelible mark.

Renan's discriminatory dichotomization of Aryan/Semite, of course, generated contemporaneous scholarly resistance. Some well-known Islamicists – such as Ignaz Goldziher, Carl Heinrich Becker (d. 1933), and Snouck Hurgronje (d. 1936) – understood *Islamwissenschaft* as countering Renan's Aryan/Semitic binary.[40] But in challenging the binary, these scholars did not necessarily abandon or reject the implicit paradigm of comparative Semitic philology. It is important to recognize that there was a moment in the nineteenth century when the notion that Islamic law was a Semitic law would have been problematic to some scholars. But even scholars like Goldziher, who would not have used the term "Semitic law," operated within a borrowing paradigm. Goldziher asserted, "even many of the provisions of Roman Law that have been adopted by Islām only found a place in *Fiḳh* through the intermediary of the Jews."[41] In other writings, Goldziher articulated Islamic law as a synthesis of Near Eastern legal systems and critiqued the notion of originality, but he used limiting terms – borrowing, formation, and influence – that perpetuated the search for "origins."[42]

Outside of Islamic studies, comparative philology made an initial impact on legal studies through methodology – specifically, the search for proto-Semitic laws. In 1903, David H. Müller (d. 1912) published his hypothesis about an *Ur-Gesetz*, from which the Hammurabi Code, the Mosaic law, and the XII Tables are all derived.[43] A few years later, he published *Semitica. Sprach- und rechtsvergleichende Studien*, in which Müller sought to identify an *Ur-Semitic* law by connecting Mosaic law to the Hammurabi code.[44] This is indicative of broader trends: comparative legal

[39] This conjecture is necessary because I was unable to identify an explicit textual reference to Semitic law in Renan's works.

[40] Goldziher sought to distinguish between medieval and modern, rather than Aryan and Semite. See David Moshfegh, "Ignaz Goldziher and the Rise of Islamwissenschaft as a 'Science of Religion,'" PhD dissertation, University of California, Berkeley, 2012.

[41] Goldziher, "Fiḳh," 102.

[42] Moshfegh, "Ignaz Goldziher and the Rise of *Islamwissenschaft*."

[43] David Heinrich Müller, *Die Gesetze Hammurabis und ihr Verhältnis zur mosaischen Gesetzgebung sowie zu den XII Tafeln: text in Umschrift, deutsche und hebräische Übersetzung, Erläuterung und vergleichende Analyse* (Vienna: A. Hölder, 1903).

[44] David Heinrich Müller, *Semitica. Sprach- und rechtsvergleichende Studien* (Vienna: Hölder, 1906).

scholars sought to pinpoint the legal equivalent of proto-Indo European – the original Aryan law, known as the *Ur-Recht*.[45] Some scholars of legal history understood Semitic law as evolving from the Hammurabi Code through Biblical, rabbinic Jewish, and Islamic legal systems in a process of linear evolution.[46] It appears to have been taken for granted that Semitic law was a coherent analytical category.

The prevalence of the term "Semitic law" in legal scholarship increased in the twentieth century, but with little discussion of its meaning. That is, few scholars appear to have offered substantively concrete explanations of Semitic law during the twentieth century, when the term "Semite" was relatively prevalent. In his essay, "The Semitic conception of absolute law," Toy claimed, "[t]he absolute law of the Jews and Moslems is an external one, imposed on man from without by a superhuman Power."[47] Here, Semitic law appears to be divine law. Vesey-Fitzgerald (d. 1954) delineated some of the ideas circulating about the nature of Semitic law. On the occasion of his being named Professor of Oriental Laws at the University of London in 1948, he identified Jewish and Islamic legal systems as Semitic.[48] He claimed, "In the theocentric Semitic societies it may be that the personal responsibility of the individual to God was a reason why constitutional checks on this despotism were never so fully developed as they were in the Indo-Germanic systems."[49] Reflecting Renan's formulation of Semitic societies as despotic, Vesey-Fitzgerald made explicit the deficiency of Semitic law by describing Islamic law as "the most static of all legal systems"[50] and an "immobile formalist doctrine."[51] Thus, theocracy and stasis became identified as the key characteristics of Semitic law. (These characterizations of Semitic law have obvious contemporary resonance.)

Philological categories and their influence on legal scholarship were not, of course, limited to the nineteenth and twentieth centuries. In the late twentieth century, Western scholars continued to implement components of the Aryan/Semitic myth in religious studies and in legal studies. By way of example, the mythology of Western legal history assumes a continuous

45 Pier G. Monateri. "Black Gaius: a quest for the multicultural origins of the 'Western legal tradition'." *Hastings Law Journal* 51:3 (2000): 479–555 at 493–4.

46 See, for example, Chilperic Edwards and Hammurabi, *The oldest laws in the world: being an account of the Hammurabi code and the Sinaitic legislation* (London: Watts & Co., 1906), 4.

47 Toy, "The Semitic conception of absolute law," 804.

48 Seymour Gonne Vesey-FitzGerald, "The future of oriental legal studies: an inaugural lecture delivered at University College London on February 4th, 1948" (London, 1948), 2. See also Schacht, "Pre-Islamic background," 85.

49 Vesey-Fitzgerald, "The future of oriental legal studies," 17.

50 *Ibid.*, 4.

51 *Ibid.*, 9.

line between Roman law and the legal systems of contemporary European nation-states; the myth of Roman law as *Ur-Recht* has not entirely disappeared.[52] The invention of "Semites" as a philological and religious category in nineteenth-century European scholarship lingers in contemporary constructions of "religious" legal systems.[53] Unlike Aryan (or secular) legal traditions, Semitic (or religious) legal traditions are limited by their rigidity and anti-democratic nature. Thus, the European invention of Semites as oppositional figures to Aryans parallels the differentiation between secular and religious legal systems. Fundamentally, the secular/religious distinction is about state versus non-state, liberty versus despotism, Aryan versus Semite. The prejudicial assumptions underlying "Semitic law" were transferred to Islamic law: the two classifications of Semitic and religious are equally embedded within a broader discourse in which race, religion, and language are inseparable. This is because the terms of comparative philology were used "interchangeably to refer to a people, a race, a nation, or a family of languages."[54] We see this clearly in the confusion about the meaning of the term "Islamic," as much scholarship implies that Islam is both a religion and a race. The derogatory attitudes that are embedded in Western thinking about Semites continue to shape understandings of religious law in general and Islamic law in particular.

Politics and Ideology: Authenticity, Ethnicity, and "Religion"

Just as comparative philology searched for the "origins" of languages, scholarship on Islam's beginnings searches for Islam's "origins." And just as comparative philology confused the distinctions between categories of language and race, scholars of late antique Islamic history conflate the terms and concepts "Islamic" and "Arab." Consequently, Islamic law, a socio-political construct, is perceived in ethnic terms. Whether the so-called "origin" is Aryan law or Semitic law, the scholarly interest in identifying the paternity or lineage of Islamic law is often motivated by an interest in evaluating legitimacy and ethnic authenticity. Scholars who describe Islamic law as having "borrowed" from some other legal system are claiming that Islamic law is not "purely" Arab (misunderstood as equivalent to Islamic) in ethnic/intellectual "origin."

52 See Monateri, "Black Gaius."

53 On the transformation of Semites into religions, see Gil Anidjar, *Semites: race, religion, literature* (Stanford, CA: Stanford University Press, 2008).

54 Olender, *The languages of Paradise*, 11.

Notions of purity are evident in the terminology used in contemporary scholarship. Crone repeated Schacht's use of the term "deceptive," claiming that "[t]he Arab appearance of the Sharīʿa is striking, but *deceptive*: it testifies to its ideal, not its *actual origins*."[55] Crone also claimed that Arabs "received" law from "others" and then ascribed that law to "their" internal community.[56] This notion that "Arabs falsely claimed Islamic law as their own" motivates scholars to identify the "foreign" paternity of Islamic law. In doing so, some scholars perceive themselves as countering the beliefs of orthodox Muslims; this spurs much revisionist scholarship (in the contemporary West) that is often intellectually haphazard. Hoyland describes revisionist scholarship as based on a skeptical perspective "that a major world religion could not have been *born* in such a *remote* corner of the Middle East and from a desire to root Islam's *origins* and *early development* more fully within the world of late antiquity, and so to argue against the traditional Muslim perspective that Islam's *birth* was *ontogenetic*, *untainted* by *alien* wisdom and *foreign* creeds."[57] While Hoyland is critical of revisionist scholarship, his use of the term "ontogenetic" echoes Crone's terminology.[58] Crone describes scholarly inquiries into the "Arab origins" of Islamic law as "assert[ing] the parthenogenetic *origins* of Islamic law."[59] Because parthenogenesis is asexual reproduction (i.e., virgin birth), Crone alleged that Islamic law could not be the "pure" product of Arabs in the Arabian Peninsula.

As a historical matter, these assumptions misconstrue the geographic extent of Arabs and the hybridity of Arab identity. Arabs lived beyond the imaginary borders of the Arabian Peninsula and into both the Byzantine and Sasanian regions.[60] Thus, Arabs were already integrated in both Byzantine and Sasanian cultures prior to Islam and there were likely Arabs

55 Patricia Crone. "*Jāhilī* and Jewish law: the *qasāma*." *Jerusalem Studies in Arabic and Islam* 4 (1984): 153–201 at 155.

56 Crone argues, "The tribal organisation of the Arabs on the one hand, and the collective *amnesia* whereby the Prophet's Medina came to be revered as the true home of the Sharīʿa on the other, meant that the Arabs gave an archaic stamp to the law which they received." Crone, *Roman*, 99.

57 Robert G. Hoyland, "New documentary texts and the early Islamic state." *Bulletin of the School of Oriental and African Studies* 69:3 (2006): 395–416 at 404, emphasis added.

58 Elsewhere, Hoyland describes a scholarly trend that treats Islam as "*conceived* and nourished wholly by the late antique world." Hoyland, "Early Islam as a late antique religion," 1069, emphasis added.

59 Crone, *Roman*, 5, emphasis added.

60 Sijpesteijn notes that "[d]ocumentary and narrative sources show Arabs as having been present in Egypt, including the Fayyūm, before the Muslim conquest." Petra M. Sijpesteijn, "Shaping a Muslim state: papyri related to a mid-eighth-century Egyptian official," Dissertation, Princeton University, 2004, 89. See also Jan Retsö, *The Arabs in antiquity: their history from the Assyrians to the Umayyads* (London; New York: Routledge Curzon, 2005).

who identified with more than one communal or ethnic group.[61] Moreover, late antique Arabs were heterogeneous, including pagans, monotheists, Christians, Zoroastrians, and Jews.[62] Arabian Jews were not necessarily rabbinic, despite historical evidence of their communications with the Babylonian rabbinic academy.[63] And, of course, non-Arab cultures did not disappear when Islam began; Graeco-Roman culture, for example, continued to thrive in the post-Islamic era and was part of Islamicate society.[64] Still, demarcating the actual geographic presence of Arabs or the hybridity of Arab culture perpetuates the false notion that Islam has a "birthplace." The underlying and deep problem is that the very notion of "foreign" is based on an erroneous definition of Islam (as Arab) and on a mistaken presumption of clear boundaries between Islamic and non-Islamic.[65] Modern scholars using modern identity categories to describe the past often draw those boundaries.[66] For example, recent studies of biographical dictionaries have suggested that the majority of Muslim jurists (in both late antiquity and the medieval period) were identifiably Arabs; the purpose of such study has been to establish that converts or non-Arabs did not comprise a substantial portion of jurists.[67] But searching for the ethnic "origins" of

[61] Trimingham notes that "the Arabs inhabited all the regions lying to the north of the Peninsula proper, Syria and Palestine, Mesopotamia and Babylonia, even parts of western Persia, intermingled with the Aramaic-speaking peoples of these regions." John Spencer Trimingham, *Christianity among the Arabs in pre-Islamic times* (London: Longman Group Limited, 1979), 1. Similarly, Shahīd asserted, "The Arab element in the Orient and the Fertile Crescent was constantly replenished by waves of penetrators and immigrants, both seasonal and unseasonal, from Arabia. It was this constant flow from the Peninsula that was the most important element in reinforcing the Arab presence in the Orient demographically and keeping it alive culturally." Irfan Shahīd, *Rome and the Arabs: a prolegomenon to the study of Byzantium and the Arabs* (Washington, DC: Dumbarton Oaks Research Library and Collection, 1984), 11.

[62] Retsö, *The Arabs in antiquity*. See also Michael Lecker, *Muslims, Jews, and pagans: studies on early Islamic Medina*, Islamic history and civilization, vol. XIII (Leiden; New York: E.J. Brill, 1995).

[63] Newby notes, "From the Mishnah we know that the concerns of Arabian Jewry were sufficient to attract the attentions of the Babylonian rabbis. Issues of kosher dress, clothing, and food in the Arabian context were debated by the rabbis. Jewish women and presumably men, wore veils when outside to protect themselves from the windborn sand, a custom adopted from the Arabs and allowed by the rabbis." Gordon Newby, *A history of the Jews of Arabia: from ancient times to their eclipse under Islam* (Columbia, SC: University of South Carolina, 1988), 54.

[64] This is why Bowersock observes in Islamic late antiquity "a remarkable continuity of Hellenism in both its cultural and pagan aspects." G. W. Bowersock, *Hellenism in late antiquity*, Jerome lectures; 18th ser. (Ann Arbor, MI: University of Michigan Press, 1990), 80.

[65] As Boyarin explains, "Borders themselves are not given but constructed by power to mask hybridity, to occlude and disown it." Boyarin, *Border lines*, 15.

[66] On these issues, see further Lena Salaymeh. "Between scholarship and polemic in Judeo-Islamic studies." *Islam and Christian–Muslim Relations* 24:3 (2013): 407–18.

[67] Motzki observes "The results of this study suggest only that we can no longer take for granted the idea that scholars of non-Arab descent were the most natural vehicles of borrowings from pre-Islamic non-Arab legal systems … It is certainly possible that there were scholars who received their education in their culture of origin, then converted and introduced legal solutions of their former

jurists neglects the probability that regional legal practices were familiar to the late antique Muslim community because of proximity.[68] Simply put, while it is indisputable that non-Arabs converted to Islam, it is not possible to measure how that assimilation process shaped Islamic law and it is inaccurate to describe those converts as conveying "originally" non-Arab materials.[69] The ostensible competition to determine which "foreign" legal system was more "influential" on Islamic law is a symptom of identity politics and not a productive scholarly practice.[70] Islamic law is not Arab law; Muslims created Islamic law, which cannot be pure because no legal system can be pure.

Contrary to "origins"-based fixations on identity, there is common and open Muslim acknowledgment of the relevance of pre-Islamic practices to Islamic traditions.[71] Muslim recognition of the hybridity of Islamic traditions is so pervasive that Schacht criticized Muslims as wrong for considering "the retention of pre-Islamic legal practices as normal."[72] Of course, all societies recycle the practices of their ancestors, so it actually is not only normative, but improbable that Muslims would not retain prior practices. This is because "all cultures are involved in one another; none is single and pure, all are hybrid, heterogeneous, extraordinarily differentiated, and unmonolithic."[73] Moreover, the discourse on influence and borrowing does not take into account accidents in the preservation of historical evidence, which can easily skew our perception of the complex realities of Near Eastern legal systems by insinuating the idea of "influence"

law systems into Islamic jurisprudence. Such cases must, however, be demonstrated. I do not know of such a case from the first two centuries AH." Motzki, "The role of non-Arab converts," 316.

[68] See, for example, Ze'ev Maghen, *After hardship cometh ease: the Jews as backdrop for Muslim moderation*, Studien zur Geschichte und Kultur des islamischen Orients; Beihefte zur Zeitschrift "Der Islam", Neue Folge, Bd. 17 (Berlin; New York: De Gruyter, 2006), 3.

[69] Newby notes, "converted Jews like Ubayy b. Kaʿb [21/642] and Kaʿb al-ʿAḥbâr [or, sometimes, *ḥibr*, the probable paradigm for Ibn ʿAbbâs's appellation], who converted to Islam under Abû Bakr, transmitted much information *originally* derived from rabbinic tradition. Some of this material can be found in the Talmud and the Midrashîm, but some of it is preserved only in Islamic versions." Newby, *A history of the Jews of Arabia*, 66, emphasis added.

[70] This interest in measuring the amount of "influence" is discernible in Crone's claim that "the conclusion of the present work is that provincial practice contributed far more to the Sharīʿa than did Roman law. But it would nonetheless be a mistake to preclude the possibility of Roman influence on the ground that Roman law was not really practised in the Roman Near East at all." Crone, *Roman*, 14.

[71] By way of example, some Islamic jurisprudential texts included sections that consider the precedential value of pre-Islamic legal systems. See ʿAbd al-Salām, *Sharʿ man qablanā*; Darwīsh, *al-Sharāʾiʿ al-sābiqah*.

[72] Schacht, *An introduction*, 20.

[73] Edward Said, *Culture and imperialism* (New York: Vintage Books, 1993), xxv.

rather than shared history.[74] The debate about "borrowing" reveals that answering the "origins" question requires defining culture in an impossibly monolithic way, often based on the fallacy of a single cause. Not surprisingly, recent scholarship has critiqued the limitations of scholarly identifications of "borrowing" or "influence."[75] For instance, studies on Arabic translations of Graeco-Roman and other texts have shifted away from the "borrowing" paradigm and toward an understanding of translation as a non-passive act of creation.[76] Just as translation is not a derivative, but rather inventive practice, so too is cultural assimilation. Similarly, Islamic legal institutions may resemble pre-Islamic ones, but this is both an inevitable and universal phenomenon.[77] Because cultures are always assimilating and translating cultural practices, "there is no such thing as authenticity," as Asad emphasizes.[78]

Another reason why Islamic law's "parental origins" became a topic of inquiry is that scholars struggled to make sense of the combination of "religious" and "secular" dimensions of Islamic law. On the one hand, Islamic law includes ritual laws that seem similar to Jewish law; on the other hand, Islamic law includes administrative laws that seem similar to Roman law. Confused by this phenomenon, Schacht asserted that "[t]he sacred law of Islam is an all-embracing body of religious duties rather than a legal system proper; it comprises on an equal footing ordinances regarding cult and ritual, as well as political and (in the narrow sense) legal rules."[79] Similarly, Jokisch alleged that Islamic law "was an Imperial

[74] Crone and Silverstein provide an example: "if it had not been for the chance preservation of the two Greek papyri, one might have taken lot-casting for the distribution of land in early Islamic society and classical law to represent a case of Jewish *Fortleben* in Islam" rather than shared Near Eastern customs. Crone and Silverstein, "The ancient Near East and Islam," 431. Although they provide this specific example of shared customs, the article generally assumes an influence paradigm.

[75] An excellent critique is Michael L. Satlow, "Beyond influence: toward a new historiographic paradigm." In *Jewish literatures and cultures: context and intertext*, ed. by Anita Norich and Yaron Z. Eliav (Providence, RI: Brown Judaic Studies, 2008), 37–53.

[76] Gutas critiques "essentializing conceptualizations and explanations, such as the extent of the 'originality' of Arabic science and philosophy, or the 'creativity' or lack thereof of Arabs and Semites." Dimitri Gutas, *Greek culture, Arabic thought* (New York: Routledge, 1998), 150 (note the relevance of the term 'Semites'). Similarly, Vagelpohl discusses "the status of translations as *literary creations in their own right*." Uwe Vagelpohl, *Aristotle's Rhetoric in the East: the Syriac and Arabic translation and commentary tradition*, Islamic philosophy, theology and science, vol. LXXVI (Leiden; Boston, MA: Brill, 2008), 209, emphasis in original.

[77] Hennigan makes this point about Islamic trusts, arguing "that the *waqf* is a distinctly Islamic institution that developed organically within an increasingly heterogeneous Muslim community." Peter C. Hennigan, *The birth of a legal institution: the formation of the waqf in third-century A.H. Ḥanafī legal discourse*, Studies in Islamic law and society, vol. XVIII (Leiden; Boston, MA: Brill, 2004), xxii.

[78] Asad, *Genealogies*, 10.

[79] Schacht, *The origins*, v.

law in a religious guise."[80] Jokisch's claim imposes certain misconceptions about the nature of "religious law." Thus, both Schacht and Jokisch sought explanations for Islamic law's breadth in the notion of "origins." Because Islamic law was, from its beginning, simultaneously part of a socio-political movement and a state-based legal system, it is incongruent with the modern bifurcation of "religion" and "secularism." "Religious" is a problematic way to describe Islamic legal systems.[81] Specifically, the nineteenth-century scholarly invention of "Semite" and the concept of Semitic law are precursors to religious law. Since "Aryan/Semite" corresponds to "secular/religious" in contemporary Western discourse, the category of religious law is implicated in a racial/colonialist discourse that continues to influence the way that Islamic legal systems are conceptualized in contemporary scholarship.[82] Because Islamic law is frequently compared to secular law (whether explicitly or implicitly), it is important to recognize how these analytical categories shape scholarship. I contend that the category of religious law is imposed upon, and misjudges, Islamic legal systems.

An Aryan/Secular Methodology

In Chapter 1, I outlined how positivist methodologies construct "original" sources just as they search for Islam's "origins." And I suggested that the dominant methodology of dating tradition-reports is a linear exercise, based on textual criticism, that subordinates (or subalternizes) late antique Islamic sources. The reliability or authenticity of these sources is evaluated not only in terms of the form of their composition or transmission, but also in terms of the identity of their composers or transmitters. Consequently, the intermixing of textual criticism and comparative philology results in an entanglement of philological and racial categories. Just as comparative philology instantiated a positivist methodology that expressed prejudicial assumptions, contemporary Islamic studies is permeated with similarly discriminatory ideas – albeit much subtler. I want to offer one specific example that reflects wide-ranging but deeply embedded trends.

In the eyes of many scholars in the field of Islamic studies, the strict scrutiny of tradition-reports (*aḥadīth*) is the subject of empirical research, often motivated by an interest in forging a middle path between skeptics

80 Jokisch, *Islamic imperial law*, 3.
81 See, generally, Asad, *Genealogies*.
82 See, generally, Anidjar, *Semites*.

(who reject the sources) and non-skeptics (who accept the sources).[83] "Non-skeptics" is my term of choice because I suspect that for scholars in the field, the term "believers" has a double meaning: believing in the reliability of the historical sources and believing in Islam. As a case in point, Motzki describes contemporary scholars "who place considerable trust in source statements on the early period and, on this basis, attempt to describe or reconstruct the historical beginnings of Islam and Islamic law" as "born Muslims," citing F. Sezgin, A. Hasan, and M. M. Azami, and "non-Muslims," citing only N. Abbott.[84] The fact that Motzki did not identify the religious or ethnic identities of the scholars who are "skeptics" or those who "try to tread a path between the two extremes,"[85] implies that it is primarily Muslims who would be so naïve or uncritical as to "trust" Islamic sources. Motzki, of course, is a casualty of the identity politics discourse that dominates contemporary popular and academic discussions. This example illustrates how the Aryan/Semite distinction is instantiated in scholarly debates: the identity of the scholar becomes an ideological object of inquiry because "Semites" are viewed as lacking secular (Aryan) methodologies. While there is always a relationship between a scholar's identity and her scholarship, there is no simple causal relationship that can be imputed to all members of a particular group (religious, racial, ethnic, etc.).

These intricate nuances usually escape scrutiny. Motzki is a highly-respected and meticulous scholar who certainly did not intend any discriminatory effect; he undoubtedly presumes, like many other scholars in the field, that "believers" are more likely to "believe" a tradition. And, admittedly, this is a byproduct of the problematic category of religion, since it validates the assumption that a "believer" cannot be a critical scholar. In comparison, this presumption is not applied to secular actors. (Would it be acceptable to assume that certain specialists in U.S. history place too much confidence in U.S. government archives only because they are U.S. citizens?) Motzki did not ascribe to skeptics the ulterior motives of non-believers: are the skeptics (presumably non-Muslims) concerned not with methodology or historical truth, but rather with discrediting Islam? Of course not. To make these kinds of assumptions about identity dictating methodology disavows scholarship.[86] *Regardless of any scholar's*

[83] Motzki, "Theme issue," 1.
[84] *Ibid.*, 1–2.
[85] *Ibid.*, 2.
[86] A similarly problematic claim is that "Muslim" scholars, because of their identities, resist certain methodologies that can reveal Islam's "true origins." See Herbert Berg. "The implications of, and opposition to, the methods and theories of John Wansbrough." *Method & Theory in the Study of Religion* 9:1 (1997): 3–22.

motivations or biases, it is unethical to evaluate a scholar's research based on the scholar's identity. More importantly, this conflation of scholarly methodology and identity is at the heart of the methodological dispute itself: at issue is not the reliability of late antique Islamic society's sources, but rather the reliability of late antique Muslims – specifically, the believing Muslim scholars who compiled, verified, redacted, and transmitted oral narratives during the late antique and medieval eras. Contemporary scholars do not distinguish between the message (the text) and the messenger (the transmitter) because, in an ethnocentric view, the two are so intimately intertwined. This is why contemporary scholarly methods – of empirically analyzing historical sources, or of identifying the ethnic "source" for Islamic law, or of discounting oral, non-contemporaneous, and multivalent sources (described in Chapter 1) – are "tool[s] of political intervention."[87] These methods colonize the study of Islamic law. Because it is only the identity of the subaltern subject that is placed under scrutiny, the unexamined identity (of the Western scholar) is presumed to be normative and objective. Just as scholars identify the "foreign origins" of Islamic law, they identify the "subjective" (religious or non-Western) position of Islamic studies scholars.

Alternatives: Hybrid Law in Islamicate Societies

It is not my objective to offer answers to the "origins" questions – birthdate, birthplace, or paternity. Instead, I dispose of the "origins" questions entirely because they are philosophically untenable, prejudiced, and ultimately irrelevant. The modern discipline of comparative philology has changed significantly since its beginnings and, to some extent, the tree model has been replaced by a model of wave theory. Wave theory offers an alternative framework for understanding legal similarities not as derivative of an "origin," but rather as reflective of regional dynamics.[88] My objective is to develop a way to study Islamic law that is historical, contextual, and disentangled from the framework of comparative philology (with all of its prejudicial implications). To do this, I assert two interrelated modifications in scholarly discourse.

[87] Asad, "Ethnographic representation, statistics and modern power," 76.

[88] Boyarin explains, "Wave theory posits that linguistic similarity is not necessarily the product of a common origin but may be the product of convergence of different dialects spoken in contiguous areas, dialects that are, moreover, not strictly bounded and differentiated from each other but instead shade one into the other. Innovations at any one point spread like the waves created when a stone is thrown into a pond, intersecting with other such waves produced in other places and leading to the currently observed patterns of differentiation and similarity." Boyarin, *Border lines*, 18.

First, I seek to replace the problematic discourse of "borrowing" or "influence" with a historically nuanced recognition of the assimilation of shared customary practices. As Wasserstrom astutely asserted, "the debtor-creditor model of influence and borrowing must be abandoned in favor of the dialectical analysis of intercivilizational and interreligious process."[89] In late antique Islamic societies, customs included an amalgamation of tribal, Roman-Byzantine, Zoroastrian, Jewish, and Syriac Christian traditions. Documentary evidence confirms shared legal traditions; for instance, Frantz-Murphy's thorough studies of Arabic and Byzantine Greek contract formularies demonstrate that there was a shared, regional contractual discourse used by inhabitants of the region in late antiquity.[90] Because Islamic law began in a hybrid socio-historical space, any historical inquiry into Islamic legal beginnings must recognize that Muslim jurists fused regional legal traditions. However, recognizing is not the same as fixating. Insofar as we may postulate a scholarly notion of "proto-Semitic" as a legal language shared by a variety of peoples in the Near East, it should be used not with a linear assumption, but rather a recognition of the impossibility of clearly delineating the borders of legal systems that share the same socio-historical space.[91] Provincial Roman, Jewish, and Islamic legal systems do not exist in linear derivation. Islamic legal traditions did not emerge in a vacuum: they are the continuations, with modifications, of earlier Near Eastern legal practices.[92] Indeed, neglecting thorough exploration of pre-Islamic Arabian legal traditions is the result of polemics, as well as scarce and difficult sources.[93] The boundary between inside and outside is more porous and imaginary than often presumed: Muslims,

[89] Steven M. Wasserstrom, *Between Muslim and Jew: the problem of symbiosis under early Islam* (Princeton, NJ: Princeton University Press, 1995), 11.

[90] Gladys Frantz-Murphy. "A comparison of the Arabic and earlier Egyptian contract formularies, part II: terminology in the Arabic warranty and the idiom of clearing/cleaning." *Journal of Near Eastern Studies* 44:2 (1985): 99–114 at 114.

[91] A non-linear proto-Semitic understanding is what I discussed in Lena Salaymeh, "Thoughts on near eastern legal culture," (September 19, 2011), http://thetalmudblog.wordpress.com/2011/09/19/thoughts-on-near-eastern-legal-culture-guest-post-by-lena-salaymeh/.

[92] Robert Roberts noted that "[t]here are many customs which are common to all Eastern nations and cannot be traced to the code of any particular people." Robert Roberts, *The social laws of the Qorân: considered and compared with those of the Hebrew and other ancient codes* (London: Curzon Press, 1971), 2. Walter Young has made a similar assertion: "Islamic law is a natural outgrowth of its Near Eastern Semitic heritage." Walter Young, "Stoning and hand-amputation: the pre-Islamic origins of the ḥadd penalties for zinā and sariqa," Master's thesis, McGill University, Montreal, 2005, 7.

[93] To my knowledge, no legal scholar has systematically compiled pre-Islamic Arabian legal materials or compared them with their successor Islamic equivalents. On ancient Near Eastern legal systems, see Raymond Westbrook and Gary Beckman, *A history of ancient Near Eastern law* (Leiden; Boston, MA: Brill, 2003). On Arabian law, see Robert G. Hoyland, *Arabia and the Arabs: from the bronze age to the coming of Islam* (London: Routledge Press, 2001), 210.

Jews, Christians, Zoroastrians, and Arab monotheists shared a common Near Eastern legal culture and altered their normative orders in ways that reflect both the internal dynamics of legal communities and their external, socio-political situations.[94] While other scholars have acknowledged regional traditions as a source for "similarities" between Jewish and Islamic legal traditions, they did so without relinquishing the problematic framework of "influence."[95]

Second, I advocate an inherently hybrid, deracialized definition of Islam. Much of the scholarship on Islam's beginnings associates "Islam" with "Arabs" and defines "Arab" in unreasonably narrow ways. It is clear that Arabs prior to Islam practiced multiple religions and that "Arab" refers not to an ethnicity, but to a linguistically-based culture. In addition to paganism, Arabs practiced Judaism, Christianity, Zoroastrianism, and a monotheism that integrated many aspects of regional practices.[96] Islam's beginning might have been "revolutionary," but it was not a total revolution that erased the late antique context; instead, it was a revolution that integrated many aspects of the late antique Near East. Late antique Islamic legal culture was undeniably heterogeneous.[97] Although some aspects of late antique Islamic law may have integrated Arabian tribal, monotheistic, Jewish, Christian, Zoroastrian, or pagan practices, this does not mean that Islamic law was not Islamic; it only means that Islamic law is hybrid and syncretic. Specifically, I dismiss the arbitrary, but common, notion that "Islamic" can only be identified through references to the Prophet, the Qur'ān, or tradition-reports (*aḥadīth*); these are orthodox ideas that

94 Meron similarly suggested that "le droit musulman est en réalité la cristallisation d'un droit coutumier, notamment celui qui régissait la vallée du Tigre et de l'Euphrate, bien avant l'avènement de l'Islam" and identified "un droit coutumier commun aux droits juif et musulman." Yaakov Meron, "Points de contact des droits juif et musulman." *Studia Islamica* 60 (1984): 83–117 at 84–85, 117.

95 For example, referencing similarities between Jewish and Islamic legal norms, Wegner asserts that "[s]everal hypotheses will be advanced, including common semitic tribal origins, common environmental influences on the development of both systems, independent development (convergence), and strong evidence especially in Shāfiʿī's case, of borrowing from talmudic sources." Wegner, "Islamic and Talmudic jurisprudence," 30. Other scholars mention continuity of Near Eastern legal practices, without it altering a core assumption of "influence." See also Judith Romney Wegner, "The status of women in Jewish and Islamic marriage and divorce law." *Harvard Women's Law Journal* 5: (1982): 1–33 at 4.

96 See Khalil Athamina. "Abraham in Islamic perspective: reflections on the development of monotheism in pre-Islamic Arabia." *Der Islam* 81:2 (2004): 184–205.

97 With modification, Crone's notion of hybrid indigenous law is useful here: "What they [Muslim jurists] reshaped was essentially provincial practice. This practice contained elements of Roman law in Syria and Egypt, just as it contained elements of Sasanid law in Iraq; and Roman law certainly, and Sasanid law probably, entered the Sharīʿa as a result. But substantially it was of ancient Near Eastern and Greek *origin*, or in other words it was the indigenous law of the Near East as it had developed after Alexander." Crone, *Roman*, 99, emphasis added.

impose medieval expressions of "Islamicness" on the late antique period. In short, Islamic law began when Muslims claimed it. Notably, situating Islamic law in its late antique context does not render Islamic law indefinite or meaningless. What Islamic law meant simply changed (and continues to do so) over time and according to region.

The comparative philological methods that aim to identify "origins" continue to influence Islamic historiography. Given my critique of "origins"-oriented historiography, the reader may wonder what this book's objective is in juxtaposing Jewish and Islamic legal history. In critiquing these methods, Lévi-Strauss noted that the weakness of traditional linguistics was in "consider[ing] the terms, and not the relations between the terms."[98] This is evident in the scholarship discussed here, which attempts to define "Islamic law" in isolation from "other Near Eastern legal customs." Correspondingly, we can achieve a deeper understanding of what makes Islamic law *Islamic* by evaluating the relationship between Islamic law and Jewish law (or Roman law or Zoroastrian law) in the same time and place. The relationship between these legal systems is their sociopolitical and historical setting – the Islamicate world. Hodgson defined Islamicate as referring "not directly to the religion, Islam, itself, but to the social and cultural complex historically associated with Islam and the Muslims, both among Muslims themselves and even when found among non-Muslims."[99] The category of "Islamicate" is a means of enriching our understanding of a shared historical space. Islamicate refers to the shared cultural practices of people living in the social space and avoids the identity-based notion of cultural ownership that have been critiqued here.

In addition, there is something unique about the relationship between Islamic law and Jewish law: these two legal communities continued to practice and to modify their legal systems in the same social space (the Islamicate Near East) for roughly a millennium (the late antique through early modern periods). It is not my objective to suggest that Jewish legal traditions were relatively more "influential" than other legal traditions; such an inquiry is both impossible to measure and based on imagined boundaries of separation. Instead, understanding the relationships between Islamic and Jewish legal traditions clarifies the process of Islamic self-articulation. Most importantly, these relationships are not uniform across all areas of law. As I illustrate in this book's case studies, the interactions or overlaps between Jewish and Islamic legal traditions vary

[98] Lévi-Strauss, *Structural anthropology*, 46.
[99] Hodgson, *The venture of Islam*, I, 59.

depending on the type of law; international, ritual, and family law constitute different fields of law with distinct links to customary practices, states, and socio-political or economic changes.

Undoubtedly, some scholars in Islamic studies are fundamentally uncomfortable with the juxtaposition of Jewish and Islamic legal history.[100] This is, in part, a justified reaction against the ideological and political underpinnings of the false notion that Islamic law is derived from Jewish law (or that Islamic law's "origins" are in Jewish law). However, some of this resistance can be attributed to intellectual anti-Semitism (which I have encountered repeatedly). Studying Jewish jurisprudence is relevant to studying Islamic jurisprudence because the combination provides important historical evidence of Islamicate law. Integrating Jewish and Islamic ideas enhances knowledge production in Islamic studies. Late antique Islamic law was a composite of multiple legal systems, including Jewish. The modern European scholarly invention of the categories "Semites" and "religion" continues to influence scholarship, such that resistance to how these prejudicial categories are used must account for their limiting effects. To explore fully the political or ideological implications of "religious law," we must scrutinize Jewish and Islamic legal systems together. In other words, analyzing Islamic and Jewish legal history concurrently is both historically and contemporaneously necessary.

Searching for "origins," as discussed in Chapter 1, results not only in seeking to identify an anthropomorphic date of Islamic law's "birth," but also its parentage. The notion of parentage is embedded in scholarly discussions of "borrowing" and "influence." In this chapter, as in Chapter 1, I have argued that these metaphors for historical theory reflect a linear methodology. I illuminated the connection between the notion of parentage and comparative philology. The distinction between Islamic and non-Islamic practices is nearly indiscernible in the beginning of Islamic history; late antique Islamic society is a fusion of several Near Eastern elements. Islam was and is always hybrid. The next chapter will implement the ideas presented here in order to illuminate the kaleidoscope of Islamic hybridity through the ritual of circumcision. Muslims practiced and legitimated male circumcision in multiple ways, drawing upon, resisting, and integrating diverse pre-Islamic practices that defy the notion of "origins."

[100] Obviously, this group of scholars does not include those cited above (Crone, Goldziher, Libson, Maghen, and Meron). Instead, I am here referring to scholars who have not published about their opposition to juxtaposing Jewish and Islamic legal traditions, but have expressed it to me in various ways.

CHAPTER 4

Legal Custom – a Case Study in Ritual Law

During the Islamic movement's beginnings, being Muslim necessarily entailed adapting regional customary practices (as the previous chapter outlined). However, the assimilative and syncretic processes that shaped Muslim identity cannot be reduced to a linear model of "origins" and "borrowing." As I presented in Chapter 3, conventional understandings of the relationship between Islamic law and predecessor legal traditions do not account for shared customary practices. In this chapter, I extend Chapter 3's claims to illustrate the mishmash of customary practices underlying Islamic circumcision, noting its flexibility and diversity. The story of how Muslims came to accept male circumcision as normative offers a glimpse into how a quintessential Abrahamic practice was legitimized as Islamic through a variety of hermeneutic strategies.[1] (My use of the term 'Abrahamic' refers specifically to the figure of Abraham and is by no means a validation of the modern category of 'Abrahamic,' which functions as a strategy for assimilating Jews, Christians, and Muslims.[2]) In this chapter, I illustrate commonalities, assimilation, and boundary definition through the ritual of male circumcision. Islamic regulations of circumcision were in dialogue with Jewish practices.

I explore temporal and spatial dimensions of ritual circumcision: its initial articulation, its late antique practice, and its late antique and medieval dissemination. Throughout this chapter, I distinguish between late antique (610–800 CE) and medieval (800–1400 CE) perspectives. The primary text I use to reference medieval perspectives is *Tuḥfat al-mawdūd*

[1] Unless otherwise indicated, I will use the term circumcision to refer to male circumcision.

[2] For a critique of the problematic, modern category of Abrahamic, see Salaymeh, "'Comparing' Jewish and Islamic legal traditions."

bi-aḥkām al-mawlūd by the Ḥanbalī jurist Ibn Qayyim al-Jawzīyah (d. 1350; Syria); this text is the most extensive and comprehensive discussion of circumcision from the medieval era.[3] My objective is to situate the silences and inconsistencies of Islamic texts within their late antique frameworks and to explore some of the ways Muslim scholars combined a variety of explanations for the "why and how" of male circumcision.

Ritual Comparisons

In Chapter 3, I outlined how outmoded comparative philological practices have shaped "origins"-oriented historiography by focusing attention on the imaginary "parentage" of Islamic law in Roman (i.e., Aryan) law or Jewish (i.e., Semitic) law. I reviewed presumptions in conventional comparative studies of Islamic and Jewish legal systems that Islamic law "borrowed from" or was "influenced by" Jewish law. Exploring horizontal, communal practices is necessary to contest the dominant, vertical model of a language family tree.[4] As the family tree model illustrates, it is tempting for scholars to assume a temporal hierarchy in which the "earlier" Jewish practice is presumed to be the "origin" of the "later" Islamic practice. But this model of derivation presumes Jewish "exclusivity" over certain practices that were "borrowed," thereby neglecting both the hybrid beginnings of Jewish practices and the non-Jewish instantiations of those practices. In addition, this model suggests that Jewish circumcision and Islamic circumcision are identical or are associated with similar meanings. The realities of Jewish practices and shared Near Eastern practices complicate any notion of simple linearity.

To challenge the common linear and derivative model, this chapter explores alleged "borrowing" in ritual law. Goldziher claimed, "The receptive character that marks the formation and development of Islām also found expression, naturally first of all in matters of ritual ... in borrowings from Jewish law."[5] Schacht asserted that "[t]he influence of Talmudic law

[3] Ibn Qayyim al-Jawzīyah's status as an innovative or unique scholar is not germane to my use of his text in this chapter. Rather, I refer to Ibn Qayyim al-Jawzīyah to offer an outline of possible medieval legal opinions on circumcision, without concern for the particularity of his text. On Ibn Qayyim al-Jawzīyah, see now Caterina Bori, *A scholar in the shadow: essays in the legal and theological thought of Ibn Qayyim al-Ǧawziyyah* (Roma: Istituto per l'Oriente, 2010); Muḥammad ibn Abī Bakr Ibn Qayyim al-Jawzīyah (d. 1350; Syria), *On taqlid: Ibn al Qayyim's critique of authority in Islamic law*, trans. by Mustafa Abdul Rahman (Oxford; New York: Oxford University Press, 2013); Alina Kokoschka, Birgit Krawietz, and Georges Tamer (eds.), *Islamic theology, philosophy and law: debating Ibn Taymiyya and Ibn Qayyim al-Jawziyya* (Berlin: De Gruyter, 2013).

[4] See further Chapter 3.

[5] Goldziher, "Fiḳh," 102.

[on Islamic law] manifested itself above all in matters of ritual and worship."[6] Admittedly, these assumptions of "Jewish origins" are not limited to modern scholars; for example, Maimonides (d. 1204; Andalusia) "saw the Islamic practice of circumcision, most prevalent among Muslim Arabs, as coming from Judaism and something which Judaism sees as a requirement for Arabs, and a requirement not originally Islamic."[7] Maimonides specifically identified ritual circumcision as an example of "borrowing" – or, "the true Judaic source of all that is truly valid in Islam."[8]

Still, the idea of "borrowing" of rituals is not universally accepted. Maghen has refuted the hypothesis of "ritual borrowing" as it relates to purity:

> it is difficult to know where to begin in order to refute Schacht's assertion of cross-the-board *halakhic* influence on *sharī'a* in matters of *ṭahāra* [ritual purity] (or Crone's claim that 'in a subject such as ritual purity there is virtual identity of both overall category and substantive provisions' between the Jewish and Muslim systems), since the preeminent characteristic of the relationship between the Judaic and Islamic purity codes is neither sameness, nor oppositeness, nor even the alleviation of the former by the latter, but rather *complete and total non-sequitur*.[9]

In this chapter, I will build upon Maghen's observations without confirming or refuting his conclusion about the relationship between Jewish and Islamic purity laws. By highlighting distinct voices and genres in Islamic literature, I implement the "anti-influence" model delineated in the previous chapter and reveal that discussions and implementations of circumcision are so inconstant as to render the "borrowing" paradigm inapplicable.

An important challenge for scholars is to recognize shared ritual practices without imposing a "borrowing" paradigm. While this chapter will explore male circumcision to interrogate how a practice that was so firmly associated with Judaism came to be practiced by Muslims, most shared ritual practices are regional (rather than solely confessional). While some ritual laws may be particular to Jews and Muslims, in this chapter, I will focus on male circumcision and the muddled realities of shared Near Eastern customary practices.

[6] Joseph Schacht, "Fiḳh." In *Encyclopaedia of Islam*, ed. by P. Bearman *et al.* (Leiden; Boston, MA: Brill, 2007) 887.

[7] David Novak, "The treatment of Islam and Muslims in the legal writings of Maimonides." In *Studies in Islamic and Judaic traditions*, ed. by William M. Brinner and Stephen D. Ricks, Brown Judaic studies; no. 110 (Atlanta, GA: Scholars Press, 1986), 233–50 at 241.

[8] *Ibid.*, 243.

[9] Maghen, "Dead tradition," 332, emphasis in original.

Ritual Meaning

Medieval Muslim jurists distinguished between laws regulating acts of worship (*ʿibādāt*) and transactions (*muʿāmalāt*). It is unlikely, however, that this distinction existed at the beginning of Islamic history. Likewise, modern Western thought not only constructed a category of "religion," but also reduced religion to ritual.[10] Thus, the term ritual may have problematic implications. For these reasons, I advocate for an open understanding of ritual based on a rough distinction between transcendental and mundane acts. I draw upon Catherine Bell's assertion that "ritualization is a way of acting that specifically establishes a privileged contrast, differentiating itself as more important or powerful."[11] By analyzing historical layers and specific genres pertaining to the ritual of circumcision, I demonstrate that late antique Muslims were monotheists in an abstract and traditional sense, whereas their medieval counterparts sought to differentiate Islamic monotheism from other monotheisms. This historical shift corresponds to the geographic and social shifts of Muslim communities: whereas in late antiquity pagans were the primary "other" for Muslims, in the medieval era, Christians and Jews were the main "other"; consequently, Muslim scholars rationalized the ritual of circumcision in ways that reflect social transformations. Drawing upon the notion of ritual as distinguishing the quotidian from the transcendent, I focus, in this chapter, on how Islamic genres ritualized circumcision.

Ritual Genealogy: Late Antique Circumcision

To understand the possible historical meanings of a specific ritual practice (male circumcision) in a particular socio-historical space (late antique Muslim society), I will begin with a brief overview of the history of circumcision in the pre-Islamic Near East. In addition to Near Eastern customs, biblical and rabbinic textual sources provide evidence for circumcision's varied expressions in the region. The specific place of circumcision in the process of Christian differentiation from Judaism suggests that circumcision was relevant to articulating a distinct group identity. In exploring these precedents for circumcision, it is important to keep in mind Bell's observation that "ritual acts must be understood within a semantic framework whereby the significance of an action is dependent upon its place and

[10] See Asad, *Genealogies*, Ch. 2.
[11] Catherine M. Bell, *Ritual theory, ritual practice* (New York: Oxford University Press, 1992), 90.

relationship within a context of all the other ways of acting: what it echoes, what it inverts, what it alludes to, what it denies."[12] Similarly, the Islamic ritual act of circumcision is embedded within expansive, multi-layered, and regional practices. Thus, when Muslim scholars regulated circumcision, they did so in intertextual worlds, referencing, modifying, and adapting various approaches to circumcision.[13] Because there are more numerous Jewish and Christian sources than pre-Islamic Arabian sources and because Jewish and Christian texts discuss male circumcision in some detail, whereas pre-Islamic Arabic sources mention it only sporadically, it is tempting to presume "more influence" from Jewish and Christian practices. I seek to give due import to practices that left relatively less textual evidence.

Ancient and Arabian Circumcision

Circumcision was practiced in ancient Egypt several millennia before the Common Era; it is commonly assumed that Egyptians practiced circumcision for cleanliness, as well as "moral, spiritual, and intellectual refinement" that may have been associated with elite status.[14] Whether or not circumcision directly spread from Egypt to Arabia, it appears to have been present throughout Arabia prior to Islam's beginning. Pagan Arabs likely practiced circumcision in pre-Islamic Arabia.[15] Josephus (d. 100; Jerusalem) observed that Arabs circumcised boys at age thirteen, following the precedent of Ishmael.[16] (In the Hebrew Bible, Genesis 17:23–26 describes Ishmael's circumcision at the age of thirteen.) Arab monotheists who followed Abrahamic traditions probably practiced circumcision.[17] Bardaisan (d. 222; Edessa), a Syriac philosopher and gnostic, noted that the Romans prohibited the "Arab" customary practice of circumcision when they conquered parts of Mesopotamia in the third century.[18]

[12] *Ibid.*, 220.

[13] Here again it is worth remembering that late antique Muslims did not "borrow" practices that existed in their very own pre-Islamic traditions!

[14] David Gollaher, *Circumcision: a history of the world's most controversial surgery* (New York: Basic Books, 2000), 6. Herodotus (d. fifth century; Turkey) suggested Egyptian beginnings and a purity concern surrounding circumcision. Sandra Jacobs, *The body as property: physical disfigurement in biblical law* (New York: Bloomsbury T&T Clark, 2014), 29. I use 'cleanliness' instead of 'hygiene' because the latter term is associated with modern practices.

[15] Retsö, *The Arabs in antiquity*, 606–7.

[16] Kathryn Kueny, "Abraham's test: Islamic male circumcision as anti/ante-covenantal practice." In *Bible and Qur'ān: essays in scriptural intertextuality*, ed. by John C. Reeves (Atlanta, GA: Society of Biblical Literature, 2003), 161–82 at 163.

[17] Athamina, "Abraham in Islamic perspective," 197.

[18] Retsö, *The Arabs in antiquity*, 490.

Origen (d. 253/4; Alexandria/Lebanon), a Christian theologian, visited Arabia and observed that Arabs circumcised boys at the age of thirteen.[19] The Babylonian Talmud includes two specific references to a "circumcised Arab."[20] Still, circumcision may not have been a universal practice in pre-Islamic Arabia. Mandeans, a gnostic community in Mesopotamia in the third century, did not practice circumcision.[21] In addition, Christian Arabs may not have practiced circumcision.[22]

Near Eastern Circumcision: Biblical, Rabbinic, and Christian

Biblical, rabbinic, and Christian textual sources point to prolonged and extensive scrutiny of ritual circumcision in the Near East. While a variety of groups practiced circumcision in antiquity, it came to be identified as an essentially Jewish practice after early Christian groups discarded the practice.[23] The Hebrew Bible is strikingly direct and engaged with the symbolic significance of circumcision. Genesis 17:10–11 declares, "This is my covenant, which you [Abraham] shall keep, between me and you and your offspring after you: Every male among you shall be circumcised. You shall circumcise the flesh of your foreskins, and it shall be a sign of the covenant between you and me."[24] The Hebrew Bible is replete with narratives that emphasize the importance of circumcision and suggest that circumcision is an important symbol of accepting divine authority.[25] In addition, circumcision has a variety of allegorical meanings in the Bible, such as disturbed speech (Exodus 6:12) or an unreasonable hearing/ear (Jeremiah 6:10; 9:25).[26] Biblical commands and narratives indicate that circumcision is a significant ritual that symbolically represents man's obedience to God's will.

19 *Ibid.*, 487.

20 References to circumcised Arabs are found in Yevamot 71a and ʿAvodah Zarah 27a, as well as in the Mekhilta de-Rabbi Ishmael. I thank Elimelech Westreich for these references.

21 Everett Ferguson, *Baptism in the early church: history, theology, and liturgy in the first five centuries* (Grand Rapids, MI: William B. Eerdmans Pub. Co., 2009), 75.

22 On Christianity among northern Arab tribes, see Trimingham, *Christianity among the Arabs in pre-Islamic times*, 6.

23 See also David A. Bernat, "Circumcision." In *The Encyclopedia of Ancient History* (Malden, MA: John Wiley & Sons, Inc., 2013).

24 *NRSV Bible.*

25 The relevant narratives are Genesis 34:14 (Hivites must be circumcised); Exodus 4:25 (Zipporah circumcises Moses' son); Joshua 5:2 (Joshua circumcised the Israelites). I thank Rhiannon Graybill for these references.

26 Gollaher, *Circumcision*, 10–1.

When Greco-Roman society spread to the Near East in antiquity, the ancient practice of circumcision became a pretext for denouncing and discriminating against Jews.[27] Greco-Romans disparaged the circumcised penis, which was on display during nude athletic events.[28] In the second century BCE, Antiochus Epiphanes, a Seleucid ruler of Palestine, "imposed severe penalties for circumcision as part of his assault on Judaism."[29] Some Jews attempted to "reverse" circumcision in order to avoid identification or persecution for being Jewish.[30] To prevent reversion of circumcision, rabbis appear to have modified circumcision by requiring that the corona (i.e., *perīʿah*) be "uncovered," thus precluding reversion.[31] While most Jews were circumcised, as Shaye Cohen noted, "we cannot assume that all Jewish men everywhere and always will have been circumcised."[32] Circumcision came to be identified with Jews as an ethno-religious group and, in turn, became an important marker of Jewish identity in the late antique era (if not earlier).[33] Rabbinic literature reflects the increased importance of circumcision.

Rabbinic literature of the antique and late antique periods points to sustained confirmation of circumcision's significance to Judaism. The Mishnah (second/third centuries CE) details aspects of the circumcision ritual that may be performed on the Sabbath.[34] The Palestinian Talmud lists the virtues of circumcision, pointing out that it supersedes Sabbath laws and that Abraham did not become perfect until after he was circumcised.[35] A fourth-century rabbinic commentary on the Book of Numbers obliges converts to Judaism to undergo circumcision, immersion, and sacrificial atonement.[36] The same text declares that opposition to circumcision is equivalent to violating a divine commandment.[37] In the Babylonian Talmud, Shabbat 137a delineates the timing of circumcision as the eighth day, unless the infant is sick or other considerations necessitate a short delay.[38] Shabbat 137b provides

[27] Bernat, "Circumcision."

[28] Gollaher, *Circumcision*, 13–4.

[29] *Ibid.*, 15.

[30] *Ibid.*, 16–7.

[31] Shaye J. D. Cohen, *Why aren't Jewish women circumcised? Gender and covenant in Judaism* (Berkeley, CA: University of California Press, 2005), 25–6.

[32] Shaye J. D. Cohen, "Judaism without circumcision and 'Judaism' without 'circumcision' in Ignatius." *The Harvard Theological Review* 95:4 (2002): 395–415 at 397.

[33] Gollaher, *Circumcision*, 13.

[34] *Mishnah*, Shabbat 18:3–19:6.

[35] *Palestinian Talmud*, Nedarim 3:9.

[36] *Sifre on Numbers*, 108.

[37] *Ibid.*, 112.

[38] *Babylonian Talmud*, Shabbat 137a.

the ritual recitation that accompanies the circumcision.[39] As Boyarin has emphasized, circumcision was essential to Jewish genealogy.[40] In general, rabbinic ideas emphasized the biblical covenant with the Israelites, linking divine obedience and community. Still, rabbinic law recognized an uncircumcised Jewish man (*ʿarel*) as Jewish, but ritually impure; thus, despite its significance, circumcision was not perceived as essential to Jewishness.[41] And the converse was also true: circumcision did not make one Jewish since late antique rabbis who were aware that Arabs practiced circumcision "did not see any Jewish religious significance in it."[42]

Rabbinic elaborations of the circumcision ritual occurred in tandem with early Christian resistance to the practice. Although Jesus was circumcised (according to Luke 2:21), early Christian authorities did not assume that circumcision was incumbent upon Christians, but rather treated circumcision as a means of differentiating Christians from Jews.[43] In his Letter to the Galatians, apostle Paul (d. *c.* 67 CE) developed a notion of spiritual circumcision as an alternative to Jewish circumcision.[44] The apostle Paul and other early Christian figures may have viewed obligatory circumcision as limiting the proselytizing potential of Christianity. In Galatians 6:15, Paul suggests that spiritual circumcision supersedes not only the ritual of circumcision, but also the broader commandments that it represents. He appears to have been arguing against Jewish Christians who assumed that converts should first be circumcised and then baptized. By spiritualizing circumcision, Paul articulated an understanding of ritual that would reverberate in later Christian notions of being "liberated" from Jewish laws.[45] In Romans 4:9–13, Paul noted that Abraham had achieved perfection prior to circumcision.[46] Several early Christian writers – including Justin (d. 165; Rome), Tertullian (d. 220; Tunisia), and Cyprian (d. 258; Tunisia) – emphasized that many prophets "pleased God" without being circumcised.[47]

39 *Ibid.*, Shabbat 137b.
40 Daniel Boyarin, *A radical Jew: Paul and the politics of identity* (Berkeley, CA: University of California Press, 1997).
41 Cohen, *Why aren't Jewish women circumcised?* 184–5.
42 Novak, "The treatment," 242.
43 Gollaher, *Circumcision*, 31. Andrew S. Jacobs, *Christ circumcised: a study in early Christian history and difference* (Philadelphia, PA: University of Pennsylvania Press, 2012).
44 Gollaher, *Circumcision*, 31. Galatians 5.6 observes, "For in Christ Jesus neither circumcision nor uncircumcision counts for anything; the only thing that counts is faith working through love." *NRSV Bible*.
45 Gollaher, *Circumcision*, 34.
46 *Ibid.*, 33.
47 Ferguson, *Baptism in the early church*, 273.

Over time, Pauline Christianity came to dominate Christian traditions. Thus, after Paul articulated Christianity's new covenant with God, many early Christians accepted the notion of spiritual circumcision and resisted the assumed ethnic dimension of circumcision. Tertullian (d. *c.* 225 CE; Carthage), as well as other early Christian writers, viewed circumcision as a specific Israelite practice that Christ abrogated with spiritual circumcision (understood as a form of salvation).[48] Similarly, Origen (d. 253/4; Alexandria/Lebanon), specified that circumcision is incumbent only on the descendants of Abraham.[49] Some early Christian writers connected spiritual circumcision with baptism through the figure of Joshua, who circumcised the Israelites after crossing the River Jordan.[50] Nevertheless, these Christians did not presume that baptism was equivalent to spiritual circumcision, but rather that it facilitated it.[51] In early Christian texts, including the *Didascalia* (*c.* third century CE; Syria), it was asserted that "the Christian equivalent to circumcision is not baptism but spiritual heart surgery, and the multiple Jewish washings for ceremonial purity are distinguished from the single Christian baptism for forgiveness of sins."[52] (The metaphor of an uncircumcised heart as being incapable of accepting the divine message appears in critiques of Jews and Christians in a major biography of the Prophet.[53]) Christian articulations of bodily rituals were in conscious dialogue with Jewish rituals.

In the late antique Near East, on the eve of Islam's beginning, several communities practiced circumcision and several communities opposed it for multiple reasons. More importantly, theological significance was ascribed to the ritual of circumcision, both by those who practiced it and those who did not. Just as Jews elaborated rituals around circumcision, Christians elaborated rituals replacing circumcision. Bell notes that a "dimension of constructed tradition concerns the delineation of group identity, which is based not only on generating a shared consensus concerning an authoritative past but also on a set of distinctions, seen as rooted in the past, which differentiates this group from other groups."[54] How did late antique Muslim scholars demarcate Muslim group identity in light of these multi-layered traditions surrounding circumcision?

[48] *Ibid.*, 272.
[49] *Ibid.*, 306, 405.
[50] *Ibid.*, 690. (Joshua's circumcision of the Israelites is described in Joshua 5:2.)
[51] *Ibid.*, 416.
[52] *Ibid.*, 274.
[53] Ibn Isḥāq and Ibn Hishām, *The life*, 254.
[54] Bell, *Ritual theory*, 121.

Islamicizing Circumcision

When the Prophet began forming a Muslim community in late antique Arabia in the early seventh century, circumcision was at once widely known and not universally practiced among the diverse tribes of the Arabian Peninsula.[55] Neither Christian nor Zoroastrian Arab tribes on the peripheries of the region likely practiced circumcision. In the central areas of the peninsula, Arabs likely practiced circumcision in accordance with tribal customs, Abrahamic monotheism (*ḥanīfiyyah*), or Judaism.[56] Some tradition-reports explicitly identify circumcision as a practice of Abrahamic monotheism in Arabia.[57] In Medina, where Judaism was prevalent and the Prophet established a Muslim community, circumcision was also probably a normative practice (for Jews, semi-Jews, and non-Jews). Thus, in the context of seventh-century Arabia, the Prophet might have met resistance if he had attempted to ban circumcision – if this possibility had even occurred to him. Given the Prophet's general acceptance of regional customary practices, he probably did not see any reason to articulate a theological defense of circumcision as legitimate or necessary.[58]

In light of Abraham's symbolic significance and the multiple and protracted regional controversies about circumcision, we might expect the Islamic scripture to include some reference to the practice. Yet no Qurʾānic verses explicitly mention or require circumcision for Muslims.[59] Instead, there are approximately seventy instances in which the Qurʾān refers to Abraham as an exemplar who should be followed; some of these "Abrahamic verses" became the basis for identifying circumcision as an Islamic practice.[60] Within exegetical literature, there appears to have been a historical shift in the understanding of Abrahamic and other verses that were associated with circumcision. Specifically, a fourteenth-century compilation of the exegesis of Ibn ʿAbbās (d. 687; Arabia) suggests that Ibn ʿAbbās did not associate circumcision with key Qurʾānic verses referring to

55 I reject the developmental notion that this community consisted of "believers" or "monotheists" rather than Muslims. As I explained in the previous chapter, this community was Muslim and what it meant to be Muslim simply changed over time.

56 Athamina, "Abraham in Islamic perspective," 201.

57 By way of example, see Muḥammad ibn Yaʿqūb al-Kulaynī (d. 941; Iran), *al-Kāfī*, ed. by Shams al-Din Muhammad Jaʿfar, 8 vols. (Beirut: Dār al-Taʿāruf, 1993), 6:37–8.

58 On the Prophet's adaptation of Arab understandings of Abrahamic monotheism, see Athamina, "Abraham in Islamic perspective," 202.

59 The absence of Qurʾānic references to circumcision does not pose a historiographic or theological dilemma since many Islamic practices are not mentioned in the Qurʾān.

60 Athamina, "Abraham in Islamic perspective," 184.

Abraham. In addition, neither Mujāhid ibn Jabr (d. *c.* 720) nor Muqātil ibn Sulaymān al-Balkhī (d. 767; Iraq) references circumcision in their respective commentaries on Abrahamic verses. By comparison, al-Ṭabarī (d. 923; Iraq) mentions circumcision as a monotheistic obligation in the exegesis of at least four verses, Q 2:124, Q 2:135, Q 2:138, and Q 98:5. A closer examination of these verses will clarify these distinctions.

Qur'ān 2:124 states, "And remember that God tested Abraham with certain commands." Ibn 'Abbās explained that Abraham was commanded to fulfill ten commands, five pertaining to his head and five pertaining to his body.[61] (These commands are identified in a widely circulated tradition-report discussed below; they most probably did not include circumcision.) Neither Mujāhid ibn Jabr nor Muqātil ibn Sulaymān mentions Abrahamic commands and neither exegete refers to circumcision.[62] By comparison, commenting on Q 2:124, al-Ṭabarī identifies circumcision as one of the bodily forms of purity that God commanded Abraham to fulfill.[63] He based this explanation on reports from Abū Qatādah (al-Ḥārith, d. 674; Arabia), Ibn 'Abbās, and al-Sha'bī (d. 721/2; Kūfah). One of al-Ṭabarī's reports is from Abū al-Jald Jīlān (d. late seventh century; Arabia), who was reportedly of Jewish heritage and read the Torah regularly.[64] (al-Jald may have provided Ibn 'Abbās with information about biblical figures or ideas.[65]) Other tradition-reports suggest that the Abrahamic commands to which the verse refers are broad theological obligations, particularly related to pilgrimage, which draws upon Abraham's role in building the Ka'bah in Mecca.[66] al-Ṭabarī's exegesis of this verse is reflected in the genre of Qur'ānic rulings (*aḥkām al-qur'ān*); both Aḥmad ibn 'Alī al-Jaṣṣāṣ (d. 982; Iraq) and Muḥammad ibn Aḥmad al-Qurṭubī (d. 1273; Andalusia) identified circumcision as one of the Abrahamic obligations referred to in Q 2:124.[67]

Qur'ān 2:135 states, "They say: 'Become Jews or Christians if you would be guided (to salvation).' Respond: 'No, the community (*millah*) of Abraham is true and he was not a polytheist." Ibn 'Abbās interpreted this verse as identifying Abraham as a Muslim.[68] Neither Mujāhid nor Muqātil

[61] al-Fīrūzābādī, *Tanwīr*, 18; al-Fīrūzābādī, *Tafsīr Ibn 'Abbās*, 25.
[62] Mujāhid, *Tafsīr al-Imām Mujāhid*, 214; Muqātil, *Tafsīr Muqātil*, 1:135.
[63] al-Ṭabarī, *Tafsīr*, 2:499–506.
[64] Ḥasan al-Mūsawī Kharsān, *Mawsū'at 'Abd Allāh ibn 'Abbās: ḥabr al-ummah wa-tarjumān al-Qur'ān*, 5 vols., Silsilat Radd al-shubuhāt, 5 (Najaf: Markaz al-Abḥāth al-'Aqā'idīyah, 2007/8), 2:149–51.
[65] Kharsān refutes this possibility explicitly in *Ibid.*, 2:165–7.
[66] al-Ṭabarī, *Tafsīr*, 2:502–3.
[67] Najāshī 'Alī Ibrāhīm, *Khiṣāl al-fiṭrah fī al-fiqh al-islāmī* (Cairo: al-Taqadum, 1980), 9.
[68] al-Fīrūzābādī, *Tanwīr*, 19; al-Fīrūzābādī, *Tafsīr Ibn 'Abbās*, 28.

ibn Sulaymān mentioned circumcision in connection with this verse.[69] (Notably, Muqātil consistently glosses the phrase "Abrahamic community" as *islām*.[70]) Here again, al-Ṭabarī's exegesis of Q 2:135 further linked the practice of Abraham to both pilgrimage and circumcision.[71] But al-Ṭabarī did not provide an authority for describing Abraham's monotheism as entailing circumcision.[72]

Qur'ān 2:138 mentions "the Baptism of God; and who can baptize better than God?" Ibn ʿAbbās explained that Muslim baptism is monotheism or the law (*dīn*) of God.[73] Mujāhid identified this baptism as the Islamic "natural predisposition" (*fiṭrah*) and Muqātil ibn Sulaymān defined it as Islam. None of these three late antique exegetes mentions circumcision.[74] Sufyān al-Thawrī (d. 778; Kūfah) defined this baptism as *dīn allāh*, which may refer to belief (or Islam).[75] In addition to Mujāhid, Ibrāhīm al-Nakhaʿī, Saʿīd bin Jubayr (d. 714; Kūfah), and other late antique traditionists and jurists defined baptism as the natural predisposition (meaning Islam).[76] By comparison, al-Ṭabarī claimed that the Islamic version of Christian baptism is circumcision – without citing an authority – while recognizing that numerous commentators identified it as law (*dīn*).[77] He cited several authorities who interpreted baptism as the "natural predisposition" (*fiṭrah*) and suggested that it is equivalent to law (*dīn*), but provided no tradition-report on why circumcision is necessary for a monotheistic body.[78] A medieval text conveyed that Ibn ʿAbbās identified baptism as the Christian ritual of immersion, which takes place on the seventh day (after birth), replaces circumcision, and renders the infant a true Christian.[79]

Qur'ān 98:5 states, "And they have been commanded to do no more than worship God, offering Him sincere devotion, being true (in monotheistic faith); to establish regular prayer; and to practice regular charity;

69 Mujāhid, *Tafsīr al-Imām Mujāhid*, 214; Muqātil, *Tafsīr Muqātil*, 1:141.
70 Muqātil, *Tafsīr Muqātil*, 1:141.
71 al-Ṭabarī, *Tafsīr*, 2:593–4.
72 *Ibid.*, 2:594.
73 al-Fīrūzābādī, *Tanwīr*, 19; al-Fīrūzābādī, *Tafsīr Ibn ʿAbbās*, 28. On the term baptism (*ṣibghah*), see Sean W. Anthony. "Further notes on the word *ṣibghah* in Qur'ān 2:138." *Journal of Semitic Studies* 59:1 (2014): 117–29. This verse, and others, are discussed in Hamza M. Zafer, *The ummah: Quranic and early Muslim communalism* (University of Pennsylvania Press, forthcoming).
74 Mujāhid, *Tafsīr al-Imām Mujāhid*, 214; Muqātil, *Tafsīr Muqātil*, 1:142.
75 Sufyān ibn Saʿīd al-Thawrī (d. 778; Kūfah), *Tafsīr Sufyān al-Thawrī* (Beirut: Dār al-Kutub al-ʿIlmīyah, 1983), 49–50.
76 ʿUthmān Miṣbāḥ, *Mafhūm al-fiṭrah: dirāsah naqdīyah li-maqālāt al-islāmīyīn*, Dirāsāt fī al-fiṭrah, 1 (al-Qunayṭirah: Maʿhad al-Gharb al-Islāmī, 2012), 46.
77 al-Ṭabarī, *Tafsīr*, 2:603–4.
78 *Ibid.*, 2:606.
79 al-Wāḥidī, *Asbāb*, 28.

and that is the right and straight faith." Ibn ʿAbbās explained "being true in monotheistic faith" as belief in the right faith, or divine oneness, and defined monotheism as the Abrahamic community.[80] There is no commentary for this verse by Mujāhid and Muqātil ibn Sulaymān did not mention circumcision.[81] Again, by contrast, al-Ṭabarī specifically identifies circumcision as a sign of monotheistic faith.[82] To explain the meaning of monotheism (*ḥanīfiyyah*), al-Ṭabarī cites Ibn ʿAbbās referring to pilgrimage and he cites Abū Qatādah (d. 674; Arabia) referring to circumcision (as well as to degrees of incest and pilgrimage).[83]

Each of these four verses illuminates a subtle gap between late antique silence or ambiguity and medieval specificity concerning circumcision. While Ibn ʿAbbās, Mujāhid, and Muqātil may have viewed circumcision as normative or even as essential to the natural predisposition (*fiṭrah*), none of them appears to have expressly associated the Abrahamic verses with circumcision. Moreover, although Mujāhid reportedly studied exegesis with Ibn ʿAbbās, he did not cite any of Ibn ʿAbbās' tradition-reports about circumcision as a key component of Abrahamic monotheism. Late antique exegesis seems to be missing tradition-reports that explicitly link the command to follow Abraham with the command to circumcise. Relevant tradition-reports, however, are included in pre-canonical collections (*muṣannafāt*). For example, some tradition-reports describe Abraham's self-circumcision at the age of 80 (or possibly 120); they are included in pre-canonical collections (*muṣannafāt*) and referenced in later medieval legal texts.[84] Similarly, some tradition-reports emphasize that Abraham was the first man to be circumcised.[85] It is difficult to determine if these tradition-reports about Abraham's circumcision were circulated at the same time as the traditions cited in the exegetical texts or later. But what is notable is that these two aspects of Abraham's circumcision echo some biblical ideas and rabbinic Midrash that were part of the Islamicate world.

[80] al-Fīrūzābādī, *Tanwīr*, 516; al-Fīrūzābādī, *Tafsīr Ibn ʿAbbās*, 885.

[81] Mujāhid, *Tafsīr al-Imām Mujāhid*, 741; Muqātil, *Tafsīr Muqātil*, 4:780–1.

[82] al-Ṭabarī, *Tafsīr*, 24:554.

[83] *Ibid.*

[84] ʿAbd Allāh ibn Muḥammad Ibn Abī Shaybah (d. 849; Iraq), *al-Kitāb al-muṣannaf fī al-aḥādīth wa-al-āthār*, ed. by Muḥammad ʿAbd al-Salām Shāhīn, 9 vols. (Beirut: Dār al-Kutub al-ʿIlmīyah, 1995), 5:317; Ibn Abī Shaybah, *Kitāb al-adab*, 223, 225; Muḥammad ibn Abī Bakr Ibn Qayyim al-Jawzīyah (d. 1350; Syria), *Tuḥfat al-mawdūd bi-āḥkām al-mawlūd* (Cairo: al-Maktabah al-Qayyimah, 1977), 120–6.

[85] Ibn Abī Shaybah, *Muṣannaf*, 5:317.

By comparison, al-Ṭabarī connected the Abrahamic verses to circumcision directly and explicitly.[86] al-Ṭabarī seems to have been doing more than simply identifying circumcision as a customary practice that was not overruled by the Prophet or as a ritual that was permissible according to Islamic law; al-Ṭabarī seems to have been responding to late antique debates about circumcision between Jews and Christians. The relevant Qurʾānic verses describe monotheistic faith, but it is al-Ṭabarī (and others) who pinpointed circumcision as a sign of monotheism. I suspect that al-Ṭabarī associated Abrahamic monotheism with circumcision because he interpreted Abrahamic practices under the shadow of the Bible and its commentaries and in dialogue with Jews and Christians. Genesis 17 specifies that maintaining the covenant between God and Abraham entails male circumcision. Accordingly, al-Ṭabarī emphasized circumcision as a primary Abrahamic obligation.[87] In doing so, al-Ṭabarī did not invent or concoct tradition-reports; instead, he connected and emphasized tradition-reports in ways that are distinct from his predecessors. It is not uncommon in Qurʾānic studies to point out the Jewish backgrounds of transmitters (such as Abū al-Jald Jīlān, who glossed verse 2:124) or to emphasize the influence of Israelite narratives (*isrāʾīlīyāt*) on transmitters (especially Ibn ʿAbbās) or authors of exegesis (particularly al-Ṭabarī).[88] However, this kind of identity-based and text-based search for "origins" cannot account for the multivalence that is inherent in the interpretive process. As I have sought to demonstrate by summarizing distinct exegetical approaches to these four verses, exegetes do not convey univocal interpretations. Moreover, if we are to understand why a particular exegetical interpretation became dominant, we must focus on the power or influence of the exegete and his relationship to a specific audience, rather than emphasizing pre-Islamic "origins."

In general, a focus on textual evidence often leads to placing texts in vertical, linear relationships, rather than in horizontal, intertextual ones.

[86] Kueny has also made this observation. Kueny, "Abraham's test," 180.

[87] The assumption that Muslims must circumcise as part of their Abrahamic obligations would be articulated by Maimonides as placing Muslims within the Abrahamic covenant. See Josef Stern, "Maimonides on the covenant of circumcision and the unity of God." In *The Midrashic imagination: Jewish exegesis, thought, and history*, ed. by Michael A. Fishbane (Albany, NY: State University of New York Press, 1993), 131–54.

[88] See, for example, Āmāl ʿAbd al-Raḥmān Rabīʿ, *al-Isrāʾīlīyāt fī tafsīr al-ṭabarī: dirāsah fī al-lughah wa-al-maṣādir al-ʿibrīyah* (Cairo: Jumhūriyat Miṣr al-ʿArabīyah, Wizārat al-Awqāf, al-Majlis al-ʿAlá lil-Shuʾūn al-Islāmīyah, 2001). On *isrāʾīlīyāt* see Michael E. Pregill, "The Hebrew Bible and the Quran: the problem of the Jewish 'influence' on Islam." *Religion Compass* 1:6 (2007): 643–59; Roberto Tottoli. "Origin and use of the term Isrāʾīliyyāt in Muslim literature." *Arabica* 46:2 (1999): 193–210.

Thus, conventional methods examine "earlier" Jewish texts and "later" Islamic texts and thereby demarcate a "borrowing" process. This is particularly evident in exegesis, as much conventional scholarship has sought to identify the Jewish "origins" of Islamic exegetical materials.[89] However, neither transmission nor reception is a linear process. Against conventional approaches, I suggest that biblical stories should be understood as regional traditions transcending confessional lines; I do not presume absolute "Jewish ownership" of biblical narratives and I avoid undervaluing the Near Eastern pre-history and circulation of these narratives.[90] Indeed, biblical ideas circulated throughout pre-Islamic Arabia without being associated exclusively with Jewish traditions. Late antique and medieval exegetes established circumcision as an Islamic ritual through an intertextual process in which Qurʾānic exegesis integrated biblical themes.

What happened between the late seventh century and the early tenth century to result in a strengthening of the correlation between Abrahamic monotheism and circumcision? Many scholars have established exegetical shifts in response to societal changes. As El Cheikh observed, "Qur'anic exegetes adopted interpretations negative to Byzantium as the empire became increasingly involved in an adversarial relationship with the Islamic state."[91] When the late antique exegetes were glossing the Qurʾān in Arabia and Iraq, their objective may have been to clarify its meaning for a primarily Arab audience for whom circumcision was normative. But as the Islamic empire grew and conversion increased, the parameters of Muslim discourse expanded to include more non-Arabs and more Christians. Thus, al-Ṭabarī's Iraqi audience was likely more heterogeneous than the audiences of his late antique predecessors – particularly those predecessors in Arabia. And this heterogeneity included groups (Zoroastrians, Manicheans, and Christians) who did not practice circumcision. If so, al-Ṭabarī may have sought to emphasize and to justify the significance of circumcision. Moreover, consumers of exegesis may have themselves asked questions and insisted upon clarifications that shaped

89 Shari L. Lowin. "Abraham in Islamic and Jewish exegesis." *Religion Compass* 5:6 (2011): 224–35 at 225–6 (summarizing "reductionist" scholarship on Islamic borrowing of Jewish exegesis).

90 On these issues, see Frank Moore Cross, *Canaanite myth and Hebrew epic: essays in the history of the religion of Israel* (Cambridge, MA: Harvard University Press, 1973); Mark S. Smith, *The origins of biblical monotheism: Israel's polytheistic background and the Ugaritic texts* (New York: Oxford University Press, 2001); Megan Bishop Moore and Brad E. Kelle (eds.), *Biblical history and Israel's past: the changing study of the Bible and history* (Grand Rapids, MI: William B. Eerdmans Pub. Company, 2011).

91 Nadia Maria El Cheikh, *Byzantium viewed by the Arabs* (Cambridge, MA: Harvard University Press, 2004), 33.

the exegetical tradition toward more direct justification of circumcision. The "semantic framework" of Islamic circumcision was not limited to Jewish and Christian ideas and the Islamic ritualization of circumcision drew upon pre-Islamic, Arabian monotheism.

Beyond Abraham: Ritualizing Customary Practice

In ritualizing circumcision, Muslim exegetes interlinked Abrahamic practice, the notion of a natural predisposition (*fiṭrah*), and ritual purity. In doing so, they combined the rituals of Arabian monotheists, Jews, and Christians, creating a syncretic practice by fusing multiple late antique rituals. Just as "the counterpoint in Judaism of Christian baptism is not circumcision but ritual washings,"[92] the counterpoint in Islam of Jewish circumcision and Christian baptism is ritual grooming and washing. But what was the objective or purpose in developing an Islamic ritual of circumcision? As Bell has explained, "[t]he implicit dynamic and 'end' of ritualization – that which it does not see itself doing – can be said to be the production of a 'ritualized body.' A ritualized body is a body invested with a 'sense' of ritual."[93] But circumcision alone did not produce a ritualized male Muslim body; the ritualization of the male Muslim body was an incremental process that reflects shifting and varying emphases in Muslim self-understandings. Despite the continued practice of circumcision, the ritualized (male) Muslim body – its conceptualization and its actualization – was distinct from that of its monotheist, or Christian, or Jewish predecessors. The syncretism of Islamic circumcision is evident not in its tenuous connection to Abrahamic circumcision (as outlined in the exegetical works above), but in its association with natural predisposition and ritual purity.

The notion of "natural predisposition" (*fiṭrah*) is defined distinctly in different texts: in the Qur'ān, it primarily refers to creation; in tradition-reports, it consists of itemizing bodily rituals that establish the natural predisposition.[94] Medieval sources suggest at least five meanings for natural predisposition: normative practices (*sunnah*), law (*dīn*), beginning state, natural disposition, and submission (*islām*).[95] Natural predisposition glossed as "Islam" appears, however, to have been the majority opinion of

[92] Ferguson, *Baptism in the early church*, 214.

[93] Bell, *Ritual theory*, 98.

[94] Ibrāhīm, *Khiṣāl al-fiṭrah*, 8–9.

[95] *Ibid.*, 13.

late antique Muslim scholars.[96] Tradition-reports that delineate the physical manifestations of natural predisposition (*fiṭrah*) report inconsistent lists of three, five, or ten rituals; the commonly accepted acts of ritual cleanliness include trimming the mustache, growing a beard, cleaning teeth, inhaling water to clean the nose, gargling, trimming nails, washing finger joints, removing underarm hair, trimming pubic hair, and washing the genitalia.[97] This list demarcates the etiquette of grooming and is categorized as the practices of natural predisposition (*sunnat al-fiṭrah*). Some tradition-reports include circumcision as part of this idealized physical and mental state,[98] while others do not include it among the inventory of physical acts that contribute to the natural predisposition.[99] This inconsistency reflects the uneasiness with which circumcision was incorporated into the category of natural predisposition. Most importantly, Shīʿī sources do not include circumcision in lists of grooming practices.[100] This may explain why some tradition-reports explicitly seek to justify circumcision as a component of *fiṭrah*.[101] In the medieval, canonical collections of tradition-reports, circumcision was consistently included in the natural predisposition list (most commonly five practices).[102] Thus, as Kueny observed, "circumcision appears to be a late addition to an already-established chain of purity practices."[103]

I want to elaborate on three aspects of what I would describe as the uneasy inclusion of circumcision in the state of *fiṭrah*. First, the fact that some tradition-reports do not include circumcision in the list of *fiṭrah*'s physical manifestations may not be a mere accident of transmission. Every item on the list is a temporary or repetitive act of cleanliness – except circumcision. In other words, the consistency of the list as a daily or regular ritual is lost when circumcision is added to it, suggesting that it may not have been part of the initial transmission of the tradition-report. Related to this point, many of the cutting or trimming acts (including the mustache, nails, underarm hair, and pubic hair) involve things that grow back, unlike the foreskin. Second, unlike circumcision, the specific acts of washing and shaving included in this list do not appear to have parallels in

[96] Miṣbāḥ, *Mafhūm al-fiṭrah*, 54.
[97] These tradition-reports are collected in *Ibid.*, 37. Underarm and pubic hair likely attracted body lice, which may explain why they were selected for grooming.
[98] Ibn Abī Shaybah, *Muṣannaf*, 5:318.
[99] *Ibid.*, 1:178. See also Ibrāhīm, *Khiṣāl al-fiṭrah*, 10.
[100] Kueny, "Abraham's test," 176.
[101] Ibn Abī Shaybah, *Kitāb al-adab*, 224.
[102] Kueny, "Abraham's test," 174.
[103] *Ibid.*, 177.

Jewish practices. While there are biblical shaving rituals that are paired with trimming nails, those rituals do not appear to have included underarms or armpits.[104] Indeed, the Babylonian Talmud prohibits men from shaving their armpit hair (and probably pubic hair).[105] There is, however, a parallel in the function of grooming rituals: biblical shaving rituals marked transitions into or out of ritual states[106] and the *fiṭrah* rituals were critical for entering the ritual state (*iḥrām*) preceding the pilgrimage.[107] Third, no pre-Islamic sources suggest an Abrahamic precedent for any of these grooming practices; there may be a gap between Abrahamic practices and this list defining the physical components of *fiṭrah*. There is an unusual tradition-report claiming that Abraham was the first person to clean his body by cutting his nails, trimming his mustache, or circumcising.[108] Muslim transmitters may have felt the need to associate directly the *fiṭrah* rituals with an Abrahamic precedent.

The possibility that Islamic circumcision is not a theological obligation, but rather a matter of etiquette, is evident in how circumcision is included under purity – rather than theological – concerns. The history of circumcision in the Near East is relevant here. Ancient and Greco-Roman Egyptians may have practiced both male and female circumcision for reasons of cleanliness.[109] Pre-Islamic Arabs likely practiced circumcision for the same reason, although Arabian monotheists may have justified circumcision by integrating cleanliness concerns and emulating Abrahamic practice. The notion of circumcision as necessary for cleanliness is one that predated Islam and continued to resonate even while Muslim scholars associated circumcision with Abrahamic practices; indeed, circumcision (*khitān*) is commonly identified in Arabic today as purification (*tuhūr*) and there is no Islamic equivalent for the rabbinic Jewish emphasis on circumcision blood.[110] Put simply, I contend that late antique Muslims *experienced* circumcision as a matter of ritual purity, but

104 Saul M. Olyan. "What do shaving rites accomplish and what do they signal in biblical ritual contexts?" *Journal of Biblical Literature* 117:4 (1998): 611–22.

105 *B. Talmud*, Nazir 59a.

106 Olyan, "What do shaving rites accomplish," 621.

107 Ibrāhīm, *Khiṣāl al-fiṭrah*, 16.

108 Ibn Abī Shaybah, *Kitāb al-adab*, 223. See also Ibrāhīm, *Khiṣāl al-fiṭrah*, 10.

109 Mary Knight, "Curing cut or ritual mutilation?: some remarks on the practice of female and male circumcision in Graeco-Roman Egypt." *Isis* 92:2 (2001): 317–38 at 334. See also Cohen, *Why aren't Jewish women circumcised?* 19 (citing Herodotus, who claimed that Egyptians circumcised for cleanliness).

110 To fulfill the rabbinic Jewish ritual requirements of circumcision, there must be blood; this is why previously circumcised converts to Judaism are still obligated to have a drop of blood drawn during a ritual circumcision (the ceremony is *hatafat dam brit*).

rationalized it as an Abrahamic practice. I am not arguing that late antique Muslims disregarded Abrahamic practices, but rather that they may not have relied upon them to justify circumcision. Instead, circumcision likely seemed self-evident to late antique Muslims as a matter of cleanliness, which may explain why the practice was incorporated into the natural predisposition list.

It should be acknowledged that these grooming practices contained social codes that were likely relevant to distinguishing Muslim identity. Kueny has noted that the "cumulative effect of these purity practices makes one easily identifiable as a believer."[111] This is reflected in later historical reports pertaining to Muslim–Christian interactions, wherein a Christian's status as uncircumcised was perceived as unclean. In a recent study of Umayyad Cordoba, Coope refers to a tenth-century Christian source, which reports:

> Muslims at the palace refused to work with men who did not respect Muslim food restrictions or who were uncircumcised. The fact that a man was a Christian was not necessarily a problem for Muslims, but a Christian who was physically polluted by the eating of pork or by not being circumcised was intolerable.[112]

In other words, Muslims associated circumcision with the grooming practices enumerated in lists about the *fiṭrah.* But this *fiṭrah* list demarcates the etiquette of grooming and, as such, constitutes recommended, but not obligatory, practices. After all, there are no legal or spiritual repercussions for failing to abide by these grooming recommendations – with the exception of circumcision, as will be discussed below. The question I want to explore now is, how did circumcision come to be perceived as an obligatory Islamic ritual?

Legalizing an Islamic Ritual

An additional Qurʾānic verse would become particularly important in the medieval era for the articulation of a legal basis for circumcision; that verse is 16:123: "Follow the people of Abraham in monotheism."[113] Neither Ibn ʿAbbās, Mujāhid, Muqātil, nor al-Ṭabarī mentions circumcision in

[111] Kueny, "Abraham's test," 178.

[112] Jessica A. Coope, "Religious and cultural conversion to Islam in ninth-century Umayyad Córdoba." *Journal of World History* 4:1 (1993): 47–68 at 56.

[113] This verse is cited in Ibn Qayyim al-Jawzīyah, *Tuḥfat al-mawdūd*, 128.

reference to this verse.[114] Instead, all four exegetes gloss this verse as being about Abrahamic monotheism's rejection of polytheism, with some of them explicitly defining Abrahamic monotheism as Islam. I suspect that the basis for articulating circumcision as a legal command was a gradual process, in which this verse initially played a minor (if any) role. One of the earliest and most comprehensive Islamic monographs dedicated to legal rulings pertaining to children, *Tuḥfat al-mawdūd bi-āḥkām al-mawlūd* by the Ḥanbalī jurist Ibn Qayyim al-Jawzīyah, links the command to follow Abraham with circumcision. Ibn Qayyim emphasized that circumcision is essential to fulfilling the monotheistic demands of the Abrahamic path and to representing one's membership in the Abrahamic community.[115] He identified circumcision as part of man's "natural predisposition" (*fiṭrah*) and as equivalent to the baptism of the monotheist (*ḥanīf*).[116] In short, circumcision may have become a legally-required act over time. Yet, this process of legalization left several regulatory aspects of circumcision unspecified: the age at which a boy should be circumcised; who should perform the circumcision; how much of the foreskin should be removed; what relationship circumcision has to the Prophet's revelation. In other words, if circumcision was an obligatory Islamic ritual practice, how did law ritualize it? With that in mind, I want to shift now from exegetical texts to other sources. In doing so, I will explore some legal dimensions of circumcision: its status as obligatory or recommended, its timing, its role in conversion, and its implications.

Ritual Precedent

Qur'ānic exegesis suggests that the key precedent for Muslim circumcision was Abraham. In late antique Islamic society, the characterization of a practice or an idea as Abrahamic gave it precedential value. Indeed, the exegetical works analyzed above did not justify why Muslims should adopt an Abrahamic practice. For late antique Muslims, it was self-evident that they should follow Abrahamic practices – unless some Islamic scriptural tradition had abrogated them. (This is one component of a broader Qur'ānic acceptance and modification of Mosaic law.) Yet, was the Prophet circumcised? Biographical sources do not provide any tradition-reports

[114] al-Fīrūzābādī, *Tanwīr*, 232; al-Fīrūzābādī, *Tafsīr Ibn ʿAbbās*, 346; Mujāhid, *Tafsīr al-Imām Mujāhid*, 427; Muqātil, *Tafsīr Muqātil*, 2:493; al-Ṭabarī, *Tafsīr*, 14:398.

[115] Ibn Qayyim al-Jawzīyah, *Tuḥfat al-mawdūd*, 145.

[116] *Ibid.*, 126–7.

about the Prophet's circumcision.[117] The silence of biographical literature on this question is telling because it points to the possible inconsequentiality of circumcision within late antique Islamic society. While some medieval sources report that the Prophet was born circumcised, this narrative did not circulate widely in late antiquity.[118] An additional important question: are there precedents for circumcision from the era of the Prophet, his Companions, or Successors? If circumcision were a crucial aspect of late antique Muslim practice, surely there would be narratives about the Prophet, the Companions, or the Successors overseeing (or instructing) a circumcision. Yet, ʿAbd al-Razzāq al-Ṣanʿānī (d. 827; Yemen) and Ibn Abī Shaybah (d. 849; Iraq) do not include any reports about circumcision as a communal event during the Prophetic era.

Instead of narratives providing an Islamic ritual precedent for circumcision, we find a variety of statements that indirectly discuss circumcision as a crucial practice. Indeed, the primary Prophetic-era narrative that implies Muslims were circumcised is a tradition-report narrated on the authority of the Prophet's wife, ʿĀʾishah; purportedly responding to an inquiry about post-sexual purification, ʿĀʾishah asserted that "[i]f the two circumcised parts have been in touch with one another, ritual washing is necessary."[119] Muslim scholars interpreted this tradition-report as meaning that if the circumcised male and female genitalia come into contact with each other, then both the man and the woman must wash themselves to be ritually pure. This tradition-report was then used to establish a normative presumption of circumcision for both men and women. But the historical veracity of the report is questionable because there is little evidence that Meccan or Medinan Arabs practiced female circumcision in antiquity. (There is, by contrast, evidence that female circumcision was practiced in parts of Africa and in southern regions of the Arabian peninsula.[120]) Moreover, several versions of the report refer explicitly to the vulva instead of describing "two circumcised parts."[121] The historical context and variants together point to the possibility that the phraseology ("two circumcised parts") may have been used euphemistically or been added by later

[117] Kueny, "Abraham's test," 169–72. See also M. J. Kister. "". . . and he was born circumcised. . .": Some notes on circumcision in Ḥadīth." *Oriens* 34 (1994): 10–30.

[118] al-Qurṭubī cites this tradition-report. Ibrāhīm, *Khiṣāl al-fiṭrah*, 23.

[119] Ibn Abī Shaybah, *Muṣannaf*, 1:84–6 (multiple tradition-reports indicating that ritual washing is necessary when the two circumcised parts meet); Mālik Ibn Anas (d. 795; Arabia), *al-Muwaṭṭaʾ*, ed. by Muḥammad Fūʾād ʿAbd al-Bāqī, 2 vols. (Beirut: Dār al-Turāth al-ʿArabī, 1985), 1:45–7. See also Maghen, "First blood."

[120] Knight, "Curing cut," 321.

[121] Ibn Abī Shaybah, *Muṣannaf*, 1:84–6.

transmitters. Regardless of the tradition-report's precise wording, it is striking that the primary Prophetic-era tradition-report about circumcision is a type of negative evidence. That is to say, there are no tradition reports about a circumcision that went wrong, was delayed, was attended by notable figures, etc. As a historical matter, we might assume that late antique Muslims practiced male circumcision, but we have little direct historical evidence of it.

Ritual Obligation or Recommendation?

The absence of an explicit Qur'ānic command requiring circumcision and the indirect evidence of circumcision in tradition-reports suggest that the practice was not obligatory for late antique Muslims. Yet the status of circumcision as obligatory, recommended, or neutral was central to Jewish–Christian polemics on the topic. As previously mentioned, a significant component of Paul's critique of circumcision was its manifestation of "Jewish legalism."[122] Consequently, Paul insisted that a convert would neither be forced to circumcise nor be uncircumcised.[123] This, of course, contrasted with the rabbinic insistence on the legal necessity of circumcision. It is therefore imperative to observe how late antique Muslim legal authorities legalized circumcision within the conversion process.

A significant number of late antique Muslim authority figures classified circumcision as a recommended, but not an obligatory practice. A tradition-report suggests that the Prophet characterized circumcision as recommended (*sunnah*) for men and a noble deed for women.[124] The fourth caliph/first Shī'ī Imām 'Alī ibn Abī Ṭālib (d. 661) identified circumcision as a recommended but not obligatory practice (*sunnah*).[125] Mujāhid and Ibrāhīm al-Nakha'ī concurred in categorizing circumcision as a recommended practice.[126] al-Ḥasan al-Baṣrī (d. 728; Iraq) classified circumcision as recommended, but not obligatory (*sunnah*).[127] Abū Ḥanīfah (d. 767; Iraq) considered circumcision to be a non-obligatory *sunnah*.[128]

By contrast, numerous jurists viewed circumcision as an obligation, including Ibn 'Abbās, al-Sha'bī (d. 723/4; Kūfah), Rabī'ah (dc. 753/4;

[122] Gollaher, *Circumcision*, 32.
[123] *Ibid.*
[124] Ibn Abī Shaybah, *Muṣannaf*, 5:318; Ibn Abī Shaybah, *Kitāb al-adab*, 224.
[125] Qal'ah'jī, *'Alī ibn Abī Ṭālib*, 242.
[126] Ibn Abī Shaybah, *Muṣannaf*, 5:318.
[127] Qal'ah'jī, *al-Ḥasan al-Baṣrī*, 1:373. Cited in Ibn Qayyim al-Jawzīyah, *Tuḥfat al-mawdūd*, 128.
[128] Ibn Qayyim al-Jawzīyah, *Tuḥfat al-mawdūd*, 128.

Medina), Awzāʿī (d. 774; Syria), and Yaḥyá bin Saʿīd al-Anṣārī (d. 761/2; Medina). The eponyms of three of the orthodox legal schools – Mālik ibn Anas (d. 795; Medina), al-Shāfiʿī (d. 820; Arabia/Egypt), and Aḥmad ibn Ḥanbal (d. 855; Baghdad) – also classified circumcision as obligatory.[129] (The Mālikī position on circumcision requires some clarification: Mālikī jurists characterized circumcision as *sunnah* and, for their legal school, this means that it falls between an obligatory and a recommended practice.[130]) Nevertheless, by the end of late antiquity, the majority of jurists likely held that circumcision is a recommended (not obligatory) practice.[131] Those jurists who claimed it was an obligation pointed to ritual purity as their strongest evidence; they argued that an uncircumcised man cannot be ritually pure because the prepuce retains dirt.[132]

These Muslim jurists did not rely on the Abrahamic command as the sole or most significant source for Islamic circumcision. This is not to imply that Abrahamic precedent was irrelevant, but rather that it was insufficient. That insufficiency is quite telling: it may explain why medieval Muslim jurists struggled to compile multiple justifications for the obligatory status of circumcision; Islamic scriptural authority was not strong enough to support the ruling. Ḥanbalī jurist Ibn Qayyim al-Jawzīyah summarizes common juristic arguments for why circumcision is an obligation:[133] (1) it is an Abrahamic, monotheistic practice, which is obligatory for Muslims; (2) converts must be circumcised; (3) since an uncircumcised man's prayers, pilgrimage, testimony, and slaughter are invalid, circumcision is obligatory; (4) circumcision is obligatory to distinguish between Christians and Muslims or between pagans and Muslims;[134] (5) if circumcision were not obligatory, then a boy would not be legally permitted to expose his genitals and the person who performs the circumcision would not be legally permitted to view the boy's genitals; (6) it would not be permissible for a guardian to expose a minor to the pain and expense of circumcision if it were not an obligatory practice; (7) circumcision removes a part of the body that does not grow back, so if it were not obligatory, it would not be permitted to remove it; (8) the foreskin that is removed during circumcision retains impurity, such that not removing it would make one perpetually ritually impure; (9) circumcision is the essential sign

[129] Qalʿahʾjī, *ʿAbd Allāh ibn ʿAbbās*, 304; Ibn Qayyim al-Jawzīyah, *Tuḥfat al-mawdūd*, 127.
[130] Ibn Qayyim al-Jawzīyah, *Tuḥfat al-mawdūd*, 127–8.
[131] Ibrāhīm, *Khiṣāl al-fiṭrah*, 26.
[132] *Ibid.*, 26–7.
[133] These arguments are outlined in Ibn Qayyim al-Jawzīyah, *Tuḥfat al-mawdūd*, 128–31.
[134] *Ibid.*, 129.

of monotheism that differentiates followers of Abraham (Muslims and Jews) from Christians. The very length and variation of the list suggests a notable anxiety to prove that circumcision is an obligatory practice precisely because it was neglected or resisted. This list also suggests that by the fourteenth century, jurists had developed a set of arguments for justifying circumcision that differed significantly from late antique notions – particularly in terms of emphasizing differentiation of group identity. If circumcision had been legalized as an obligatory ritual in order to differentiate Muslim identity, how did jurists relate to Jewish circumcision?

Ritual Performance

The prescribed time for a ritual offers another angle through which to view Islamic circumcision. Jewish circumcision occurs on a clearly stipulated day, in conformity with Leviticus 12:3, which specifies, "On the eighth day the flesh of his foreskin shall be circumcised."[135] By comparison, for pre-Islamic monotheist Arabs (and possibly for some ancient Israelites), circumcision may have been a puberty initiation rite.[136] Late antique Muslim scholars did not specify a date for circumcision.[137] Medieval sources provide multiple opinions on the timing of circumcision, ranging between seven days and puberty; this range of ages seems to correspond both to Jewish and to pre-Islamic customary practices.[138] (Notably, the "eighth day" in Jewish sources refers to the eighth day of the infant's life, whereas the "seventh day" in Islamic sources means the seventh day after the infant's birth. Thus, these units of time are equivalent.) Imāmī Shīʿī sources report that the sixth Imām, Jaʿfar al-Ṣādiq (d. 765; Medina) advised that circumcision should be on the seventh day.[139] ʿAlī ibn Yaqṭīn (d. 798; Baghdad) reportedly asked Imām Musá ibn Jaʿfar (d. 799; Medina) about the recommended time for circumcision and the Imām responded that performing the ritual on the seventh day is recommended, but circumcising at a later date is inconsequential.[140]

[135] *NRSV Bible*. Other biblical sources for this prescribed day of circumcision are Genesis. 17:12 (circumcision is at eight days old) and Genesis 21:4 (Isaac was eight days old when Abraham circumcised him).

[136] Retsö, *The Arabs in antiquity*, 606. Some scholars have suggested that ancient Israelites also practiced circumcision as an initiation rite, pointing to Genesis 17:25 (Ishmael was thirteen when he was circumcised) and Exodus 4:24–26 (Zipporah's circumcision of her son).

[137] ʿAbd al-Razzāq al-Ṣanʿānī (d. 827; Yemen) and Ibn Abī Shaybah do not include narratives prescribing the timing of circumcision.

[138] Ibrāhīm, *Khiṣāl al-fiṭrah*, 32–3.

[139] al-Kulaynī, *al-Kāfī*, 6:36.

[140] *Ibid.*, 6:37.

Indeed, some Muslim scholars disapproved of circumcision on the seventh day after birth precisely because it was a Jewish practice. For some Muslim scholars, the obligation of male circumcision was not in and of itself an emulation of Jewish practices; in contrast, the timing of *when or what day* to circumcise came dangerously too close to Jewish tradition. Thus, al-Ḥasan al-Baṣrī discouraged Muslims from circumcising on the seventh day after birth, on the grounds that this was a Jewish practice.[141] Makḥūl (d. 731; Syria), and other traditionists, reported that Abraham circumcised Isma'īl when he was thirteen years old and Isḥāq when he was seven days old.[142] This tradition-report suggests an interest in differentiating between Muslim circumcision and Jewish circumcision through the figures of Abraham's sons. al-Layth ibn Sa'd (d. 791; Egypt) recommended circumcision between the ages of seven and ten.[143] Mālik ibn Anas also reportedly advised against circumcising on the seventh day in order to distinguish Muslim and Jewish practices.[144] Some jurists held that it was necessary to distinguish between Jews and Muslims through ritual practices.[145]

In addition to ritual timing, an additional dimension of circumcision's potential obscuration of Jewish–Muslim identity was the circumciser. In one tradition-report, Imām Ḥasan al-Askarī (d. 874; Medina) was asked, "May a Jewish cupper circumcise a Muslim child?"[146] Imām Ḥasan responded, "The normative practice (*sunnah*) is the seventh day. Do not contradict it."[147] This narrative suggests that there may have been Muslims in the ninth century who did not practice circumcision regularly or did not have Muslim circumcisers readily available. Moreover, some Muslims themselves were concerned that if the circumciser were Jewish and the circumcision took place on the seventh day, the circumcision might be "Jewish" rather than "Muslim." Imām Ḥasan's response quashes that concern.

Many Muslim jurists perceived the issue of confusing Muslims and Jews through circumcision as inconsequential. Aḥmad ibn Ḥanbal rejected the

[141] Qal'ah'jī, *al-Ḥasan al-Baṣrī*, 1:373.
[142] Ibn Qayyim al-Jawzīyah, *Tuḥfat al-mawdūd*, 121, 44.
[143] *Ibid.*, 144.
[144] *Ibid.*
[145] There are many other examples of Muslims defining themselves against Jews by adopting distinct practices. See, for example, Haggai Mazuz. "Menstruation and differentiation: how Muslims differentiated themselves from Jews regarding the laws of menstruation." *Der Islam* 87:1–2 (2012): 204–23.
[146] A cupper performs cupping therapy, which uses heat and suction to treat a variety of physical ailments.
[147] al-Kulaynī, *al-Kāfī*, 6:36.

notion that circumcising on the seventh day would conflate Muslims and Jews.[148] And Ibn Mundhir al-Naysābūrī (d. 930; Nishapur/Arabia) argued that there was no conclusive evidence to prohibit circumcision on the seventh day.[149] By the medieval era, the question of when to perform the circumcision ritual seems to have become less pressing. In *Aḥkām al-ṣighār*, Ustarūshanī (d. 1234/5; Samarqand) identifies the maximum age of circumcision as twelve years old and concedes that there is no consensus on the minimum age.[150] Ibn Qayyim al-Jawzīyah cites Wahb ibn Munabbih (d. *c.* 730; Yemen) – who may have had a Jewish background – as claiming that circumcision on the seventh day is preferable because it inflicts the least pain on the child.[151] Ibn Qayyim cites additional authorities as evidence: Imām Muḥammad ibn ʿAlī al-Bāqir (d. 733; Medina) reported that the Prophet's daughter, Fāṭimah (d. 632; Mecca), circumcised her sons on the seventh day.[152] (Ibn Qayyim includes another version of this report, in which the Prophet had his grandsons circumcised on the seventh day.[153]) Ibn Qayyim notes that jurists differed on the validity of circumcising boys on the seventh day after their birth, acknowledging the dispute over Jewish practice and citing al-Ḥasan al-Baṣrī as explicitly rejecting it.[154] Ibn Qayyim al-Jawzīyah concluded that all boys must be circumcised prior to reaching puberty.[155] The various tradition-reports cited by medieval jurists indicate that there was a debate in late antique and medieval Islamic societies about when to perform circumcision and that this debate was at least partially concerned with the dynamics of group identity vis-à-vis Jews.

Ritual Conversion

An important dimension of Jewish–Christian polemic in antiquity was the place of circumcision in the conversion process. Circumcision was so central to Jewish conversion that the Rabbis debated the necessity of a "symbolic circumcision" for converts who were already circumcised. The Babylonian Talmud reports that Beit Shammai (the dissenting rabbinic opinion) ruled that a few drops of the "covenant blood" must be

[148] Ibn Qayyim al-Jawzīyah, *Tuḥfat al-mawdūd*, 144.
[149] *Ibid.*, 144–5.
[150] Muḥammad ibn Maḥmūd Ustarūshanī (d. 1234/5; Samarqand), *Aḥkām al-ṣighār* (Beirut: Dār al-Kutub al-ʿIlmīyah, 1997), 144–5.
[151] Ibn Qayyim al-Jawzīyah, *Tuḥfat al-mawdūd*, 144.
[152] *Ibid.*
[153] *Ibid.*, 145.
[154] *Ibid.*, 143.
[155] *Ibid.*, 142.

drawn from the convert; in comparison, Beit Hillel (the normative opinion) ruled that this symbolic circumcision was unnecessary.[156] Against this juristic difference of opinion, the Geonim apparently made a symbolic conversion incumbent on previously circumcised converts.[157] (It is possible that this Geonic ruling was a response to circumcised Arabs converting to Judaism.) As Ferguson explains, "The heart of the rabbinic conversion ceremony was circumcision, not baptism; baptism was the central act in Christian conversion."[158] By comparison, it is difficult to know what the process for conversion to Arab paganism might have entailed. Still, it is clear that many late antique communities in the Near East made bodily rituals a necessary element of the conversion process. I suspect that for Muslims, the bodily ritual of circumcision was not only secondary to conversion, but probably not viewed as necessary in late antiquity.

Late antique Islamic sources do not provide a clear regulation on circumcision's role in conversion. The Qur'ān lacks an explicit command and Prophetic traditions do not provide conclusive or distinct guidelines. One tradition-report depicts a new convert approaching the Prophet for instructions: in one version, the Prophet approves when the new convert performs ablutions and prays; but in another version (possibly a later variant), the Prophet instructs him to shave and to be circumcised.[159] Late antique pious Muslim figures offer conflicting perspectives. Imām ʿAlī ibn Abī Ṭālib reportedly made circumcision an obligatory component of conversion.[160] (Following Imām ʿAlī's opinion, the sixth Imām, Jaʿfar al-Ṣādiq [d. 765; Medina], asserted that a convert to Islam may not perform the pilgrimage unless he has been circumcised.[161]) But al-Ḥasan al-Baṣrī did not obligate adult converts to undergo circumcision.[162] Reportedly, al-Ḥasan al-Baṣrī expressed his opinion on the non-obligatory status of circumcision in response to a historical event: when the governor of Baṣrah "inspected" some Muslims in his region and found them to be uncircumcised, he ordered that they be circumcised. Some of them died. In response, al-Ḥasan al-Baṣrī reportedly stated, "In the time of Muḥammad, Byzantines, Persians, and Abyssinians converted to Islam and no one inspected them

[156] *B. Talmud*, Shabbat 135a. See footnote 110.
[157] Novak, "The treatment," 243.
[158] Ferguson, *Baptism in the early church*, 82.
[159] ʿAbd al-Razzāq ibn Hammām al-Ḥimyarī al-Ṣanʿānī (d. 827; Yemen), *al-Muṣannaf*, ed. by Ḥabīb al-Raḥmān al-ʿAẓamī, 2nd edn., 11 vols., Manshūrāt al-Majlis al-ʿIlmī, 39 (Beirut: al-Maktab al-Islāmī, 1983), 6:10.
[160] al-Kulaynī, *al-Kāfī*, 6:38.
[161] *Ibid.*, 4:279–80.
[162] Qalʿah'jī, *al-Ḥasan al-Baṣrī*, 1:374.

[to verify if they were circumcised]."[163] While there were multiple opinions concerning if a convert should be circumcised, it is interesting to note that no late antique Muslim scholar appears to have given an opinion on the status of a previously circumcised convert. Simply put, there is no Islamic equivalent of a "symbolic circumcision" and no late antique discussion of the blood of circumcision as being crucial to conversion.

However, in the medieval era, the notion that circumcision is obligatory for converts seems to have become the majority opinion, despite the absence of clear precedential authority.[164] Here again, circumcision's role in conversion was less symbolic and more physical. As noted, in tenth-century Cordoba, circumcision was viewed not only as a necessary component of the conversion process, but also a sign of cleanliness.[165] Ibn Qayyim cited multiple opinions on the circumcision of converts, indicating that there was no consensus on it as an obligation for conversion.[166] (However, in line with the eponym of his school, he argued that circumcision is an obligation unless the adult convert fears for his health.[167])

Ritual Implications

Isolated tradition-reports emphasizing that conversion is incomplete without circumcision substantiate the tenuousness of circumcision's role in conversion to Islam. Some tradition-reports – and the historical narrative about forced conversions cited above – imply that men (possibly Christian or Zoroastrian) were converting to Islam without being circumcised. ʿAlī ibn Abī Ṭālib reportedly asserted that the funeral prayer should not be performed for someone who was not circumcised, unless there was a health reason that prevented him from being circumcised.[168] Many reports suggest that Ibn ʿAbbās invalidated the testimony of an uncircumcised witness, in addition to invalidating his prayer, pilgrimage, and ritual slaughter.[169] Late antique figures did not provide Qurʾānic or Prophetic evidence for their opinions. This may be why Ibrāhīm al-Nakhaʿī (d. 717; Kūfah) and al-Ḥasan al-Baṣrī reportedly did not invalidate animal slaughter by an uncircumcised Muslim. By the medieval era, juristic opinion

163 Ibn Qayyim al-Jawzīyah, *Tuḥfat al-mawdūd*, 132.
164 Ibrāhīm, *Khiṣāl al-fiṭrah*, 33–6.
165 Coope, "Religious and cultural conversion."
166 Ibn Qayyim al-Jawzīyah, *Tuḥfat al-mawdūd*, 128.
167 *Ibid.*, 139.
168 Qalʿahʾjī, *ʿAlī ibn Abī Ṭālib*, 414.
169 Qalʿahʾjī, *ʿAbd Allāh ibn ʿAbbās*, 305.

seems to have shifted toward elaborating a set of negative implications for an uncircumcised convert. By the fourteenth century, Ibn Qayyim would cite multiple opinions invalidating an uncircumcised man's prayers, pilgrimage, testimony, and slaughter.[170] Ibn Qayyim relied primarily on a tradition-report attributed to Ibn ʿAbbās.[171] Muslim scholars who drew upon Ibn ʿAbbās' perspective may have sought to prevent "fake" conversions by individuals seeking to avoid paying the poll tax; by requiring circumcision, some medieval jurists made conversion more complicated, in hopes that it would encourage only "genuine" conversions. Of course, that these legal opinions on circumcision's implications were necessary indicates that there were uncircumcised Muslim converts. In addition, it is notable that the enumerated implications entailed invalidating a Muslim's ritual acts, but not declaring the Muslim an apostate. Thus, not being circumcised did not imply that a man was not Muslim.

Gender of Ritual

Thus far, I have focused on male circumcision, with only modest references to the practice of female circumcision. There is no consensus on what constitutes female circumcision, with some practices involving removal of the clitoris and others including the labia minora or labia majora.[172] As Charlotte Fonrobert has pointed out, "discussions of late antique religio-ethnic identities focus on ethnic markers such as circumcision, which reinforce constructions of male identities as the center of conflicts over the constitution of ethnic or religious identities in the culture of late antiquity."[173] If circumcision is the sign of the covenant, then women are excluded from it.[174] In focusing on circumcision as a marker of identity, I have sought to demonstrate that it was not fundamental to being Muslim in late antiquity. Indeed, rather than being a bodily ritual that symbolized Abraham's covenant, Islamic circumcision was a grooming practice that was a prerequisite for Muslim men to perform particular rituals. Female circumcision may have confused medieval Muslim jurists

170 Ibn Qayyim al-Jawzīyah, *Tuḥfat al-mawdūd*, 129.
171 *Ibid.*, 154–5.
172 Knight, "Curing cut," 323.
173 Charlotte Elisheva Fonrobert, *Menstrual purity: rabbinic and Christian reconstructions of Biblical gender* (Stanford, CA: Stanford University Press, 2000), 12.
174 For a detailed and nuanced exploration of the relationship between circumcision and the covenant, see Cohen, *Why aren't Jewish women circumcised?* See also Ilona N. Rashkow, *Taboo or not taboo: sexuality and family in the Hebrew Bible* (Minneapolis, MN: Fortress Press, 2000), Ch. 4.

because it was not an Abrahamic practice, but could be justified as necessary for ritual purity.[175] Berkey has outlined the arguments presented by medieval Muslim jurists for permitting female circumcision and demonstrated that most jurists presumed that male circumcision is obligatory and female circumcision is recommended.[176] But the key reason why jurists did not prohibit female circumcision is because they viewed it as a matter of cleanliness, disassociated from the Abrahamic covenant's relevance to men only. In other words, in Islamic discourse, male and female circumcisions are entangled in bodily ritual purity, which is a different justification for circumcision than Abraham's covenant.

A Ritual of "Conclusion"

I have sought to demonstrate that the meaning of "Muslim" changes not only over time and space, but also within Islamic literary genres and practices. The Qur'ān does not explicitly mention circumcision, but medieval exegetes built upon the commentaries of their late antique predecessors by specifying that male circumcision is a prerequisite for fulfilling Abrahamic commands. Biographical and historical texts provide relatively little information about circumcision among late antique Muslims. While Abraham's covenant resonates in Islamic literature, it does not neatly correspond to its connotations in Jewish and Christian texts. In marking circumcision as a component of ritual purity, late antique Muslim traditionists seem to have interlinked grooming practices and notions of cleanliness from pre-Islamic Arabian customs. The legal parameters that legitimated and demarcated the ritual of circumcision likewise demonstrate a mélange of precedential authorities and legal arguments. These legal considerations suggest that in the late antique Islamic world, male circumcision was not a clear obligation (including for converts), lacked a precise time of performance, and may not have hindered other acts (such as ritual slaughter or performance of the pilgrimage). In short, circumcision was not a crucial aspect of late antique Muslim identity.

Tracking changes in ritual practices offer a window through which to understand how what it meant to be Muslim changed over time. In this chapter, I explored how circumcision was given scriptural authority, associated with ritual purity, and elaborated as a ritual act with significant

[175] Kueny, "Abraham's test," 173.

[176] Jonathan P. Berkey. "Circumcision circumscribed: female excision and cultural accommodation in the medieval Near East." *International Journal of Middle East Studies* 28:1 (1996): 19–38 at 25.

legal consequences. In so doing, I have avoided any assumption of an "original" practice of circumcision. Much scholarship in Islamic studies has focused on uncovering a presumed "origin" of Islam in order to demonstrate that what moderns now recognize as "Islamic" is a "later" product. As I outlined in the previous chapter, this way of thinking is based on a false linearity in which scholars identify an essentialized "Islam" and then seek to identify an equally essentialized "pre-Islam."[177] The distinct ways in which the circumcision ritual was elaborated over time suggests a different understanding of this process: initially, Muslims defined themselves as monotheists against polytheists; later, they defined themselves as differentiated monotheists. This shift is not evidence of "influence," but rather of the intermingling between practices, their textual elaborations, and audiences.

The kaleidoscope of Islamic ritual practice that I have explored here eschews any simple linear narrative. As Bell noted, "ritualization is, in itself, a creative act of production, a strategic reproduction of the past in such a way as to maximize its domination of the present."[178] I have illustrated how that strategic reproduction of the past draws upon a multitude of Near Eastern notions and practices – including ritual purity and Abraham's covenant-based circumcision. It was not my intention to disentangle these interwoven elements or to claim an "Arab" or "Jewish" (two categories that are not mutually exclusive) "origin" for Islamic circumcision; instead, I have sought to emphasize that Islamic circumcision is so syncretic and shifting as to deny any "origins" analysis. The meaning of "Muslim" shifted as orthodoxy and orthopraxy shaped and reshaped ritual acts and their legal boundaries. Depending on what aspect of circumcision we analyze – its scriptural justifications, normative legitimations, legal status, performance, or implications – we will find a different "color" to the relationship between Islamic circumcision and its multiple predecessors and contemporaries. As we turn the Islamic kaleidoscope, the color – if it is even discernible – may look monotheistic, pagan, Jewish, or Christian; but when the colors combine into whiteness, that is Islamicate.

[177] Alternatively, Donner claimed that Islam began as a movement of "believers" that eventually distinguished themselves as Muslims; but his thesis is predicated on a developmental paradigm, since he remarks that "ritual practices were not at first so rigidly defined as they later became, so it seems likely that some of these rituals evolved under the influence of the practices of Jewish or Christian Believers of the Fertile Crescent (or even of Arabia in Muhammad's day)." Fred M. Donner, *Muhammad and the believers: at the origins of Islam* (Cambridge, MA: The Belknap Press of Harvard University Press, 2010), 215. As I have sought to clarify in this chapter, all rituals change – rather than "develop" – within hybrid historical contexts.

[178] Bell, *Ritual theory*, 123.

CHAPTER 5

Legal Historicizing: Moments in Macro-histories

Thus far, I have used the terms late antique and medieval to imply broad historical changes and to delineate some of the profound distinctions in Islamic law during these two eras. As the case studies in Chapters 2 and 4 demonstrate, contrasting late antique Muslim jurists and medieval Muslim jurists reveals that they interpreted law in distinct ways and engaged dissimilar legal consumers. Of course, neither late antique jurists nor their medieval counterparts constituted homogenous groups and a diversity of legal opinions and approaches are evident throughout Islamic legal history; but, undoubtedly, the range of legal options narrowed between the late antique and medieval eras. The broad outlines of this process are fairly well known. By the medieval era, four main surviving schools of law (*madhāhib*) among Sunnīs and two among Shīʿīs became dominant in the Islamic legal landscape. The phrase "diversity within unity" is often used to describe Islamic law. However, this (medieval) diversity is relatively narrow in comparison to the diversity of late antiquity. A recent empirical study has demonstrated that up until the late ninth century CE, more than 50 percent of jurists were unaffiliated with any of the surviving Sunnī schools of law.[1] It was not until the beginning of the eleventh century that more than 50 percent of jurists became affiliated with one of the four surviving Sunnī schools of law. An extensive change occurred between the mid-seventh and the eleventh centuries as Muslim jurists organized into increasingly professional legal schools characterized by some degree of internal homogeneity. Explaining how and why this happened is an important question in the field of Islamic legal studies. This is because the

[1] Monique Bernards and John Nawas. "The geographic distribution of Muslim jurists during the first four centuries AH." *Islamic Law and Society* 10:2 (2003): 168–81.

result of these changes was legal conformity – not a singular conformity, but legal conformity nonetheless.

The heterodoxy of late antiquity became the orthodoxy of the medieval era and, consequently, what it meant for jurists to dissent in Islamic societies fundamentally changed. As the Islamic empire expanded, its bureaucracy, including the administration of courts, intensified. When the state's courts appointed judges from particular legal schools, they signaled the legitimacy of those legal schools; in turn, this attracted more students or adherents in search of employment opportunities. In addition, the elites associated with the state and the elites who prospered from an increasingly complex urban market system acted as patrons for legal scholarship. As in the case of judicial appointments, the sponsorship of certain legal schools strengthened them. Simultaneous to this political and economic support from the state and elites, gradual processes of conversion and social change created demands for predictable legal opinions and approaches. As a result of these and other changes, the hundreds of Islamic legal schools that existed in late antiquity consolidated into the several that dominated in the medieval period. This was accompanied by a transformation in the internal dynamics of Islamic jurisprudence. In late antiquity, dissenting legal opinions were fettered by accusations of heresy; but in the medieval era, dissenting opinions were fettered by majoritarian rule. Thus far, I have pointed to some of the reasons for these shifts in particular case studies. In this chapter, I will outline some of the far-ranging changes in Islamic law by delineating a rough framework for how legal education, the legal profession, and the everyday implementation of law transformed.

Metaphors for Historical Theory: Maturity/Formative

"Origins"-oriented historiography identifies multiple anthropomorphic aspects of Islamic law: its conception (see Chapter 1), its parentage (see Chapter 3), and its "maturity." The anthropomorphic notion of maturity informs the conventional periodization of Islamic law into "formative" and "classical" periods. Conventional Islamic legal historiography characterizes the seventh through tenth centuries CE as the "formative" period of Islamic law and investigates its "evolution" or "development." (The usage of the term "formative" in "origins"-oriented scholarship on Islamic law parallels the prevalence of this term in the field of Islamic studies more broadly.[2])

[2] To be clear, the term "formative" is applied generally in Islamic historiography to refer roughly to the first century and a half of Islamic history. Most scholars distinguish between a "formative" and a "classical" period. See Chase F. Robinson, "Conclusion: from formative Islam to classical Islam," in *The formation of the Islamic world, sixth to eleventh centuries*, ed. by Chase F. Robinson, The new Cambridge history of Islam (Cambridge: Cambridge University Press, 2011), 683–95.

This period is the focus of what is arguably disproportionate academic interest.[3] The subsequent period in the conventional periodization of Islamic legal history is the so-called "classical" period, roughly the tenth through fourteenth centuries.[4] Here again, Schacht provided the plot for the field's master-narrative: Schacht framed "the *development* of Muhammadan jurisprudence from its *origins* through its *formative* period to its apex which it reached in Shāfi'ī."[5] Similarly, Crone claimed, "Islamic law, it would seem, evolved from *embryonic* beginnings to *classical* shapes within less than two hundred years."[6] In between "embryonic" and "classical," Crone demarcated "the *formative* first century of Islamic law."[7] Melchert's work explored the "formation" of Sunnī legal schools and identified their "classical" forms.[8] Dutton identified "the *formative* period of Islamic law in the first to third centuries AH."[9] Hallaq defined "the '*formative* period' as that historical period in which the legal system arose from rudimentary beginnings and then developed to the point at which its constitutive features had acquired an identifiable shape."[10] He associated those constitutive features with "the mature form" of Islamic law.[11] While the terms "formative" and "classical" are pervasive in Islamic studies, they are problematic descriptive terms because they simultaneously essentialize and anthropomorphize Islamic law. These metaphors suggest that Islamic law is conventionally perceived as "developing" from "infancy" to a "mature" legal system in a unilinear process.[12] Consequently, scholarship commences with a preconceived notion of Islamic law as it existed in its "classical" form and anachronistically searches for its "formative" version. What this "origins"-oriented historiography inescapably presumes is that "classical" Islamic law was the inevitable outcome, as if other possibilities did not exist. As the case studies in Chapters 2 and 4

[3] Hallaq, "The quest for origins or doctrine?," 3 (confirming that "the 'origins' of Islam in general and of Islamic law in particular were and continue to be, comparatively speaking, the focus of much of the writing in the field.").

[4] By contrast, El Shamsy contends that Islamic law's "*formative* period" began in the eighth century CE and "lasted about a century and a half" before Islamic law acquired its "*classical* form." El Shamsy, *The canonization of Islamic law*, 2–3, emphasis added.

[5] Schacht, *The origins*, 329, emphasis added.

[6] Crone, *Roman*, 26, emphasis added.

[7] *Ibid.*, 2, emphasis added.

[8] Christopher Melchert, *The formation of the Sunni schools of law, 9th-10th centuries C.E.*, ed. by Ruud Peters and Bernard Weiss, Studies in Islamic Law and Society, 4 (Leiden: Brill, 1997), *passim*.

[9] Ibn Anas, *Original Islam*, 2, emphasis added.

[10] Hallaq, *The origins*, 2–3, emphasis added.

[11] Hallaq, *Sharī'a*, 56. See also Hallaq, *The origins*, 24.

[12] Gordon explains the problems and inaccuracies of viewing legal history as progressive development in Robert W. Gordon, "Historicism in legal scholarship." *The Yale Law Journal* 90:5 (1981): 1017–56 at 1035–6.

have already demonstrated, there are significant distinctions in the jurisprudence ascribed to the "formative" and "classical" eras.

Linearity: From Progress and Decline to Orthodoxy

The emphasis on "origins" in Islamic legal historiography reflects an implicitly evolutionary theory of history.[13] Evolutionary theories of history are linear, irreversible, and often reductive. Typically, evolutionary theories of history characterize broad social changes as moving from "simple to complex." I contend that this narrative arc reflects the influence of post-Enlightenment historiography, with its assumption of progress or social evolution.[14] When we juxtapose the "origins" metaphors discussed in Chapter 1 (conception) and Chapter 3 (parentage) with metaphors of development (formative) and maturity (classical), the resulting image is of an anthropomorphic Islamic law. As Gordon explained, evolutionary "legal history is often written as the story of the genetic ancestors or '*origins*' of the legal forms of the present and of the gradual developing of these *embryos* into their *mature* modern condition."[15] This evolutionary perspective is precisely what animates the conventional narrative of Islamic historiography both terminologically and conceptually. Of course, evolutionary legal histories are not unique to Islamic legal studies. One of the most influential legal historians of the nineteenth century, Henry J. S. Maine (d. 1888; UK), presented an evolutionary ancient legal development by applying Darwinian evolution to legal history.[16] While Maine's widely influential work did not discuss Islamic law, his ideas about law's progress were dominant for generations and shaped much modern comparative legal scholarship.

In addition to being philosophically untenable, evolutionary legal histories conceal prejudices and preconceptions. It is important to investigate what value meanings are embedded within the terms "formative" and "classical" because, as Rouland noted, "evolutionism carries a value

[13] By way of comparison, this correlates to Whiggish understandings of history that were prevalent among scholars of Western legal systems. See the relevant critique in Robert W. Gordon, "The past as authority and as social critic: stabilizing and destabilizing functions of history in legal argument." In *The historic turn in the human sciences*, ed. by Terrence J. McDonald (Ann Arbor, MI: University of Michigan Press, 1996), 339–78 at 343.

[14] On the influence of evolutionary ideas of history in legal studies, see Rouland, *Legal anthropology*, 27.

[15] Gordon, "The past as authority and as social critic," 343, emphasis added.

[16] Henry Sumner Maine, *Ancient law; its connection with the early history of society and its relation to modern ideas* (Boston, MA: Beacon Press, 1963).

judgment of a discriminatory nature."[17] In Chapters 1 and 3, I explored how the related metaphors of birth and parentage signified the absence and derivativeness of Islamic law.[18] The dating and borrowing implications of these metaphors are furthered by the notion of "formative," which conveys a sense of crudeness or parochialism. While the term "classical" is commonly perceived as positive, it functions as a precursor for "post-classical," which is associated with decline, stagnation, or a failure to become modern.[19] Schacht, for instance, claimed that "the *classical* system of legal theory" was followed by "a long period of scholasticism."[20] Schacht's identifies "scholasticism" (probably, *taqlīd*) as a stagnant period – or to use an anthropomorphic metaphor in line with the scholarship of the field, the "aging" – of Islamic law.[21] In other words, the conventional narrative's identification of a post-evolutionary moment of stagnation is viewed as the period when Islamic societies "ceased progressing." Evolutionary characterizations of Islamic legal historiography have extensive implications that are simultaneously difficult to discern and problematic in their implications.

The evolutionary notions that underlie the terms "formative" and "classical" result in four common limitations in conventional scholarship. First, in the problematic evolutionary framework, any law that existed prior to the "development" of medieval orthodox jurisprudence (*uṣūl al-fiqh*) is immature and insufficient. This is why much Islamic legal scholarship characterizes late antique Muslim societies as either not having a legal system, or having a legal system that was not Islamic, or having a legal system that was immature. All these interpretations are problematic because they are based on a narrow definition of law. Law is a changing body of norms operating in a social context. While there are differences between late antique, medieval, early modern, and modern law, those differences are not equivalent to evolutionary progress.[22] The conventional definition of Islamic law as equivalent to medieval orthodox jurisprudence is historically inaccurate because the establishment and dominance of orthodox legal schools were not inevitable.[23]

[17] Rouland, *Legal anthropology*, 26.

[18] On the Orientalist assumptions of absences, see Bryan S. Turner, *Marx and the end of Orientalism* (London: George Allen & Unwin Ltd, 1978), 81.

[19] On these themes, see *Ibid.*, 81–2.

[20] Schacht, *The origins*, 329, emphasis added.

[21] For a critique of Islamic "legal stagnation," see Hallaq, *Sharīʿa*, 355–70.

[22] Rouland notes that "In spite of evolutionist prejudices, there is no radical distinction, in nature, between law in modern societies and traditional societies." Rouland, *Legal anthropology*, 243.

[23] "Having severed Islamic legal concepts from both their origins and their operational frameworks, orientalist scholars concluded that *fiqh* products and Islamic law were one and the same, a divine dictation, which was incapable of change." Haifaa Khalafallah. "The elusive 'Islamic

Second, and relatedly, the presumed "problem" of the sources (discussed in Chapter 1) is intrinsically related to the assumed absence of institutions, including a legal system.[24] Too often, texts that do not appear overtly legal – including biographical, exegetical, and non-canonical sources – are dismissed. In a different context, Gordon explains, "This is why, long after the discrediting of evolutionary theories of history, legal history was still so frequently written as if these theories still held sway. For the historian who restricts his sources to the strictly legal, there often is no explanation available other than the genetic."[25] In the case of Islamic legal history, there is significant evidence of legal practice during the first Islamic century in a variety of historical texts (including *sīrah, maghāzī, muṣannafāt,* and *masānīd*) that have not been investigated exhaustively. Third, the evolutionary framework results in discounting jurists from the "formative" period and overemphasizing jurists from the "classical" period. This "great men" narrative of history concentrates on specific, orthodox jurists (particularly al-Shāfiʿī, d. 820; Arabia/Egypt). It is not uncommon for contemporary Islamic legal scholarship to mention some influential late antique jurists in passing.[26] Some recent scholarship has investigated specific jurists or networks of jurists who were active in late antiquity.[27] Still, overall, investigations of late antique Muslim jurists remain limited. This book attempts to begin the complicated process of re-inscribing late antique Muslim jurists and their legal practices in Islamic legal historiography. Fourth, the evolutionary narrative of Islamic law's "developing

law': rethinking the focus of modern scholarship." *Islam and Christian-Muslim Relations* 12:2 (April 2001): 143–52 at 143.

24 Chamberlain noted this phenomenon in a different context: "Where the sociological emphasis has been on the 'lack' of formal institutions and group structures, the historiographical problem has been to grapple with the 'scarcity' of original document collections." Chamberlain, *Knowledge and social practice*, 2.

25 Robert W. Gordon. "Introduction: J. Willard Hurst and the common law tradition in American legal historiography." *Law & Society Review* 10:1 (Autumn 1975): 9–55 at 20.

26 Some examples: Abou El Fadl notes, "there are many extinct schools such as the schools of Ibn Abī Laylā (d. 148/765), Sufyān al-Thawrī (d. 161/778), al-Ṭabarī (d. 310/923), al-Layth b. Saʿd (d. 175/791), al-Awzāʿī (d. 157/774), Abū Thawr (d. 240/854), Dāwūd b. Khalaf (the Zāhirī) (d. 270/884) and many more." Khaled Abou El Fadl, *And God knows the soldiers: the authoritative and authoritarian in Islamic discourses* (Lanham, MD: University Press of America, Inc., 2001), 27. Dutton mentions legal schools from "the *formative* period of Islamic law in the first to third centuries AH, such as those of al-Awzāʿī (d. 157/774), al-Layth ibn Saʿd (d. 175/791), Dāwūd al-Ẓāhirī (d. 270/884), and 'the two Sufyāns', i.e. Sufyān al-Thawrī (d. 161/778) and Sufyān ibn 'Uyayna (d. 198/813)" Ibn Anas, *Original Islam*, 2, emphasis added. See also Crone, *Roman*, 23–4.

27 See Mūsá, *Tārīkh al-fiqh*. See also Raif Georges Khoury. "Al-Layth Ibn Saʿd (94/713–175/791), grand maître et mécène de l'Egypte, vu à travers quelques documents islamiques anciens." *Journal of Near Eastern Studies* 40:3 (1981): 189–202. See also Muḥammad Rawwās Qalʿah'jī's edited series, *Silsilat mawsūʿat fiqh al-salaf*; Judd, *Religious scholars*.

complexity" often too simplistically parallels the growth or complexification of an Islamic empire (or, more broadly, state). By implying that the state is a primary causal agent in Islamic legal changes, scholars render law and the state as synonymous.[28] When law is defined narrowly as state law, legal pluralism is discounted. While I recognize the significant role of the state in shaping the legal profession and legitimating legal orthodoxy, I seek to balance these insights with awareness of how legal consumers, social conditions, and economic factors also affected law.

Against constructions of history as foreseeable or preordained, a genealogically oriented (rather than origins-oriented) historiography scrutinizes the historical paths not followed. A primary objective of genealogical historical inquiry is challenging assumptions about the inescapability (or evolutionary normalcy) of history by exploring the myriad contingencies of historical change. Genealogy rejects anthropomorphic characterizations of an object of historical inquiry (Islamic law's conception, parentage, development, and maturity) because these interpretations presume an inescapable, linear progression from conception to maturity.

Orthodox Stories

The ideas underlying the conventional periodization of "formative" and "classical" not only express developmental understandings of history, they also intersect with – and legitimate – orthodox narratives. Specifically, evolutionary historiography intersects with Islamic orthodoxy in conceptualizing historical changes as inevitable and correct. Thus, the emplotment of scholarly and orthodox legal histories overlap. What makes orthodox Islamic legal historiography problematic is not that "believers" ascribe to it; critiquing historiography based exclusively on the identity of those who composed it is illegitimate – as I discussed in Chapter 3. Instead, the limitations of orthodox legal historiographies parallel the limitations of evolutionary theories of history: they ignore contingency and legitimize the legal perspectives of historical victors. Orthodox law is legitimated by normativity and continuity – that is, by its habitual, ancient, presumably uninterrupted practice. Indeed, orthodox legal histories about Jewish law and Islamic law are emplotted in analogous ways and they legitimate orthodox positions by narrating continuity and preservation of tradition.[29]

[28] Rouland, *Legal anthropology*, 3 ("the ethnocentricism of Western law: the identification of law with the state").

[29] See Peter Brooks, *Reading for the plot: design and intention in narrative* (New York: A. A. Knopf, 1984).

Orthodox legal histories are not unique features of Islamic legal historiography because they reflect broader tendencies to narrate history through the eyes of triumphant groups. Orthodox groups obtain power through socio-political and economic contests with other groups. Those contests are components of regional dynamics. Thus, the contextual factors that enabled the orthodoxy of certain factions of Muslims also enabled the orthodoxy of certain factions of Jews in Islamicate society. I contend that some of what is perceived as "similar" in Jewish and Islamic jurisprudence is the result of orthodoxies coalescing in the same social space, the Islamicate world. To clarify the content of these emplotted stories, I will outline extremely abbreviated and over-simplified versions of the orthodox stories of Jewish law and Islamic law. These stories are not comprehensive or the subjects of any explicit consensus; however, they are prevalent in the discourse of orthodox Muslim and Jewish communities, as well as of Jewish studies and Islamic studies. It is important to emphasize that these stories fuse internal and external perspectives. In other words, the stories I will outline here are strategic reductions of orthodox narratives.[30]

The "story of Jewish law" is the story of orthodox rabbinic Judaism, so non-rabbinic Jewish sects (such as Qaraites) are effectively absent.[31] It typically begins with the rabbinic sages (the Tannaim and the Amora'im, 70 through 500 CE) who preserved and elaborated ancient Jewish legal traditions; their authority is generally unquestioned. The redaction of the Babylonian Talmud is assumed to have been completed by the early seventh century (by the Savora'im or Stammaim, 500–620 CE) and is conceptualized as the culmination of the rabbinic tradition. Orthodox elites perceive the Geonic period (620–1050 CE) as having preserved rabbinic-talmudic teachings. The medieval commentators, known as the Rishonim (1050–1400 CE), authored the definitive commentaries of rabbinic literature that remain canonical today. This somewhat standard periodization of Jewish law is based on classifying or grouping generations of rabbinic scholars as playing particular roles in Jewish legal authority. Each generation of rabbinic scholars legitimates itself by claiming that its legal output preserves orthodox customs.

The "story of Islamic law" is likewise the story of orthodox Sunnī Islam, so Shīʿī and other sectarian legal expressions are marginalized. The late antique period (roughly seventh and eighth centuries, roughly equivalent

30 I am invoking the idea of "strategic essentialism" as a component of subaltern historiography.

31 Qaraism is a Jewish sect that rejects oral rabbinic law. See Meira Polliack (ed.), *Karaite Judaism: a guide to its history and literary sources* (Leiden; Boston, MA: Brill, 2003).

to "formative") of Islamic law is categorized in terms of generations of authority: the Prophet, the Companions, and the Successors. The traditional story then identifies a period (roughly the ninth and tenth centuries) of authoritative legal scholars, with particular emphasis on the eponyms (or their most influential students) of the surviving Sunnī legal schools (Ḥanafī, Mālikī, Shāfiʿī, Ḥanbalī) as having laid the foundations for later legal practice. In the medieval period (roughly ninth to fourteenth centuries, equivalent to "classical"), it gradually became normative for Muslim jurists to be committed to a canonized jurisprudential methodology (*ijtihād fī al-madhhab* or *taqlīd*). As in the case of the Jewish law story, this story classifies every generation of jurists as playing a certain role in Islamic legal authority and each generation of jurists legitimates itself by claiming to preserve orthodox practices.

These reductive narratives are not comprehensive or completely representative. But multiple forms of these condensed stories of Jewish legal history and Islamic legal history do circulate. The significance of these stories is manifold. First, these stories are insular: they present law as entirely disconnected from socio-political contexts; legal systems are presumed to march along a linear continuum from "point a" to "point b" without any interference from non-legal conditions. Second, these stories are incomplete representations of legal systems: they fail to consider the substantive changes within legal literature, legal education, and legal professionalization. Third, these orthodox stories are ideologically one-sided: they voice the perspective of an orthodox elite, including its biases against groups it deems heretical. The theme of continuity in Jewish and Islamic legal historiography has significant socio-political ramifications. While most jurists – both Muslim and Jewish – in the late antique and medieval periods likely perceived themselves as continuing or maintaining legal traditions, gradual changes nevertheless occurred. If we understand orthodoxy as being the ideology of a particular class – in this context, traditional Muslim scholars, particularly those affiliated with the dominant political power – then this class narrates its own victory by declaring its practices as being the **same** as the practices of its predecessor classes.[32] Thus, there are two dilemmas for legal historians: the first is uncovering the changes that underlie juristic narratives of legal continuity in both Jewish and Islamic legal traditions; the second is accounting for continuity across generations of jurists without legitimating the orthodox narrative. A genealogy of Islamic legal orthodoxy has the potential to illuminate both how Islamic

[32] Benjamin, "Theses," 256.

legal heresy was constructed over time and how orthodox Islamic jurisprudence was differentiated from the diversity of Islamicate legal culture.[33]

Politics and Ideology: Scholarly Orthopraxy

Alongside equivalent sections in Chapters 1 and 3, this chapter's section on metaphors for historical theory revealed the evolutionary assumptions embedded in conventional scholarly narratives about Islamic law. In addition, the previous section on orthodox narratives of Islamic and Jewish legal histories examined some of the intersections and equivalences in evolutionary and orthodox narratives. These associations, I argue, are not random, but rather the outcome of similar methods. Both orthodox and scholarly practices fetishize orthopraxy. Just as "ritual practices transform knowledge into belief and membership into belonging,"[34] orthoprax methodologies transform much Islamic studies scholarship into orthodox scholarship and scholarly belonging. Orthoprax rituals emphasize "right practice" to reinforce orthodox beliefs; likewise, orthoprax scholarly methods emphasize positivist methodologies to reinforce orthodox scholarship.

The parallel between orthoprax rituals and orthoprax methods is one that needs emphasis. Positivist tendencies in Islamic studies present "scientific (i.e., disciplinary) rationality" as an antidote to the unscientific aspects of Islamic sources (as discussed in Chapter 1) or of Islamic legal identity (as discussed in Chapter 3). However, orthoprax methods are not neutral. Latour and Woolgar's investigation of "the way in which the daily activities of working scientists lead to the *construction* of scientific facts"[35] offers a useful framework for understanding subtle dynamics in scholarship that claims neutrality. Latour and Woolgar demonstrated that the methods of scientists shape their "factual" conclusions; I propose that the methods of Islamic studies scholars shape their substantive conclusions. In other words, as presented in Chapters 1 and 3, historical method and philosophy of history are interlinked. The positivist methods of orthoprax scholarship result in orthodox (or conventional) historiography. The conventional emphasis on rigor in form (i.e., proper diacritics, specific

[33] What I propose is a parallel implementation of Boyarin's observation that "the discourse we know of as orthodoxy and heresy provides at least one crucial site for the excavation of a genealogy of Judaism and Christianity." Boyarin, *Border lines*, 2.

[34] Douglas A. Marshall, "Behavior, belonging, and belief: a theory of ritual practice." *Sociological Theory* 20:3 (2002): 360–80 at 361.

[35] Bruno Latour and Steve Woolgar, *Laboratory life: the construction of scientific facts* (Princeton, NJ: Princeton University Press, 1986), 40, emphasis added.

citation practices, exact transliteration of Arabic, etc.) often sublimates rigor in content (i.e., conceptual framing). In general, the discipline of Islamic legal studies mistakes philology for historiography. Orthoprax methods – from perfecting transliterations to creating visual representations of every variant tradition-report's chain of transmission – do not result in the discovery of Islamic "origins," they construct those "origins." Debates about methodology are so contentious in Islamic studies precisely because they are entangled within orthodox beliefs.

Orthoprax scholarly methods contribute to the semblance of neutrality or objectivity; in turn, these orthoprax methods neglect the political and ideological dimensions of academic knowledge production. I am not arguing that all scholarship is political, but rather that we have an ethical obligation to recognize and to consider the political and ideological implications of scholarship. Presenting orthoprax scholarship as "correct" corresponds to orthodoxy's advocacy of "right" practice, which neglects that "right" practices were determined through a historical process in which orthodox groups (i.e., those with power) silenced or marginalized dissenting practices. Implementing orthopraxy in scholarship has the (perhaps unintended) consequence of being a political tool to silence dissenting views. Resisting orthoprax methods (as outlined in Chapters 1 and 3) is a form of heresy within the field. In other words, orthodox scholars perceive unorthodox scholarship as "incorrect." The method of details and "correctness" polices scholarly boundaries. In response, this book emphasizes scholarly tactics of resistance that challenge orthoprax scholarly strategies.[36]

Alternatives: Contingent Historical Moments

On the one hand, I have argued that the conventional scholarly macro-narrative of Islamic law is inappropriately evolutionary. On the other hand, I have argued that orthoprax scholarly methods of attending to details stifle macro-thinking. I want to turn now to presenting an alternative to both of these problems: a non-evolutionary, macro-narrative of Islamic legal history. A macro-historical narrative that explores broad processes of legal change is a form of resistance against the field's evolutionary theories of history and habitus of detailed orthopraxy. In proposing a chronological framework, I am sensitive to the necessity of balancing

[36] On strategies and tactics, see Michel de Certeau, *The practice of everyday life*, trans. by Steven Rendall (Berkeley, CA: University of California Press, 1984).

emphasis on contingency (instead of "evolutionary" process), with incremental changes, with continuity, and with rupture. The periodization I present is an evolving framework based on observable changes in legal literature, in the identity and training of jurists, in the role of the state, and in modes of legal reasoning. I acknowledge at least three risks to my periodization. First, demarcating blocks of time and labeling them can have historiographically limiting effects because it provokes debates about the classification labels and the cut-off dates that can be unproductive. (The above discussion of scholarly orthopraxy resonates here.) Second, I do not describe these periods either comprehensively or exhaustively because my objective is not substantiation with a surplus of historical evidence. The changes within and between periods are contingent upon a variety of social, economic, political, and legal factors that need further, critical elaboration; therefore, this periodization is provisional and intentionally imprecise. Third, although my genealogical approach defines these periods as historical moments (rather than evolutionary periods of development), some may still perceive "progress" because the very structure of periodization invokes evolutionary ideas of history that are linear and downplay contingency. Because "historical time is not linear and homogeneous but complex and multilayered,"[37] periodization is a limiting framework.

Moments in Islamic Legal History

Despite the limitations of periodization, it is necessary to counter conventional narratives. As Hayden White has noted, "every history, even the most 'synchronic' or 'structural' of them, will be emplotted in some way."[38] The conventional plot of Islamic legal history ascribes a tangible "origin" or "evolution." However, these misleading notions obfuscate that there are only shifts and transformations in Islamic legal traditions and systems within concrete and existing Muslim communities. Consequently, I advocate for alternatives to the internal periodization of "formative" and "classical" that is dominant in the field of Islamic studies. Islamic law's beginnings are more substantively delineated in an internal periodization that I use in this book: Legal circles and networks (*c.* 610–800 CE), Islamic legal beginnings; Professionalization of legal schools (*c.* 800–1000 CE);

[37] Helge Jordheim, "Against periodization: Koselleck's theory of multiple temporalities." *History and Theory* 51:2 (2012): 151–71 at 170.

[38] Hayden White, *Metahistory: the historical imagination in nineteenth-century Europe* (Baltimore, MD: Johns Hopkins University Press, 1975), 8.

Consolidation and formalization (*c.* 1000–1200 CE); Technocratization (*c.* 1200–1400 CE).[39] This schematization of Islamic legal history avoids the "evolutionary" notions underlying terms like "origins" and "formative" by emphasizing beginnings (rather than origins) and transformations (rather than maturity). In addition, this periodization integrates contingency by acknowledging aspects of Islamic law that did not continue from Islamic law's beginnings into the professionalization period. The periodization I present here is simplified intentionally for a general (rather than specialist) reader.

Legal Circles and Networks (c. *610–800* CE): *Islamic Legal Beginnings*

When the Prophet began his movement in Mecca, the region was already a medley of legal traditions with tribal, Sasanian, Byzantine, and customary practices shaping distinct areas of law (taxation, family, property, criminal, etc.). Islamic legal history begins with the Prophet Muḥammad's judgments over the first Muslim community in both Mecca (*c.* 610–622) and Medina (*c.* 622–632). Some of these laws were recorded in the Qur'ān; others were orally transmitted as tradition-reports; others were not preserved. To derive legal rulings, the Prophet's Companions and the first generation of Muslims after them (known as the Successors) relied on the Qur'ān, normative practices (*sunnah*), and their own personal opinions (*rā'y*) or interpretations of Islamic law; in generating Islamic law, they both innovated and followed legal precedents (of the Prophet, of Arabian customs, and of broader Near Eastern legal practices). The caliphs who were the Prophet's initial successors sent Qur'ān teachers to garrison towns where they not only taught the scripture, but also its legal implications. These caliphs were not merely political leaders because they promulgated laws and shaped normative legal practices. For example, Caliph ʿUmar standardized the text of the Qur'ān, which had far-reaching legal consequences. As was the case for the general transmission of knowledge in the region, legal education occurred primarily in study circles around particular scholars (Companions or Successors), who sometimes served as judges in local courts. Judges often relied upon independent judgment and customary arbitration principles in resolving disputes. Jurists with a reputation for piety or learning attracted larger circles of students.

[39] I began to elaborate this periodization in Lena Salaymeh, "Islamic law." In *The International Encyclopedia of Social and Behavioral Sciences*, ed. by James D. Wright (Oxford: Elsevier, 2015), 746–53. I will continue to modify this periodization in my future work.

With the Arab/Muslim conquests and the establishment of the Umayyad Empire (661–750 CE), Muslims created a burgeoning empire and integrated the region's diverse religious and ethnic communities – as well as some of their legal practices. While legal education initially took place in legal circles (local schools), they evolved into legal networks (both regional and personal schools, following a reputed jurist), and later consolidated into legal schools (*madhāhib*, groups of legal professionals following a particular jurisprudential method).[40] Legal circles were informal groups of students who sat around a teacher (in a circle) to memorize and to discuss wide-ranging Islamic legal and historical traditions; these local legal circles often met in mosques or private homes. Legal networks were larger, more formal groups of students who studied with a teacher to memorize and to discuss a limited set of legal and historical traditions. Meeting in mosques, homes, and informal academies, these networks comprised both students who were local to the teacher's community and those who traveled from afar in order to study with the teacher. Many of these teachers were also jurists who served the legal needs of their communities. Rather than there being one or a few influential jurists, there were numerous jurists involved in the transmission of legal knowledge – some of whom were recognized for their learning. These jurists reflected the geographic diversity of Islamic law.[41] Traditional Islamic sources identify seven jurists in Medina as having been influential: Abū Bakr ibn ʿAbd al-Raḥmān al-Makhzūmī (d. 712/13), Khārijah ibn Zayd ibn Thābit (d. 717–19), ʿUrwah ibn al-Zubayr (d. *c.* 715), Sulaymān ibn Yasār al-Ḥilālī (d. 718/19), ʿUbayd Allāh (d. 716/17), Saʿīd ibn al-Musayyab (d. 712/13), and al-Qāsim ibn Muḥammad (d. 728). Jurists outside Medina also gained fame; for example, famous jurists in Mecca included ʿAṭāʾ ibn Abī Rabāḥ (d. 723) and Mujāhid ibn Jabr (d. *c.* 720) and in Kūfah included Ibrāhīm al-Nakhaʿī and Ḥammād ibn Abī Sulaymān (d. 737).[42] The eponyms of three surviving legal schools were active in this era: Abū Ḥanīfah (d. 767; Kūfah, Iraq), Mālik ibn Ānas (d. 795; Medina), al-Shāfiʿī (d. 820; Egypt).

[40] I distinguish between legal circles (regional or local schools), legal networks (personal schools), and legal schools (doctrinal schools), but they can and did coexist. This classification is an adaptation of Hallaq's terminology: "During the second/eighth century, therefore, the term '*madhhab*' meant a group of students, legists, judges and jurists who had adopted the doctrine of a particular leading jurist." Hallaq, *Sharīʿa*, 63.

[41] Hallaq observed, "Each locale, from Syria to Iraq to the Hejaz, established its own legal practices on the basis of what was regarded as the sunna of the forefathers, be they the Companions or the Prophet, although the Prophet more often than not merely sanctioned the ancient Arabian sunan." *Ibid.*, 47.

[42] Hallaq, *The origins*, 65.

It is not entirely clear what it meant in the Umayyad era to be a specialist in law; however, few jurists had the luxury of dedicating themselves entirely to the pursuit of knowledge. While Umayyad judges often served additional administrative functions simultaneously or successively, Umayyad courts were institutionalized.[43] Umayyad judges could be tax collectors, police chiefs, preachers, military commanders, distributors of military stipends, and experts in customary law.[44] Despite the multiplicity of roles performed by Umayyad judges, the administrative functions of the courts were in some general way regulated by the Umayyad council of judges (*diwān al-quḍāh*). That Umayyad judges did not follow specific legal schools resulted in similar cases being decided differently; this situation provoked demands for the systematization of Islamic legal practice that eventually generated consolidated legal schools.[45] Umayyad appointment of judges played a role in the spread of certain legal networks that parallels ʿAbbāsid influences in the consolidation of legal schools. The first "centralized" chief judge was the Ḥanafī jurist Abū Yūsuf (d. 798) in Baghdād under the Caliph Hārūn al-Rashīd (r. 786–809).[46] There is inconclusive evidence about which caliph formalized courts of equity (i.e., *maẓālim*), with some attributions to the Umayyad caliph ʿAbd al-Malik ibn Marwān (r. 685–705) and others to the ʿAbbāsid caliphs al-Mahdī (r. 775–785) or al-Hādī (r. 785–786).[47]

As is the case for many other legal traditions, there was a spectrum of Muslim juristic approaches, with one end comprising rationalists (*ahl al-rāʾy*, primarily in Iraq) and the other end consisting of traditionists (*ahl al-ḥadīth*, primarily in Ḥijāz). Rationalists anchored jurisprudence in logical thinking, whereas traditionists anchored jurisprudence in sacred, textual sources.[48] Muslim jurists of this period cannot easily be

[43] See the discussion of non-judicial functions of Umayyad and early ʿAbbāsid judges in Irit Bligh-Abramski. "The judiciary (qāḍīs) as a governmental-administrative tool in early Islam." *Journal of the Economic and Social History of the Orient* 35:1 (1992): 40–71 at 43–9. "The earliest qāḍīs not only resolved disputes but also performed non-judicial functions, serving as governors, tax collectors, military commanders, leaders of prayer, and supervisors of the Public Treasury and the land tax." Muhammad Khalid Masud, Rudolph Peters, and David Stephan Powers, "Qāḍīs and their courts: an historical survey." In *Dispensing justice in Islam: qadis and their judgements*, ed. by Muhammad Khalid Masud, Rudolph Peters, and David Stephan Powers, Studies in Islamic law and society, 22 (Leiden; Boston, MA: Brill, 2006), 1–44 at 9.

[44] Bligh-Abramski, "The judiciary," 49.

[45] Muḥammad Muṣṭafá Zuḥaylī, *Tārīkh al-qaḍāʾ fī al-islām* (Damascus; Beirut: Dār al-Fikr, 1995), 215.

[46] Masud, Peters, and Powers, "Qāḍīs and their courts," 12.

[47] Mathieu Tillier, "Qāḍīs and the political use of the maẓālim jurisdiction under the ʿAbbāsids." In *Public Violence in Islamic Societies*, ed. by Christian Lange and Maribel Fierro (Edinburgh University Press, 2009), 42–66.

[48] Hallaq, *Sharīʿa*, 55–60.

categorized as belonging to one camp or the other because most jurists likely combined approaches, by both relying on textual authorities and engaging in logical reasoning in formulating legal opinions. Shīʿī sectarianism led to the development of another approach, based on the legal authority of Caliph/Imām ʿAlī and his Imāmī successors. The largest Shīʿī legal school was the Imāmī one – sometimes identified as the Jaʿfarī school, after the fifth and sixth Imāms who lived in the late seventh through mid-eighth centuries; it was initially strongest in Medina and Kūfah.

A genre of Islamic legal literature specifically dedicated to juristic disagreement (*ikhtilāf*) appears to have begun in the mid-eighth century. Abu Ḥanifah (d. 767) wrote a text dedicated to disagreements between the Companions; his student, Abu Yusuf (d. 798), wrote a text about disagreements between Abu Ḥanifah and Ibn Abi Layla. al-Shāfiʿī wrote about disagreements between Abu Ḥanifah and al-Awzāʿī (d. 774) and recorded his own disagreements with Mālik (d. 795). Why is there no mention of (*ikhtilāf*) texts prior to the mid-eighth century, meaning for the first century of Islamic history? It likely only became necessary to record differences of opinion when jurists sought to impose their laws beyond their local communities. In other words, certain jurists sought to overrule other jurists by identifying legitimate jurisprudential methodology and opinions. The genre of (*ikhtilāf*) may have been intended to limit legal pluralism.

Professionalization of Legal Schools (c. *800–1000* CE)

After the ʿAbbāsids (r. 750–1258) established (in 762 CE) Baghdad as the political-intellectual capital of the Islamic empire, Islamic law gradually became more centralized. Jurists shifted from associating with legal circles or networks to identifying with professional legal schools (*madhāhib*). Parallel to the ʿAbbāsid empire's development of an increasingly more widespread and professionalized bureaucratic system, Muslim jurists became professionalized – as evidenced in their literature, education, and organizational structures. Islamic legal literature initially integrated historical narratives and recorded legal judgments, but Muslim scholars gradually intensified the distinctions in genres (such as historiography, Qurʾānic exegesis, *ḥadīth* studies, and law) as the juristic profession became more specialized. Muslim jurists debated the role of oral law (the orally transmitted traditions about the legal practices of the earliest generations of Muslims) in Islamic jurisprudence; challenges to the authority of oral reports led to the increasing importance of recorded (written) *ḥadīth*. The broad synthesis of rationalist and traditionist approaches to jurisprudence took place in this period.

Islamic legal education became more professionalized. Islamic law was initially taught in mosques and in private homes, but the demands of students and scholars traveling in search of knowledge led to the establishment of hostels and the organization of more dedicated spaces of learning. The college of legal studies (*madrasah*) gradually emerged in Iran and Iraq to provide spaces for instruction and libraries, in addition to housing for professors and students. But these buildings served additional communal functions, as they often included tombs or public fountains. Law students studied with many scholars in many places, not being limited to one legal school; in turn, their travels resulted in the diffusion of legal ideas to new areas. Beginning in the tenth century, legal education became increasingly formalized as professional law colleges (*madāris*) were established with the financial support of endowments. Colleges were often endowed with permanent sources of income, such as land or rent-bearing urban property, set aside in perpetuity. These endowed trusts (*awqāf*) funded faculty salaries, student stipends, clerical staff, administrative staff, and maintenance staff (janitors, gatekeepers, etc.).

Over the course of the first four centuries of Islam, hundreds of legal circles and networks emerged and disappeared. The legal reasoning and doctrines of these now extinct legal circles and networks are difficult to reconstruct from the available historical sources. They were superseded incrementally by legal schools, for which we have more historical evidence – particularly those that survive. Among the extinct legal schools, some scholarly attention has been focused on the schools of three jurists: al-Awzāʿī (d. 773; Syria), al-Ẓāhirī (d. 883; Iraq), and al-Ṭabarī (d. 922; Iraq). The ʿAbbāsid state's demand for professional jurists and sectarian resistance encouraged the consolidation of Islamic legal schools from hundreds to several. Aḥmad ibn Ḥanbal (d. 855; Baghdad, Iraq), the eponym for one of the surviving orthodox legal schools, was active in this era. Each school became known for a particular characteristic: Ḥanafīs for their reliance on personal opinion, analogical reasoning (*qiyās*), and juristic preference (*istiḥsān*); Mālikīs for their prioritization of Medinan practice (*ʿamal*) and consensus (*ijmāʿ*); Shāfiʿīs for their synthesis of rationalist and traditionist methodologies; Ḥanbalīs for their avoidance of reasoning in favor of textual sources. Still, it would be a mistake to reduce the complexity of these legal schools to these common motifs or to assume that these jurists and their students represent all Islamic legal activity of this period. It was not until the beginning of the tenth century, at the earliest, that these legal schools became identified clearly, especially in terms of a particular jurisprudential methodology.[49] The influences of popular support on the consolidation of legal schools are particularly difficult to determine.

Coinciding with the rise of formal institutions of learning and the consolidation of the schools of law was an increase in the importance of the jurisconsult (*muftī*) – a jurist qualified to formulate Islamic legal opinions. A legal decree consisted of both the question sent in writing to the jurisconsult and his answer. In addition, judges often consulted with jurisconsults for their expertise in complicated cases, as evidenced by the inclusion of a jurisconsult's legal decree within the court register. The earliest surviving collections of a jurisconsult's decrees (plural, *fatāwá;* singular, *fatwá*) date to the tenth century. The general public consulted a jurisconsult in ways similar to how we now consult attorneys for legal advice; some individuals "shopped" for a legal decree (*fatwá*), asking several jurisconsults until they obtained a desired outcome.

The ʿAbbāsids centralized and bureaucratized courts by creating a more hierarchical administrative structure.[50] The appointment of judges is an example of this centralizing process, since under the ʿAbbāsids provincial judges were appointed increasingly by caliphs (or by the chief judge or the minister) rather than provincial governors.[51] The ʿAbbāsids made being a judge more lucrative, as reflected in the doubling of judicial salaries soon after the establishment of the empire.[52] One reason for the elaboration of a specialized legal-administrative system was the simple increase in the number of consumers of ʿAbbāsid government services; the ʿAbbāsid empire created more administrative positions to fill those needs. ʿAbbāsid appointments of Ḥanafī judges influenced the distribution and expansion of that legal school.[53] But that process of state endorsement of a legal school did not begin with the ʿAbbāsids, since the Umayyads similarly promoted particular legal networks. As under pre-Islamic rule, market inspectors acted on behalf of the state to ensure fair dealings in

49 Hallaq, *Sharīʿa*, 60–71.

50 On ʿAbbāsid courts, see Mathieu Tillier, *Les cadis d'Iraq et l'état abbasside, 132/750–334/945* (Damascus; Lebanon: IFPO, 2009).

51 Bligh-Abramski, "The judiciary," 49, 57.

52 "Two decades into ʿAbbāsid rule, change started to show with the salaries more than/almost doubling to 30 dinārs." al-Qāḍī, "The salaries of judges in early Islam," 28.

53 Tsafrir notes, "one of the conclusions emerging from this evidence is that the ʿAbbasids contributed considerably to the spread of the Hanafi school. This was pronounced, among other things, in their appointment of Hanafi qadis." Nurit Tsafrir, *The history of an Islamic school of law: the early spread of Hanafism*, Harvard Series in Islamic Law, 3 (Cambridge, MA: Islamic Legal Studies Program, Harvard Law School, 2004), xv.

the marketplace, which evolved into enforcing proper moral behavior. Reflecting the professionalization of legal knowledge, jurists produced a genre of legal literature (*ḥisbah*) that delineated the duties and limitations of a market inspector.

Consolidation and Formalization (c. *1000–1200 CE*)

Professionalization of jurists and institutionalization of learning contributed to the growing dominance of an Islamic legal orthodoxy. Diversity of opinions on a variety of legal and theological matters gradually became narrower and, after the tenth century, a legal canon becomes discernible. As previously noted, prior to the eleventh century, the majority of Muslim jurists identified with one of the many legal circles or networks that no longer survive. But, by the eleventh century, the majority of Muslim jurists appear to have identified with one of the still extant Sunnī legal schools (Ḥanafī, Shāfiʿī, Ḥanbalī, or Mālikī). Legal schools succeeded or failed based on popular support, the socio-political influence of the school's jurists, and the compatibility between local, customary practices and the school's legal opinions. A legal orthodoxy emerged through the consolidation of the main legal schools and the gradual marginalization of peripheral or minority legal schools. The four surviving Sunnī legal schools grew in terms of number, power, and influence for a variety of both internal (i.e., legal education, popular appeal) and external (i.e., state support) reasons. For example, in eleventh- and twelfth-century Nishapur, Ḥanafīs and Shāfiʿīs struggled for local political power over the judiciary, academies, and charitable endowments; these struggles affected the influence of each legal school in the region. Yet, an individual Muslim's identification with a legal school did not necessarily indicate a commitment to the legal school's jurisprudence; the common people were loyal to local leaders and not necessarily to the abstract principles of the legal school.

Within this consolidation process, identification with a particular legal school was not necessarily exclusive. Law students studied with scholars outside their own legal school – particularly transmission of tradition-reports – and freely switched legal school affiliation. Since caliphs appointed a chief judge who, in turn, oversaw the appointment of judges throughout the empire, jurists increasingly tended to associate with the larger, state-endorsed legal schools. Some jurists shifted their legal school affiliation in order to procure administrative or judicial appointments. Indeed, as legal education became more systematized and salaries of judges increased, the legal profession most likely attracted students drawn to the pragmatic – rather than spiritual or intellectual – aspects of the vocation of law. In terms of producing the most influential jurisprudential texts, the most important jurists were unaffiliated with the state.

The formalization and professionalization of the legal schools are reflected in changing genres of legal literature. Whereas previously legal texts tended to compile the opinions of a single jurist, in later periods, the legal opinions of groups of jurists who belonged to the same legal school were compiled. Then, Muslim jurists wrote commentaries on canonized or codified legal texts of groups of predecessor jurists (who had been identified as authoritative) and created condensed legal manuals (*mukhtaṣarāt*). These legal manuals abbreviated earlier legal texts to offer straightforward legal answers based on each school's most authoritative or widely accepted legal opinions; these abridgments became the main texts of study for students and became increasingly prevalent after the eleventh century. By selectively choosing which legal opinions would be considered authoritative, these compendia created an official resource for later jurists to perpetuate and to disseminate the rulings and the methodology of their school. Another genre of legal literature that intensified in this period is texts on the etiquette of judging (*adab al-qāḍī*). Based on earlier court practices, these texts outlined the duties and proper behavior of a judge and general court procedures, thereby further formalizing the legal profession.

Jurist-professors designed the curriculum of law schools, which varied according to local practice and the legal school affiliation. In previous centuries, jurists typically had earned their living through trade or craft work, but with the institutionalization of education in the form of endowed colleges, scholars became professionals, administrators, and salaried employees. Through state patronage, salaries and the administration of endowments, scholars became a professional class. Islamic legal education was basically informal, flexible, and built on individual teacher and student relationships, rather than institutional ties; students did not earn grades or receive degrees. Learning revolved around the reputation of a respected scholar, who in his individual capacity could give students a specific license to teach, to transmit *ḥadīth*, to judge, or to participate in scholarly debates – depending on the course of study. In addition to law, many colleges taught Qur'ān, *ḥadīth*, Arabic grammar, theology, Sufism, medicine, and philosophy. These colleges consolidated informal legal instruction into an official institution with a physical center and permanently endowed funds, thereby facilitating professional full-time study of Islamic law and the expanded training of cadres of Islamic law teachers and administrators.

Still, a typical student "heard" (i.e., listened to and memorized oral lectures) his subjects from a variety of teachers on a variety of topics in a variety of places. Education occurred beyond colleges and the function of colleges extended beyond education (into propaganda and political action). In addition to endowed colleges, the transmission of knowledge took place in informal study circles (*ḥalaqāt*; s. *ḥalqah*), in public mosques, and in private homes; students could come to a college without being a resident or receiving a stipend. College professors, Qur'ān and *ḥadīth* reciters, and story-tellers all had audiences with the general public. Both formal colleges and informal learning circles encouraged the consolidation of the surviving legal schools by training students to propagate further the law school's methodology. Niẓām al-Mulk (d. 1092), a Seljuq minister, made it the state's policy to support Islamic educational institutions and endowed both Ḥanafī and Shāfiʿī colleges in all of the empire's major cities.

Technocratization (c. 1200–1400 CE)

By the thirteenth century, Muslim jurists were increasingly becoming technocrats, meaning that they were skilled in knowing the doctrinal rulings of a particular school – rather than applying the Islamic jurisprudential methodology of a particular school.[54] While the colleges were initially dedicated to only one legal school, the Mustanṣiriyyah college (founded in Baghdad in 1233) was devoted to several legal schools. In this era, Muslim jurists composed more abridged versions of canonical legal commentaries and the locus of jurisprudential activity was shifting away from the Iraqi sphere of influence (both geographically and intellectually). This was likely a result of the Mongol destruction of Baghdad (capital of the ʿAbbāsid Caliphate) and its libraries in 1258. The city's role as an intellectual center gradually ended as regional centers of intellectual production arose to replace it. In provincial centers of legal activity, legal manuals and their commentaries were produced; in particular, the type of abridged Islamic legal text – sometimes identified as a "common law *mukhtaṣar*" – became prevalent.[55]

The Mamluk Sultanate (r. 1250–1517) of Egypt appointed a chief judge for each of the four main Sunnī legal schools, solidifying the position of the largest schools and confirming the demise of the once numerous

[54] I do not use the term technocrat pejoratively.

[55] Mohammad Fadel, "The social logic of *taqlīd* and the rise of the *mukhtaṣar*." *Islamic Law and Society* 3:2 (1996): 193–233.

smaller schools. A potential consequence of these juristic appointments was that the Mamluk Sultan used these four legal options to his advantage, by selectively seeking legal decrees from the legal school most likely to meet his needs. Some of the daily operations of Mamluk courts are preserved in fourteenth-century court documents archived in Jerusalem's Islamic museum. While generally jurisconsults were not affiliated with or regulated by the state, the Mamluks did appoint some jurisconsults to courts of equity. In the eleventh century, jurists had defined a jurisconsult as being a *mujtahid* (i.e., one who has the ability to independently reason; the highest rank of a jurist). By the middle of the thirteenth century, however, it appears that the prerequisites were lowered and a jurisconsult was expected – by most, but not all scholars – to be a *muqallid* (i.e. able to articulate a legal opinion based on the precedents and methodology of a particular legal school; a lower rank than *mujtahid*). This reflects a far-reaching phenomenon as many (though not all) Muslim jurists preferred to follow the legal opinions of their predecessors in orthodox legal schools (*taqlīd*), rather than developing legal opinions based on the jurisprudential methodology of an orthodox legal school (*ijtihād fi al-madhhab*).

Moments in Islamicate Legal History

The periodization of Islamic legal history presented above attempts to counter the evolutionary tendencies of conventional scholarly narratives. What about the orthodox narratives of Jewish law and Islamic law? As I demonstrated, these orthodox stories are parallel in their basic structure. Thus, to challenge these orthodox stories, we need a periodization that accounts for why they seem so similar. As noted, these orthodox stories resemble each other because they took shape in the same socio-historical space. Islamicate legal history challenges the inevitability of orthodox narratives by demonstrating that some of the same processes occurred in both Islamic and eastern Jewish legal traditions, which defies the hermetic assumptions of orthodoxy. Islamicate should be understood as a component of global history.

The periods delineated below are intentionally rough and I recognize that there are aspects of Islamic and Jewish legal history that do not neatly correspond. (An obvious distinction, for example, is Islamic law's integration in various states and Jewish law's independence from states.) Despite exceptions to the parallelisms I outline here, an Islamicate-based periodization is necessary to account for how and why legal literature and legal reasoning in these two traditions parallel each other. An Islamicate periodization is also necessary to challenge the evolutionary and orthodox master narratives in Islamic legal studies. The "periods" of Islamicate legal history that I identify are historical moments in which certain jurisprudential modes became dominant. Not intended to be exhaustive or comprehensive, this periodization broadly indicates why and how Islamic and Jewish legal orthodoxies began to dominate in the Islamicate world at roughly the same time. I expect that there are parallels in Byzantine legal history, but exploring them is beyond the scope of this periodization.

Diffusion and diversity (c. *610–800* CE)

During this transformative period, legal education occurred primarily in study circles around particular jurists, who sometimes served as judges in local courts. In addition, private jurists in academies organized legal education.[56] While the Roman law school in Beirut had been destroyed by an earthquake in the mid-sixth century, legal education took place in rabbinic academies (probably including in Medina) and other forums.[57] Jewish and Islamic legal literature integrated narrative and legal content, which jurists gradually differentiated as their profession became more specialized.[58] After the ʿAbbāsid empire was established, Iraqi schools of legal thought began a gradual rise to dominance in both Jewish and Islamic legal systems.[59] Debates about the role of oral law (or juristic customs) occurred in both Jewish and Muslim communities. For instance, during this period, Qaraites presented their opposition to rabbinic oral law.[60] Indeed, the redaction of the Babylonian Talmud may be understood as a response to Qaraite opposition by elevating the legal significance of the Mishnah (as embodying the oral Torah) to be on par with

[56] The transformation of study circles or networks into academies was a regional process evident among both Muslims and Jews. On the apprenticeship or study circle model of rabbinic legal education prior to the Islamic period, see David M. Goodblatt, *Rabbinic instruction in Sasanian Babylonia* (Leiden: Brill, 1975). For a similar narrative history of Islamic legal instruction, see Hallaq, *The origins*, 57–78.

[57] On the Beirut law school, see Kathleen McNamee. "Another chapter in the history of scholia." *The Classical Quarterly* 48:1 (1998): 269–88.

[58] See Barry S. Wimpfheimer, *Narrating the law: a poetics of talmudic legal stories* (Philadelphia, PA: University of Pennsylvania Press, 2011).

[59] This move soon resulted in a shift of authority as Iraq-based jurisprudence gradually gained ascendancy. See Shelomo Dov Goitein, "The interplay of Jewish and Islamic laws." In *Jewish law in legal history and the modern world*, ed. by Bernard S. Jackson, The Jewish law annual. Supplement 2 (Leiden: Brill, 1980), 61–77 at 62. See also Robert Brody, *The geonim of Babylonia and the shaping of medieval Jewish culture* (New Haven, CT: Yale University Press, 1998), 116.

[60] I reject the linear, evolutionary assumption underlying use of the term proto-Qaraite. See Fred Astren, *Karaite Judaism and historical understanding* (Columbia, SC: University of South Carolina Press, 2004).

the (written) Torah.[61] This parallels a similar debate and process occurring in Muslim circles about the significance of "oral law," which manifests itself in the increasing importance of (recorded/written) tradition-reports in Islamic legal literature.[62] Traditionalism (i.e., the emphasis on textual traditions) in Islamic jurisprudence gradually gained significance and this likely reflects a broader process of textual materiality that influenced Jewish jurisprudence. Generally, legal practice was both diffuse and diverse, largely based on customary practice and on the legal conventions of antecedent jurists.

Synthesis and systematization (c. 800–1000 CE)

Jurists – both rabbinic and Muslim – in this period synthesized legal education and legal literature.[63] Among both Muslim and Jewish jurists, a clear separation between literary and legal materials became prevalent as they further organized the pragmatic legal rulings of previous generations. Jurists systematized the transmitted legal opinions of predecessor jurists in texts that would be identified later as canonical. Among Muslim jurists, a transition from legal networks to legal schools occurred as part of a broader synthesis of Islamic legal reasoning.[64] Consolidation of Islamic legal schools occurred in reaction to/against sectarian resistance. Similarly, rabbinic jurists articulated their interpretations of Jewish law in reaction to or against Qaraite and other sectarian challenges. Jewish and Muslim jurists based in Iraq became stronger centers of legal authority by the beginning of the ninth century, if not earlier.[65] Babylonian rabbinic

[61] While I do not want to delve into the complicated issue of historically dating the redaction of the Babylonian Talmud, I suspect that sectarian conflict played a role in the elevation of the text's importance. Moreover, the parallel debates and shifts from oral to written legal authority among Muslims and Jews are unlikely to be merely coincidental.

[62] For instance, Muslim juristic circles debated the authority of Companion or Successor jurists. See Mohammad Hashim Kamali, *Principles of Islamic jurisprudence*, rev. edn. (Cambridge: Islamic Texts Society, 1991), 313–22 (discussing the legal opinions of Companions).

[63] Codification is only one form of systematization; codification began prior to this period. For example, "Two important codificatory works were written in the early part of the geonic period, around the mid-eighth century: the She'iltot and Halakhot Peṣuḳot." Gideon Libson, "Halakhah and law in the period of the Geonim." In *An introduction to the history and sources of Jewish law*, ed. by Neil S. Hecht *et al.* (Oxford; New York: Clarendon Press; Oxford University Press, 1996), 197–250 at 204.

[64] Hallaq observes, "The intellectual and legal history of Islam between 150 and 350 H (c. 770 and 960 AD) represents a dynamic competition among several forces that crystallized in the opposing movements of traditionalism and rationalism, movements out of which emerged the Great Synthesis." Hallaq, *Sharīʿa*, 57.

[65] See Bernards and Nawas, "The geographic distribution of Muslim jurists during the first four centuries AH," 174. See also Brody, *The geonim of Babylonia*, 36.

Judaism became increasingly authoritative and dominant, as reflected in treatises and commentaries of individual Geonic rabbis.[66] The power of particular law schools (or academies) became entrenched and nominally linked to state power as legal education became focused on emerging legal canons.

Legal structure (c. *1000–1200 CE*)

This moment consisted of further systemization of both rabbinic and Islamic legal literature.[67] Structured jurisprudential frameworks were widespread in the Islamicate world; this is why the writings of the rabbinic jurist and philosopher Maimonides (d. 1204) adapted the structure prevailing in contemporaneous Islamic legal texts.[68] Generally, in this period, rabbinic and Muslim jurists wrote commentaries on canonized or codified legal texts of predecessor jurists (who had been identified as authoritative) and created condensed legal manuals. An example is the *Hilkhot ha-Rif* (by Isaac ben Jacob Alfasi ha-Cohen, d. 1103), which presents practical legal decisions in an abridged form – following the order of the Talmud but presenting only the conclusions or definitive opinions (as determined by Rabbi Alfasi). This resembles the Islamic *mukhtaṣar* genre of abridged legal manuals; these abridgments became the main texts of study for students.[69] The technical literature of both legal traditions in this period indicates abbreviation. An increasing number of Muslim jurists

[66] These include *Halakhot Pesuqot* by Yehudai Gaon, *She'iltot* by Achai Gaon, and *Halakhot Gedolot* by Simeon Qayyara. (Zvi Septimus has pointed out to me that Rashi cited or relied on these texts rather than Geonic responsa.) Libson noted that "Rav Saadya's [d. 942; Iraq] major innovation was the composition of halakhic monographs." Libson, "Halakhah and law," 231.

[67] A canonization process has been identified for this period: "the tenth through the thirteenth centuries of the common era, which witnessed also the acme of Jewish-Islamic symbiosis. It was the time when everything we regard as Judaism: Jewish law and ritual, the text of the Hebrew Bible and the synagogue service, Jewish thought and ethics, were put into their final shape and received authoritative status." Goitein, "The interplay of Jewish and Islamic laws," 62.

[68] See Sarah Stroumsa, *Maimonides in his world: portrait of a Mediterranean thinker* (Princeton, NJ: Princeton University Press, 2009); Michael Schwarz, "Al-Fiqh, a term borrowed from Islam used by Maimonides for a Jewish concept in his Sefer haMizwoth and in the Guide of the Perplexed." In *Adaptations and innovations: studies on the interaction between Jewish and Islamic thought and literature from the early Middle Ages to the late twentieth century*, ed. by Joel L. Kraemer, Y. Tzvi Langermann, and Jossi Stern, Collection de la Revue des études juives, 44 (Paris; Dudley, MA: Peeters, 2007).

[69] The Rif removed all *haggadic* materials and kept only *halakhic* passages. Similarly, *mukhtaṣar* texts abbreviate earlier legal texts to offer straightforward legal answers. Hallaq explains that "abridgments (*mukhtasars*) were generally preferred after the fifth/eleventh century when they became abundant. Some of these abridgments were specifically produced by professors for teaching purposes, their intent being to sum up *fiqh* doctrine by invoking legal principles and alluding to 'cases' that supported these principles." Hallaq, *Sharīʿa*, 138.

were employed by the state in this period and this likely further bureaucratized the legal profession.[70]

Legal autonomy (c. 1200–1400 CE)
By the thirteenth century, Muslim and Jewish jurists were creating abridged versions of canonical legal commentaries and the locus of jurisprudential activity was shifting away from the Iraqi sphere of influence (both geographically and intellectually). Provincial centers of legal activity emerged after the Mongol invasion of Baghdad (in 1258). Legal manuals and their commentaries were produced. By way of example, the legal compilation of Mordechai ben Hillel (d. 1298) corresponds to a type of abridged Islamic legal text known as "common law *mukhtaṣars*."[71] By this period, a type of process theory had gained ascendancy as jurists identified their role in legal-algorithmic terms.[72]

In the late antique and medieval Islamicate world, Jews and Muslims practiced, modified, and transformed legal pluralism. They perceived their own legal systems as continuing earlier practices and only slightly modifying those practices when necessary. They did not do so in isolated spaces, disconnected from their predecessors or neighbors – of any religious, ethnic, or political grouping.

Implications and Applications

This chapter built upon the critical explorations of "origins" in previous chapters in order to illustrate how metaphors of maturity signify a unilinear theory of history. In turn, this linearity serves to reify the notion of "classical Islamic law." Similarly, orthodox stories present linear narratives that validate "orthodox law." Against these tendencies, this chapter posits that "Islamic legal orthodoxy" shaped the everyday practice of law, legal education, and the organization of the legal profession. This orthodoxy

[70] Hallaq clarifies that "By the end of the eleventh century, a substantial segment of the legal elite was in the pay of government. With the incorporation of the professors into the madrasa system, the political domain encroached further into the terrain of the law, subordinating a considerable segment – even the elite – of the professorial profession and contributing to the increasing diminution of the 'moral community' of the legists." Hallaq, *An introduction*, 53.

[71] I use the term "common law *mukhtaṣar*" as defined by Fadel, "The social logic." An example of a Mālikī *mukhtaṣar* is that of Khalīl b. Isḥāq al-Jundī (d. 1365).

[72] By process theory, I mean a structured procedure for generating or identifying legal opinions that seeks to minimize differences. For a modern example, see Henry Melvin Hart and Albert M. Sacks, *The legal process: basic problems in the making and application of law*, ed. by William N. Eskridge and Philip P. Frickey (Westbury, NY: Foundation Press, 1994).

was not a natural or inevitable occurrence, but rather the result of a socio-political struggle for power. The situated construction of orthodoxy is reflected in the parallel construction of Jewish legal orthodoxy. Hence, I argue that both Jewish and Islamic legal systems formulated a legal orthodoxy during roughly the same period, in roughly the same space, and the same socio-political context – an Islamicate context. Thus, this chapter offered two loose periodizations, of Islamic and of Islamicate legal changes, as scaffolds for understanding the transformations of law in the region.

The next chapter refers to both my Islamic and my Islamicate periodizations in order to clarify how an orthodox perspective on wife-initiated divorce came to dominate. The next chapter also intentionally offers a macro-narrative of wife-initiated divorce by blending legal opinions and practices into an accessible narrative. To do so, I have placed textual discussions and citations in the footnotes in order to provide the reader with an opportunity to experience a macro-narrative flow.

CHAPTER 6

Legal Comparisons – a Case Study in Family Law

Chapter 5 suggested broad-scale periodizations of legal history to replace evolutionary and orthodox storylines. This chapter demonstrates that reexamining conventional periodizations can clarify parallel changes in divorce practices among Jews and Muslims in the Near East.[1] I tell a story about the laws surrounding wife-initiated (and acquired) divorce in Jewish and Islamic legal systems in the late antique and medieval eras.[2] In doing so, I contest "orthodox" stories that claim a woman's minimal agency in divorce as essential both to Jewish and to Muslim communities.[3] This chapter uses documentary and literary-legal sources to present evidence of both Jewish and Muslim women divorcing their husbands in late antiquity (roughly, 250–800 CE). I offer some provisional explanations for why women's divorce options became more limited in the medieval period (roughly, 800–1450 CE). I argue that changes in women's divorce options

[1] For reading and commenting on versions of this chapter, I thank Daniel Boyarin, Charlotte Fonrobert, Rhiannon Graybill, Wael Hallaq, Ira Lapidus, Maria Mavroudi, Laurent Mayali, William Ian Miller, and Zvi Septimus. I would also like to thank Menachem Butler, the indefatigable Jewish studies bibliographer, for sending me numerous articles used throughout this chapter. Errors are mine alone. Translations from original sources are my own, unless otherwise indicated; translated texts have been cited whenever possible.

[2] I narrate this story in two voices: the text of this chapter for the general reader and most (though not all) of the footnotes for the specialist reader. For more extensive citations to sources, see the previous version of this chapter, Lena Salaymeh. "Every law tells a story: orthodox divorce in Jewish and Islamic legal histories." *UC Irvine Law Review* 4:1 (2014): 19–63.

[3] The reader may wonder what motivates this particular focus on Jewish and Islamic legal systems, or why Christian legal systems are not represented in this study. This research was built around a specific point of intersection between these two legal systems, which is explored in the Disenchanting the Orthodox Narratives section of this chapter.

are manifestations of multidimensional historical processes that illustrate law's profoundly contingent contexts. Divorce in Jewish and Islamic legal systems underwent parallel transformations between the late antique (roughly, 250–800 CE) and medieval (roughly, 800–1400 CE) periods as the result of common socio-political and jurisprudential dynamics.[4] This chapter combines historicism and thick descriptions of law to tell a story about legal heterodoxy and the growing dominance of legal orthodoxy.

As discussed in the previous chapter, legal communities create orthodox narratives about their legal systems. Orthodox Jewish and Muslim jurists construct ahistorical narratives that legitimate their own authority; both historical actors and contemporary scholars espouse these narratives. By placing Jewish and Islamic legal systems into historical conversation with each other, this chapter demonstrates that orthodoxy is historically situated. This case study indicates that comparative legal history – as implemented in this chapter – illuminates dynamics of legal change that would otherwise remain unnoticed. Studying a legal system in isolation from its context, which includes contiguous legal systems, obscures expansive and long-term changes. By plotting parallel changes over time in divorce practices among Jews and Muslims in the Islamicate world, this chapter demonstrates that legal orthodoxy is not timeless or uniform. Jewish and Islamic divorce laws tell stories that are sporadic, unpredictable, and barely audible under the faux euphony of orthodoxy.

Defining Wife-initiated Divorce

It is widely presumed that men have unlimited access and women have restricted access to initiate divorce in both Jewish and Islamic law.[5] This presumption, however, simplifies a complicated historical process – only part of which I will briefly explore here – in which a woman's access to divorce changed over time. I will focus primarily on jurisprudential texts and only secondarily on how these jurisprudential ideas were implemented because the surviving documentary sources make it difficult to reconstruct what kind of access to divorce women – both Muslim and

[4] While the medieval era extends beyond 1400 CE, this chapter will not present material beyond this date.

[5] I will not fully discuss the rabbinic limitations placed on a husband's ability to divorce because it is beyond the scope of my analysis. But see *Mishnah*, Gīṭṭīn 9:10 (debate between Shammai and Hillel about a husband's legitimate grounds for divorcing his wife – adultery or any reason). See also *B. Talmud*, Gīṭṭīn 90a. Generally, Islamic law does not restrict a husband's ability to divorce his wife, except by limiting the number of times a husband can divorce the same wife after remarriage.

Jewish – actually had in the late antique and medieval periods. In what follows, I will present two concise chronologies of Judaic legal changes and Islamic legal changes in women's access to divorce.

We cannot differentiate between a wife's ability to "initiate" a divorce and her ability to "execute" a divorce. It is possible that women could "cause" a divorce without a husband's divorce decree – a written one in the Judaic tradition or an oral one in the Islamic tradition.[6] As will become evident, the two procedural moves – of initiating and of executing divorce – likely overlapped in the late antique era. That is, the act of initiating a divorce may have been simultaneous with effecting a divorce. While family members were often involved in a Jewish or Muslim woman's marriage, women were frequently independent actors during divorce.[7] In describing women as autonomous legal actors, this chapter does not project modern notions of women's agency.

A Judaic Chronology of Wife-initiated Divorce

The periodization of Jewish legal history and dates of rabbinic texts used in this section are modified versions of the dates used in contemporary Jewish studies.[8]

Rabbinic (70–620 CE)

There is a thorny scholarly debate surrounding the evidence for Jewish women obtaining divorces or actually divorcing their spouses in antiquity and late antiquity,[9] but it is evident that the diverse and varied situations of pre- and non-rabbinic Jewish women included wife-initiated divorce.[10]

[6] Avishalom Westreich. "History, dogmatics and hermeneutics: the divorce clause in Palestinian *Ketubbōt* and the Geonic compulsion of divorce." Working Papers of the Agunah Research Unit (March 2009): 2.

[7] Shelomo Dov Goitein, *A Mediterranean society: the Jewish communities of the Arab world as portrayed in the documents of the Cairo Geniza*, 6 vols. (Berkeley, CA: University of California Press, 1967–1993), 3:270. Muslim women also frequently represented themselves in divorce, as will be discussed below, in the Islamic chronology of wife-initiated divorce.

[8] See Charlotte Elisheva Fonrobert and Martin S. Jaffee, *The Cambridge companion to the Talmud and rabbinic literature*, Cambridge companions to religion (Cambridge; New York: Cambridge University Press, 2007), xiii–xvi.

[9] David Instone Brewer. "Jewish women divorcing their husbands in early Judaism: the background to papyrus Ṣe'elim 13." *The Harvard Theological Review* 92:3 (1999): 349–57; Robert Brody. "Evidence for divorce by Jewish women?" *The Journal of Jewish Studies* 50:2 (1999): 230–4; Bernard S. Jackson, "Some reflections on family law in the papyri." In *Jewish Law Association Studies XIV*, ed. by Hillel Gamoran (Binghamton, NY: Global Academic Pub.; Binghamton University, 2002), 141–77.

[10] Brewer, "Jewish women divorcing their husbands," 354.

The key documentary evidence is Aramaic marriage contracts of the Elephantine Jewish community dated to the fifth century BCE, which include a stipulation that a wife may initiate divorce and pay her husband a divorce settlement (i.e., not collect her dower, which is whatever the husband gave or granted his wife as part of the marriage contract).[11] At least some Jewish women were able to divorce their husbands in the antique and late antique periods.

Thus, Jewish legal practice contrasted somewhat with rabbinic legal texts.[12] Rabbinic jurisprudence on divorce builds upon one Biblical verse, Deuteronomy 24:1, "Suppose a man enters into marriage with a woman, but she does not please him because he finds something objectionable about her, and so he writes her a certificate of divorce, puts it in her hand, and sends her out of his house."[13] The verse does not specify if this divorce procedure is the only legally valid form of divorce.[14] But rabbinic jurists elaborated a variety of justifications for divorce. A survey of rabbinic literature indicates that the following types of divorce were recognized in late antiquity:

(1) A husband divorces his wife for whatever reason and pays her dower.[15]
(2) A rabbinic court compels a husband to divorce his wife[16] and pay the dower because the husband:

[11] Mordechai A. Friedman, *Jewish marriage in Palestine: a Cairo genizah study* (Tel-Aviv; New York: Tel-Aviv University, Chaim Rosenberg School of Jewish Studies; Jewish Theological Seminary of America, 1980), 1:313; *Geniza studies in Jewish marriage law* (s.l.: s.n., 1970), 4; and "Babatha's 'ketubba': some preliminary observations." *Israel Exploration Journal* 46:1/2 (1996): 55–76; Yigael Yadin *et al.*, *The documents from the Bar Kokhba period in the cave of letters: Hebrew, Aramaic, and Nabatean-Aramaic Papyri*, 2 vols., Judean Desert Series (Jerusalem: Israel Exploration Society; Hebrew University of Jerusalem: Shrine of the Book, 2002), 1:118–41; Goitein, *A Mediterranean society*, 3:264.

[12] Bernard S. Jackson. "The 'institutions' of marriage and divorce in the Hebrew Bible." *Journal of Semitic Studies* 56:2 (2011): 221–51 at 243.

[13] *NRSV Bible.*

[14] For a brief introduction to Jewish divorce laws, see Rachel Biale, *Women and Jewish law: an exploration of women's issues in halakhic sources* (New York: Schocken Books, 1984), 70–101. For a more extensive examination, see Shlomo Riskin, *A Jewish woman's right to divorce: a halakhic history and a solution for the agunah* (Jersey City, NJ: KTAV Pub. House, 2006). Riskin is a major modern orthodox rabbinic figure and the arguments he presents in his text come from within an orthodox perspective.

[15] See footnote 5. The House of Shammai's argument to limit a husband's ability to divorce was refuted by the House of Hillel. See *Mishnah*, Gīṭṭīn 9:10. But the *ketubbah* payment was perceived as an impediment to the husband's otherwise unencumbered right to divorce. See *B. Talmud*, Ketubbōt 11a and Yevamot 89a.

[16] *Mishnah*, Gīṭṭīn 9:8. See also *B. Talmud*, Gīṭṭīn 88b (a Jewish court may compel a divorce, but a non-Jewish court may only do so based on the decision of a Jewish court; specific type of divorce decree, השועמ טג). See also *B. Talmud*, Arakhin 5:6 (a husband is compelled to give a writ of divorce to his wife until he says he wills it).

a. has physical defects[17]
b. imposes unreasonable restrictions or makes unreasonable demands[18]
c. is sterile, impotent, or refuses to provide conjugal rights[19]
d. works in a profession considered disgusting[20]
e. or because the wife has made a vow prohibiting her husband from touching her.

(3) A husband divorces his wife and does not pay the dower because the court has declared the wife to be recalcitrant (i.e., a *moredet* or in breach of contract)[21] or because the wife:
a. apostatized, ignored a Jewish precept, or acted immorally[22]
b. refused sexual relations with her husband or performance of "wifely duties"[23]
c. has blemishes or physical defects that impinge the marital relationship[24]

The practical consequences of these rabbinic ideas on divorce likely varied from community to community.[25] Since the Palestinian tradition included a wife's right to divorce in the marriage contract, there may have been distinctions between Palestinian and Babylonian divorce practices.[26] Moreover, the rabbinic prerogative of annulling a marriage may have been a means of granting a woman a divorce (without the husband's deliverance of a divorce decree).[27] Still, this brief schema delineates the basic ideas circulating about divorce within late antique rabbinic legal communities.

[17] *B. Talmud*, Ketubbōt 7:9.
[18] *Ibid.*, Ketubbōt 7:1–5.
[19] *Ibid.*, Ketubbōt 5:6. See also *B. Talmud*, Ketubbōt 91a.
[20] *Mishnah*, Ketubbōt 7:10.
[21] *Ibid.*, Ketubbōt 5:5–7 (defining a recalcitrant wife). *P. Talmud*, Ketubbōt 5:8 (a "writ of rebellion" is a charge against or a deduction of the wife's ketubbah payment). *B. Talmud*, Ketubbōt 63a (the ketubbah of a recalcitrant wife is reduced to depletion and she is divorced).
[22] *Mishnah*, Ketubbōt 7:6.
[23] *Ibid.*, Ketubbōt 5:7.
[24] *Ibid.*, Ketubbōt 7:8.
[25] For a broad overview, see Tal Ilan, *History of Jewish women in late antiquity* (Jerusalem: The Hebrew University of Jerusalem, Rothberg School for Overseas Students, 1994).
[26] Friedman, *Jewish marriage in Palestine*, 1:313. See also Westreich, "History, dogmatics and hermeneutics," 18–21.
[27] *B. Talmud*, Ketubbōt 3a and Gīṭṭīn 33a (rabbis can annul betrothal by returning the dower money or by declaring the sexual act as non-marital, which corresponds to the two means of enacting a marriage). See Avishalom Westreich, "Umdena as a ground for marriage annulment: between mistaken transaction (kiddushei ta'ut) and terminative condition." *Jewish Law Association Studies* 20 (June 10, 2010): 330–52.

Geonic Era (620–1050 CE)

In 650/651 CE, Geonic rabbis issued a decree (*taqqanah*) that a recalcitrant wife (*moredet*) could procure a divorce immediately and not lose her dower (*ketubbah*).[28] This decree is documented in the Geonic responsa of Rav Sherira Gaon (d. 1006, Babylon).[29] This decree abandoned the twelve-month waiting period and loss of dower stipulated for a recalcitrant wife in the Babylonian Talmud.[30] Historical sources indicate that the majority of Geonim viewed this decree as a legal enactment validated by judicial authority and social need.[31] Genizah evidence[32] indicates that in the medieval Near East, Jewish women could initiate divorce by forfeiting some of their rights – what is often described as a "ransom" divorce, in line with the equivalent Arabic terminology.[33] This historical evidence should be emphasized: the Geonic practice of coercing a husband to divorce a "recalcitrant" wife was normative for centuries until its gradual undermining in the late medieval period. In other words, when compared to the Rabbinic period (or, more precisely, rabbinic texts), an additional option *may* have been introduced, in which a woman could obtain a divorce decree immediately (instead of waiting twelve months) in exchange for relinquishing part (or all) of her economic rights. This differs from the contract stipulation described in the Palestinian Talmud because an explicit marriage contract stipulation does not appear to have been required and because

[28] Libson, *Jewish and Islamic law*, 111. Brody, *The geonim of Babylonia*, 9, 62–3. While I translate *taqqanah* as decree in this chapter, it is to avoid confusing the reader. The literal meaning of *taqqanah* is to straighten and it has the connotation of establishing, instituting, or ordaining a legal rule.

[29] Benjamin Menasseh Lewin, *Otsar ha-ge'onim: teshuvot ge'one bavel u-ferushehem `al pi seder ha-talmud* (Haifa; Jerusalem: Hebrew University, 1928–1943), 8:99–102. Cited in Riskin, *A Jewish woman's right to divorce*, 56–9. Rav Sherira Gaon also mentions this decree in Rav Sherira Gaon (d. 1006; Babylonia), *The Iggeres of Rav Sherira Gaon*, trans. by Rabbi Nosson Dovid Rabinowich (Jerusalem; Brooklyn, NY: Rabbi Jacob Joseph School Press, Ahavath Torah Institute; Moznaim, 1988), 126.

[30] In this chapter, I assume that by 650 CE either the Babylonian Talmud had been redacted or much of the material in it was associated with a corpus that would later be identified as the Babylonian Talmud. *B. Talmud*, Ketubbōt 63b and 64a. See also Avishalom Westreich. "Compelling a divorce? Early Talmudic roots of coercion in a case of *moredet*." Working Papers of the Agunah Research Unit (May 2008): 12.

[31] Simeon Qayyara (ninth century; Iraq), *Halakhot Gedolot* (ninth century), sec. 36, laws of marriage.

[32] Genizah marriage contracts include explicit stipulations that a wife may relinquish her dower and be divorced "by the authorization of the court." Friedman, *Jewish marriage in Palestine*, 2:56. (For an example of Genizah evidence, see Taylor-Schechter Cairo Genizah Collection (Cambridge University Library) TS 13 J 3, fol. 22, copied from S. D. Goitein's Typed Texts. 07-09-90, N.H. (p).)

[33] See in particular the Judeo-Arabic documents cited in Mordechai A. Friedman, "Divorce upon the wife's demand as reflected in manuscripts from the Cairo Geniza." *Jewish Law Annual* 4 (1981): 103–26. See also Mordechai A. Friedman, "The ransom-divorce: divorce proceedings initiated by the wife in medieval Jewish practice." *Israel Oriental Studies* 6 (1976): 288–307 at 296, 301; Goitein, *A Mediterranean society*, 3:267–8.

women appear to have been able to initiate divorce proceedings as a result of the Geonic decree.[34] The Geonim appear to have implemented this form of wife-initiated divorce as an extension of the Talmudic category of a recalcitrant wife.[35]

To summarize, Geonic divorce practices included:

(1) a husband divorcing his wife for whatever reason and paying her dower.[36]
(2) a rabbinic court compelling a husband to divorce his wife and pay the dower because the husband:[37]
   a. has physical defects
   b. imposes unreasonable restrictions or behavior
   c. is sterile or impotent
   d. works in a profession considered disgusting
(3) a husband divorcing his wife and not paying the dower because the court has declared the wife to be recalcitrant (i.e., a *moredet* or in breach of contract) or because the wife:
   a. apostatized, ignored a Jewish precept, or acted immorally
   b. refused sexual relations with her husband or performance of "wifely duties"
   c. has blemishes or physical defects that impinge the marital relationship
(4) a wife divorcing her husband, receiving either her full dower or part of it and without waiting twelve months. In practice, it is unclear if the wife actually received the dower or relinquished it.[38]

It is unclear precisely who (husband or court) delivered the divorce decree when a wife initiated divorce by relinquishing her dower.[39] As in the case of evidence of Jewish women divorcing in antiquity, the interpretation of

[34] As will become clear, I challenge the view that this Geonic practice "deviated" from talmudic practice and argue that it should be understood as a customary practice, rather than an "innovative" enactment.

[35] Friedman, *Jewish marriage in Palestine*, 1:324. See also Friedman, "The ransom-divorce," 302.

[36] But note that Rabbeinu Gershom (d. 1028; Germany) "enacted a decree which made it impossible for a husband to divorce his wife against her will." Riskin, *A Jewish woman's right to divorce*, xii, 109.

[37] These grounds for compelling a husband to divorce his wife are discussed in Geonic responsa. See, for example, Albert Harkavy, *Teshuvot ha-geonim: sheelot u-teshuvot* (New York: Menorah, Makhon le-mehkar ule-hotsaat kitve-yad u-sefarim `atikim, 1959), sec. 451.

[38] Goitein notes that the Genizah contains numerous documents indicating that Jewish wives initiated divorce proceedings by renouncing their financial claims (i.e., their dowers) against their husbands. Goitein, *A Mediterranean society*, 3:265.

[39] Qaraites permitted judicial divorce decrees. See footnote 118. In addition, it is unclear if Islamic courts only coerced Jewish husbands to deliver divorce decrees or if they also provided judicial divorce decrees. Goitein mentions Genizah evidence of a Jewish woman who went to a Muslim judge to divorce her husband against his will; the judge may have issued the divorce decree. *Ibid.*

the historical record is obfuscated by an orthodox presumption that only husbands – not rabbinic courts – can deliver the divorce decree. But the evidence of substantive flexibility (i.e., Jewish wives initiating divorces) implies some procedural flexibility (i.e., less formalism than the presumption that only husbands may deliver divorce decrees). Since there is limited surviving historical evidence, we cannot be certain which divorce types were most prevalent.

Era of the Rishonim (1050–1400 CE)

In the post-Geonic era, the Rishonim (roughly, medieval rabbis) further elaborated rabbinic opinions on when a woman could be divorced from her husband.[40] (It should be noted that the spread of Jewish communities to Europe resulted in two centers of rabbinic authority, one Western and one Eastern.) Two sub-categories in this period appear to have supplemented the rabbinic "short list" of grounds that warrant a court ordering a husband to divorce his wife: (1) the husband's adultery[41] and (2) the husband's transgression of the laws of Moses (or apostasy).[42] A woman's ability to initiate a divorce without citing one of the grounds specified in the Babylonian Talmud became, during the period of the Rishonim, an issue debated by jurists that generated a variety of regional practices.[43]

Generally, the Rishonim debated a rabbinic court's ability to coerce a husband to divorce his recalcitrant wife by making conflicting assertions about the so-called "origin" of the law: the Talmud or the Geonic decree. Rashi (d. 1105, France) suggested that the Talmud was the source of the practice.[44] His grandson (Rashbam, d. 1158, France) upheld the decree by

[40] Elaboration of Talmudic discussions include: (a) refusal or inability to provide a wife sufficient maintenance (Joseph ben Ephraim Karo (d. 1575; Ṣafad), *Shūlḥan ʿarūkh* (1563), Even Haʿezer, Ketubbōt 70:3.); (b) refusal of conjugal rights (*Ibid.*, Even Haʿezer, Ketubbōt 76:11.); (c) husband's inability to provide maintenance or sex (*Ibid.*, Even Haʿezer, Gīṭṭīn, 154:3.); (d) husband is compelled to divorce his wife if he engages in a disgusting profession (*Ibid.*, Even Haʿezer, Gīṭṭīn, 154:1.)

[41] *Ibid.*

[42] Mūsá ibn Maymūn Maimonides (d. 1204; Andalusia/Egypt), *Mishneh Torah*, 14 vols., Yale Judaica series (New Haven, CT: Yale University Press, 1949), Hilkhot Ishut 4:15. See also Karo, *Shūlḥan ʿarūkh*; Even Haʿezer, Gīṭṭīn, 154:1.

[43] For a thorough discussion of the medieval debates on the recalcitrant wife doctrine, see Elimelech Westreich, "The rise and decline of the law of the rebellious wife in medieval Jewish law." In *Jewish Law Association studies, XII (Zutphen conference)*, ed. by Hillel Gamoran. (Binghamton, NY: Global Publications, State University of New York at Binghamton, 2002), 207–18.

[44] Rashi (d. 1105; France) offers the following gloss of Ketubbōt 63b: "*One who says 'I want him'* – we should force her by reducing her ketubbah. *But if she said 'he is repulsive to me'* – I do not want either him or his ketubbah. *No pressure is placed on her* – to delay her, but rather he gives her a divorce document and she is divorced without a *ketubbah*." See also Westreich, "The rise and decline," 212 (citing Rashi, Ketubbōt 63b).

ruling that a husband should be coerced to divorce his recalcitrant wife.[45] However, Rashbam's brother, Rabbeinu Tam (d. 1171, France) rejected the Geonic decree of coercing the husband to divorce his wife and effectively claimed that the Geonic practice was unorthodox.[46]

In comparison, Maimonides (d. 1204, Andalusia/Egypt) criticized, but did not entirely reject, Geonic practices pertaining to a wife's ability to demand a divorce as a recalcitrant wife (*moredet*).[47] Viewing the Geonic decree as based on Talmudic practice, Maimonides differentiated between two types of recalcitrant wives: (a) one who "loathes" her husband must forfeit her dower in order for the husband to "be compelled to divorce her immediately"[48] and (b) one who "rebels against her husband merely in order to torment him" becomes the subject of a daily public announcement threatening the forfeiture of her dower if she persists in her recalcitrance;[49] if she persists, then she is prohibited from receiving maintenance (i.e., alimony) for twelve months, when she finally receives her divorce decree.[50] A practical application of his legal opinions is evident in a Maimonidean responsum, which makes clear that a woman who chooses to divorce leaves her home without her dower and the husband is forced to divorce her.[51]

The debate among Rishonim about the legitimacy of the Geonic decree was fundamentally related to broader questions of juristic authority.[52] Medieval divorce in eastern Jewish communities paralleled divorce in Muslim communities: it was normative, uncomplicated, and often initiated by wives. Still, "the majority of divorces in Mamluk [1250–1517]

[45] Westreich, "The rise and decline," 212 (citing Rashbam in *Ṭur*, Even Ha'ezer, ch. 77).

[46] Riskin, *A Jewish woman's right to divorce*, 98–9 (citing *Ṣefer ha-yashar*, Responsa sec. 24 by Rabbeina Tam (d. 1171)). See also Westreich, "The rise and decline," 212 (citing *Ṣefer ha-yashar*, Responsa sec. 24 and *Toṣafot*, Ketubbōt 63b).

[47] In *Hilkhot Ishut* 14:14, Maimonides claims, "The Geonim reported that in Babylonia they have different customs pertaining to the recalcitrant wife, but those customs did not spread to the majority of Israel and many great scholars in many places disagree with them. We ought to recognize and to rule according to Talmudic law." Maimonides, *Mishneh Torah*, Hilkhot Ishut 14:14, p. 90.

[48] In *Hilkhot Ishut* 14:8, Maimonides explicitly states that a woman is not held captive and forced to have sex with her husband if she despises him. *Ibid.*, Hilkhot Ishut 14:8, pp. 88–9.

[49] Shai Secunda has pointed out to me that this practice of making a public announcement is evident in Zoroastrian law, discussed in the Babylonian Talmud, and mentioned in the Palestinian Talmud in reference to a Babylonian sage. Therefore, these public announcements were likely a Babylonian practice shared by many groups in that region.

[50] Maimonides, *Mishneh Torah*, Hilkhot Ishut 14:9–13, pp. 89–90.

[51] Responsum 34; a translation and discussion of this responsum is available in Reneé Levine Melammed. "He said, she said: a woman teacher in twelfth-century Cairo." *Association for Jewish Studies Review* 22:1 (1997): 19–35 at 27.

[52] This authority issue is evident in many rabbinic texts and appears explicitly in Rabbi Yitzhak Ben Moshe (d. 1250; Vienna), *Ṣefer or zaru'a*, section 1, responsa section 4354.

society were consensual separations" and women's economic independence was a key factor in facilitating divorce.[53] By the early fourteenth century, a perspective of the Western Rishonim that the Geonic decree was invalid began to dominate. By the sixteenth century, a major Jewish law code acknowledged a rabbinic court's ability to compel a divorce, but in situations of the husband's unwillingness to support his wife.[54]

It may be possible to differentiate Eastern (including Babylonian and North African) legal practices from Western (including primarily European) legal practices. Jewish communities in the East continued to coerce husbands to divorce their wives, as documented by Genizah evidence.[55] The perspective of Western rabbinic authorities appears to have arrived in the East at the end of the fourteenth century when two rabbinic jurists (Ribash and Rashbatz) moved from the southern regions of modern-day Spain to North Africa and prohibited coercion of a husband to divorce a recalcitrant wife.[56]

This condensed chronology of Jewish women's access to divorce indicates that Western Rishonim (late medieval rabbis) gradually abolished a prevalent Eastern practice of rabbinic courts coercing husbands to divorce "recalcitrant" wives by characterizing it as unorthodox. Rather than resolve the debate about the orthodoxy (or lack thereof) of the Geonic decree, I want to turn to the Islamic chronology, which may elucidate some of the confusion or questions in the Judaic chronology.

An Islamic Chronology of Wife-initiated Divorce

Legal Circles (610–800 CE)

Muslim women's divorce options in the earliest decades of Islamic history cannot be easily reconstructed, but some historical texts can illuminate the orally transmitted traditions of the late antique period. Most of the Qur'ānic verses dealing with the subject of divorce are addressed to men

[53] Yossef Rapoport, *Marriage, money and divorce in medieval Islamic society* (Cambridge: Cambridge University Press, 2005), 112.

[54] Karo, *Shūlḥan ʿarūkh*, Even Haʿezer, Gīṭṭīn, 154:3.

[55] See Taylor-Schechter Cairo Genizah Collection (Cambridge University Library), Additional Series 146 4 (court order forcing a husband to write a divorce decree for his wife; Egypt, *c.* 1240). See also Taylor-Schechter Cairo Genizah Collection (Cambridge University Library), New Series J 455 (husband forced to give his wife a divorce decree).

[56] Ribash is Rabbi Isaac Bar Sheshet (d. 1408, Valencia/Algiers) and Rashbatzh (also Tashbatz) is Simeon ben Zemah Duran (d. 1444, Aragón/Algiers). Westreich, "The rise and decline," 216–17.

and discuss the post-divorce waiting period and alimony.[57] But one key verse (2:229) declares: "if you fear that they (the couple) cannot maintain God's limits, then it will not be held against them (the couple) if she (the wife) forfeits something."[58] Major exegetical texts and other historical sources interpret this verse as relating to an actual incident in which the Prophet approved a woman returning her dower (*mahr*) to effect a divorce.[59] In all versions of this narrative, the wife returns the entire dower she had received from her husband and the Prophet approves her action. Most late antique Muslim traditionists interpreted the narrative as limiting the amount a woman forfeits to the amount she received as dower, since there are no Prophetic reports permitting a husband to take more than the dower.[60] Jurists did not interpret the tradition as restricting this form of divorce to judicial intervention (i.e., equivalent to the Prophet's approval).[61] Most versions of the narrative describe the event without indicating that the woman was at fault, but rather that she found her husband intolerable.[62] Yet other variations of this narrative imply distinct conditions surrounding this particular woman's forfeiture divorce (*khulʿ*): she was abused;[63] she was recalcitrant;[64] or her husband consented to the

[57] Relevant verses include Qurʾān, 2:228–32, 2:36–7, 2:41; 65:1–7; 4:35.

[58] *Ibid.*, 2:229. The verse is commonly interpreted as referring to *khulʿ*.

[59] ʿAbd al-Razzāq ibn Hammām al-Ḥimyarī al-Ṣanʿānī (d. 827; Yemen), *Muṣannaf fī al-ḥadīth*, ed. by Ḥabīb al-Raḥmān al-ʿAẓamī, 11 vols. (Beirut: al-Maktab al-Islāmī, 1970–), 6:482–503. The same narrative is reported in numerous other collections, including by Mālik (d. 796), Bukhārī (d. 870), Muslim (d. 875), Dārimī (d. 869), Ibn Mājah (d. 887), Abū Dāwūd (d. 889), and al-Tirmidhī (d. 892).

[60] al-Ṣanʿānī, *Muṣannaf fī al-ḥadīth*, 6:501–6 (majority of reports suggest a husband may not take more than dower in *khulʿ* divorce). See also Ibn Abī Shaybah, *Muṣannaf*, 4:128–9 (the majority of reports suggest a husband may not take more than dower in *khulʿ* divorce).

[61] al-Ṣanʿānī, *Muṣannaf*, 6:494–5 (the majority of reports indicate that *khulʿ* is permissible without court intervention); Ibn Abī Shaybah, *Muṣannaf*, 4:124–5 (the majority of reports indicate that *khulʿ* is permissible without court intervention); Qalʿahʾjī, *ʿAbd Allāh ibn ʿUmar*, 324 (*khulʿ* is permissible without a judge); Qalʿahʾjī, *ʿUthmān ibn ʿAffān*, 162–3 (*khulʿ* is permissible without a judge). But see Qalʿahʾjī, *al-Ḥasan al-Baṣrī*, 1:386 (*khulʿ* is not permissible without court intervention). Ibn al-Mundhir reports a consensus that wife-initiated divorce does not require court intervention. Muḥammad ibn Ibrāhīm Ibn al-Mundhir al-Naysābūrī (d. 930), *al-Ijmāʿ* (Beirut: Dār al-Kutub al-ʿIlmīyah, 1985), 46.

[62] al-Ṣanʿānī, *Muṣannaf*, 6:483; Qalʿahʾjī, *ʿAlī ibn Abī Ṭālib*, 246 (*khulʿ* is permissible if wife states that she finds husband intolerable).

[63] al-Ṣanʿānī, *Muṣannaf*, 6:482–4. It should be noted that this and the majority of texts cited in this chapter do not define abuse; therefore, I will also not specify what constitutes abuse, which is beyond the scope of this chapter.

[64] *Ibid.*, 6:495–8 (majority of reports indicate that husband can only accept payment from wife if she finds him intolerable or she is recalcitrant). Ibn Abī Shaybah, *Muṣannaf*, 4:120–1 (a wife's recalcitrance is a condition for forfeiture divorce). Qalʿahʾjī, *ʿAlī ibn Abī Ṭālib*, 246 (*khulʿ* is permissible if wife is recalcitrant). Some reports limit the forfeiture divorce to a wife who has committed a grave sin (such as adultery).

divorce settlement.[65] In discussing a woman's potential fault, some jurists were concerned with preventing an injustice prohibited in the Qur'ān: a woman relinquishing her dower right without cause in order to divorce her husband.[66] Late antique jurists ruled that if a husband abuses his wife in order to pressure her to pursue a forfeiture divorce, then that divorce is void and the wife receives her full dower.[67]

That this wife-initiated divorce was historically practiced is corroborated by a report that 'Umar (d. 644), the second Caliph, condemned criticism of women who demanded a divorce by forfeiting their dowers.[68] (This type of criticism is apparent in reports that women who pursue forfeiture divorces are morally compromised.[69]) There were four basic late antique Islamic divorce practices:

(1) The most frequently discussed situation is of a husband divorcing his wife and paying a divorce settlement.[70] According to some jurists, he could avoid paying the post-divorce alimony if she was deemed recalcitrant.[71]
(2) A husband offers his wife the option of choosing divorce or staying with him; if she chooses divorce, he pays her the full divorce settlement.[72]

65 The implication of consent is that this divorce was not unilaterally imposed on the husband either by the wife or by the Prophet. al-Ṣanʿānī, *Muṣannaf*, 6:502–3.

66 The Qur'ānic verse is 4:19 ("do not compel them (women) to give away part of what you have given them unless they commit an obvious sin").

67 Qalʿah'jī, *'Abd Allāh ibn 'Abbās*, 312–13 (if a wife is not at fault, then it is impermissible for her husband to take money in a forfeiture divorce). Qalʿah'jī, *Sufyān al-Thawrī*, 378 (*khul'* is void under duress of husband's abuse; husband must return dower).

68 Ibn Abī Shaybah, *Muṣannaf*, 4:201; Ibn Abī Shaybah, *Muṣannaf*, 4:185 (do not criticize women who want *khul'* divorces); Qalʿah'jī, *'Umar ibn 'Abd al-'Azīz*, 268 (*khul'* divorce permitted where wife finds husband intolerable). See also Aḥmad ibn al-Ḥusayn al-Bayhaqī (d. 1066; Khurasan), *al-Sunan al-kubrá*, 17 vols. (Beirut: Dar al-Fikr, 1996), 11:182 (do not criticize women who want *khul'* divorces).

69 Ibn Abī Shaybah, *Muṣannaf*, 4:201.

70 *Ibid.*, 4:*kitāb al-talāq*, passim. Muḥammad ibn Idrīs al-Shāfiʿī (d. 820; Arabia/Egypt), *al-Umm*, 11 vols. (al-Manṣūrah: Dār al-Wafā', 2001), 6: passim.

71 Qalʿah'jī, *Sufyān al-Thawrī*, 780–1 (recalcitrant wife does not receive post-divorce alimony; no mention of dower reduction or loss).

72 This is based on a Prophetic precedent. Abū Yūsuf Yaʿqūb ibn Ibrāhīm al-Anṣārī al-Kūfī (d. 798; Iraq), *Kitāb al-āthār* (Beirut: Dār al-Kutub al-'Ilmīyah, 1978), 139–41; al-Ṣanʿānī, *Muṣannaf*, 6:515–26 and 7:8–15. Ibn Abī Shaybah, *Muṣannaf*, 4:92–4; Muḥammad ibn Yazīd Ibn Mājah (d. 887; Iran), *Sunan al-Muṣṭafá*, ed. by Abī al-Ḥasan Muḥammad Ibn 'Abd al-Hādī al-Sindī Ḥanafī, 2 vols. (Beirut: Al-Fikr, 1975), 1:632 (Prophet offered his wives divorce option); Muḥammad ibn Yazīd al-Qazwīnī Ibn Mājah (d. 887; Iran), *Sunan Abī 'Abd Allāh Muhammad ibn Yazīd al-Qazwīnī Ibn Mājah*, ed. by Muhammad Fu'ād 'Abd al-Bāqī, 2 vols. (Cairo: Dār Ahyā' al-Kutub al-'Arabīyah, 1952–54), 1:661–2 (Prophet gave wives option to divorce and receive full dower). See also the following late antique jurists who validated giving a wife the option to divorce without relinquishing her dower: Qalʿah'jī, *'Alī ibn Abī Ṭālib*, 440–3; Qalʿah'jī, *'Uthmān ibn 'Affān*, 257; Qalʿah'jī, *'Abd*

(3) A wife divorces her husband and she pays some form of divorce settlement by relinquishing part or all of her dower.[73]
(4) A court divorces a couple because the husband is unable to provide his wife with sufficient maintenance,[74] is missing,[75] or is impotent.[76]

This historical evidence unambiguously records a wife's ability to initiate and to effect a divorce (*khulʿ*) in late antique Arabia, but the conditions surrounding a wife's divorce option were imprecise.

Professionalization of Legal Schools (800–1000 CE)

Professional jurists replaced the imprecision surrounding wife-initiated divorce with elaborate juridical categories. In comparison to earlier collections (*muṣannafāt*), slightly later, canonical compilations of tradition-reports reduce the number of reports about wife-initiated divorce (*khulʿ*) and limit these divorces to situations where a wife has sufficient grounds.[77]

Allāh ibn ʿUmar, 562–4; Muḥammad Rawwās Qalʿahʾjī, *Mawsūʿat fiqh Zayd ibn Thābit wa-Abī Hurayrah*, Fī sabīl mawsūʿah fiqhīyah jāmiʿah; Silsilat mawsūʿat fiqh al-salaf (Beirut: Dār al-Nafāʾis, 1993), 197–8; Qalʿahʾjī, *Sufyān al-Thawrī*, 614–6. Qalʿahʾjī, *ʿAbd Allāh ibn ʿAbbās*, 510.

[73] al-Ṣanʿānī, *Muṣannaf*, 6:490–1, 94–5, 500–6; Ibn Abī Shaybah, *Muṣannaf*, 4:120–3, 28–9; Qalʿahʾjī, *ʿUthmān ibn ʿAffān*, 162 (the first four caliphs all permitted *khulʿ* divorce). See also al-Bukhārī, *Ṣaḥīḥ al-Bukhārī*, 7:149–51; ʿAlī ibn Jaʿfar al-Madanī (d. 825), *Masāʾil ʿAlī ibn Jaʿfar wa-mustadrakātuhā*, Silsilat maṣādir biḥār al-anwār, 8 (Beirut: Muʾassasat Āl al-Bayt li-Iḥyāʾ al-Turāth, 1990), 283 (Imāmī Shīʿī: a woman relinquishes any monetary claims against the husband in wife-initiated divorce). (There was a minority opinion that prohibited forfeiture divorces and another minority opinion that only permitted it with judicial intervention; but neither of these positions was normative. ʿAblah Kaḥlāwī, *al-Khulʿ: dawāʾ mā lā dawāʾ la-hu: dirāsah fiqhīyah muqāranah* [Cairo: Dār al-Rashād, 2000], 68–9.)

[74] Ibn Abī Shaybah, *Muṣannaf*, 4:174–5; Qalʿahʾjī, *ʿAlī ibn Abī Ṭālib*, 456 (a judge may issue divorce if husband is unable/unwilling to provide maintenance). But see Qalʿahʾjī, *Sufyān al-Thawrī*, 781 (a judge does not divorce a couple if the husband is unable to provide sufficient maintenance for the wife).

[75] Qalʿahʾjī, *ʿAbd Allāh ibn ʿAbbās*, 520 (a judge may issue divorce with sufficient grounds, such as abandonment).

[76] Qalʿahʾjī, *ʿAlī ibn Abī Ṭālib*, 454–5 (divorce granted if husband is impotent or cannot provide wife with conjugal rights). On sexual impotence as a ground for divorce, see the excellent piece, Benkheira, "L'impuissance sexuelle."

[77] I compared the compilations of al-Ṣanʿānī (d. 827) and Ibn Abī Shaybah (d. 849) to Scott Lucas's schematic study of the texts of Bukhārī (d. 870), Muslim (d. 875), Dārimī (d. 869), Ibn Mājah (d. 887), Abū Dāwūd (d. 889), and al-Tirmidhī (d. 892). The later texts have fewer reports about *khulʿ* and suggest the necessity of sufficient grounds (such as spousal abuse or a husband's consent) that were not explicit in earlier texts. Scott C. Lucas. "Divorce, ḥadīth-scholar style: from al-Dārimī to al-Tirmidhī." *Journal of Islamic Studies* 19:3 (2008): 325–68 at 368. Later sources include more versions implying that it is wrong for a woman to demand a divorce without sufficient "justification." Ibn Mājah, *Sunan Ibn Mājah*, 1:662 (a woman who demands a divorce without grounds will be punished in the hereafter). And see Muḥammad ibn ʿĪsá al-Tirmidhī (d. 892; Khurāsān), *Sunan al-Tirmidhī wa-huwa al-Jāmiʿ al-ṣaḥīḥ*, ed. by ʿAbd al-Wahhāb ʿAbd al-Laṭīf and ʿAbd al-Raḥmān Muḥammad ʿUthmān, 5 vols. (Medinah: al-Maktabah al-Salafīyah, 1965), 2:429–30 (narratives about the evils of a woman demanding a divorce without sufficient justification).

There are conflicting opinions about what constituted reasonable justification for a wife to pursue a divorce, with some jurists identifying her expressed statement of abhorrence as sufficient.[78] Yet most Muslim jurists interpreted the narratives about the Prophetic precedent permitting wife-initiated divorce as including a requirement of the husband's consent[79] or as being prompted by a situation of abuse.[80] Many legal texts of this period also imposed a close association between wife-initiated divorce (*khulʿ*) and recalcitrant wives, which was less evident in earlier texts.[81] Consequently, the legal possibility that seems to prevail in this period is a husband's option to divorce his wife and not pay the full dower if she is considered recalcitrant (*nāshizah*). This juristic elaboration of the forfeiture divorce is remarkable because no Prophetic legal precedent substantiates the legal option of husbands paying less than the divorce settlement.[82] There is no indication in the historical sources that a Muslim man in the Prophetic period could divorce a woman without paying the full dower. Muslim jurists appear to have elaborated the forfeiture divorce in this period.

[78] See footnote 62. Some canonical Sunnī texts seem to have understood a wife's disgust for her husband as sufficient grounds: Ibn Mājah, *Sunan Ibn Mājah*, 1:663 (implying that Ḥabībah pursued *khulʿ* because her husband was repulsive). Note that Imāmī Shīʿī sources make the wife's explicit statement of disgust for her husband incumbent in a *khulʿ* divorce. al-Ḥurr al-ʿĀmilī *Wasāʾil al-shīʿah ilá taḥṣīl masāʾil al-sharīʿah*, 7:487–9 (Imāmī Shīʿī). This resembles the rabbinic discussions of a wife who seeks a divorce because her husband is repulsive. See footnotes 44 and 48.

[79] Most versions of the narrative suggest that the husband was not consulted, but rather that the Prophet simply agreed to the woman's (Ḥabībah's) suggestion of giving back the garden she had received as her dower and the husband, upon learning of the Prophet's approval, acquiesced. See footnote 65. This is a key procedural issue, since a husband's unilateral prerogative to effect the divorce is not substantiated by all versions of this narrative.

[80] There are several different versions of this narrative; see footnote 63. The version that includes abuse subsequently became more dominant. While Dārimī, Ibn Mājah, Abū Dāwūd, and al-Tirmidhī include a category of reports preventing a woman from seeking to divorce a non-abusive husband, the other texts (i.e., Bukhārī and Muslim) do not. See Lucas, "Divorce, ḥadīth-scholar style: from al-Dārimī to al-Tirmidhī," 368. See also Sulaymān ibn al-Ashʿath al-Sijistānī Abū Dāwūd (d. 889; Iraq), *Sunan Abī Dāwūd*, ed. by Muḥammad Muḥyī al-Dīn ʿAbd al-Ḥamīd, 4 vols. (Beirut: Dār Iḥyāʾ al-Turāth al-ʿArabī, 1970), 1:462 and 4:310–11 (different narratives: Ḥabībah's husband was/was not abusive).

[81] Again, this is based on my comparison of tradition-report collections. See the beginning of the section on *khulʿ* in Saḥnūn, *al-Mudawwanah*, 2:241–51. Reports about a recalcitrant wife and wife-initiated divorce are juxtaposed in al-Shāfiʿī, *al-Umm*, 6:*kitāb al-khulʿ wa al-nushūz*. The section on recalcitrance (*nushūz*) appears immediately before the section on wife-initiated divorce (*khulʿ*) in al-Shīrāzī, *al-Muhadhdhab*, 2:71–8 (Shāfiʿī: section on recalcitrance immediately precedes section on *khulʿ*); in a different edition: Abū Isḥāq Ibrāhīm ibn ʿAlī ibn Yūsuf Fīrūzābādī al-Shīrāzī (d. 1083; Iran), *al-Muhadhdhab fī fiqh al-imām al-shāfiʿī*, ed. by Zakarīyā ʿUmayrāt and Muḥammad ibn Aḥmad Baṭṭāl, 3 vols. (Beirut: Dār al-Kutub al-ʿIlmīyah, 1995), 2:486–99. Some Muslim jurists viewed *khulʿ* as being only permissible in situations of recalcitrance or loathing. Kaḥlāwī, *al-Khulʿ*, 68.

[82] There are no references to this practice in biographical or historical texts; in addition, the jurisprudential texts do not cite a Prophetic precedent.

By the end of the professionalization period, the following divorce practices were recognized:

(1) A husband divorces his wife for whatever reason and pays the divorce settlement in full.
(2) A husband divorces his wife and pays less than the divorce settlement under the category of *khulʿ*, because the wife is recalcitrant or immoral.[83]
(3) A court declares a wife divorced and the husband pays the divorce settlement for the following reasons:
  a. if he is impotent or has a severe defect or disease[84]
  b. if he deserts his wife, fails to provide her maintenance, or is cruel[85]
  c. if he is insane[86]
(4) A wife divorces her husband[87] and forfeits the divorce settlement (dower) partially or completely, or even pays in excess of the dower under specific circumstances. According to many jurists, the husband's consent is required.[88]
(5) Less prevalent than in late antiquity,[89] a husband offers his wife the option of choosing divorce or staying with him; if she chooses divorce, he pays her a divorce settlement.[90]

83 Ibn al-Mundhir reports a juristic consensus that a husband can only collect from a wife's dower if she is recalcitrant. Ibn al-Mundhir, *al-Ijmāʿ*, 46. Many late antique jurists and Aḥmad ibn Ḥanbal prohibit a husband from taking more than the wife's dower; Ḥanafīs do not recommend his taking more; Mālikīs, Shāfiʿīs, and Imāmī Shīʿīs permit husbands to take as much as, less than, or more than the dower amount he gave her. The two main juristic opinions (for and against a husband taking more than the dower in a *khulʿ* divorce) are summarized in Kaḥlāwī, *al-Khulʿ*, 140–3.

84 ʿAlī ibn Abī Bakr al-Marghīnānī (d. 1197; Farghāna), *The Hidāyah: commentary on the Islamic laws*, trans. by Zahra Baintner, 2 vols. (Karachi: Darul Ishaat, 2007), 2:217 (Ḥanafī).

85 See footnote 74. See also al-Nawawī, *al-Majmūʿ*, 17:110–2 (Shāfiʿī: if a husband cannot support his wife, they are divorced).

86 However, there is a Ḥanafī opinion that a woman cannot demand judicial divorce if her husband is mentally incompetent or has a serious disease. al-Marghīnānī, *The Hidāyah*, 2:219 (Ḥanafī).

87 Ibn Ḥazm synopsizes juristic opinions by noting that some jurists prohibit *khulʿ*, while others make it conditional upon one of the following factors: (a) a political leader permits it; (b) the wife is having an affair; (c) the husband is abusive; (d) she refuses to purify herself; (e) she claims that her husband is repulsive; (f) she dislikes him and he is not compelling her (to relinquish her dower). Ibn Ḥazm, *Marātib*, 74–5 (Ẓāhirī). See also Ibn Ḥazm, *al-Muḥallā*, 10:286–97 (Ẓāhirī).

88 While all the legal schools accept the validity of *khulʿ*, most legal schools view it as a negotiated settlement. Ibn Ḥazm, *al-Muḥallā*, 10:286 (Ẓāhirī: *khulʿ* only by mutual consent). Ḥanafīs require the husband to accept the wife's *khulʿ* offer in order for a divorce to be valid. ʿAbd al-Raḥmān al-Jazīrī, Muḥammad Gharawī, and Yāsir Māziḥ, *Kitāb al-fiqh ʿalá al-madhāhib al-arbaʿah wa madhhab ahl al-bayt*, 5 vols. (Beirut: Dār al-Thaqalayn, 1998), 4:494. This requirement that the husband must explicitly effect the divorce resembles the common – although likely not universal – rabbinic perspective that a husband must deliver a *get* for a divorce to occur.

89 See footnote 72. Earlier texts discuss this option more than later texts.

90 Mālik Ibn Anas (d. 795; Arabia), *Muwaṭṭaʾ al-Imām Mālik*, ed. by ʿAbd al-Wahhāb ʿAbd al-Laṭīf, 2nd edn. (Beirut: al-Maṭbaʿah al-ʿIlmīyah, 1979), 191–2 (giving wife divorce option with full dower); Abū

When compared to the previous period (of legal circles and networks), a wife's ability to initiate divorce was circumscribed.

Consolidation (1000–1200 CE) and Technochratization (1200–1400 CE)

By the eleventh century, Muslim jurists had elaborated more details surrounding divorce practices.[91] Wife-initiated divorce continued, as papyrological evidence from divorce documents indicate.[92] While there is no indication that jurists prohibited any of the divorce types previously practiced,[93] the distinctions between earlier and later legal texts imply that a woman's access to divorce became limited to particular circumstances.[94] In theory, women still had the legal right to divorce their husbands by paying a divorce settlement.[95] Yet, juristic restrictions (as outlined in jurisprudential texts) seem to have limited this right to cases where a wife could establish grounds for divorce or to situations where the husband concedes to the divorce settlement.[96] Notably, juristic discussions of wife-initiated

Yūsuf, *Kitāb al-āthār*, 139–41 (Ḥanafī: women given choice to divorce and receive dowers); Bishr ibn Ghānim al-Khurāsānī al-Ibāḍī (d. *c.* 815; Khurāsān), *Mudawwanah al-kubrá*, 2 vols. (Oman: Wizārat al-Turāth al-Qawmī wa-al-Thaqāfah, 1984), 2:56–67 (Ibāḍī); Muḥammad ibn Aḥmad Shams al-Dīn al-Sarakhsī (d. eleventh century; Transoxania), *Kitāb al-mabsūṭ*, 30 vols. (Beirut: Dār al-Kutub al-ʿIlmīyah, 1993), 6:210–23 (Ḥanafī: giving wife divorce option with full dower); Ibn ʿAbd al-Barr, *Kitāb al-kāfī*, 2:587–91 (Mālikī: giving wife divorce option with full dower).

91 Ibn Rushd summarizes medieval juristic perspectives: "Five opinions are, thus derived for *khulʿ*. First, that it is not permitted at all. Second, it is permitted in all circumstances, that is, even under duress. Third, it is not permitted unless fornication is witnessed. Fourth, it is permitted when there is fear that the limits imposed by Allāh will not be maintained. Fifth, that it is permitted in all circumstances, except under duress, which is the most widely accepted (*mashhūr*) opinion." Ibn Rushd, *Distinguished Jurist's Primer*, 2:81. (Duress here refers to a husband forcing his wife to accept less than the divorce settlement.)

92 A divorce document dated 1069 CE indicates a wife relinquished her dower and is cited in Grohmann and Khoury, *Chrestomathie*, 44–5.

93 Jurists distinguished between "*takhyīr* (granting a choice) and *tamlīk* (granting possession of the right)." Ibn Rushd, *Distinguished Jurist's Primer*, 2:84 (summarizing the juristic debates on these divorce types).

94 Abuse and repulsiveness continued to be cited as grounds for a woman to pursue a *khulʿ* divorce. al-Nawawī, *al-Majmūʿ*, 16:3–6 (Shāfiʿī: physical abuse as provoking wife-initiated divorce). See also Nūr al-Dīn ʿAlī ibn Abī Bakr Haythamī (d. 1405), *Ghāyat al-maqṣūd fī zawāʾid al-musnad*, ed. by Khalāf Maḥmūd ʿAbd al-Samīʿ, 4 vols. (Beirut: Dār al-Kutub al-ʿIlmīyah, 2001), 2:267–8 (Shāfiʿī: implying that Ḥabībah, the woman from the Prophetic-era tradition-report, pursued *khulʿ* because her husband was repulsive).

95 Ibn Rushd noted that "there is no dispute that a woman possessing discretion (a *rashīda*) has a right to transact redemption for herself." Ibn Rushd, *Distinguished Jurist's Primer*, 2:82. See also Ibn Qudāmah, *al-Mughnī*, 10:267 (Ḥanbalī: wife has the right to "ransom" divorce); al-Nawawī, *al-Majmūʿ*, 16:2 (Shāfiʿī: "if a woman loathes her husband … she may remove him by [paying] compensation").

96 Referring to *khulʿ*, Ibn Rushd explains "the majority held that it [redemption divorce] is permitted with the mutual consent of the parties, unless consent to pay him is obtained by fear of injury to her." Ibn Rushd, *Distinguished Jurist's Primer*, 2:81; al-Marghīnānī, *The Hidāyah*, 2:194 (Ḥanafī: implying that *khulʿ* necessitates mutual consent).

divorce often occur adjacent to or in conjunction with the topic of recalcitrance.[97] Still, late medieval and early modern Islamicate court records establish that women continued to acquire divorces by forfeiting part or all of their dowers.[98] Indeed, it is possible that *khulʿ* divorces superseded judicial grants of divorce in which women were given full dowers.

What this condensed chronology of Muslim women's access to divorce suggests is that jurists gradually limited a wife's ability to divorce her husband. Notably, husbands gained the option of divorcing and paying less than the standard divorce settlement in a variety of situations.

Disenchanting the Orthodox Narratives

Thus far, I have presented two distinct chronologies – one Judaic and the other Islamic – in which I have outlined historical changes in how jurists of each community conceptualized a woman's right to divorce. In both of these chronologies, jurists interpreted the legal opinions and practices of their predecessors within a juristic construction of historical "truth" that informs legal orthodoxy. The historical evidence presented in these two chronologies contrasts with the "orthodox" stories – of both historical actors and contemporary scholars. The orthodox Islamic legal story elides distinctions between the legal practices of the late antique and medieval periods, creating a seamless narrative of women being able to negotiate a divorce primarily by forfeiting their dowers – or more. However, the Islamic chronology detailed above implies that medieval Muslim jurists construed a Prophetic precedent about wife-initiated divorce as requiring a husband's consent or necessitating the determination of fault; consequently, they elaborated a variety of restrictions on wife-initiated divorce.

The orthodox Jewish legal story selects legal changes that legitimate normative practices.[99] In what is described as the Rabbinic period (70–620 CE), women did not have a no-fault divorce option because they

[97] Majd al-Dīn Abī al-Barakāt ʿAbd al-Salām ibn ʿAbd Allāh ibn al-Khiḍr ibn Taymīyah al-Ḥarrānī (d. 1254/5; Syria/Iraq) and Shams al-Dīn Ibn Mufliḥ al-Ḥanbalī al-Maqdisī (d. 1362; Syria) *Muḥarrar fī al-fiqh ʿalá madhhab al-imām Aḥmad ibn Ḥanbal*, ed. by Muḥammad Ḥasan Muḥammad Ḥasan Ismāʿīl and Aḥmad Maḥrūs Jaʿfar Ṣāliḥ, 2 vols. (Beirut: Dār al-Kutub al-ʿIlmīyah, 1999), 2:95 and 97 (Ḥanbalī: section on recalcitrance immediately precedes section on *khulʿ*); ʿUthmān ibn ʿAlī al-Zaylaʿī al-Ḥanafī (d. 1342/3), ʿAbd Allāh ibn Aḥmad al-Nasafī (d. 1310; Iraq), and Aḥmad ibn Muḥammad Shalabī (d. 1612/13), *Tabyīn al-ḥaqāʾiq; sharḥ kanz al-daqāʾiq*, ed. by Aḥmad ʿAzzū ʿInāyah, 7 vols. (Beirut: Dār al-Kutub al-ʿIlmīyah, 2000), 3:185 (Ḥanafī: Prophetic precedent concerning Ḥabibah's *khulʿ* divorce is explicitly interpreted as an example of a woman's recalcitrance).

[98] See, for example, Ronald C. Jennings, "Divorce in the Ottoman sharia court of Cyprus, 1580–1640." *Studia Islamica* 78 (1993): 155–67.

[99] In its basic form, this orthodox story is validated by Libson, *Jewish and Islamic law*, 111.

could initiate a divorce only if they could prove just cause. According to the orthodox story, in the Geonic period (620–1050 CE), the rabbis felt "pressured" by the influence of Islamic courts to change existing practices by facilitating a no-fault divorce option for women. In the era of the Rishonim (1050–1400 CE), the rabbis corrected the "deviant" Geonic practice and returned Jewish law to its "original" foundations by prohibiting women from no-fault divorce.

The orthodox Islamic narrative obscures the strong possibility that the specific procedural requirement of obtaining a husband's acquiescence to the wife's divorce initiation emerged in the medieval period. The orthodox Jewish narrative hides that the Geonic practice of coercing a husband to divorce a "recalcitrant" wife was normative for centuries until its gradual undermining in the late medieval period. When these two orthodox stories and the two chronologies enumerated above are all juxtaposed, a pattern begins to emerge.

I want to problematize a specific point of intersection between these two narratives: the orthodox Jewish narrative characterizes the Geonic enactment (*taqqanah*) as an innovation (i.e., lacking talmudic precedent) caused by Islamic "influence" and many scholars accept this perspective.[100] The question I want to explore is why this Geonic decree has been interpreted – both by some Rishonim and by some contemporary scholars – as having deviated from Talmudic practice or from pre-Geonic Jewish practice. My claim is that the characterization of the Geonic decree as deviating from the Talmud or as exceeding the limits of Geonic authority is implicitly based on an evaluation of the Islamicate setting. In other words, those who rejected the Geonic ordinance as an innovation did so because they believed it was "caused" by Islamic influence.[101] That is, viewing this Geonic decree as the outcome of "influence" implicitly accepts the orthodox narrative about its legitimacy. This Geonic decree's classification is the site of a contest for legal authority and I will provide historical and critical evidence to offer an alternative understanding of this Jewish law in its presumed "Islamic" context.

As I will clarify below, a late medieval rabbinic consensus gradually developed in the West that viewed the Geonic decree as an "innovation"

100 See footnote 34. But see Friedman, who argued that wife-initiated divorce was a pre-Islamic Jewish custom. Friedman, "The ransom-divorce," 298.

101 For example, Westreich describes the opinion of Rishonim: "Halakhic sources explicitly indicate that the aim of this ruling was to prevent malicious manipulations in Moslem [*sic*] courts that forced Jewish men to grant a divorce demanded by women claiming 'repulsion.'" Westreich, "The rise and decline," 217 (citing Hilkhot ha-Rosh, Ketubbōt 85, sec. 35).

caused by the "influence" of Gentile courts. Contemporary scholars who presume that the Gentile courts were Islamic characterize the Geonic decree as being caused by Islamic pressure – of some kind.[102] But these two characterizations of "innovation" and "influence" must be reevaluated because they obscure a complicated historical struggle for legal authority. Discrediting the Geonic legal practice of facilitating a recalcitrant wife's divorce claim may be a manifestation of Western rabbinic authority overpowering Eastern rabbinic authority.[103]

The implications of the two characterizations that I will challenge are manifest in a specific example. There is suggestive evidence of Jewish women divorcing their husbands prior to the Islamic period and the interpretation of that evidence is driven by interpretations of the Geonic decree. In other words, those who view the decree as an extension of a continuous practice (i.e., the Talmud sanctions the practice of coercing husbands to divorce a wife) thus recognize that Jewish wives had a long-standing ability to initiate unilateral divorce.[104] In contrast, those who view the decree as a legal "innovation" based on "foreign influence" thereby negate the possibility that Jewish wives could initiate divorce outside the judicially recognized justifications.[105] Therefore, the historical and contemporary interpretation of this decree has significant stakes for Jewish legal practice and the conventional narratives should be scrutinized.

Reevaluating Causal Influence

At the time of the Geonic decree (mid-seventh century),[106] a minority of the population was Muslim and Islamic courts were not adjudicating

[102] Contemporary scholars perpetuate these assumptions about "innovation" and "influence." For instance, like other contemporary scholars, Brody characterizes the Geonic decree as "dictated by profound changes in the circumstances affecting Jewish life in the Muslim world, and more particularly in Babylonia, which necessitated a *departure* from Talmudic law." Brody, *The geonim of Babylonia*, 62, emphasis added.

[103] Libson suggests, "Rejections of geonic rulings are more common among Ashkenazi scholars, who allowed themselves more latitude in legal decisions than the Sephardim." Libson, "Halakhah and law," 241.

[104] See footnote 10. Jewish wives appear to have been able to initiate divorce in Babylonia (possibly prior to the Geonic decree) and in Palestine (based on a practice of including a stipulation in the marriage contract). See also Westreich, "The rise and decline," 207.

[105] See footnote 9. See also Brody, "Evidence for divorce by Jewish women?." Libson, *Jewish and Islamic law*, 158.

[106] Libson dates the decree to 650 or 651 and while it may be possible to date it to a slightly later period, these historical observations hold true. Libson, *Jewish and Islamic law*, 111. In other words, the precise accuracy of this dating is less important than its issuance within a relatively short amount of time after the conquests.

outside the garrison towns established during the Arab/Muslim conquests.[107] That a minority Muslim presence could have such significant effect on Jewish legal practice as to provoke the enactment within decades of the beginning of Iraq's conquest is improbable. In other words, the orthodox narrative's claim that the Geonim "deviated" from Talmudic practice in order to defend against the threat of Muslim "influence" – coercive or otherwise – is based on inaccurate interpretations of historical evidence.[108] The majority population at this time was actually Christian or Zoroastrian; among Eastern Christians and Zoroastrians, women returning their dowers in order to effect a divorce is a historically verified practice. Since local communities operated courts, the "Gentile" courts that provoked the Geonic decree may not have been Islamic even after the Muslim conquests.[109] Indeed, wife-initiated divorce may not have been the dominant Islamic legal practice, since it was the subject of intense juristic debate among Muslims and possibly only one of many legal positions.[110] Moreover, it is particularly improbable that any potential Islamic legal "influence" was coercive. The orthodox Jewish narrative inaccurately assumes the existence of Islamic influence that is negated by historical evidence.

[107] Hallaq explains that Islamic law was only applied to Muslims in the garrison towns and parts of the Arabian peninsula for the first several decades after the Prophet's death. Hallaq, *The origins*, 54–5. Morony observes that Islamic law was not applied to Jews and he suggests that rabbinic authority increased as a result of the non-involvement of Muslims in their internal legal affairs. Michael G. Morony, *Iraq after the Muslim conquest* (Princeton, NJ: Princeton University Press, 1984), 320, 518. By contrast, Libson rejects the idea that the decree's proximity in time to the Arab/Muslim conquests weakens the assumption of influence. Libson, "Halakhah and law," 238. But Libson does not provide historical evidence about the administration of Islamic courts in the mid-seventh century to substantiate his influence claim.

[108] Indeed, common interpretations of the Geonic decree suggest prejudicial and anachronistic assumptions. For example, a contemporary scholar argues that the Geonic decree does not represent "absorption of legal concepts of one culture into another culture, but rather a defensive act of a minority culture against the destructive influence of the surrounding majority culture" (my translation). Yehudah Zvi Stampfer, "Islamic influence in the divorce laws of Rav Samuel Ben Hofni Gaon and the Rambam." In *ʿAle ʿasor: divre ha-veʿidah ha-ʿasirit shel ha-hevrah le-heker ha-tarbut ha-ʿArvit-ha-yehudit shel yeme-ha-benayim*, ed. by Congress Society for Judaeo-Arabic Studies *et al.* (Beer-Sheva: University of Ben Gurion, 2008), 312. These assumptions about the destructive nature of the majority culture are based on an inaccurate understanding of history: the majority of the population in Iraq (or the Near East more generally) was Christian and did not become Muslim until several centuries later.

[109] Simonsohn, *A common justice*.

[110] For instance, Muslim jurists debated the necessity of having a legal justification or court involvement for *khulʿ*. Two late antique Muslim jurists – al-Ḥasan al-Baṣrī (d. 728) and Ibn Sīrīn (d. 729) – had an exceptional opinion that *khulʿ* is only permissible with judicial oversight. Kaḥlāwī, *al-Khulʿ*, 69; al-Sarakhsī, *al-mabsūṭ*, 6:173 (Ḥanafī: court involvement not necessary for *khulʿ*); Ibn Qudāmah, *al-Mughnī*, 10:268–9 (Ḥanbalī: conflicting reports about the necessity of court involvement in *khulʿ*).

More probable than the existence or prevalence of Islamic courts is the possibility that Jewish women simply knew that non-Jewish women who demanded divorces did not have to wait one year, in addition to having relatively more expansive inheritance and property rights. Threatened by the possibility of Jewish women converting (to any religion), Geonic rabbis likely reduced the waiting period; this practical modification can be interpreted as reacting to an internal social demand – not necessarily "influence." This type of legal change – motivated by "social welfare" or "public interest" – is endemic to all legal systems. Moreover, forum shopping by legal consumers shaped legal changes. While Jewish women in the Near East and North Africa were able to acquire divorces in rabbinic courts under a recalcitrant wife claim throughout the medieval period,[111] they apparently still frequented state (such as Islamic) courts.[112] Even in places where rabbinic courts facilitated wife-initiated divorce, Jewish women availed themselves of state (i.e., Islamic) courts; the Geonic enactment did not prevent Jewish women from accessing other legal options.[113] To appreciate the dynamics of legal pluralism, we need to recognize such complexities as venue shopping and socio-economic barriers to legal consumerism.

In addition, the "influence" theory does not sufficiently explain how the Geonic enactment "protected" the Jewish community from two realities: the availability of state (i.e., Islamic) courts that facilitated a Jewish wife's divorce and the possibility of conversion.[114] The orthodox narrative claims that Jewish women who had to wait twelve months for a divorce fell into indecency (i.e., illicit affairs) or apostatized (presumably becoming Muslim).[115] Ostensibly, the Geonim dispensed with the long waiting period in order to hasten a Jewish woman's divorce and prevent her apostasy (for the purpose of divorcing her Jewish husband).[116] Yet a Jewish

[111] Westreich, "The rise and decline," 216; Goitein, *A Mediterranean society*, 3:266.

[112] Goitein mentions a Jewish woman who divorced her husband in an Islamic court. Goitein, *A Mediterranean society*, 3:265. On Jews frequenting Islamic (state) courts for divorce, see Simonsohn, *A common justice*, 178–80. See also Aryeh Shmuelevitz, *The Jews of the Ottoman Empire in the late fifteenth and the sixteenth centuries: administrative, economic, legal, and social relations as reflected in the responsa* (Leiden: E.J. Brill, 1984), 67 ("sixteenth century matrimonial cases were frequently referred to Muslim law courts.").

[113] It may be the case, however, that (rabbinic) Jewish women continued to seek judicial divorce decrees from state (i.e., Islamic) courts in situations where a Jewish husband refused to deliver a divorce decree.

[114] Libson, *Jewish and Islamic law*, 111.

[115] An anonymous thirteenth-century text identifies both moral indecency and apostasy as causal factors motivating the Geonic decree. Riskin, *A Jewish woman's right to divorce*, 52–3.

[116] By the early medieval era, the consensus of Muslim jurists was that a married woman who became Muslim would be divorced unless her husband also converted within her divorce waiting period.

woman who became Muslim would not necessarily have been automatically divorced because this Islamic doctrine was not clearly established in the mid-seventh century.[117]

How might the Geonic rabbis have compelled a husband to deliver a divorce decree instantaneously when husbands very often delayed the process? If the Geonic practice removed the twelve-month waiting period and then relied on coercing the husband to grant a wife a divorce, the "threat" of conversion to Islam remained. That is, a Jewish woman might simply become Muslim and demand a judicial divorce decree from an Islamic court, rather than wait for her husband to deliver her divorce decree under coercion. It is no coincidence then that the Qaraites – in the eleventh century or earlier – accepted judicial divorce decrees and that Maimonides denounced the practice as heretical.[118] Qaraite Judaism's tension with rabbinic Judaism was both intellectually and geographically located in the Islamicate world. Notably, the specific wording of several Geonic texts implies that courts granted or gave Jewish women divorces, without explicitly delineating that the courts coerced husbands to deliver divorce decrees.[119] While we cannot make conclusions based on this precise terminology, it is likely that judicial divorce decrees became a site of Jewish orthodox contestation in the medieval period. It was not only Muslim "influence" that concerned the rabbis, but the sectarian influence of Qaraites. Western rabbinic jurists may have marked the boundaries of rabbinic orthodoxy against Qaraite "heresy" through this particular legal issue. The extent to which generalizations may be made from this case study to broader processes of sectarian resistance and regional competition in the shaping of rabbinic Jewish orthodoxy is a matter for further research.

117 It is unclear if the seventh-century Muslim community viewed the conversion of a wife as automatically resulting in a divorce.

118 Judith Olszowy-Schlanger, "La lettre de divorce caraïte et sa place dans les relations Caraïtes et Rabbanites au Moyen Age." *Revue des Études Juives* 155:3 (1996): 337–62 at 342. The Qaraite judicial divorce decree is also discussed in Judith Olszowy-Schlanger, *Karaite marriage documents from the Cairo Geniza: legal tradition and community life in mediaeval Egypt and Palestine* (Leiden; New York: Brill, 1998), 126. See also Maimonides' critique of non-Jewish courts coercing Jewish husbands, evidence that the practice existed, but not a negation of the possibility that non-rabbinic courts provided judicial divorce decrees. Maimonides, *Mishneh Torah*, Hilchot Gerushin, 2:20, pp. 177–8.

119 By way of example, see the following responsum: "After the gemara, our rabbis decreed that even what she holds (from him) *we* take from her and *we* give her a divorce immediately." Harkavy, *Teshuvot ha-geonim*, section 71, emphasis added. See also footnote 31.

Giving Voice to the Geonim

Most Geonim did not view their practice of facilitating wife-initiated divorce as divergent from Talmudic traditions.[120] The Geonic enactment included two components: (a) the removal of the twelve-month waiting period (stipulated in the Babylonian Talmud) for the recalcitrant wife and (b) coercion of the husband to grant a recalcitrant wife a divorce.[121] The Geonim perceived the first component as new, but not the second.[122] Yet, later rabbinic authorities interpreted both components of the decree as "innovative," despite the Geonic perspective that they had preserved rabbinic Jewish tradition. This assumption of "innovation" is reflected in much of the scholarly literature.[123] The orthodox narrative thereby marks as heretical the prolonged practice of Geonic communities who facilitated wife-initiated divorce.[124]

The characterization of the Geonic decree as an "innovation" is motivated by the causal presumption of "influence." It is commonly assumed that the availability of divorce for women in contemporaneous Islamic courts led Geonic rabbis to modify divorce practices.[125] However, Geonic texts do not explicitly identify Islamic courts as being a causal influence on the decree. For example, Naṭrōnāī ben Hilāī (or Natronai Gaon,

[120] Westreich notes that "according to the Geonim, the source of the halakha coercing the husband to grant a divorce to his rebellious wife is the Talmud itself. Several geonic writings indeed state so specifically." Westreich, "The rise and decline," 209. See also Friedman, *Jewish marriage in Palestine*, 1:324.

[121] A third component concerns the dower payment, which the Geonim made collectable on movable property. Libson, "Halakhah and law," 237. I suspect that it may be possible to add a fourth component: the possibility that rabbinic courts granted Jewish women divorces without requiring a formal deliverance of the divorce decree from the husband. But this possibility necessitates more research than the scope of this chapter allows.

[122] Since the Geonim identified the Talmud as the source for (b), only (a) was perceived by them as innovative. Libson explains, "Rav Sherira holds – and this seems to be the view of all the Geonim – that the compulsory nature of the divorce had already been laid down in the *Talmud*, the only new element in the *takkanah* being the stipulation that divorce be granted forthwith, without delay." *Ibid.* See also Westreich, "The rise and decline," 209.

[123] By way of example, Libson claims, "since the talmudic text itself could not be easily interpreted and the details of the *takkanah* itself were not known, the interpretation became a matter of controversy among the Geonim themselves. It is therefore difficult to determine the *takkanah*'s precise degree of *deviation* from Talmudic law proper." Libson, "Halakhah and law," 236, emphasis added.

[124] By way of example, Genizah evidence indicates that in Palestinian marriage contracts of the tenth and eleventh centuries, "Either party was empowered, thereby, to demand a divorce for purely subjective reasons and was not compelled to prove cause." Friedman, *Jewish marriage in Palestine*, 1:330.

[125] "There is no doubt that the redress open to women in the Shariʿa courts spurred the geonim to provide similar redress in Jewish law." Libson, *Jewish and Islamic law*, 111. See also Westreich, "The rise and decline," 217–18.

d. ninth century, Iraq) explained the rationale for the decree as "so that Jewish women should not stray towards lewdness and indecency."[126] Some Geonic sources do not mention a reason for the enactment.[127] Of course, these Geonim may have recognized Islamic legal practices, but simply did not acknowledge them. But in analyzing the issuance of the Geonic decree, we should focus on the consistency and plausibility of historical interpretations. In light of the aforementioned historical evidence, early Geonim did not cite Islamic "influence" for the decree because no such "influence" existed in their time.

By contrast, Sherira ben Ḥanina, writing in the late tenth century, identified the decree as intended to prevent Jewish women from asking Gentile courts to coerce their husbands because only a Jewish court can legitimately coerce a Jewish husband to divorce his wife.[128] In Sherira Gaon's lifetime, Islamic courts were prevalent and, when petitioned by Jewish wives, they probably did coerce Jewish husbands to deliver divorce decrees – or possibly granted divorce decrees to Jewish wives. Sherira Gaon may have anachronistically interpreted the reasons for the seventh-century Geonic decree based on his own reality; that is, since Sherira was surrounded by Islamic courts, he may have simply assumed that his Geonic predecessors were likewise "competing" with Muslim jurists for Jewish litigants. Notably, Sherira Gaon is the only known Geonic figure to attribute the influence of Gentile courts to the Geonic decree.[129]

Which Context?

What is problematic about "influence" as a characterization for a particular historical event? "Influence" is very often code for "infiltration" or "impurity." The orthodox understanding of the Geonic decree focuses on the causal factors (rather than context) that led to its enactment and presents the decree's gradual overturning as if it occurred in the absence of causal factors (or a context). The orthodox Jewish narrative validates a specific bias that can be identified in terms of time (medieval era) and space (the West): it was Western Rishonim who characterized the Geonic decree as unorthodox. It is possible, of course, that the Rishonim would have invalidated the Geonic decree even if they had not suspected or assumed

[126] Riskin, *A Jewish woman's right to divorce*, 51.

[127] *Halakhot gedolot* does not explain the enactment's rationale. *Ibid.*, 48–9.

[128] *Ibid.*, 58. See also Menachem Elon, *Jewish law: history, sources, principles* [Ha-mishpat ha-Ivri], trans. by Bernard Auerbach and Melvin J. Sykes (Philadelphia, PA: Jewish Publication Society, 1994), 2:659–60.

[129] Riskin, *A Jewish woman's right to divorce*, 74 (citing Tykocinski as having made this observation).

"Islamic influence." But it is notable that the orthodox narrative does not acknowledge (or minimizes) Western Christian "influences," while Islamic "influences" are vilified – and both legal systems are drastically oversimplified.[130] Notably, the distinctions within Christian teachings on divorce may reflect discrete regional practices.[131]

While it is not surprising that Western Rishonim did not describe their annulling of the Geonic decree as being the result of Western "influence," it is remarkable that contemporary scholars perpetuate this selective application of the notion of "influence." Westreich, for instance, noted that "the process of erosion [of the recalcitrant wife divorce] moved along the lines of advance of Christian society, which gradually conquered and dominated areas that had so far been under Moslem [*sic*] influence and control, at least in Spain."[132] Westreich explicitly observes that Rabbeinu Tam's legal opinion against the recalcitrant wife divorce occurred "as Christian society became monogamous and imposed Catholic laws making divorce impossible."[133] Moreover, it is possible that Rabbeinu Tam (d. 1171) felt compelled to oppose wife-initiated divorce because his German predecessor, Rabbeinu Gershom (d. 1028) had "enacted a decree which made it impossible for a husband to divorce his wife against her will."[134] Since Western Jewish men had lost their ability to divorce their wives unilaterally, it became necessary to limit the divorce options of Western Jewish women in similar ways. Contemporary scholars pose a question about the "influences" that provoked the Geonic decree, but not about the "influences" that led to the overturning of that decree.

To be clear, I am not arguing for Western Christian "influence" on the Western Rishonim; to do so would replace one problematic "influence" paradigm with another. Instead, all legal communities produce law in social

[130] In reference to (Christian) Europe, Westreich, for example, claims that "the influence of the Gentile environment also affected the decline of the rebellious woman ground, ultimately leading to its abolition. This influence, however, is indirect, as Jewish society internalizes the social norms of the Gentile environment as a result of a prolonged encounter, and projects them onto Jewish law through a complex mutual relationship whose stages cannot be traced." Westreich, "The rise and decline," 218. Compare this to Westreich's description of Islamic influence: "Halakhic sources explicitly indicate that the aim of this ruling was to prevent malicious manipulations in Moslem [*sic*] courts that forced Jewish men to grant a divorce demanded by women claiming 'repulsion' … the geonic ordinance clearly originated as a result of factors that, although directly affecting Jewish circumstances, were extraneous to *Halakhah*." *Ibid.*, 217–18. The historical evidence presented above establishes that no such Islamic "influence" existed for the Geonic decree.

[131] The Greek, but not the Hebrew, version of the Gospel of Matthew 5:31–32 limits a husband's grounds for divorcing his wife to adultery. George Howard, *The Gospel of Matthew according to a primitive Hebrew text* (Macon, GA: Mercer University Press, 1987), 204.

[132] Westreich, "The rise and decline," 218.

[133] *Ibid.*

[134] Riskin, *A Jewish woman's right to divorce*, xii, 109.

contexts; indeed, law *cannot* be disentangled from society. Just as the Geonim read the Talmud through the intellectual concerns and socio-political realities of their times, so too did the Western Rishonim. These two historical moments – the enactment of the Geonic decree and its abolition by Western Rishonim – are both reflective of, and mediated by, jurists enmeshed in their societies. Late medieval, Western jurists marked a seventh-century Geonic decree as an "innovation" caused by Gentile "influence" within a struggle for legal authority: the Geonic decree was marked as "deviant" not because it occurred under Gentile "influence," but because its revocation occurred in a Western-Christian context. This case study only touches upon a broader disjuncture between Western and Eastern Judaic practices that is beyond the scope of this chapter. For our purposes, it is important to note that contemporary scholars delineated the "other" by placing a Jewish law in an imagined "Islamic" context – instead of a historical one. Both some Western Rishonim and some contemporary scholars employ a notion of "influence" that manifests reductive causality and, thereby, is an impediment to deeper and more complex understanding of legal change. Probing relationships and contextualization can move us beyond simplified notions of "influence" that are themselves legal-political strategies.

The extent to which generalizations may be made from this case to broader processes of sectarian resistance and regional competition in the shaping of rabbinic Jewish orthodoxy is a matter for further research.[135] To understand each legal system's transformations, we need to recognize the unending dialectic between internal legal logic and changing socio-political circumstances. In the next section, I narrate wife-initiated divorce outside the orthodox framework, with the background of Near Eastern legal culture.

An Interwoven Narrative of Wife-initiated Divorce

Antiquity and Late Antiquity (up to 800 CE)

While most Near Eastern legal systems in antiquity appear to have granted men an unencumbered right to divorce,[136] women were not

[135] Libson observed that "Although it [the recalcitrant wife decree] was recorded in geonic codificatory works, such as *Halakhot Peṣuḳot* and *Halakhot Gedolot*, it did not win acceptance in later rabbinic literature – a fate similar to that of many other *taḳḳanot* and customs from the geonic period." Libson, "Halakhah and law," 238.

[136] David L. Lieber, Ben-Zion Schereschewsky, and Moshe Drori, "Divorce." In *Encyclopaedia Judaica*, ed. by Michael Berenbaum and Fred Skolnik (Detroit, MI: Macmillan Reference USA, 2007), 710–21 at 710–11.

precluded from divorcing their husbands. Indeed, there is evidence of women initiating divorces,[137] which may have taken place by the act of the wife leaving the home.[138] Common Near Eastern customs are apparent in some surviving ancient Mesopotamian legal texts; as in the case of Jewish divorce practices in antiquity, there is a scholarly debate on the issue of a woman's ability to divorce in ancient Mesopotamian law.[139] The nature of the surviving historical evidence (primarily legal texts and some court records) results in this inconsistency in the historical interpretation surrounding women and divorce in the ancient Near East. But it may be concluded that the ambiguous nature of the historical evidence itself reflects a diverse legal reality in which some wives could divorce their husbands and others could not.[140] Despite a male, jurisprudential rhetoric legitimating divorce as a male prerogative, women could and did divorce their husbands in practice. At least in some cases, women in the ancient Near East had to seek judicial intervention in order to divorce their husbands.[141] Even this condensed "pre-history" suggests that, by the late antique period, there were diverse Near Eastern customary practices of men divorcing women, women divorcing men, and judges intervening to effect divorces.

Underlying these practices is a specific economic reality: men paid for both marriages and divorces. Ancient Near Eastern legal texts consistently

[137] Roman provincial law recognized wife-initiated divorce and was likely practiced throughout the Near East. Gillian Clark, *Women in late antiquity: pagan and Christian life-styles* (Oxford: Clarendon Press, 1993), 18. Jewish women divorced their husbands in second-century Egypt and in Palestine under Roman law. See Brewer, "Jewish women divorcing their husbands," 354. The main source for Zoroastrian law is the Mādigān ī hazār dādistān and it is commonly dated to approximately 620 CE. *Das sasanidische Rechtsbuch "Matakdan i hazar datistan" (Teil II)*, trans. by Maria Macuch (Wiesbaden: Deutsche Morgenländische Gesellschaft: Kommissionsverla g, F. Steiner, 1981), 25–9, 97–120.

[138] By way of example, Sealey points out that marriage in ancient Greece was not public and did not necessitate judicial involvement. Raphael Sealey, *The justice of the Greeks* (Ann Arbor, MI: University of Michigan Press, 1994), 68, fn. 30.

[139] Raymond Westbrook, *Old Babylonian marriage law*, Archiv für Orientforschung, Beiheft 23 (Horn, Austria: F. Berger, 1988), 79. See also Russ VerSteeg, *Early Mesopotamian law* (Durham, NC: Carolina Academic Press, 2000), 88.

[140] Westbrook, *Old Babylonian marriage law*, 85.

[141] The Laws of Hammurabi (*c.* 1750 BCE) mention that if a wife repudiates her husband, an inquiry is made; if she is found to be not at fault, then she takes her dowry and leaves, but if she is found to be at fault, she is thrown into the water. Martha Tobi Roth, Harry A. Hoffner, and Piotr Michalowski, *Law collections from Mesopotamia and Asia Minor* (Atlanta, GA.: Scholars Press, 1997), 108. Likewise, Johns asserts that "It was far harder for a woman to secure a divorce from her husband. She could do so, however, but only as the result of a lawsuit. As a rule, the marriage-contracts mention death as her punishment, if she repudiates her husband." C. H. W. Johns, *Babylonian and Assyrian laws, contracts and letters* (Edinburgh: T. & T. Clark, 1904), 143.

reference divorce in terms of men paying divorce settlements.[142] Since the default Near Eastern norm was for husbands to pay dowers to their wives as part of the marriage process, they maintained stronger privileges to divorce, which also entailed payment of a divorce settlement to the wife. This is why women who divorced their husbands paid for this prerogative in nearly all late antique Near Eastern legal cultures – Jewish, Byzantine, and Islamic.[143] Indeed, a basic presumption in the region seems to have been that if a wife returned her entire dower, then that act in and of itself constituted divorce.[144] For example, late antique divorce documents (written in Greek on papyrus) from Nessana indicate that Christian women – both prior to and soon after the Arab/Islamic conquest – relinquished their dowers in order to acquire a divorce.[145] Juxtaposed with the evidence from Jewish and Islamic sources cited above, this suggests that women in the late antique Near East – regardless of confessional identity – relinquished dowers in order to divorce their husbands.

These divorce-based monetary exchanges resemble the conceptually related slavery and ransoming practices of the region. At the level of terminology, slaves could financially redeem themselves to receive a manumission decree in a manner that mimics a divorce decree in Jewish law.[146]

[142] Laws of Ur-Namma (*c.* 2100 BCE) sec. 9–11 (man pays upon divorcing wife, based on wife's status), Roth *et al.*, *Law collections*, 18; Laws of Lipit-Ishtar (*c.* 1930 BCE) sec. 28, 30 (limits a man's ability to divorce his first wife; indicates that men pay divorce settlement), *Ibid.*, 31–2; Sumerian Laws Handbook of Forms (*c.* 1700 BCE) iv 12–16 (husband pays divorce settlement), *Ibid.*, 50; Laws of Eshnunna (*c.* 1770 BCE) sec. 59 (husband is financially punished for divorcing a wife who is mother of his children), *Ibid.*, 68; Laws of Hammurabi (*c.* 1750 BCE) sec. 137–41 (husband who divorces wife with whom he has children pays her dowry and half of his assets; husband who divorces wife who is childless pays a divorce settlement that varies depending on the status of the wife), *Ibid.*, 107. One exception is Middle Assyrian Laws (*c.* 1076 BCE) A sec. 37–8 (husband may divorce wife without paying divorce settlement), *Ibid.*, 167.

[143] In late antique Roman provincial (or Christian) law: "A woman who divorced without grounds lost dowry and gifts and had to wait five years to remarry; a man who divorced without good reason merely lost dowry and gifts." Clark, *Women in late antiquity*, 24. See also Judith Evans Grubbs, "'Pagan' and 'Christian' marriage: the state of the question," in *Christianity and society: the social world of early Christianity*, ed. by Everett Ferguson, Recent studies in early Christianity (New York: Garland, 1999), 185–236 at 190 (noting that after Constantine, husbands could financially benefit if divorce was the wife's "fault").

[144] As a case in point: while the word *ketubbah* means marriage contract, it is commonly used in rabbinic literature to refer specifically to the dower payment. In other words, the marriage contract and the dower are equivalent.

[145] Casper J. Kraemer, *Excavations at Nessana. Non-literary papyri*, Colt Archaeological Expedition, 1936–1937 (Princeton, NJ: Princeton University Press, 1958), 104–6, 161–7.

[146] *Mishnah*, Giṭṭīn 1.4 (comparing delivery of divorce and emancipation documents); *P. Talmud*, Giṭṭīn 1:3 (writs of divorce and writs of manumission are treated the same). The slave's emancipation decree is *geṭ shikhrūr* and a woman's divorce decree is *geṭ nashīm*. See also *B. Talmud*, Giṭṭīn 9a (similarities between divorce and emancipation documents) and Qīddūshīn 16a (discussing slaves redeeming themselves by payment).

Similarly, the Qur'ānic verse that grants women the option of initiating divorce indicates that women may "ransom" themselves.[147] There is a late antique exception that, perhaps, proves the rule: according to the late antique *Corpus Juris Civilis* (Roman legal code), a wife may repudiate her husband, but the husband does not pay a dower; a wife pays a dowry in order to marry and her husband profits from it during the marriage.[148] Moreover, Near Eastern women of higher social status had relatively more access to divorce, further indicating that financial means figured into a woman's ability to procure a divorce.[149]

Recognition of the diversity of late antique Near Eastern legal practices and premodern forms of women's agency suggests that there were a variety of legal maneuvers for women to obtain divorces. It should be noted that judicial involvement likely varied according to region – with some areas functioning without an official court. We may characterize this period as being legally heterodox.

Medieval Era (800–1400 CE)

Legal systematization and professionalization transformed legal practice in the Near East. Marriage and divorce became institutionalized in the medieval era. By the twelfth century, divorce became a primarily court-mediated process and some court intervention became normative for most divorce situations.[150] The professionalization and centralization of legal education resulted in the consolidation of juristic opinions. Some form of legal orthodoxy is evident in both Jewish and Islamic legal texts that present a hierarchy of divorce practices:

(1) husband divorces wife and pays full divorce settlement;
(2) court divorces husband and wife because of husband's impotence, defects, or unreasonable behavior; husband pays full divorce settlement;

[147] Qur'ān 2:229 (a wife may "redeem" herself from a marriage). See also Kecia Ali, *Marriage and slavery in early Islam* (Cambridge, MA: Harvard University Press, 2010).

[148] Dig. 23.3.1 *et seq.* (woman pays dowry at marriage); Dig. 24.3.1 *et seq* (elaborating various dowry-related cases and husband's rights to dowry's profits); Dig. 24.2.1 *et seq.* (wife or husband may repudiate spouse) in *Digest of Justinian or Digest. English.* Although redacted in the sixth century, the *Digest of Justinian* contains legal traditions dating to earlier generations of jurists, including to the Roman republican period.

[149] Muhammad A. Dandamayev, Mansour Shaki, Sachiko Murata, Akbar Aghajanian, Jenny Rose, and Mujan Momen, "Divorce," in *Encyclopaedia Iranica* (London: Routledge & Kegan Paul, 1983). See also Brewer, "Jewish women divorcing their husbands," 356.

[150] That wife-initiated divorce occurred in an earlier period without court intervention is substantiated by juristic texts. See footnote 110.

(3) husband divorces wife or wife divorces husband; husband does not pay divorce settlement or pays only part of the settlement because wife has agreed to accept less or has been declared recalcitrant.

In the third category, I intentionally collapse two distinct forms of divorce that became ambiguous in the medieval period. The divorce of a recalcitrant wife in the Jewish legal tradition and the forfeiting wife in the Islamic legal tradition are procedurally the same: in both cases, women acted to divorce their husbands and lost some money in the process. Similarly, the formalist expectation that a Jewish husband deliver a divorce decree or that a Muslim husband consent to the wife's divorce settlement are both legal-formalist perspectives that gained ascendancy in the medieval periods.

It may be possible to discern similar shifts in juristic views of marriage and divorce in how jurists adjudicated temporary marriage: widely practiced in late antiquity, temporary marriages were gradually marked as deviant in the medieval era. Both Jews and Muslims appear to have practiced temporary marriages throughout the late antique period, but gradually marked it as heretical. The legitimacy of temporary marriages became a sectarian issue between Sunnīs and Shīʿīs after the tenth century.[151] One of the reasons Sunnī jurists offered as evidence of temporary marriage's illegitimacy is that, since the marriage automatically expired at the end of the specified duration, it did not end with a divorce.[152] Orthodox jurists appear to have been anxious about women being able to end marriages without going to court; they made a woman's status the subject of institutional oversight.

In all the divorce types enumerated above, men or women pay a divorce settlement depending on which party was considered – by the court or customary norms – to be the breaching party. Generally, women who initiated or demanded divorce in the absence of judicially recognized justifications lost money in the divorce process. Between late antiquity and the middle ages, these judicially recognized justifications became more formalized. There is a substantive difference in how the exchange is abstracted: whereas earlier divorce was akin to a contract

[151] See Lena Salaymeh and Zvi Septimus, "Temporalities of marriage: medieval Jewish and Islamic legal debates." In *Talmudic Transgressions: Essays in Honor of Daniel Boyarin*, ed. by C. Fonrobert *et al.* (Leiden: Brill, forthcoming).

[152] ʿAlī ibn Muḥammad Ṭabāṭabāʾī (d. *c.* 1816), *Riyāḍ al-masāʾil fī bayān al-aḥkām bi-al-dalāʾil* (Beirut: Dār al-Hādī, 1992), 7:25 (Imāmī Shīʿī: there is no divorce in a temporary marriage); al-Shīrāzī, *al-Muhadhdhab*, 2:54 (Shāfiʿī: temporary marriages are void because divorce, inheritance, and other characteristics of marriage are not present).

dissolution (modeled after ransoming or receiving an emancipation decree), in the medieval era, divorce became a contractual breach (modeled after a market procedure, or termination of a labor contract). Just as the employer–employee relationship is a legally rationalized version of the master–slave relationship, so too is medieval divorce a judicially rationalized version of late antique divorce in the Near East. Market dynamics and property-ownership indisputably changed between late antiquity and the medieval era in ways that directly influenced the daily lives of women. While there is undoubtedly a connection between the region's legal and economic history, these economic changes cannot be reconstructed with the available historical sources. It is possible that the changes enumerated here reflect broader shifts in the relationships between contract and property.

Jurisprudential rhetoric about recalcitrant wives should be understood as disguising situations of women demanding divorces and using a variety of legal strategies to obtain a divorce. Restrictions on a wife's ability to initiate a divorce created a fault system of divorce that is familiar in a variety of other contexts.[153] Late medieval debates about Geonic practices were not unique, but rather reflect a socio-legal process that is evident in both Jewish and Islamic legal texts: a wife's ability to divorce her husband became embedded more deeply within legal procedures that complicated a late antique (or earlier) practice of women simply "paying" for a divorce. This process is discernible in the increasing emphasis on identifying one of the spouses as being "at fault" with the consequence of "paying" for the divorce.

By appreciating that the relationship between these legal systems was one of a shared social space and historical tradition, we can begin to investigate what parallel legal transformations can tell us about their socio-political contexts. Muslim and Jewish jurists did not elaborate comparable legal schemata for divorce because they were building on similar scriptural texts or legal precedents – indeed, they were not. Nor did they "borrow" from the "influencing" legal system of the "other." Instead, the schemata are essentially alike because they reflect the comparable customary practices, socio-political circumstances, and jurisprudential logic of Near Eastern legal culture more generally and Islamicate legal culture more specifically.

[153] Lawrence M. Friedman, "A dead language: divorce law and practice before no-fault." *Virginia Law Review* 86:7 (October 2000): 1497–536.

Speculating on the Interwoven Narrative

I have presented a Judaic chronology, followed by an Islamic chronology, and then finally a Near Eastern story. The narrative of Islamicate legal pluralism is a more exact and coherent interpretation of the historical evidence than the two preceding chronologies. Moreover, the interwoven narrative is not implicated in any particular self-justificatory or orthodox belief; it is then relatively more objective. The crux of the interwoven narrative is that changes occurred between the eighth and twelfth centuries that resulted in limitations on women's abilities to initiate divorces.[154] I described the general outlines of these changes in the previous chapter's Islamicate periodization, which discussed the shift from diffusion and diversity (roughly 610–800 CE), to synthesis and systematization (roughly 800–1000 CE), to legal structure (roughly 1000–1200 CE), to legal autonomy (roughly 1200–1400 CE). The historical sources presented in the previous section demonstrate that whereas in late antiquity women had more flexibility to simply divorce their husbands without state (whether Byzantine, Sasanian, or, later, Islamic) involvement, by the medieval era divorce had become a state-dominated procedure. I want briefly to consider what broad political and social processes shaped this legal change.

In both legal systems, the role of jurists in declaring divorces intensified and jurists thereby staked more control for themselves and, by extension, for husbands.[155] In late antiquity, divorce often occurred without judicial intervention: Jewish men delivered notarized divorce decrees and Muslim men pronounced an oral divorce statement, but neither procedure necessarily necessitated court registration or involvement; Jewish or Muslim women simply left the homes of their husbands and refused to return.[156] But in the medieval era, local courts – proliferating throughout the empire – gradually came to process most divorces. Jurists who had been trained in institutions of learning that were becoming more technical and bureaucratic, in turn, staffed the courts. The informal legal circles and

[154] Not coincidentally, more historical evidence survives from the twelfth century than from the eighth century. This certainly has an effect on how we perceive historical change, but the changes enumerated here do not appear to be fabrications of the historical evidence.

[155] Among Western Jews, however, there is an exception: Rabbeinu Gershom (d. 1028) in Germany "enacted a decree which made it impossible for a husband to divorce his wife against her will." Riskin, *A Jewish woman's right to divorce*, xii, 109.

[156] While papyri containing marriage contracts survive from the late antique Islamic period, I was unable to locate divorce documents in the Arabic Papyrology Database. This could be an accident of historical survival, but I suspect it reflects that divorce was less institutionalized in late antiquity than in the medieval era, from which both marriage and divorce documents survive.

networks of the late antique period were transformed into the grand academies of learning that dictated the form and substance of legal education. The numerous legal circles, networks, and schools that had emerged gradually at the beginning of Islamic history consolidated into the few that came to dominate in the medieval era; likewise, numerous Jewish sects disappeared as rabbinic Judaism came to ascendancy. While the diversity of academies of learning preserved some of the region's legal plurality, the boundaries between legal orthodoxy and legal heresy were being defined ever more narrowly. These changes in the transmission of knowledge and identification of religious authority were occurring simultaneously among Muslims and Jews in the Near East, indicating a shared Islamicate culture.

What the interwoven narrative further reveals is that modifications in a woman's access to divorce is one site where we can witness Jewish and Muslim jurists responding to regional, socio-economic and political changes. In both legal systems, the notion that the breaching party should suffer a financial loss underlies the medieval juristic discourse on divorce. Changes in women's financial autonomy likely corresponded to their ability to initiate divorce by paying out divorce settlements. But the available historical evidence does not permit a clear analysis of the economic changes that accompanied the legal changes described here. As previously mentioned, the medieval processes of urbanization and commercialization – and their effects on law – cannot be easily measured. It should be noted that consumers of these legal systems likely demanded more judicial intervention as a means of clarifying domestic relationships that had significant financial implications (inheritance, post-divorce alimony, maintenance, etc.). But without sources that give "voice" to these consumers, it is difficult to reconstruct how, why, or when they sought court involvement in marriage and divorce. Consequently, the micro-histories presented above offer limited explanations and it is necessary to consider the macro-context of this case study on wife-initiated divorce. Likewise, it is unclear if a demographic shift in the number or age of men resulted in increased limitations on women's divorce options or protection of men's status; for instance, there may have been an interest in preventing women from divorcing their husbands while the latter were away at war. Many questions cannot be answered.

But there is a specific question for which we can articulate a relatively substantive answer: how did the legal profession change? Broad transformations in the state and in religious institutions had concrete consequences for the legal profession. Recent research has revealed not only that the number of judges increased, but also that their salaries doubled in the mid-eighth century as the ʿAbbāsid Empire (750–1258 CE) began a gradual process of systematizing and centralizing its empire.[157] These ʿAbbāsid judges received higher salaries because the empire was more prosperous, there was greater demand for judicial services, and these judges had more training than their predecessors. This legal professionalization resulted from the growing strength and diffusion of institutions of religious learning and training, which appointed or designated jurists for both Muslim and Jewish subjects. Judges transformed a late antique practice of divorce as mediation into a medieval practice of divorce as judicial procedure.

Conclusion

The syncretic framework presented here emphasizes understanding legal traditions as multivalent and dynamic traditions embedded in and inseparable from social settings. Through historicization and contextualization, this mode of inquiry contests the reification of religions that leads to false assumptions about the religion's "essence" or "primordial nature." Religious communities, like all communities, are the products of their contexts and cannot be understood as transhistorical (or universal) categories. In the late antique and medieval eras, Jewish and Muslim jurists continued, modified, and practiced Islamicate legal pluralism. Conventional models of comparative legal studies assume clear boundaries between legal systems; this assumption does not correspond to the historical fluidity and porousness of Jewish and Islamic legal traditions. The evaluation of historical evidence by jurists, laypeople, and historians of both Jewish and Islamic legal traditions is embedded within an inherited tradition of unchallenged presumptions. In presenting this historical evidence, I have attempted to illustrate how understandings of law are entangled within orthodox narrative assumptions. In so doing, I have chosen to elucidate aspects of Jewish and Islamic legal historiography silenced by orthodoxy. There are more stories of Jewish and Islamic laws that remain untold.

[157] al-Qāḍī, "The salaries of judges in early Islam."

Conclusion

This book began with a question about how to encounter Islamic law from the perspective of the society that began elaborating it. I asserted that the first Muslim community enacted Islamic law and I stressed that defining Islamic law must begin with *law*, rather than with *Islamic*. To recognize evidence of law, Chapters 1 and 2 examined both how to mine and to interpret multiple genres of Islamic sources. To define law historically, Chapters 3 and 4 focused on exploring Islamic law in relation to Jewish law and to Islamicate legal culture. To analyze broad changes in legal history, Chapters 5 and 6 offered macro-historical frameworks for analyzing Islamicate legal culture. Together, these chapters illustrated, in line with the definition offered in the Introduction, that law is an interpretive praxis.

Besides implementing the definition of *law* offered in the Introduction, I proposed a definition of *Islamic*. *Islamic* is syncretic. Islamic law's syncretism opens up the possibility of understanding *law* more profoundly. It is interesting to consider, for instance, if we should classify all of the Prophet's acts as constituting Islamic law. Among his many legal acts, the Prophet entered into treaty agreements, collected taxes,[1] sent numerous expeditions to tribes, redistributed property, and acted as an arbitrator/judge.[2] In matters of treaty negotiations, was the Prophet articulating Islamic international law or abiding by customary international law?[3] In adjudicating the case of a Jewish adulteress, did he apply Jewish law (since the tradition-report narrates that he relied on the Torah) or Islamic law?[4] In the case of the Banū Qurayẓah incident (discussed in Chapter 2), did he apply Islamic law or condone tribal arbitration?

[1] See Salaymeh, "Taxing citizens."

[2] Expeditions are enumerated throughout the biographical literature. Redistribution of property is mentioned in Ibn Isḥāq and Ibn Hishām, *The life*, 438.

[3] *Ibid.*, 198, 203, 08, 31.

[4] *Ibid.*, 267 (applying Jewish law).

There are no definitive historical or analytical answers to these questions. While these legal acts might appear "liminal," they are actually normative because legal pluralism (non-Islamic legal traditions coexist with Islamic ones) and legal polycentricity (Islamic law is generated by multiple groups and institutions) exist in most legal systems. Recognizing these Prophetic legal acts as *Islamic* illuminates a universal legal logic – not limited to Islamic jurisprudence – of reusing and inventing legal traditions. Rather than answering these or similar questions, this book maintains that scholarly inquiries should be oriented toward observing how jurists responded to these hypothetical questions. How did jurists interpret the Prophet's acts and how did they harmonize them (or not) with scripture or with their social, economic, and political conditions?

In the sober and intricate jurisprudential debates of the late antique and medieval eras, we find innovative legal reworking. Like artists who use a combination of recycled and new materials, jurists crafted their legal opinions by fusing ancient norms, scripture, Prophetic precedents, local practice, and contemporaneous needs in unexpected ways.[5] The recycled artwork of Islamic law transformed and combined many sources to create inventive compositions. The craft of legal recycling produced works whose component parts are not easily identifiable or classifiable; much law was simultaneously Islamic and tribal, Jewish, or customary. Rather than labeling a law's presumed "identity," each of the three case studies in this book illustrated instead the recycled art of Islamic jurisprudence. Each case study scrutinized how jurists combined the legal resources at their disposal. Chapter 2 showed how the juristic treatment of war prisoners connected Prophetic precedents, Qur'ānic exegesis, customary practices, and political concerns. Chapter 4 showed that juristic ideas about circumcision fused Arabian Abrahamic traditions with Jewish and customary practices. Chapter 6 showed that juristic changes in the regulations pertaining to wife-initiated divorce linked customary practices and a Prophetic precedent. These case studies presented glimpses of Islamic legal syncretism. The juristic craftwork observed in this book could have been quite different because it was contingent on a variety of factors, many of which are historically unrecoverable.

[5] Or, as Marx described it: "Men make their own history, but they do not make it as they please; they do not make it under self-selected circumstances, but under circumstances existing already, given and transmitted from the past. The tradition of all dead generations weighs like a nightmare on the brains of the living." Karl Marx, "The Eighteenth Brumaire of Louis Bonaparte." In *Karl Marx: selected writings*, ed. by David McLellan (Oxford: Oxford University Press, 2000), 329–55 at 329.

Despite the conditional nature of juristic crafting, legal recycling reflects broad regional trends in law. In providing samples of Islamic legal recycling processes, the case studies tracked a shift in the starting point of legal authority. Whereas late antique legal authority was concentrated in the expertise of scholars and their understandings of oral and written sources, medieval legal authority was concentrated in interpretation of written sources. This shift was made evident in the case studies. Chapter 2 suggested that late antique Muslim jurists who prohibited the execution of war prisoners based their opinions on Prophetic precedents; by comparison, their medieval counterparts who permitted execution of war prisoners based their opinions on Qur'ānic verses that reinterpreted Prophetic acts and minimized opposing historical evidence. Similarly, Chapter 4 pointed out that many late antique figures did not consider circumcision an obligatory act for Muslims. Yet most medieval jurists, interpreting Qur'ānic verses about Abrahamic practices, designated circumcision as obligatory. Correspondingly, Chapter 6 highlighted how medieval jurists, in contrast to their late antique predecessors, interpreted the tradition-report about a Prophetic precedent on wife-initiated divorce as including a fault-based justification (such as spousal abuse) or the husband's consent. Here again, medieval jurists focused on analyzing a Prophetic precedent in ways that resulted in their augmenting (perhaps introducing?) legal conditions for wife-initiated divorce.

Large-scale changes in "Islamic legal recycling" are evident in the slow, incremental transition from the authority of scholars in late antiquity to the authority of texts in the medieval era.[6] Medieval jurists relied on more textual authority than their late antique predecessors and this altered the shape and substance of Islamic jurisprudence. As Muslim legal actors gradually and incrementally relied upon more textual sources for legal opinions, they gained interpretive autonomy. This jurisprudential turn toward textual sources was, in part, the consequence of changes in the availability of materials for composing, transmitting, and distributing Islamic legal knowledge. Materiality played a crucial, as yet underexamined, role in the transformation of Islamic jurisprudential logics. By alternately zooming in to observe intricate details and zooming out to observe broad trends, this book has identified how the craft of legal recycling changed over time.

[6] In the modern era, legal authority shifted to the modern nation-state; this had profound implications for Islamic law, which I will elaborate in future work.

In their minutiae, the case studies illustrated that Islamic law is not stable, fixed, or undifferentiated. Certain expressions – a judiciary, positive legal doctrines, science of legal methodology, or doctrinal legal schools – are not "essential" to Islamic law.[7] Chapter 2 reconstructed Islamic history on warfare and integrated it with legal opinions on the status of war prisoners prior to the consolidation of orthodox Islamic legal schools. Many late antique legal figures prohibited execution of war prisoners, but most medieval jurists permitted it, despite relying on the same Prophetic precedents and Qurʾānic verses as their late antique predecessors. Chapter 4 searched for late antique perspectives on circumcision and identified some ambivalence or ambiguity about the practice. By the medieval era, jurists had bolstered circumcision as an obligatory practice based on Abrahamic precedent and notions of ritual purity. Chapter 6 isolated late antique practices of wife-initiated divorce to elucidate that they were less formalized than medieval juristic opinions. Each chapter pinpointed a legal option that disappeared or was weakened over time: war prisoners may not be executed; men do not have to be circumcised; women can divorce their husbands by returning their dowers. I offered several accounts for why these changes occurred, with particular emphasis on legal orthodoxy and legal culture.

Legal Orthodoxy and Islamic Jurisprudence

Islamic law does not have specific features or innate characteristics and it does not develop. Conventional notions about Islamic law conflate the presumed "essence" of Islamic law with orthodoxy. Islamic legal orthodoxy was not inevitable. In all three case studies, I contrasted late antique legal heterodoxy with medieval legal orthodoxy as an imperfect means of expressing the narrowing of legal options that occurred over time. In Chapter 2, the late antique perspective prohibiting execution of war prisoners became a minority opinion in the medieval era. In Chapter 4, the late antique variations on the legal status of circumcision contrasts with medieval expectations that circumcision is an obligation. There was some late antique juristic ambivalence in classifying circumcision as an obligatory act; yet medieval jurists overwhelmingly assumed that circumcision is an obligation. Chapter 6 showed that late antique Muslims understood wife-initiated divorce as taking effect through the return of the dower, but

[7] These dimensions are enumerated in Hallaq, *The origins*, 3.

medieval jurists made judicial intervention or spousal approval incumbent components of this type of divorce. These three case studies suggest that, over time, legal options were narrowed. Legal orthodoxy gives a name to this process.

The rise of Islamic legal orthodoxy was a multi-faceted process. Legal orthodoxy resulted from juristic professionalization, bureaucratization, and canonization, as well as "consumer" demands. The materiality of the juristic craft changed both figuratively and literally: the widespread consolidation of legal opinions coincided with the intensification of materiality. Yet, this materiality did not *fix* legal texts, nor did it render jurisprudence a science. The increasing availability and affordability of materials for writing and recording legal knowledge profoundly contributed to legal orthodoxy, but the craft of legal hermeneutics can never be fully rationalized. In delving into the intricacies of juristic analyses of substantive areas of doctrinal law, I chose to illuminate the richness of the jurisprudential craft, which differs significantly from both orthodox assumptions and scholarly depictions.

While it is often recognized that Islamic law is contingent, multivalent, and changing, that recognition remains rather thin and needs constant reinforcement. In part, this is because the presumption of Islamic otherness orients scholarship toward identifying difference and uniqueness. For example, much scholarly literature seems to ask and to answer the questions, "what, when, and how did Islamic law innovate?" This is peculiar because law inculcates tradition, not innovation. The legal consumers of Arabia would undoubtedly have rejected the Prophet and his movement if he had introduced an entirely new legal system or if he had proposed considerable innovations in law. Some amount of legal continuity is both inevitable and necessary. And the interplay of tradition and innovation in any legal system is haphazard. This is why, in selecting the case studies, I made no assumptions about the continuity (or discontinuity) of pre-Islamic legal systems; instead, I sought to discover relationships between pre-Islamic, late antique, and medieval legal traditions in order to *explore* Islamic law as a site for constant discovery and rediscovery. These explorations revealed that Islamic law is an intertextual space in which historical precedents, exegesis, and legal opinions shape each other.

An important observation about the craft of Islamic legal recycling needs to be emphasized: the art of Islamic jurisprudence is primarily functional. The juristic perspectives cited in this book were engaged with social realities. The legal issues surveyed (treatment of war prisoners, circumcision, and wife-initiated divorce) were examples of jurists grappling with legal issues of immediate social concern. (This observation does not imply that there were no abstract, theoretical jurisprudential discussions, but rather that they were marginal.) Islamic law is the product of interpretations of and interactions among legal texts, jurists, judges, bureaucrats, and other legal actors. Jurists, courts, the state, consumers, and socio-political changes negotiate and transform Islamic law. As the case studies made clear, jurists are not isolated from the everyday practice of law and the everyday practice of law is enacted through engagement with jurisprudential ideas.

Indeed, Islamic law – like any other legal tradition – has always been an amalgamation of theory and practice. In the twentieth century, the notion of a gap between "law on the books" and "law in action" was popularized by socio-legal studies, which presented the study of legal practice in social contexts as a corrective to the study of jurisprudential texts.[8] This polarization of law and society impossibly presumes that each is a separate and independent sphere. Because the "gap thesis" imposes a narrow conceptualization of law, it implies that law must be what is "in action" and whatever is "on the books" (meaning in jurisprudential texts) must be ivory tower discourse. This assumed division has been refuted by more recent legal scholarship that explores law's inextricability from society.[9] In line with this scholarship, this book has shown that law is both what is on the books and what is in action because legal texts cannot be interpreted in isolation from their interpretive communities, which includes both the scholars and the communities that apply them.

Legal Historiography and Sources

This book applied interdisciplinary heuristics to extract evidence of Islamic law from a variety of late antique and medieval sources. Intertwining biography, exegesis, tradition-reports, and legal texts, I showed that multiple genres inform Islamic legal history. In critically reading these diverse sources, I did not impose a particular method or make sweeping claims about the nature of the sources. Instead, I read and interrelated the sources closely, paying attention both to consensus and to dispute. In doing so, I challenged positivist methods that result from and result

[8] See, for example, Roscoe Pound, "Law in Books and Law in Action." *American Law Review* 44 (1910):12–36.

[9] An abbreviated discussion is in Christopher Tomlins, "How Autonomous Is Law?" *Annual Review of Law and Social Science* 3:1 (2007): 45–68.

in "origins"-oriented historiography. Chapter 1 demonstrated that the dating of "original" Islamic sources in traditional textual criticism corresponds to scholarly identifications of Islamic law's "birthdate." Chapter 3 presented how the quest for an "original" Semitic language in traditional comparative philology resembles scholarly classifications of Islamic law's "parentage." Chapter 5 argued that the naming of a "classical period" in traditional, evolutionary historiography relates to scholarly emphasis on Islamic law's "maturity." These three distortions in conventional Islamic legal historiography are embedded in the notion of "origins" and they are overcome by the alternative periodizations presented in this book.

By interpreting and connecting multiple sources, this book exposed the overlaps between exegesis, history, and law – particularly in the late antique period. During the late antique era, Muslim scholars gradually became more specialized – as exegetes, historians, or jurists. Medieval, specialized scholars operated in intertextual worlds, but they interpreted those texts differently from their late antique counterparts. This is evident in how medieval jurists understood Prophetic precedents and exegesis about prisoners of war; how medieval jurists understood Abrahamic traditions and exegesis; and how medieval jurists understood a Prophetic precedent on wife-initiated divorce. How jurists interpret historical narratives cannot be separated from historical writing or legal reasoning. These intertextual processes are the site of the transformation of late antique heterodoxy into medieval orthodoxy.

Legal Culture and Islamicate Society

Interpretive communities give meaning to legal texts in ways that cut across social, geographic, or confessional boundaries. This is evident when we inspect subtle dynamics of legal thinking and legal practice in late antique and medieval Islamicate societies. Because Islamicate refers to the social complex created by the Islamic movement, it encompasses Muslims and non-Muslims and directs us toward scrutinizing socio-historical situations. Placing (eastern) Jewish and Islamic legal traditions in conversation with each other illuminated the ways in which they responded to comparable socio-political dynamics and intellectual questions – as well as the ways in which they changed independently. Apparent similarities in orthodox Jewish law and Islamic law are the products of specific spaces and periods. The Islamicate setting explains the shift from late antique heterodoxy to medieval orthodoxy in both Islamic and eastern Jewish legal systems.

While I have emphasized the shared Islamicate legal culture, I have also highlighted variances. Islamic juristic rulings on prisoners of war may be unrelated to biblical law. As a purity ritual, Islamic circumcision may have a meaning that is distinct from Jewish circumcision's basis in the Abrahamic covenant. Limitations on wife-initiated divorce in medieval Islamic law may be unrelated to the bible's neglect of the topic. The case studies simultaneously pointed out that a common social space generated some overlaps between Islamic and Jewish legal traditions, but this shared space cannot explain all aspects of either legal tradition. There are limits to the conceptual framing provided by Islamicate legal culture.

Legal Moments and Periodization

The three periodizations – global, Islamic, and Islamicate – used in this book presented three vantage points for viewing Islamic legal history. The global periodization identified late antique society as shaping legal heterodoxy and medieval society as forming legal orthodoxy. These two rough characterizations (heterodoxy and orthodoxy) of changes in Islamic legal history were not developmental stages, but rather the outcomes of specific social, political, and economic circumstances. The Islamic periodization emphasized the professionalization of the legal profession as a contingent and conditional process.[10] The steady consolidation and rise of orthodox legal schools was not an evolutionary process, but rather one that coincided with and resulted from broad contextual changes. The Islamicate periodization reoriented conventional comparison by identifying the situational changes that resulted in Islamic and eastern Jewish legal systems intersecting or overlapping.[11] This periodization revealed that Islamic law changed in ways that paralleled changes in neighboring legal systems because law is molded by contextual factors. These three periodizations challenged the conventional, developmental narrative of Islamic legal historiography, which, relying on the notion of "origins," assumes linear development. All of these periodizations link narratives about Islamic law to specific times and places. Instead of completely substantiating them, I offered these periodizations as potentially liberating models for

[10] As presented in Chapter 5, the Islamic periodization is: legal circles and networks (*c.* 610–800 CE): Islamic legal beginnings; professionalization of legal schools (*c.* 800–1000 CE); consolidation and formalization (*c.* 1000–1200 CE); technocratization (*c.* 1200–1400 CE).

[11] As presented in Chapter 5, the Islamicate periodization is: diffusion and diversity (roughly 610–800 CE); synthesis and systematization (roughly 800–1000 CE); legal structure (roughly 1000–1200 CE); legal autonomy (roughly 1200–1400 CE).

reimagining Islamic and Islamicate legal history. Their efficacy will not be determined by my scholarship alone, but rather by many future scholars, hopefully working in collaboration.

Structure

The two main structural problems in conventional Islamic legal historiography are linear developmentalism and the imposition of modern categories.

In opposition to conventional linearity, the case studies in this book offer some tools for articulating Islamic legal historiography in its own terms. To resist linear (evolutionary) assumptions, the case studies did not present historical evidence in a simple chronological fashion. To resist oversimplified comparative impulses, the case studies eschewed the conventional terms of comparative legal studies (such as legal transplants, borrowing, and influence) because they mistakenly assume clear boundaries between Jewish and Islamic law. A crucial limitation in conventional comparisons is presuming that legal systems are uniform across diverse areas of law. The case studies in this book were different because the relationship between Jewish and Islamic legal systems is *not* consistent across all areas of law. Because international law (Chapter 2), ritual law (Chapter 4), and family law (Chapter 6) are based on distinct scriptural sources, customary practices, socio-political contexts, and economic factors, the relevance of Jewish law to Islamic legal practices is not uniform. In addition, the case studies did not seek to provide consistent or parallel information about Islamic and Jewish laws; instead, Jewish laws were strategically mined for material relevant to the historical questions being explored about Islamic law. Because the length and approach of each chapter were based on the individual chapter's particular objectives, the chapters were intentionally dissimilar. Thus, the substance, organization, and structure of the case studies together offered alternatives to conventional scholarship.

To resist modern categories, this book has promoted rigorous recalibrations of terms and concepts because contemporary assumptions restrain scholarly inquiries. A significant difficulty in writing about Jewish law and Islamic law is avoiding the politicized trope of "Jews versus Muslims." This trope renders these two identity classifications as both inseparable and equivalent; it perpetuates the false notion that "Muslims" and "Jews" are part of the same category ("religious" groups). The equivalence leads to the incorrect identification of Muslims as an ethnic group. The trope also implicates contemporary geo-politics in ways that severely limit scholarship.[12] Likewise, the modern category of "religion" makes it difficult to understand pre-modern Islamic law (or Jewish law) as *law* – as a legal tradition much like any other. The prevalent presumption that religious legal traditions – or, more broadly, religious societies – are fundamentally different from secular ones is embedded within a broader way of thinking that has prejudicial roots and consequences.[13]

Subtexts

The politics of academic knowledge production lies at the heart of methodological debates in Islamic studies, as elaborated in the odd-numbered chapters of this book. While many scholars of Islamic history and law assume the neutrality or objectivity of their methodologies, this book illustrated that the present can never be extricated fully from historical research. I have made no claims to objectivity (or to neutrality) in the positivist sense of the term. Nevertheless, this book does claim a post-foundational objectivity infused with an ethical commitment to acknowledging the implications of academic scholarship.[14] In writing this book, I have sought to provide future scholars with some necessary tools to dismantle hegemonies in Islamic legal studies. These were the tools I wish I had had when my own path began; it is recognition of those many years of struggles and scuffles that impelled me to enumerate my approach in detail. I hope that some readers will find this book constructive as they pursue their own scholarship. And I hope that this book might prevent recurrence of some of the conflicts and controversies I encountered.

Further Directions

We live in an era of perplexing legal questions. The media bombards us with images of law's failure, of law's exploitation by violent states and groups. Concurrently, powerful groups propagate the "rule of law" ideology – that modern liberal law is an antidote to contemporary global problems because it provides both liberty and security – in order to legitimate and to intensify their power. Underlying these contemporary depictions

[12] I discussed some of these limitations in Salaymeh, "Between scholarship and polemic in Judeo-Islamic studies."

[13] I discussed these limitations in Salaymeh, "'Comparing' Jewish and Islamic legal traditions."

[14] Postfoundationalism rejects the notion of Truth, but acknowledges historical truth. Thus, post-foundational objectivity "arises from comparing and criticizing rival webs of interpretations in terms of facts." Bevir, "Objectivity in history," 334.

of law is a presumed polarization between modern, liberal, secular law and traditional, conservative, religious law. This polarization needs to be questioned. Law's potential as a simultaneously emancipating and ordering force is mediated by the state, jurists, and legal consumers. Secularism and modern nation-states have reconfigured the division of power within this triad (state, jurists, and legal consumers). As this book elucidated, in the late antique and medieval eras, jurists played commanding roles in determining "*what is law?*" and "*who has the authority to produce law?*" In the modern era, it is nation-states that answer these questions.[15] It is then incumbent to reiterate that law and the state are not synonymous. In the intricacies of late antique and medieval Islamic law, we find law outside the state, law that is not motivated exclusively by the interests of the state.

This book has explored how meticulous historical research can alter our ideas about law and how deep understandings of law can change our assumptions about history. My future research will continue the process begun here of resisting assumptions, scrutinizing the obvious, and reconsidering what a variety of historical-legal texts from multiple traditions can communicate about a past that is always simultaneously present and absent. Hearing that past through the dissonance of the present is an enduring challenge.

[15] Christopher Tomlins, "Framing the Field of Law's Disciplinary Encounters: A Historical Narrative." *Law & Society Review* 34:4 (2000): 911–72 at 937 ("Law's resilience as an authoritative state discourse").

Works Cited

Classical works cited

Babylonian Talmud
Mishnah
Palestinian Talmud
Sifre on Numbers

Additional works cited

'Abd al-Majīd, 'Abd al-Majīd Maḥmūd. *al-Ittijāhāt al-fiqhīyah 'inda aṣḥāb al-ḥadīth fī al-qarn al-thālith al-hijrī.* (Cairo: Maktabat al-Khānjī, 1979).

'Abd al-Salām, Anwar Shu'ayb. *Shar' man qablanā: māhīyatuhu wa-ḥujjīyatuhu wa-nash'atuhu wa-ḍawābiṭuhu wa-taṭbīqātuh.* (Kuwait: Lajnat al-Ta'līf wa-al-Ta'rīb wa-al-Nashr, 2005).

Abou El Fadl, Khaled. *And God knows the soldiers: the authoritative and authoritarian in Islamic discourses.* (Lanham, MD: University Press of America, Inc., 2001).

"The rules of killing at war: an inquiry into classical sources." *The Muslim World* 89:2 (April 1999): 144–57.

Abu-Odeh, Lama. "The politics of (mis)recognition: Islamic law pedagogy in American academia." *The American Journal of Comparative Law* 52:4 (2004): 789–824.

Abū Dāwūd, Sulaymān ibn al-Ash'ath al-Sijistānī (d. 889; Iraq). *Sunan Abī Dāwūd.* Edited by Muḥammad Muḥyī al-Dīn 'Abd al-Ḥamīd. 4 vols. (Beirut: Dār Iḥyā' al-Turāth al-'Arabī, 1970).

Adghīrī, 'Abd al-Salām bin al-Ḥasan. *Ḥukm al-asrá fī al-islām wa-muqāranatuhu bī al-qānūn al-dawlī al-'āmm.* (Rabat: Maktabat al-Ma'ārif, 1985).

Adorno, Theodor W. *The positivist dispute in German sociology.* Translated by Glyn Adey and David Frisby. (London: Heinemann, 1976).

Ahmed, Mohammed Shahab. "The Satanic verses incident in the memory of the early Muslim community: an analysis of the early riwāyahs and their isnāds." Dissertation, Princeton University, 1999.

Al-Azmeh, Aziz A. *The emergence of Islam in late antiquity: Allah and his people.* (Cambridge: Cambridge University Press, 2014).

Ali, Kecia. *Marriage and slavery in early Islam*. (Cambridge, MA: Harvard University Press, 2010).
Anidjar, Gil. *Semites: race, religion, literature*. (Stanford, CA: Stanford University Press, 2008).
al-Anṣārī al-Kūfī, Abū Yūsuf Ya'qūb ibn Ibrāhīm (d. 798; Iraq). *Kitāb al-āthār*. (Beirut: Dār al-Kutub al-'Ilmīyah, 1978).
Anthony, Sean W. "Further notes on the word *ṣibghah* in Qur'ān 2:138." *Journal of Semitic Studies* 59:1 (2014): 117–29.
Arafat, W. N. "New Light on the Story of Banū Qurayẓa and the Jews of Medina." *Journal of the Royal Asiatic Society of Great Britain and Ireland* 108:2 (1976): 100–7.
Asad, Talal. "Ethnographic representation, statistics and modern power." *Social Research* 61:1 (1994): 55–88.
Genealogies of religion. (Baltimore, MD: Johns Hopkins University Press, 1993).
The idea of an anthropology of Islam. (Washington, D.C.: Center for Contemporary Arab Studies, Georgetown University, 1986).
Astren, Fred. *Karaite Judaism and historical understanding*. (Columbia, SC: University of South Carolina Press, 2004).
Athamina, Khalil. "Abraham in Islamic perspective: reflections on the development of monotheism in pre-Islamic Arabia." *Der Islam* 81:2 (2004): 184–205.
al-Awzā'ī, 'Abd al-Raḥmān ibn 'Amr (d. 774; Syria). *Sunan al-Awzā'ī: aḥādīth wa-āthār wa-fatāwá*. Edited by Marwān Muḥammad al-Sha''ār. (Beirut: Dār al-Nafā'is, 1993).
Bagnall, Roger S. *Reading papyri, writing ancient history*. (London; New York: Routledge, 1995).
al-Balkhī, Muqātil ibn Sulaymān (d. 767; Iraq). *Tafsīr Muqātil ibn Sulaymān: 80–150 hijrīyah*. Edited by 'Abd Allāh Maḥmūd Shiḥātah. 5 vols. (Cairo: al-Hay'ah al-Miṣrīyah al-'Āmmah li al-Kitāb, 1979).
Bamyeh, Mohammed A. *The social origins of Islam: mind, economy, discourse*. (Minneapolis, MN: University of Minnesota Press, 1999).
Banakar, Reza. "Power, culture and method in comparative law." *International Journal of Law in Context* 5:1 (2009): 69–85.
al-Bayḍāwī, 'Abd Allāh ibn 'Umar (d. 1286; Shīrāz). *Anwār al-tanzīl wa-asrār al-tā'wīl. Beidhawii Commentarius in Coranum: ex codd. Parisiensibus, Dresdensibus et Lipsiensibus*. Edited by Heinrich Leberecht Fleischer. 2 vols. (Lipsiae: Sumptibus F.C.G. Vogelii, 1846–1848).
al-Bayhaqī, Aḥmad ibn al-Ḥusayn (d. 1066; Khurasan). *al-Sunan al-kubrá*. 17 vols. (Beirut: Dār al-Fikr, 1996).
Bell, Catherine M. *Ritual theory, ritual practice*. (New York: Oxford University Press, 1992).
Benes, Tuska. *In Babel's shadow: language, philology, and the nation in nineteenth-century Germany*. (Detroit, MI: Wayne State University Press, 2008).
Benjamin, Walter. "Theses on the philosophy of history." Translated by Harry Zohn. In *Illuminations*. Edited by Hannah Arendt. (New York: Schocken Books, 2007), 253–64.

Benkheira, Mohammed Hocine. "Jouir sans enfanter? Concubines, filiation et coït interrompu au debut de l'Islam." *Der Islam* 90:2 (2013): 245–305.

"L'impuissance sexuelle, motif légal de rupture du lien matrimonial." *Islamic Law and Society* 21:1–2 (2014): 1–48.

"Un libre peut-il épouser une esclave? Esquisse d'histoire d'un débat, des origines à al-Shāfiʿī (m.204/820)." *Der Islam* 84:2 (2008): 246–355.

Bentley, Jerry H. "Cross-cultural interaction and periodization in world history." *The American Historical Review* 101:3 (1996): 749–70.

Berg, Herbert. "The implications of, and opposition to, the methods and theories of John Wansbrough." *Method & Theory in the Study of Religion* 9:1 (1997): 3–22.

"The *isnād* and the production of cultural memory: Ibn Abbās as a case study." *Numen* 58:2 (2011): 259–83.

Berkey, Jonathan P. "Circumcision circumscribed: female excision and cultural accommodation in the medieval Near East." *International Journal of Middle East Studies* 28:1 (1996): 19–38.

Bernards, Monique and John Nawas. "The geographic distribution of Muslim jurists during the first four centuries AH." *Islamic Law and Society* 10:2 (2003): 168–81.

Bernat, David A. "Circumcision." In *The Encyclopedia of Ancient History*. (Malden, MA: John Wiley & Sons, Inc., 2013).

Bevir, Mark. "How to be an intentionalist." *History and Theory* 41:2 (May 2002): 166–75.

"Objectivity in history." *History and Theory* 33:3 (1994): 328–44.

"What is genealogy?" *Journal of the Philosophy of History* 2:3 (2008): 263–75.

"Why historical distance is not a problem." *History and Theory* 50:4 (December 2011): 24–37.

Bevir, Mark and R. A. W. Rhodes. *The state as cultural practice*. (Oxford: Oxford University Press, 2010).

Biale, Rachel. *Women and Jewish law: an exploration of women's issues in halakhic sources*. (New York: Schocken Books, 1984).

Bligh-Abramski, Irit. "The judiciary (qāḍīs) as a governmental-administrative tool in early Islam." *Journal of the Economic and Social History of the Orient* 35:1 (1992): 40–71.

Bloch, Marc. *The historian's craft*. (New York: Knopf, 1953).

Boekhoff-van der Voort, Nicolet. "The *kitāb al-maghāzī* of ʿAbd al-Razzāq b. Hammām al-Ṣanʿānī: searching for earlier source-material." In *The transmission and dynamics of the textual sources of Islam: essays in honour of Harald Motzki*. Edited by Harald Motzki, Nicolet Boekhoff-van der Voort, Kees Versteegh, and Joas Wagemakers. (Leiden; Boston, MA: Brill, 2011), 27–47.

Bori, Caterina. *A scholar in the shadow: essays in the legal and theological thought of Ibn Qayyim al-Ǧawziyyah*. (Roma: Istituto per l'Oriente, 2010).

Bowersock, G. W. *Hellenism in late antiquity*. Jerome lectures; 18th ser. (Ann Arbor, MI: University of Michigan Press, 1990).

Boyarin, Daniel. *Border lines: the partition of Judaeo-Christianity*. Divinations: Rereading Late Ancient Religion. (Philadelphia, PA: University of Pennsylvania Press, 2004).

A radical Jew: Paul and the politics of identity. (Berkeley, CA: University of California Press, 1997).

Brewer, David Instone. "Jewish women divorcing their husbands in early Judaism: the background to papyrus Ṣe'elim 13." *The Harvard Theological Review* 92:3 (1999): 349–57.

Brody, Robert. "Evidence for divorce by Jewish women?" *The Journal of Jewish Studies* 50:2 (1999): 230–4.

The geonim of Babylonia and the shaping of medieval Jewish culture. (New Haven, CT: Yale University Press, 1998).

Brooks, Peter. *Reading for the plot: design and intention in narrative*. (New York: A. A. Knopf, 1984).

Brown, Peter R. L. *The world of late antiquity: AD 150–750*. (New York: W. W. Norton, 1989).

The world of late antiquity: from Marcus Aurelius to Muhammad. Library of European civilization. (London: Thames and Hudson, 1971).

al-Bukhārī, Muḥammad ibn Ismāʿīl (d. 870; Khurāsān). *Ṣaḥīḥ al-Bukhārī = The translation of the meanings of Ṣahiḥ al-Bukhārī, Arabic-English* [Jamiʿ al-sahih]. Translated by Muhammad Muhsin Khan. 9 vols. (Medina: Dar al-Fikr, 1981).

Burton, John. *The sources of Islamic law: Islamic theories of abrogation*. (Edinburgh: Edinburgh University Press, 1990).

Certeau, Michel de. *The practice of everyday life*. Translated by Steven Rendall. (Berkeley, CA: University of California Press, 1984).

Chakrabarty, Dipesh. "Postcoloniality and the artifice of history." In *A subaltern studies reader, 1986–1995*. Edited by Ranajit Guha. (Minneapolis, MN: University of Minnesota Press, 1997), 263–93.

Chamberlain, Michael. *Knowledge and social practice in medieval Damascus, 1190–1350*. Cambridge Studies in Islamic Civilization. (Cambridge: Cambridge University Press, 1994).

Clark, Elizabeth A. *History, theory, text: historians and the linguistic turn*. (Cambridge, MA: Harvard University Press, 2004).

Clark, Gillian. *Women in late antiquity: pagan and Christian life-styles*. (Oxford: Clarendon Press, 1993).

Cohen, Shaye J. D. "Judaism without circumcision and 'Judaism' without 'circumcision' in Ignatius." *The Harvard Theological Review* 95:4 (2002): 395–415.

Why aren't Jewish women circumcised? Gender and covenant in Judaism. (Berkeley, CA: University of California Press, 2005).

Collier, Jane F. "Intertwined histories: Islamic law and Western imperialism." *Law & Society Review* 28:2 (1994): 395–408.

Cook, Michael. "The opponents of the writing of tradition in early Islam." *Arabica* XLIV (1997): 437–530.

Coope, Jessica A. "Religious and cultural conversion to Islam in ninth-century Umayyad Córdoba." *Journal of World History* 4:1 (1993): 47–68.

Coulson, Noel J. *A history of Islamic law.* (Edinburgh: Edinburgh University Press, 1964).

Crone, Patricia. "*Jāhilī* and Jewish law: the *qasāma*." *Jerusalem Studies in Arabic and Islam* 4 (1984): 153–201.

Roman, provincial and Islamic law: the origins of the Islamic patronate. (Cambridge: Cambridge University Press, 2002).

Crone, Patricia and Adam Silverstein. "The ancient Near East and Islam: the case of lot-casting." *Journal of Semitic Studies* 55:2 (2010): 423–50.

Cross, Frank Moore. *Canaanite myth and Hebrew epic: essays in the history of the religion of Israel.* (Cambridge, MA: Harvard University Press, 1973).

Daaïf, Lahcen. "Le prix du sang (*diya*) au premier siècle de l'islam." *Hypothèses* 1:10 (2007): 329–42.

Dandamayev, Muhammad A., Mansour Shaki, Sachiko Murata, Akbar Aghajanian, Jenny Rose, and Mujan Momen. "Divorce." In *Encyclopaedia Iranica* (London: Routledge & Kegan Paul, 1983).

Darwīsh, ʿAbd al-Raḥmān ibn ʿAbd Allāh. *al-Sharāʾiʿ al-sābiqah wa-madá ḥujjīyatihā fi al-sharīʿah al-islāmīyah.* (Saudi Arabia: ʿA. al-R. b. ʿA. A. al-Darwīsh, 1989).

Das sasanidische Rechtsbuch "Matakdan i hazar datistan" (Teil II). Translated by Maria Macuch. (Wiesbaden: Deutsche Morgenländische Gesellschaft: Kom missionsverlag, F. Steiner, 1981).

Derrida, Jacques and Eric Prenowitz. "Archive fever: a Freudian impression." *Diacritics* 25:2 (1995): 9–63.

The Digest of Justinian, Translated by Alan Watson. Revised English-language edn., 2 vols. (Philadelphia. PA: University of Pennsylvania Press, 1998).

Donner, Fred M. *Muhammad and the believers: at the origins of Islam.* (Cambridge, MA: The Belknap Press of Harvard University Press, 2010).

Narratives of Islamic origins. Studies in Late Antiquity and Early Islam 14. (Princeton, NJ: The Darwin Press, 1998).

al-Dūrī, ʿAbd al-ʿAzīz. *The rise of historical writing among the Arabs.* Translated by Lawrence I. Conrad. Modern classics in Near Eastern Studies. Edited by Charles Issawi and Bernard Lewis. (Princeton, NJ: Princeton University Press, 1983) [*Baḥth fi nashʾat ʿilm al-taʾrīkh ʿinda al-ʿarab* (Beirut, 1960)].

Dutton, Yasin. *The origins of Islamic law: the Qurʾan, the Muwaṭṭaʾ and Madinan ʿamal.* Culture and civilization in the Middle East. (Surrey, UK: Curzon, 1999).

Eaton, Richard Maxwell. *Islamic history as global history.* Essays on Global and Comparative History. (Washington, DC: American Historical Association, 1990).

Edwards, Chilperic and Hammurabi. *The oldest laws in the world: being an account of the Hammurabi code and the Sinaitic legislation.* (London: Watts & Co., 1906).

El-Hibri, Tayeb. *Parable and politics in early Islamic history: the Rashidun caliphs.* (New York: Columbia University Press, 2010).

Reinterpreting Islamic historiography: Harun al-Rashid and the narrative of the 'Abbasid caliphate. (New York: Cambridge University Press, 1999).

El Cheikh, Nadia Maria. *Byzantium viewed by the Arabs.* (Cambridge, MA: Harvard University Press, 2004).

El Shamsy, Ahmed. *The canonization of Islamic law: a social and intellectual history.* (New York: Cambridge University Press, 2013).

Elad, Amikam. "Community of believers of 'holy men' and 'saints' or community of Muslims? The rise and development of early Muslim historiography." *Journal of Semitic Studies* 47:2 (2002): 241–308.

Eldon Jay, Epp. "The multivalence of the term 'original text' in New Testament textual criticism." *The Harvard Theological Review* 92:3 (1999): 245–81.

Elon, Menachem. *Jewish law: history, sources, principles [Ha-mishpat ha-ivri].* Translated by Bernard Auerbach and Melvin J. Sykes. (Philadelphia, PA: Jewish Publication Society, 1994).

Fadel, Mohammad. "The social logic of *taqlīd* and the rise of the *mukhtaṣar.*" *Islamic Law and Society* 3:2 (1996): 193–233.

Faizer, Rizwi S. "Muhammad and the Medinan Jews: a comparison of the texts of Ibn Ishaq's *Kitāb sīrat rasūl Allāh* with al-Waqidi's *Kitāb al-maghāzī.*" *International Journal of Middle East Studies* 28:4 (1996): 463–89.

Fār, 'Abd al-Wāḥīd Muḥammad. *Asrá al-harb: dirāsah fiqhīyah wa-taṭbīqīyah fī niṭāq al-qānūn al-duwalī al-'āmm wa-al-sharī'ah al-islāmīyah.* (Cairo: 'Ālam al-Kutub, 1975).

Fatoohi, Louay. *Abrogation in the Quran and Islamic law: a critical study of the concept of "naskh" and its impact.* (New York: Routledge, 2012).

Ferguson, Everett. *Baptism in the early church: history, theology, and liturgy in the first five centuries.* (Grand Rapids, MI: William B. Eerdmans Pub. Co., 2009).

al-Fīrūzābādī, Muḥammad ibn Ya'qūb (d. 1414/5; Iran). *Tafsīr Ibn 'Abbās.* Translated by Mokrane Guezzou. (Louisville, KY; [Amman, Jordan]: Fons Vitae; Royal Aal al-Bayt Institute for Islamic Thought, 2008).

Tanwīr al-miqbās min tafsīr Ibn 'Abbās. (Beirut: Dār al-Kutub al-'Ilmīyah, 1980).

Fonrobert, Charlotte Elisheva. *Menstrual purity: rabbinic and Christian reconstructions of Biblical gender.* (Stanford, CA: Stanford University Press, 2000).

Fonrobert, Charlotte Elisheva and Martin S. Jaffee. *The Cambridge companion to the Talmud and rabbinic literature.* Cambridge companions to religion. (Cambridge; New York: Cambridge University Press, 2007).

Foucault, Michel. "Nietzsche, genealogy, history." Translated by Paul Rabinow. In *The Foucault reader.* Edited by Paul Rabinow. (New York: Pantheon, 1984), 76–100.

Fowden, Garth. *Before and after Muḥammad: the first millennium refocused.* (Princeton, NJ: Princeton University Press, 2014).

Frantz-Murphy, Gladys. "Arabic Papyrology and Middle Eastern Studies." *Middle East Studies Association Bulletin* 19:1 (1985): 34–48.

"A comparison of the Arabic and earlier Egyptian contract formularies, part II: terminology in the Arabic warranty and the idiom of clearing/cleaning." *Journal of Near Eastern Studies* 44:2 (1985): 99–114.

Friedman, Lawrence M. "A dead language: divorce law and practice before no-fault." *Virginia Law Review* 86:7 (October 2000): 1497–536.

Friedman, Mordechai A. "Babatha's 'ketubba': some preliminary observations." *Israel Exploration Journal* 46:1/2 (1996): 55–76.

"Divorce upon the wife's demand as reflected in manuscripts from the Cairo Geniza." *Jewish Law Annual* 4 (1981): 103–26.

Geniza studies in Jewish marriage law. (*s.l.*: *s.n.*, 1970).

Jewish marriage in Palestine: a Cairo genizah study. (Tel-Aviv; New York: Tel-Aviv University, Chaim Rosenberg School of Jewish Studies; Jewish Theological Seminary of America, 1980).

"The ransom-divorce: divorce proceedings initiated by the wife in medieval Jewish practice." *Israel Oriental studies* 6 (1976): 288–307.

Gafni, Isaiah. "Rabbinic historiography and representations of the past." In *The Cambridge companion to the Talmud and rabbinic literature.* Edited by Charlotte Elisheva Fonrobert and Martin S. Jaffee. (Cambridge; New York: Cambridge University Press, 2007), 295–312.

Gaon, Rav Sherira (d. 1006; Babylonia). *The Iggeres of Rav Sherira Gaon.* Translated by Rabbi Nosson Dovid Rabinowich. (Jerusalem; Brooklyn, NY: Rabbi Jacob Joseph School Press, Ahavath Torah Institute; Moznaim, 1988).

Gil, Moshe. "The earliest waqf foundations." In *Related worlds: studies in Jewish and Arab ancient and early medieval history.* (Aldershot; Burlington, VT: Ashgate, 2004), Chap. IX.

Glenn, H. Patrick. *Legal traditions of the world: sustainable diversity in law.* (Oxford; New York: Oxford University Press, 2007).

Goitein, Shelomo Dov. "The birth-hour of Muslim law?" *The Muslim World* 50:1 (1960): 23–9.

"The interplay of Jewish and Islamic laws." In *Jewish law in legal history and the modern world.* Edited by Bernard S. Jackson. The Jewish law annual. (Leiden: Brill, 1980), Supplement 2, 61–77.

A Mediterranean society: the Jewish communities of the Arab world as portrayed in the documents of the Cairo Geniza. 6 vols. (Berkeley, CA: University of California Press, 1967–1993).

Goldziher, Ignaz (d. 1921). "Fiḳh." In *The Encyclopaedia of Islam: a dictionary of the geography, ethnography and biography of the Muhammadan peoples.* Edited by M. Th. Houtsma, A. J. Wensinck, T. W. Arnold, W. Heffening, E. Lévi-Provençal, and International Association of Academies. (Leiden; London: E.J. Brill; Luzac & Co., 1913), 101–5.

Gollaher, David. *Circumcision: a history of the world's most controversial surgery.* (New York: Basic Books, 2000).

Goodblatt, David M. *Rabbinic instruction in Sasanian Babylonia.* (Leiden: Brill, 1975).

Gordon, Robert W. "Historicism in legal scholarship." *The Yale Law Journal* 90:5 (1981): 1017–56.

"Introduction: J. Willard Hurst and the common law tradition in American legal historiography." *Law & Society Review* 10:1 (Autumn 1975): 9–55.

"The past as authority and as social critic: stabilizing and destabilizing functions of history in legal argument." In *The historic turn in the human sciences.* Edited by Terrence J. McDonald. (Ann Arbor, MI: University of Michigan Press, 1996), 339–78.

Green, William A. "Periodizing world history." *History and Theory* 34:2 (1995): 99–111.

Grohmann, Adolf and Raif Georges Khoury. *Chrestomathie de papyrologie arabe: documents relatifs à la vie privée, sociale et administrative dans les premiers siècles islamiques.* (Leiden; New York: E.J. Brill, 1993).

Grubbs, Judith Evans. "'Pagan' and 'Christian' marriage: the state of the question." In *Christianity and society: the social world of early Christianity.* Edited by Everett Ferguson. Recent studies in early Christianity. (New York: Garland, 1999), 185–236.

Guha, Ranajit. *Elementary aspects of peasant insurgency in colonial India.* (Delhi: Oxford University Press, 1983).

Gutas, Dimitri. *Greek culture, Arabic thought.* (New York: Routledge, 1998).

Hallaq, Wael B. *An introduction to Islamic law.* (Cambridge; New York: Cambridge University Press, 2009).

The origins and evolution of Islamic law. (Cambridge: Cambridge University Press, 2005).

"The quest for origins or doctrine? Islamic legal studies as colonialist discourse." *UCLA Journal of Islamic and Near Eastern Law* 2:1 (2002–2003): 1–31.

"Review: The use and abuse of evidence: the questions of provincial and Roman influences on early Islamic law." *Journal of the American Oriental Society* 110:1 (1990): 79–90.

Sharīʿa: theory, practice, transformations. (Cambridge: Cambridge University Press, 2009).

"Was al-Shafiʿi the Master Architect of Islamic Jurisprudence?" *International Journal of Middle East Studies* 25:4 (1993): 587–605.

Ḥamādah, Muḥammad Māhir. *al-Wathāʾiq al-siyāsīyah wa-al-idārīyah al-ʿāʾidah li al-ʿaṣr al-umawī: 40–132 H/661–750 M.* (Beirut: Muʾassasat al-Risālah, 1974).

al-Wathāʾiq al-siyāsīyah wa-al-idārīyah al-ʿāʾidah li al-jazīrah al-ʿarabīyah khilāla al-ʿuṣūr al-islāmīyah al-mutatābiʿah: min al-ʿaṣr al-umawī ilá al-fatḥ al-ʿuthmānī li-bilād al-shām wa-miṣr wa-al-jazīrah al-ʿarabīyah 40h-922h = 661m-1516m. (Beirut: Muʾassasat al-Risālah, 1987).

Hamidullah, Muhammad. *Majmūʿat al-wathāʾiq al-siyāsīyah li al-ʿahd al-nabawī wa-al-khilāfah al-rāshidah.* (Beirut: Dār al-Irshād, 1969).

Muslim conduct of state: being a treatise on Siyar. (Malaysia: Islamic Book Trust, 2012).

Harkavy, Albert. *Teshuvot ha-geonim: sheelot u-teshuvot.* (New York: Menorah, Makhon le-mehkar ule-hotsaat kitve-yad u-sefarim `atikim, 1959).

Hart, Henry Melvin and Albert M. Sacks. *The legal process: basic problems in the making and application of law.* Edited by William N. Eskridge and Philip P. Frickey. (Westbury, NY: Foundation Press, 1994).

Haythamī, Nūr al-Dīn ʿAlī ibn Abī Bakr (d. 1405). *Ghāyat al-maqṣūd fī zawāʾid al-musnad.* Edited by Khalāf Maḥmūd ʿAbd al-Samīʿ. 4 vols. (Beirut: Dār al-Kutub al-ʿIlmīyah, 2001).

Heidemann, Stefan. "Numismatics." In *The formation of the Islamic world, sixth to eleventh centuries.* Edited by Chase F. Robinson. (Cambridge: Cambridge University Press, 2011), 648–53.

Heirbaut, Dirk. "An unknown treasure for historians of early medieval Europe: the debate of German legal historians on the nature of medieval law." In *Zeitschrift des Max-Planck-Instituts für europäische Rechtsgeschichte.* Edited by Thomas Duve. (Frankfurt am Main: Vittorio Klostermann GmbH, 2010), 87–90.

Hennigan, Peter C. *The birth of a legal institution: the formation of the waqf in third-century A.H. Ḥanafī legal discourse.* Studies in Islamic law and society, vol. XVIII. (Leiden; Boston, MA: Brill, 2004).

Herman, Geoffrey. *A prince without a kingdom: the Exilarch in the Sasanian era.* (Tübingen: Mohr Siebeck, 2012).

Hill, Enid. "Comparative and historical study of modern Middle Eastern law." *American Journal of Comparative Law* 26:2 (1978): 279–304.

Hodgson, Marshall G. S. *Rethinking world history: essays on Europe, Islam, and world history.* Edited by Edmund Burke. (Cambridge; New York: Cambridge University Press, 1993).

The venture of Islam: conscience and history in a world civilization. Vol. I (Chicago, IL: University of Chicago Press, 1974).

Holsinger, Bruce W. "Medieval studies, postcolonial studies, and the genealogies of critique." *Speculum* 77:4 (2002): 1195–227.

The Holy Qur-ān. Translated by ʿAbdāllah Yūsuf ʿAlī. (Medina: King Fahd Holy Qur-ān Printing Complex, 1989–1990).

Horovitz, Josef and Lawrence I. Conrad (eds.). *The earliest biographies of the Prophet and their authors.* (Princeton, NJ: The Darwin Press, 2002).

Howard, George. *The Gospel of Matthew according to a primitive Hebrew text.* (Macon, GA: Mercer University Press, 1987).

Howell, Martha C. and Walter Prevenier. *From reliable sources: an introduction to historical methods.* (Ithaca, NY: Cornell University Press, 2001).

Hoyland, Robert G. *Arabia and the Arabs: from the bronze age to the coming of Islam.* (London: Routledge Press, 2001).

"Early Islam as a late antique religion." In *The Oxford handbook of late antiquity.* Edited by Scott Fitzgerald Johnson. (Oxford; New York: Oxford University Press, 2012), 1053–77.

"History, fiction and authorship in the first centuries of Islam." In *Writing and Representation in Medieval Islam: Muslim horizons.* Edited by Julia

Bray. Routledge Studies in Middle Eastern Literatures. (London; New York: Routledge, 2006), 16–46.

"New documentary texts and the early Islamic state." *Bulletin of the School of Oriental and African Studies* 69:3 (2006): 395–416.

al-Ḥurr al-ʿĀmilī, Muḥammad ibn al-Ḥasan (d. 1693; Lebanon). *Wasāʾil al-Shīʿah ilá taḥṣīl masāʾil al-sharīʿah*. Edited by ʿAbd al-Raḥīm Rabbānī, Muḥammad Rāzī, and Abū al-Ḥasan Shaʿrānī. 7 vols. (Tehran: Maktabat al-Islāmīyah, 1956).

Ibn ʿAbd al-Barr, Yūsuf ibn ʿAbd Allāh (d. 1070; Andalusia). *Kitāb al-kāfī fī fiqh ahl al-Madīnah al-Mālikī*. Edited by Muḥammad Muḥammad Aḥīd Wuld Mādīk Mūrītānī. 2 vols. (Riyadh: Maktabat al-Riyāḍ al-Ḥadīthah, 1980).

Ibn Abī Shaybah, ʿAbd Allāh ibn Muḥammad (d. 849; Iraq). *Kitāb al-adab*. Edited by Muḥammad Riḍā Qahwajī. (Beirut: Dār al-Bashāʾir al-Islāmīyah, 1999).

Ibn Abī Shaybah, ʿAbd Allāh ibn Muḥammad *al-Kitāb al-muṣannaf fī al-aḥādīth wa-al-āthār*. Edited by Muḥammad ʿAbd al-Salām Shāhīn. 9 vols. (Beirut: Dār al-Kutub al-ʿIlmīyah, 1995).

Muṣannaf fī al-aḥādīth wa-al-āthār. Edited by Saʿīd Laḥḥām. 9 vols. (Beirut: Dār al-Fikr, 1989).

Ibn Abī Zayd al-Qayrawānī, ʿAbd Allāh ibn ʿAbd al-Raḥmān (d. 996; Tunisia). *The Rísâla: treatise on Mâlikî law of ʿAbdallâh Ibn-Abî-Zayd Al-Qayrawânî (922–996): an annotated translation*. Translated by Joseph Kenny. (Minna: Islamic Education Trust, 1992).

al-Risālah al-fiqhīyah. (Beirut: Dār al-Gharb al-Islāmī, 1986).

Ibn al-Mundhir al-Naysābūrī, Muḥammad ibn Ibrāhīm (d. 930). *al-Ijmāʿ*. (Beirut: Dār al-Kutub al-ʿIlmīyah, 1985).

Ibn al-Muṭahhar al-Ḥillī, al-Ḥasan ibn Yūsuf (d. 1325; Iraq). *Tadhkirat al-fuqahāʾ*. 20 vols. (Qum: Muʾassasat Āl al-Bayt li-Iḥyāʾ al-Turāth, 1993/94).

Ibn al-Ṣalāḥ al-Shahrazūrī, ʿUthmān ibn ʿAbd al-Raḥmān (d. 1245). *Muqaddamat Ibn al-Ṣalāḥ fī ʿulūm al-ḥadīth*. (Damascus: Dār al-Ḥikmah, 1972).

Ibn Anas, Mālik (d. 795; Arabia). *al-Muwaṭṭaʾ*. Edited by Muḥammad Fūʾād ʿAbd al-Bāqī. 2 vols. (Beirut: Dār al-Turāth al-ʿArabī, 1985).

Muwaṭṭaʾ al-Imām Mālik. Edited by ʿAbd al-Wahhāb ʿAbd al-Laṭīf. 2nd edn. (Beirut: al-Maṭbaʿah al-ʿIlmīyah, 1979).

Ibn Anas, Mālik and Muḥammad ibn Muḥammad Rāʿī (d. 1449). *Original Islam: Mālik and the madhhab of Madina*. Translated by Yasin Dutton. Culture and civilization in the Middle East. (London; New York: Routledge, 2007).

Ibn Ḥazm, ʿAlī ibn Aḥmad (d. 1064; Andalusia). *Marātib al-ijmāʿ fī al-ʿibādāt wa-al-muʿāmalat wa-al-ʿitiqādāt*. (Beirut: Dār al-Kutub al-ʿIlmīyah, 1970).

al-Muḥallā. Edited by Ḥasan Zaydān Ṭulbah. 12 vols. (Cairo: Maktabat al-Jumhūriyah al-ʿArabīyah, 1967–1971).

Ibn Isḥāq, Muḥammad (d. 767; Iraq), and ʿAbd al-Malik Ibn Hishām (d. 833; Egypt). *The life of Muḥammad: a translation of Isḥāq's Sīrat rasūl Allāh.*

Translated by Alfred Guillaume. (Karachi: Oxford University Press, 2004, 1955).
Ibn Jabr, Mujāhid (d. *c.* 720; Arabia). *Tafsīr al-Imām Mujāhid ibn Jabr: al-mutawaffá sanat 102 h.* Edited by Mu.ammad 'Abd al-Salām Abū al-Nīl. (Cairo: Dār al-Fikr al-Islāmī al-Ḥadīthah, 1989).
Ibn Mājah, Muḥammad ibn Yazīd (d. 887; Iran). *Sunan al-Muṣṭafá.* Edited by Abī al-Ḥasan Muḥammad Ibn 'Abd al-Hādī al-Sindī Ḥanafī. 2 vols. (Beirut: Al-Fikr, 1975).
Sunan Abī 'Abd Allāh Muhammad ibn Yazīd al-Qazwīnī Ibn Mājah. Edited by Muhammad Fu'ād 'Abd al-Bāqī. 2 vols. (Cairo: Dār Ahyā' al-Kutub al-'Arabīyah, 1952–54).
Ibn Qayyim al-Jawzīyah, Muḥammad ibn Abī Bakr (d. 1350; Syria). *On taqlid: Ibn al Qayyim's critique of authority in Islamic law.* Translated by Mustafa Abdul Rahman. (Oxford; New York: Oxford University Press, 2013).
Tuḥfat al-mawdūd bi-āḥkām al-mawlūd. (Cairo: al-Maktabah al-Qayyimah, 1977).
Ibn Qudāmah al-Maqdīsī, Muwaffaq al-Dīn 'Abd Allāh ibn Aḥmad (d. 1223; Syria). *al-Mughnī.* Edited by 'Abd Allāh ibn 'Abd al-Muḥsin Turkī and 'Abd al-Fattāḥ Muḥammad Ḥulw. 16 vols. (Imbābah, Cairo: Hajr, 1986).
al-Mughnī. Edited by 'Abd Allāh ibn 'Abd al-Muḥsin Turkī and 'Abd al-Fattāḥ Muḥammad Ḥulw. 2nd edn. 15 vols. (Cairo: Hajr, 1992).
al-'Umdah fī al-fiqh al-Ḥanbalī. Edited by al-Hawwārī and Anwar Zahrā'. (Damascus: al-Dār al-Muttaḥidah lil-Ṭibā'ah wa-al-Nashr, 1990).
Ibn Quraysh, Judah (d. tenth century; North Africa). *Risalat al-ḥakīm.* Edited by J. J. L. Bargès and Baer ben Alexander Goldberg. (Lutetiae Parisiorum: B. Duprat, D. Maisonneuve, 1857).
Ibn Rāshid, Ma'mar (d. 770; Baṣrah), and 'Abd al-Razzāq ibn Hammām al-Ḥimyarī al-Ṣan'ānī (d. 827; Yemen). *The expeditions: an early biography of Muḥammad.* Translated by Sean W. Anthony. (New York; London: New York University Press, 2014).
Ibn Rushd, Abū al-Walīd (d. 1198; Andalusia/Maghreb). *Bidāyat al-mujtahid wa-nihāyat al-muqtaṣid.* Edited by Māji al-Ḥamawī. 4 vols. (Beirut: Dār Ibn Ḥazm, 1995).
The Distinguished Jurist's Primer: a translation of Bidāyat al-mujtahid wa-nihāyat al-muqtaṣid. Translated by Imran Khan Nyazee. Edited by Muhammad Abdul Rauf. 2 vols. (Reading: Garnet Publishing, 1994).
Ibn Sa'd, Muḥammad (d. *c.* 845; Iraq). *Kitāb al-ṭabaqāt al-kabīr.* Translated by S. Moinul Haq, assisted by H. K. Ghazanfar. 2 vols. (Karachi: Pakistan Historical Society, 1967).
Ibn Taymīyah, Aḥmad ibn 'Abd al-Ḥalīm (d. 1328; Syria). *Ibn Taimiyya on public and private law in Islam; or, Public policy in Islamic jurisprudence.* Translated by Omar A. Farrukh. (Beirut: Khayats 1966).
Ibn Taymīyah al-Ḥarrānī, Majd al-Dīn Abī al-Barakāt 'Abd al-Salām ibn 'Abd Allāh ibn al-Khiḍr (d. 1254/5; Syria/Iraq) and Shams al-Dīn ibn Mufliḥ al-Ḥanbalī al-Maqdisī (d. 1362; Syria). *Muḥarrar fī al-fiqh 'alá madhhab*

al-Imām Aḥmad ibn Ḥanbal. Edited by Muḥammad Ḥasan Muḥammad Ḥasan Ismāʿīl and Aḥmad Maḥrūs Jaʿfar Ṣāliḥ. 2 vols. (Beirut: Dār al-Kutub al-ʿIlmīyah, 1999).

Ibrahim, Mahmood. *Merchant capital and Islam*. (Austin, TX: University of Texas Press, 1990).

Ibrāhīm, Najāshī ʿAlī. *Khiṣāl al-fiṭrah fī al-fiqh al-islāmī*. (Cairo: al-Taqadum, 1980).

Iggers, G. G. "Historiography and historical thought: modern history (since the eighteenth century)." In *International Encyclopedia of the Social & Behavioral Sciences*. Edited by Neil J. Smelser and Paul B. Baltes. (Oxford: Pergamon, 2001), 6798–804.

Ilan, Tal. *History of Jewish women in late antiquity*. (Jerusalem: The Hebrew University of Jerusalem, Rothberg School for Overseas Students, 1994).

The Institutes of Justinian: text, translation, and commentary. Translated by Joseph Anthony Charles Thomas. (Amsterdam; New York: North-Holland Pub. Co.; American Elsevier Pub. Co., 1975).

Jabrī, ʿAbd al-Mutaʿāl Muḥammad. *Nāsikh wa-al-mansūkh bayna al-ithbāt–wa-al-nafy*. (Cairo: Maktabat Wahbah, 1987).

Jackson, Bernard S. "The 'institutions' of marriage and divorce in the Hebrew Bible." *Journal of Semitic Studies* 56:2 (2011): 221–51.

"Some reflections on family law in the papyri." In *Jewish Law Association Studies XIV*. Edited by Hillel Gamoran. (Binghamton, NY: Global Academic Pub.; Binghamton University, 2002), 141–77.

Jacobs, Andrew S. *Christ circumcised: a study in early Christian history and difference*. (Philadelphia, PA: University of Pennsylvania Press, 2012).

Jacobs, Sandra. *The body as property: physical disfigurement in biblical law*. (New York: Bloomsbury T&T Clark, 2014).

Jaffer, I. E. "The asānid of Ibn ʿAbbās in the tafsīr of Al-Ṭabarī and Ibn Kathīr." *Journal for Semitics* 16:2 (2007): 449–70.

al-Jazīrī, ʿAbd al-Raḥmān, Muḥammad Gharawī, and Yāsir Māziḥ. *Kitāb al-fiqh ʿalá al-madhāhib al-arbaʿah wa madhhab ahl al-bayt*. 5 vols. (Beirut: Dār al-Thaqalayn, 1998).

Jennings, Ronald C. "Divorce in the Ottoman sharia court of Cyprus, 1580–1640." *Studia Islamica* 78 (1993): 155–67.

Johns, C. H. W. *Babylonian and Assyrian laws, contracts and letters*. (Edinburgh: T. & T. Clark, 1904).

Jokisch, Benjamin. *Islamic imperial law: Harun Al-Rashid's codification project*. Studien zur Geschichte und Kultur des islamischen Orients. Edited by Lawrence I. Conrad. (Berlin; New York: Walter de Gruyter, 2007).

Jordheim, Helge. "Against periodization: Koselleck's theory of multiple temporalities." *History and Theory* 51:2 (2012): 151–71.

Judd, Steven C. *Religious scholars and the Umayyads: piety-minded supporters of the Marwanid Caliphate*. (London; New York: Routledge, 2014).

Kaḥlāwī, ʿAblah. *al-Khulʿ: dawāʾ mā lā dawāʾ la-hu: dirāsah fiqhīyah muqāranah*. (Cairo: Dār al-Rashād, 2000).

Kamali, Mohammad Hashim. *Principles of Islamic jurisprudence*. Rev. edn. (Cambridge: Islamic Texts Society, 1991).

Kaplony, Andreas, Daniel Potthast, and Cornelia Römer (eds.). *From Bāwīṭ to Marw: documents from the medieval Muslim world*, Islamic history and civilization, vol. CXII. (Leiden: Brill, 2015).

Karo, Joseph ben Ephraim (d. 1575; Ṣafad). *Shūlḥan ʿarūkh*. (1563).

Kāsānī, Abū Bakr ibn Masʿūd (d. 1189; Syria). *Badāʾiʿ al-ṣanāʾiʿ fī tartīb al-sharāʾiʿ*. Edited by Aḥmad Mukhtār ʿUthmān. 10 vols. (Cairo: Zakarīyā ʿAlī Yūsuf, 1968).

Khadduri, Majid and Liebesny Herbert J. (eds.). *Origin and development of Islamic law*. (Washington, DC: Middle East Institute, 1955).

Khalafallah, Haifaa. "The elusive 'Islamic law': rethinking the focus of modern scholarship." *Islam and Christian-Muslim Relations* 12:2 (April 2001): 143–52.

Khan, Geoffrey. "An Arabic legal document from the Umayyad period." *Journal of the Royal Asiatic Society* 4:3 (1994): 357–68.

Arabic papyri: selected material from the Khalili collection. Nasser D. Khalili Collection of Islamic Art. (London; New York: Nour Foundation in association with Azimuth Editions and Oxford University Press, 1992).

Bills, letters, and deeds: Arabic papyri of the 7th to 11th centuries. Nasser D. Khalili Collection of Islamic Art. (New York: Nour Foundation in association with Azimuth Editions and Oxford University, 1993).

Kharsān, Ḥasan al-Mūsawī. *Mawsūʿat ʿAbd Allāh ibn ʿAbbās: ḥabr al-ummah wa-tarjumān al-Qurʾān*. Silsilat Radd al-shubuhāt, 5. 5 vols. (Najaf: Markaz al-Abḥāth al-ʿAqāʾidīyah, 2007/8).

al-Khaṭīb, Muʿtaz. *Raddu al-ḥadīth min jihat al-matn: dirāsah fī manāhij al-muḥaddithīn wa al-uṣūlīyīn*. (Beirut: Arab Network for Research and Publishing, 2011).

al-Khaṭīb al-Baghdādī, Abū Bakr Aḥmad ibn ʿAlī (d. 1071; Iraq). *Kitāb al-kifāyah fī ʿilm al-riwāyah*. (Cairo: Dār al-Kutub al-Ḥadīthah, 1972).

Khoury, Raif Georges. "Al-Layth Ibn Saʿd (94/713–175/791), grand maître et mécène de l'Egypte, vu à travers quelques documents islamiques anciens." *Journal of Near Eastern Studies* 40:3 (1981): 189–202.

"Papyruskunde." In *Grundriss der Arabischen Philologie*. (Wiesbaden: L. Reichert, 1983), 252–70.

al-Khurāsānī al-Ibāḍī, Bishr ibn Ghānim (d. *c*. 815; Khurāsān). *Mudawwanah al-kubrá*. 2 vols. (Oman: Wizārat al-Turāth al-Qawmī wa-al-Thaqāfah, 1984).

Kister, M. J. "'... and he was born circumcised...': Some notes on circumcision in Ḥadīth." *Oriens* 34 (1994): 10–30.

"The massacre of the Banū Qurayẓa: a re-examination of a tradition." *Jerusalem Studies in Arabic and Islam* 8 (1986): 61–96.

Knight, Mary. "Curing cut or ritual mutilation?: some remarks on the practice of female and male circumcision in Graeco-Roman Egypt." *Isis* 92:2 (2001): 317–38.

Kokoschka, Alina, Birgit Krawietz, and Georges Tamer (eds.). *Islamic theology, philosophy and law: debating Ibn Taymiyya and Ibn Qayyim al-Jawziyya*. (Berlin: De Gruyter, 2013).

Kraemer, Casper J. *Excavations at Nessana. Non-literary papyri*. Colt Archaeological Expedition, 1936–1937. (Princeton, NJ: Princeton University Press, 1958).
Kueny, Kathryn. "Abraham's test: Islamic male circumcision as anti/ante-covenantal practice." In *Bible and Qur'ān: essays in scriptural intertextuality*. Edited by John C. Reeves. (Atlanta, GA: Society of Biblical Literature, 2003), 161–82.
al-Kulaynī, Muḥammad ibn Ya'qūb (d. 941; Iran). *al-Kāfī*. Edited by Shams al-Din Muhammad Ja'far. 8 vols. (Beirut: Dār al-Ta'āruf, 1993).
LaCapra, Dominick. *History & criticism*. (Ithaca, NY: Cornell University Press, 1985).
Lakoff, George and Mark Johnson. *Metaphors we live by*. (Chicago, IL: University of Chicago Press, 1980).
Latour, Bruno and Steve Woolgar. *Laboratory life: the construction of scientific facts*. (Princeton, NJ: Princeton University Press, 1986).
Le Goff, Jacques. *Must we divide history into periods?* Translated by M. B. DeBevoise. (New York: Columbia University Press, 2015).
Lecker, Michael. "'Amr ibn Ḥāzm al-Anṣārī and Qur'ān 2, 256: 'No compulsion is there in religion'." *Oriens* 35 (1996): 57–64.
The "Constitution of Medina": Muḥammad's First Legal Document. Studies in Late Antiquity and Early Islam 23. (Princeton, NJ: The Darwin Press, 2004).
Muslims, Jews, and pagans: studies on early Islamic Medina. Islamic history and civilization, vol. XIII. (Leiden; New York: E.J. Brill, 1995).
"A note on early marriage links between Qurashīs and Jewish women." *Jerusalem Studies in Arabic and Islam* 10 (1987): 17–39.
"Wāqidī's account on the status of the Jews of Medina: a study of a combined report." *Journal of Near Eastern Studies* 54 (1995): 15–32.
"Zayd b. Thābit, 'a Jew with two sidelocks': Judaism and literacy in pre-Islamic Medina (Yathrib)." *Journal of Near Eastern Studies* 56 (1997): 259–73.
Lévi-Strauss, Claude. *Structural anthropology*. Translated by Claire Jacobson and Brooke Schoepf. (New York: Basic Books, 1963).
Lewin, Benjamin Menasseh. *Otsar ha-ge'onim: teshuvot ge'one bavel u-ferushehem `al pi seder ha-talmud*. (Haifa; Jerusalem: Hebrew University, 1928–43).
Libson, Gideon. "Halakhah and law in the period of the Geonim." In *An introduction to the history and sources of Jewish law*. Edited by Neil S. Hecht, Bernard S. Jackson, S. M. Passamaneck, D. Piattelli, and A. M. Rabello. (Oxford; New York: Clarendon Press; Oxford University Press, 1996), 197–250.
Jewish and Islamic law: a comparative study of custom during the Geonic period. Harvard series in Islamic law, 1. (Cambridge, MA: Islamic Legal Studies Program, Harvard Law School, 2003).
Lieber, David L., Ben-Zion Schereschewsky, and Moshe Drori. "Divorce." In *Encyclopaedia Judaica*. Edited by Michael Berenbaum and Fred Skolnik. (Detroit, MI: Macmillan Reference USA, 2007), 710–21.
Lorenz, C. "History: theories and methods." In *International Encyclopedia of the Social & Behavioral Sciences*. Edited by Neil J. Smelser and Paul B. Baltes. (Oxford: Pergamon, 2001), 6869–76.

Lowin, Shari L. "Abraham in Islamic and Jewish exegesis." *Religion Compass* 5:6 (2011): 224–35.

Lucas, Scott C. "Divorce, ḥadīth-scholar style: from al-Dārimī to al-Tirmidhī." *Journal of Islamic Studies* 19:3 (2008): 325–68.

al-Madanī, ʿAlī ibn Jaʿfar (d. 825). *Masāʾil ʿAlī ibn Jaʿfar wa-mustadrakātuhā*. Silsilat maṣādir biḥār al-anwār, 8. (Beirut: Muʾassasat Āl al-Bayt li-Iḥyāʾ al-Turāth, 1990).

Maghen, Ze'ev. *After hardship cometh ease: the Jews as backdrop for Muslim moderation*. Studien zur Geschichte und Kultur des islamischen Orients; Beihefte zur Zeitschrift "Der Islam", Neue Folge, Bd. 17. (Berlin; New York: De Gruyter, 2006).

"Dead tradition: Joseph Schacht and the origins of 'popular practice'." *Islamic Law and Society* 10:3 (2003): 276–347.

"First blood: purity, edibility, and the independence of Islamic jurisprudence." *Der Islam* 81:1 (2004): 49–95.

Maimonides, Mūsá ibn Maymūn (d. 1204; Andalusia/Egypt). *Mishneh Torah*. Yale Judaica series. 14 vols. (New Haven, CT: Yale University Press, 1949).

Maine, Henry Sumner. *Ancient law; its connection with the early history of society and its relation to modern ideas*. (Boston, MA: Beacon Press, 1963).

Malczycki, W. Matt. "The papyrus industry in the early Islamic era." *Journal of the Economic and Social History of the Orient* 54:2 (2011): 185–202.

al-Marghīnānī, ʿAlī ibn Abī Bakr (d. 1197; Farghāna). *Al-Hidāyah = the Guidance: a translation of al-Hidāyah fī sharḥ Bidāyat al-mubtadī, a classical manual of Ḥanafī law*. Translated by Imran Ahsan Khan Nyazee. (Bristol: Amal Press, 2006).

The Hidāyah: commentary on the Islamic laws. Translated by Zahra Baintner. 2 vols. (Karachi: Darul Ishaat, 2007).

Marlow, Louise. *Hierarchy and egalitarianism in Islamic thought*. (New York: Cambridge University Press, 1997).

Marshall, Douglas A. "Behavior, belonging, and belief: a theory of ritual practice." *Sociological Theory* 20:3 (2002): 360–80.

Marsham, Andrew. "The pact (*amāna*) between Muʿāwiya ibn Abī Sufyān and ʿAmr ibn al-ʿĀṣ (656 or 658 CE): 'documents' and the Islamic historical tradition." *Journal of Semitic Studies* 57:1 (2012): 69–96.

Marsham, Andrew and Chase Robinson. "The safe-conduct for the Abbasid ʿAbd Allāh b. ʿAlī (d. 764)." *Bulletin of the School of Oriental and African Studies, University of London* 70:2 (2007): 247–81.

Marx, Karl. "The Eighteenth Brumaire of Louis Bonaparte." In *Karl Marx: selected writings*. Edited by David McLellan. (Oxford: Oxford University Press, 2000), 329–55.

Masud, Muhammad Khalid, Rudolph Peters, and David Stephan Powers. "Qāḍīs and their courts: an historical survey." In *Dispensing justice in Islam: qadis and their judgements*. Edited by Muhammad Khalid Masud, Rudolph Peters, and David Stephan Powers. Studies in Islamic law and society, 22. (Leiden; Boston, MA: Brill, 2006), 1–44.

al-Māwardī, ʿAlī ibn Muḥammad (d. 1058; Iraq). *The ordinances of government [Al-ahkām al-sulṭāniyya w'al-wilāyāt al-dīniyya]*. Translated by Wafaa H. Wahba. The great books of Islamic civilization. (Reading: Garnet, 1996).

Mayali, Laurent. "Introduction. De la raison à la foi: l'entrée du droit en religion." *Revue de l'histoire des religions* 4 (2011): 475–82.

Mazuz, Haggai. "Menstruation and differentiation: how Muslims differentiated themselves from Jews regarding the laws of menstruation." *Der Islam* 87:1–2 (2012): 204–23.

McClintock, Anne. *Imperial leather: race, gender, and sexuality in the colonial contest.* (New York: Routledge, 1995).

McNamee, Kathleen. "Another chapter in the history of scholia." *The Classical Quarterly* 48:1 (1998): 269–88.

Melammed, Reneé Levine. "He said, she said: a woman teacher in twelfth-century Cairo." *Association for Jewish Studies Review* 22:1 (1997): 19–35.

Melchert, Christopher. *The formation of the Sunni schools of law, 9th-10th centuries C.E.* Studies in Islamic Law and Society, 4. Edited by Ruud Peters and Bernard Weiss. (Leiden: Brill, 1997).

Meron, Yaakov. "Points de contact des droits juif et musulman." *Studia Islamica* 60 (1984): 83–117.

Merry, Sally Engle. "Legal pluralism." *Law & Society Review* 22:5 (1988): 869–96.

Mikhail, Maged S. A. "An orientation to the sources and study of early Islamic Egypt (641–868 CE)." *History Compass* 8:8 (2010): 929–50.

Miṣbāḥ, ʿUthmān. *Mafhūm al-fiṭrah: dirāsah naqdīyah li-maqālāt al-islāmīyīn.* Dirāsāt fī al-fiṭrah, 1. (al-Qunayṭirah: Maʿhad al-Gharb al-Islāmī, 2012).

Modarressi, Hossein. "Early debates on the integrity of the Qurʾān: a brief survey." *Studia Islamica* 77 (1993): 5–39.

Monateri, Pier G. "Black Gaius: a quest for the multicultural origins of the 'Western legal tradition'." *Hastings Law Journal* 51:3 (2000): 479–555.

Moore, Megan Bishop and Brad E. Kelle (eds.). *Biblical history and Israel's past: the changing study of the Bible and history.* (Grand Rapids, MI: William B. Eerdmans Pub. Company, 2011).

Morony, Michael G. *Iraq after the Muslim conquest.* (Princeton, NJ: Princeton University Press, 1984).

Moshfegh, David. "Ignaz Goldziher and the Rise of *Islamwissenschaft* as a 'Science of Religion,'" PhD dissertation, University of California, Berkeley, 2012.

Motzki, Harald (ed.). *The biography of Muḥammad: the issue of the sources*, Islamic history and civilization. Studies and texts, vol. XXXII. (Leiden; Boston, MA: Brill, 2000).

Ḥadīth: origins and developments. (Aldershot; Burlington, VT: Ashgate/Variorum, 2004).

"The *muṣannaf* of ʿAbd al-Razzāq al-Ṣanʿānī as a source of authentic *aḥādīth* of the first century A.H." *Journal of Near Eastern Studies* 50:1 (1991): 1–21.

The origins of Islamic jurisprudence: Meccan fiqh before the classical schools [Die Anfange der islamischen Jurisprudenz: Ihr Entwickllung in Mekka bis zur Mitte des 2./8. Jahrhunderts (1991)]. Translated by Marion H. Katz. Islamic history

and civilization. Studies and texts, vol. XLI. (Leiden; Boston, MA: Brill, 2002).
"The question of the authenticity of Muslim traditions reconsidered: a review article." In *Method and theory in the study of Islamic origins*. Edited by Herbert Berg. (Leiden: Brill, 2003), 211–58.
"The role of non-Arab converts in the development of early Islamic law." *Islamic Law and Society* 6:3 (1999): 293–317.
"Theme issue: methods of dating early legal traditions: introduction." *Islamic Law and Society* 19:1–2 (2012): 1–10.
Motzki, Harald, Nicolet Boekhoff-van der Voort, and Sean W. Anthony. *Analysing Muslim traditions: studies in legal, exegetical and maghāzī ḥadīth*. (Leiden; Boston, MA: Brill, 2010).
Mourad, Suleiman Ali. *Early Islam between myth and history: al-Ḥasan al-Baṣrī (d. 110H/728CE) and the formation of his legacy in classical Islamic scholarship*. Islamic Philosophy, Theology and Science. Texts and Studies, 62. (Leiden; Boston, MA: Brill, 2006).
al-Muḥaqqiq al-Ḥillī, Jaʿfar ibn al-Ḥasan (d. 1277; Iraq). *Mukhtaṣar al-nāfiʿ fī fiqh al-imāmīyah*. (Tehran: Asadī, 1967).
Müller, David Heinrich. *Die Gesetze Hammurabis und ihr Verhältnis zur mosaischen Gesetzgebung sowie zu den XII Tafeln: text in Umschrift, deutsche und hebräische Ubersetzung, Erläuterung und vergleichende Analyse*. (Vienna: A. Hölder, 1903).
Semitica. Sprach- und rechtsvergleichende Studien. (Vienna: Hölder, 1906).
Mūsá, Muḥammad Yūsuf. *Tārīkh al-fiqh al-islāmī*. 2nd edn., 3 vols. (Cairo: Dār al-Maʿrifah, 1964–66).
al-Naḥḥās, Aḥmad ibn Muḥammad (d. 950; Egypt). *al-Nāsikh wa-al-mansūkh fī al-qurʾān al-karīm*. Edited by Muḥammad ibn ʿAli Udfuwī. (Egypt: al-Maktabah al-ʿAllāmīyah, 1938).
al-Nawawī, Abū Zakarīyā Muḥyī al-Dīn ibn Sharaf (d. 1277; Syria). *Rawḍat al-ṭālibīn*. Edited by ʿĀdil Aḥmad ʿAbd al-Mawjūd, ʿAlī Muḥammad Muʿawwaḍ, and Jalāl al-Dīn ʿAbd al-Raḥmān ibn Abī Bakr al-Suyūṭī (d. 1505). 8 vols. (Beirut: Dār al-Kutub al-ʿIlmīyah, 1992).
al-Nawawī, Abū Zakarīyā Muḥyī al-Dīn ibn Sharaf (d. 1277; Syria), Abū Isḥāq Ibrāhīm ibn ʿAlī ibn Yūsuf al-Fīrūzābādī al-Shīrāzī (d. 1083; Iran), and Taqī al-Dīn ʿAlī ibn ʿAbd al-Kāfī al-Subkī (d. 1355; Cairo/Damascus). *al-Majmūʿ, sharḥ al-Muhadhdhab*. Edited by Zakarīyā ʿAlī Yūsuf. 18 vols. (Cairo: Maṭbaʿat al-ʿĀṣimah, 1966–69).
The new Oxford annotated Bible with Apocrypha: new revised standard version (NRSV Bible). Edited by Michael David Coogan, Marc Zvi Brettler, Carol A. Newsom, and Pheme Perkins. 4th edn. (New York: Oxford University Press, 2010).
Newby, Gordon. *A history of the Jews of Arabia: from ancient times to their eclipse under Islam*. (Columbia, SC: University of South Carolina, 1988).
Nietzsche, Friedrich Wilhelm. *The use and abuse of history*. (New York: Liberal Arts Press, 1957).

Nikēphoros II Phōkas, Byzantine Emperor (d. 969). *Le Traité Sur la Guérilla de l'Empereur Nicéphore Phocas (963–969).* Translated by Gilbert and Haralambie Mihăescu Dagron. Le monde Byzantin. (Paris: Editions du Centre National de la Recherche Scientifique, 1986).

Nöldeke, Theodor. *Tārīkh al-Qur'ān [Geschichte des Qorans].* Translated by Georges Tamer. Edited by Friedrich Schwally, Gotthelf Bergstrasser, and Otto Pretzl. (Beirut: Konrad Adenauer Foundation, 2004).

Novak, David. "The treatment of Islam and Muslims in the legal writings of Maimonides." In *Studies in Islamic and Judaic traditions.* Edited by William M. Brinner and Stephen D. Ricks. Brown Judaic studies; no. 110. (Atlanta, GA: Scholars Press, 1986), 233–50.

Olender, Maurice. *The languages of Paradise: race, religion, and philology in the nineteenth century* [*Les langues du paradis*]. Translated by Arthur Goldhammer. (Cambridge, MA: Harvard University Press, 1992).

Olszowy-Schlanger, Judith. *Karaite marriage documents from the Cairo Geniza: legal tradition and community life in mediaeval Egypt and Palestine.* (Leiden; New York: Brill, 1998).

"La lettre de divorce caraïte et sa place dans les relations Caraïtes et Rabbanites au Moyen Age." *Revue des Études Juives* 155:3 (1996): 337–62.

Olyan, Saul M. "What do shaving rites accomplish and what do they signal in biblical ritual contexts?" *Journal of Biblical Literature* 117:4 (1998): 611–22.

Patriarch of Antioch, Michael I (d. 1199; Syria). *Chronique de Michel le Syrien: patriarche jacobite d'Antioche (1166–1199).* Translated by Jean Baptiste Chabot. 4 vols. (Paris: Ernest Leroux, 1899–1910).

Pavlovich, Pavel. *The formation of the Islamic understanding of kalāla in the second century AH (718–816 CE): between scripture and canon.* (Boston, MA; Leiden: Brill, 2016).

Pellat, Ch. "al-Naḍr b. al-Ḥāri<u>th</u> b. ʿAlḳama b. Kalada b. ʿAbd Manāf b. ʿAbd al-Dār b. Ḳuṣayy." In *Encyclopaedia of Islam.* Edited by P. Bearman, Th. Bianquis, C. E. Bosworth, E. van Donzel, and W. P. Heinrichs, s.v. (Leiden; Boston, MA: Brill, 2007).

Polliack, Meira (ed.). *Karaite Judaism: a guide to its history and literary sources.* (Leiden; Boston, MA: Brill, 2003).

Pound, Roscoe. "Law in Books and Law in Action." *American Law Review* 44 (1910): 12–36.

Powers, David S. "The exegetical genre *nāsikh al-Qur'ān wa mansūkhuhu.*" In *Approaches to the history of the interpretation of the Qur'ān.* Edited by Andrew Rippin. (Oxford; New York: Clarendon Press; Oxford University Press, 1988), 117–38.

Muḥammad is not the father of any of your men: the making of the last prophet. (Philadelphia, PA: University of Pennsylvania Press, 2009).

"On the abrogation of the bequest verses." *Arabica* 29:3 (1982): 246–95.

Pregill, Michael E. "The Hebrew Bible and the Quran: the problem of the Jewish 'influence' on Islam." *Religion Compass* 1:6 (2007): 643–59.

al-Qāḍī, Wadād. "A documentary report on Umayyad stipends registers (*dīwān al-ʿaṭāʾ*) in Abū Zurʿaʾs *Tārīkh*." *Quaderni di studi arabi* 4 (2009): 7–44.
"The names of estates in state registers before and after the arabization of the ʻdīwānsʼ." In *Umayyad legacies: medieval memories from Syria to Spain*. Edited by Antoine Borrut and Paul M. Cobb. (Leiden: Brill, 2010), 255–80.
"The salaries of judges in early Islam: the evidence of the documentary and literary sources." *Journal of Near Eastern Studies* 68:1 (2009): 9–30.
"An Umayyad papyrus in al-Kindī's *Kitāb al-Quḍāt*?" *Der Islam* 84:2 (2008): 200–45.
Qalʿahʾjī, Muḥammad Rawwās. *Mawsūʿat fiqh ʿAbd Allāh ibn ʿAbbās*. Fī sabīl mawsūʿah fiqhīyah jāmiʿah; Silsilat mawsūʿat fiqh al-salaf. (Beirut: Dār al-Nafāʾis, 1996).
Mawsūʿat fiqh ʿAbd Allāh ibn ʿUmar: ʿaṣruhu wa-ḥayātuh. Fī sabīl mawsūʿah fiqhīyah jāmiʿah, 7. (Beirut: Dār al-Nafāʾis, 1986).
Mawsūʿat fiqh Abū Bakr al-Ṣiddīq. Fī sabīl mawsūʿah fiqhīyah jāmiʿah, 1; Silsilat mawsūʿat fiqh al-salaf. (Damascus: Dār al-Fikr, 1983).
Mawsūʿat fiqh al-Ḥasan al-Baṣrī. Fī sabīl mawsūʿah fiqhīyah jāmiʿah, 9. 2 vols. (Beirut: Dār al-Nafāʾis, 1989).
Mawsūʿat fiqh ʿAlī ibn Abī Ṭālib. Fī sabīl mawsūʿah fiqhīyah jāmiʿah; Silsilat mawsūʿat fiqh al-salaf, 4. (Damascus: Dār al-Fikr, 1983).
Mawsūʿat fiqh Ibrāhīm al-Nakhaʿī. Fī sabīl mawsūʿah fiqhīyah jāmiʿah, 8. 2 vols. (Beirut: Dār al-Nafāʾis, 1986).
Mawsūʿat fiqh Sufyān al-Thawrī. Fī sabīl mawsūʿah fiqhīyah jāmiʿah; Silsilat mawsūʿat fiqh al-salaf, 10. (Beirut: Dār al-Nafāʾis, 1990).
Mawsūʿat fiqh ʿUmar ibn ʿAbd al-ʿAzīz. Fī sabīl mawsūʿah fiqhīyah jāmiʿah; Silsilat mawsūʿat fiqh al-salaf. (Kuwait: Jāmiʿat al-Kuwayt, 2001).
Mawsūʿat fiqh ʿUthmān ibn ʿAffān. Min al-turāth al-Islāmī, al-kitāb 32. (Mecca: Jāmiʿat Umm al-Qurá, Kullīyat al-Sharīʿah wa-al-Dirāsāt al-Islāmīyah, Markaz al-Baḥth al-ʿIlmī wa-Iḥyāʾ al-Turāth al-Islāmī, 1983).
Mawsūʿat fiqh Zayd ibn Thābit wa-Abī Hurayrah. Fī sabīl mawsūʿah fiqhīyah jāmiʿah; Silsilat mawsūʿat fiqh al-salaf. (Beirut: Dār al-Nafāʾis, 1993).
Qayyara, Simeon (ninth century; Iraq). *Halakhot Gedolot*.
Qurʾān.
al-Qurṭubī, Abī ʿAbd Allāh Muḥammad ibn Aḥmad al-Anṣārī (d. 1273; Cordoba). *al-Jāmiʿ li-aḥkām al-qurʾān*. 20 vols. (Beirut: Dār Iḥyāʾ al-Turāth al-ʿArabī, 2002).
al-Qushayrī, Muslim ibn Hajjāj (d. 875; Khurāsān). *Ṣaḥiḥ Muslim; being traditions of the sayings and doings of the prophet Muhammad as narrated by his companions and compiled under the title al-Jāmiʿ-uṣ-ṣaḥīh, by Imām Muslim*. Translated by ʿAbdul Ḥamīd Ṣiddīqī. 4 vols. (Lahore: Sh. Muhammad Ashraf, 1971–75).
al-Tamyīz. Edited by Ṣāliḥ ibn Aḥmad ibn Thābit Dayyān. (Ṣanʿāʾ: Maktabat al-Imām al-Albānī, 2009).
Rabīʿ, Āmāl ʿAbd al-Raḥmān. *al-Isrāʾīlīyāt fī tafsīr al-ṭabarī: dirāsah fī al-lughah wa-al-maṣādir al-ʿibrīyah*. (Cairo: Jumhūriyat Miṣr al-ʿArabīyah, Wizārat al-Awqāf, al-Majlis al-ʿAlá li al-Shuʾūn al-Islāmīyah, 2001).

al-Rāfiʿī, ʿAbd al-Karīm ibn Muḥammad (d. 1226; Iran). *al-ʿAzīz sharḥ al-wajīz: al-maʿrūf bi-al-sharḥ al-kabīr*. Edited by ʿAlī Muḥammad Muʿawwaḍ and ʿĀdil Aḥmad ʿAbd al-Mawjūd. 14 vols. (Beirut: Dār al-Kutub al-ʿIlmīyah, 1997).

Rapoport, Yossef. *Marriage, money and divorce in medieval Islamic society*. (Cambridge: Cambridge University Press, 2005).

Rashkow, Ilona N. *Taboo or not taboo: sexuality and family in the Hebrew Bible*. (Minneapolis, MN: Fortress Press, 2000).

Reinhart, A. Kevin. "On Sunni Sectarianism." In *Living Islamic history: studies in honour of Professor Carole Hillenbrand*. Edited by Yasir Suleiman. (Edinburgh: Edinburgh University Press, 2010), 209–25.

Renan, Ernest. *De la part des peuples Sémitiques dans l'histoire de la civilisation: discours d'ouverture du cours de langues Hébraïque, Chaldaïque et Syriaque, au Collége de France*. (Paris: M. Lévy Frères, 1862).

Histoire générale et système comparé des langues sémitiques. (Paris: Calmann Levy, 1928).

Retsö, Jan. *The Arabs in antiquity: their history from the Assyrians to the Umayyads*. (London; New York: Routledge Curzon, 2005).

Rippin, Andrew. *The Qur'an: formative interpretation*. Formation of the classical Islamic world, vol. XXV. (Brookfield, VT: Ashgate, 1999).

"Al-Zuhrī, *Naskh al-Qur'ān* and the problem of early *Tafsīr* texts." *Bulletin of the School of Oriental and African Studies, University of London* 47:1 (1984): 22–43.

Riskin, Shlomo. *A Jewish woman's right to divorce: a halakhic history and a solution for the agunah*. (Jersey City, NJ: KTAV Pub. House, 2006).

Roberts, Robert. *The social laws of the Qorân: considered and compared with those of the Hebrew and other ancient codes*. (London: Curzon Press, 1971).

Robin, Julien Christian. "La réforme de l'écriture arabe à l'époque du califat médinois." *Mélanges de l'Université Saint-Joseph* 59 (2006): 319–64.

Robinson, Chase F. "Conclusion: from formative Islam to classical Islam." In *The formation of the Islamic world, sixth to eleventh centuries*. Edited by Chase F. Robinson. The new Cambridge history of Islam. (Cambridge: Cambridge University Press, 2011), 683–95.

Empire and elites after the Muslim conquest: the transformation of northern Mesopotamia. (New York: Cambridge University Press, 2000).

Islamic historiography. (Cambridge; New York: Cambridge University Press, 2003).

"Reconstructing early Islam: truth and consequences." In *Method and theory in the study of Islamic origins*. Edited by Herbert Berg. (Leiden: Brill, 2003), 101–35.

(ed.). *The formation of the Islamic world, sixth to eleventh centuries*, The new Cambridge history of Islam, vol. I. (Cambridge: Cambridge University Press, 2011).

Roth, Martha Tobi, Harry A. Hoffner, and Piotr Michalowski. *Law collections from Mesopotamia and Asia Minor*. (Atlanta, GA: Scholars Press, 1997).

Rotman, Youval. *Les esclaves et l'esclavage: de la Méditerranée antique à la Méditerranée médiévale: VIe-XIe siècles.* (Paris: Belles lettres, 2004).

Rouland, Norbert. *Legal anthropology.* Translated by Philippe G. Planel. (Stanford, CA: Stanford University Press, 1994). First published in France in 1988 by Presses Universitaires de France as *Anthropologie juridique.*

Rubin, Uri. *The eye of the beholder: the life of Muḥammad as viewed by the early Muslims: a textual analysis.* Studies in late antiquity and early Islam, 5. (Princeton, NJ: Darwin Press, 1995).

al-Saḥnūn, ʿAbd al-Salām ibn Saʿīd (d. 854; Tunisia), Mālik Ibn Anas (d. 796; Medina), Muḥammad ibn Aḥmad Ibn Rushd (d. 1126), and Jalāl al-Dīn ʿAbd al-Raḥmān ibn Abī Bakr al-Suyūṭī (d. 1505; Egypt). *al-Mudawwanah al-kubrá li-Imām Mālik ibn Anas al-Aṣbaḥī.* Edited by ʿĪsá ibn Masʿad Zawāwī. 5 vols. (Beirut: Dār al-Kutub al-ʿIlmīyah, 1994).

Said, Edward. *Beginnings: intention and method.* (New York: Columbia University Press, 1985).

Culture and imperialism. (New York: Vintage Books, 1993).

Salaymeh, Lena. "Between scholarship and polemic in Judeo-Islamic studies." *Islam and Christian–Muslim Relations* 24:3 (2013): 407–18.

"Commodifying 'Islamic law' in the U.S. legal academy." *Journal of Legal Education* 63:4 (May 2014): 640–6.

" 'Comparing' Jewish and Islamic legal traditions: between disciplinarity and critical historical jurisprudence." *Critical Analysis of Law, New Historical Jurisprudence* 2:1 (2015): 153–72.

"Every law tells a story: orthodox divorce in Jewish and Islamic legal histories." *UC Irvine Law Review* 4:1 (2014): 19–63.

"Islamic law." In *The International Encyclopedia of Social and Behavioral Sciences.* Edited by James D. Wright. (Oxford: Elsevier, 2015), 746–53.

"The politics of inaccuracy and a case for 'Islamic law.'" *The Immanent Frame* (July 7, 2011). http://blogs.ssrc.org/tif/2011/07/07/the-politics-of-inaccuracy-and-a-case-for-islamic-law.

"Propaganda, politics, and profiteering: Islamic law in the contemporary U.S." *Jadaliyya* (2014). Published electronically September 29. www.jadaliyya.com/pages/index/19408/propaganda-politics-and-profiteering_islamic-law-i.

"Taxing citizens: socio-legal constructions of late antique Muslim identity." *Islamic Law and Society* 23:4 (2016), 1–35.

"Thoughts on near eastern legal culture." (September 19, 2011). http://thetalmudblog.wordpress.com/2011/09/19/thoughts-on-near-eastern-legal-culture-guest-post-by-lena-salaymeh/.

Salaymeh, Lena and Zvi Septimus. "Temporalities of marriage: medieval Jewish and Islamic legal debates." In *Talmudic Transgressions: Essays in Honor of Daniel Boyarin.* Edited by C. Fonrobert, I. Rosen-Zvi, A. Shemesh, and M. Vidas. (Leiden: Brill, forthcoming).

Ṣāliḥ, Ṣubḥī. *ʿUlūm al ḥadīth, wa-muṣṭalaḥuhu: ʿarḍ wa-dirāsah.* 2nd edn. (Damascus: University of Damascus Press, 1963).

al-Ṣanʿānī, ʿAbd al-Razzāq ibn Hammām al-Ḥimyarī (d. 827; Yemen). *Mukhtaṣar al-muṣannaf.* 4 vols. (Beirut: Dār al-Jīl, 1997).

al-Muṣannaf. Manshūrāt al-Majlis al-ʿIlmī, 39. Edited by Ḥabīb al-Raḥmān al-ʿAẓamī. 2nd edn. 11 vols. (Beirut: al-Maktab al-Islāmī, 1983).

Muṣannaf fī al-ḥadīth. Edited by Ḥabīb al-Raḥmān al-ʿAẓamī. 11 vols. (Beirut: al-Maktab al-Islāmī, 1970).

Muṣannaf fī al-ḥadīth. Edited by Ayman Naṣr Azharī. 12 vols. (Beirut: Manshūrāt Muḥammad ʿAlī Bayḍūn, Dār al-Kutub al-ʿIlmīyah, 2000).

al-Sarakhsī, Muḥammad ibn Aḥmad Shams al-Dīn (d. eleventh century; Transoxania). *Kitāb al-mabsūṭ.* 30 vols. (Beirut: Dār al-Kutub al-ʿIlmīyah, 1993).

al-Sarakhsī, Muḥammad ibn Aḥmad and Muḥammad ibn al-Ḥasan al-Shaybānī (d. 804/5; Iraq). *Sharḥ al-siyar al-kabīr.* Edited by Ṣalāḥ al-Dīn Munajjid. 5 vols. (Cairo: Maʿhad al-Makhṭūṭāt bi-Jāmiʿat al-Duwal al-ʿArabīyah, 1971/72).

al-Sarḥān, Muḥyī Hilāl. *Asrá al-ḥarb fī al-islām wa-al-qānūn al-dawlī.* (Baghdad: al-Jumhūrīyah al-ʿIrāqīyah, Wizārat al-Awqāf wa-al-Shuʾūn al-Dīnīyah, Majallat al-Risālah al-Islāmīyah, 1986).

Satlow, Michael L. "Beyond influence: toward a new historiographic paradigm." In *Jewish literatures and cultures: context and intertext.* Edited by Anita Norich and Yaron Z. Eliav (Providence, RI: Brown Judaic Studies, 2008), 37–53.

Schacht, Joseph. "Fiḳh." In *Encyclopaedia of Islam.* Edited by P. Bearman, Th. Bianquis, C. E. Bosworth, E. van Donzel, and W. P. Heinrichs (Leiden; Boston, MA: Brill, 2007).

"Foreign elements in ancient Islamic law." *Journal of Comparative Legislation and International Law* 32:3/4 (1950): 9–17.

An introduction to Islamic law. (London: Oxford University Press, 1964).

The origins of Muhammadan jurisprudence. (Oxford: Clarendon Press, 1950).

"Pre-Islamic background and early development of jurisprudence." In *Origin and development of Islamic law.* Edited by Majid Khadduri and Herbert J. Liebesny. (Washington, DC: Middle East Institute, 1955), 28–56.

Schoeler, Gregor. *The oral and the written in early Islam.* Translated by Uwe Vagelpohl. Routledge Studies in Middle Eastern Literatures. Edited by James E. Montgomery. (London and New York: Routledge, 2006).

"Writing and publishing: on the use and function of writing in the first centuries of Islam." *Arabica* 44:3 (July 1997): 423–35.

Schubert, Alexander T. and Petra Sijpesteijn (eds.). *Documents and the history of the early Islamic world.* Islamic history and civilization. (Leiden: Brill, 2015).

Schwarz, Michael. "Al-Fiqh, a term borrowed from Islam used by Maimonides for a Jewish concept in his Sefer haMizwoth and in the Guide of the Perplexed." In *Adaptations and innovations: studies on the interaction between Jewish and Islamic thought and literature from the early Middle Ages to the late twentieth century.* Edited by Joel L. Kraemer, Y. Tzvi Langermann, and Jossi Stern. Collection de la Revue des études juives, 44. (Paris; Dudley, MA: Peeters, 2007), 349–54.

Sealey, Raphael. *The justice of the Greeks.* (Ann Arbor, MI: University of Michigan Press, 1994).

Ševčenko, Ihor. "Two varieties of historical writing." *History and Theory* 8:3 (1969): 332–45.

Sewell Jr., William H. *Logics of history: social theory and social transformation.* Chicago Studies in Practices of Meaning. (Chicago, IL; London: University of Chicago Press, 2005).

al-Shāfiʿī, Muḥammad ibn Idrīs (d. 820; Arabia/Egypt). *al-Umm.* Kitāb al-Shaʿb. Edited by Ismāʿīl ibn Yaḥyá Muzanī (d. 878). Reprint of the edn. published in Cairo, 1321 (1903/4 edn.) 7 vols. (Cairo: Dār al-Shaʿb, 1968).

al-Umm. 11 vols. (al-Manṣūrah: Dār al-Wafāʾ, 2001).

Shahīd, Irfan. *Rome and the Arabs: a prolegomenon to the study of Byzantium and the Arabs.* (Washington, DC: Dumbarton Oaks Research Library and Collection, 1984).

Shalabī, Raʾūf. *al-Jihād fī sabīl allāh: majālatuhu wa-wasāʾiluhu wa-āhdāfuhu.* (Cairo: Dār al-Turāth al-ʿArabī, 1974).

al-Shāṭibī, Ibrāhīm ibn Mūsá (d. 1388; Granada). *al-Muwāfaqāt fī uṣūl al-aḥkām.* Edited by Muḥammad al-Khiḍr Ḥusayn al-Tūnisī. 4 vols. (Beirut: Dār al-Fikr, 1922).

al-Shaybānī, Muḥammad ibn al-Ḥasan (d. 804/5; Iraq). *The Islamic law of nations: Shaybānī's Siyar.* Translated by Majid Khadduri. (Baltimore, MD: Johns Hopkins Press 1966).

al-Shīrāzī, Abū Isḥāq Ibrāhīm ibn ʿAlī ibn Yūsuf Fīrūzābādī (d. 1083; Iran). *al-Muhadhdhab fī fiqh al-imām al-shāfiʿī.* 2 vols. (Cairo: Sharikat Maktabat wa-Maṭbaʿat Muṣṭafá al-Thānī al-Ḥalabī wa-Awlādahu bi-Miṣr, 1959).

al-Muhadhdhab fī fiqh al-imām al-shāfiʿī. Edited by Zakarīyā ʿUmayrāt and Muḥammad ibn Aḥmad Baṭṭāl. 3 vols. (Beirut: Dār al-Kutub al-ʿIlmīyah, 1995).

Shmuelevitz, Aryeh. *The Jews of the Ottoman Empire in the late fifteenth and the sixteenth centuries: administrative, economic, legal, and social relations as reflected in the responsa.* (Leiden: E.J. Brill, 1984).

Sijpesteijn, Petra M. "Shaping a Muslim state: papyri related to a mid-eighth-century Egyptian official." Dissertation, Princeton University, 2004.

Simonsohn, Uriel I. *A common justice: the legal allegiances of Christians and Jews under early Islam.* Divinations: Rereading Late Ancient Religion. (Philadelphia, PA: University of Pennsylvania Press, 2011).

Sizgorich, Thomas. "Narrative and community in Islamic late antiquity." *Past & Present* 185:1 (2004): 9–42.

Violence and belief in late antiquity: militant devotion in Christianity and Islam. (Philadelphia, PA: University of Pennsylvania Press, 2008).

Small, Keith E. *Textual criticism and Qurʾān manuscripts.* (Lanham, MD: Lexington Books, 2011).

Smith, Mark S. *The origins of biblical monotheism: Israel's polytheistic background and the Ugaritic texts.* (New York: Oxford University Press, 2001).

Spiegel, Gabrielle M. *The past as text: the theory and practice of medieval historiography.* (Baltimore, MD: Johns Hopkins University Press, 1997).

Practicing history: new directions in historical writing after the linguistic turn. (New York: Routledge, 2005).

Stampfer, Yehudah Zvi. "Islamic influence in the divorce laws of Rav Samuel Ben Hofni Gaon and the Rambam." In *ʿAle ʿasor: divre ha-veʿidah ha-ʿasirit shel ha-hevrah le-heker ha-tarbut ha-ʿArvit-ha-yehudit shel yeme-ha-benayim.* Edited by Congress Society for Judaeo-Arabic Studies, Daniel J. Lasker, Haggai Ben-Shammai, Studies Society for Judaeo-Arabic, and ba-Mizrah Mekhon Ben-Tsevi le-heker kehilot Yisrael. (Beer-Sheva: University of Ben Gurion, 2008), 309–16.

Stern, Josef. "Maimonides on the covenant of circumcision and the unity of God." In *The Midrashic imagination: Jewish exegesis, thought, and history.* Edited by Michael A. Fishbane. (Albany, NY: State University of New York Press, 1993), 131–54.

Strawson, John. "Encountering Islamic law." *Critical Legal Conference held in New College* (1993). www.witness-pioneer.org/vil/Articles/shariah/jsrps.html

"Islamic law and English texts." *Law and Critique* 6:1 (1995): 21–38.

Stroumsa, Sarah. *Maimonides in his world: portrait of a Mediterranean thinker.* (Princeton, NJ: Princeton University Press, 2009).

Sundelin, Lennart. "Introduction: papyrology and the study of early Islamic Egypt." In *Papyrology and the history of early Islamic Egypt.* Edited by Petra Sijpesteijn and Lennart Sundelin. (Leiden; Boston, MA: Brill, 2004), 1–19.

al-Suyūṭī, Jalāl al-Dīn ʿAbd al-Raḥmān ibn Abī Bakr (d. 1505; Egypt). *al-Itqān fī ʿulūm al-qurʾān.* Edited by Muḥammad Abū al-Faḍl Ibrāhīm. 2nd edn. (Tehran: Manshūrāt al-Raḍī, 1984).

al-Ṭabarī, Abū Jaʿfar Muḥammad ibn Jarīr (d. 923; Iraq). *Kitāb al-jihād wa-kitāb al-jizyah wa-aḥkām al-muḥāribīn min kitāb ikhtilāf al-fuqahāʾ*. Edited by Joseph Schacht. (Leiden: Brill, 1933).

Tafsīr al-Ṭabarī: jāmiʿ al-bayān ʿan taʾwīl āy al-qurʾān. Edited by ʿAbd Allāh ibn ʿAbd al-Muḥsin Turkī. 26 vols. (Riyadh: Dār ʿĀlam al-Kutub, 2003).

The victory of Islam. Translated by Michael Fishbein. *The history of al-Ṭabarī, VIII.* (Albany, NY: State University of New York Press, 1997).

Ṭabāṭabāʾī, ʿAlī ibn Muḥammad (d. *c.* 1816). *Riyāḍ al-masāʾil fī bayān al-aḥkām bi-al-dalāʾil.* (Beirut: Dār al-Hādī, 1992).

Ṭalḥah, ʿAlī ibn Abī (d. 760/1). *Ṣaḥīfat ʿalī ibn abī ṭalḥah: ʿan ibn ʿabbās fī tafsīr al-qurʾān al-karīm.* Edited by Rāshid ʿAbd al-Munʿim al-Rajjāl. (Cairo: Maktabat al-Sunnah, 1991).

Tamanaha, Brian Z. "Understanding legal pluralism: past to present, local to global." *Sydney Law Review* 30:3 (2008): 375–511.

Tanselle, G. Thomas. *Textual criticism since Greg: a chronicle, 1950–2000.* (Charlottesville, VA: The Bibliographical Society of The University of Virginia, 2005).

al-Thawrī, Sufyān ibn Saʿīd (d. 778; Kūfah). *Tafsīr Sufyān al-Thawrī.* (Beirut: Dār al-Kutub al-ʿIlmīyah, 1983).

Tillier, Mathieu. "Le cadi et le sauf-conduit (*amān*): les enjeux juridiques de la diplomatie dans l'Orient abbasside." *Islamic Law and Society* 19:3 (2012): 201–21.

Les cadis d'Iraq et l'état abbasside, 132/750–334/945. (Damascus; Lebanon: IFPO, 2009).

"Qāḍīs and the political use of the *maẓālim* jurisdiction under the ʿAbbāsids." In *Public Violence in Islamic Societies.* Edited by Christian Lange and Maribel Fierro. (Edinburgh: Edinburgh University Press, 2009).

Timpanaro, Sebastiano and Glenn W. Most. *The genesis of Lachmann's method.* (Chicago, IL: University of Chicago Press, 2005).

al-Tirmidhī, Muḥammad ibn ʿĪsá (d. 892; Khurāsān). *Sunan al-Tirmidhī wa-huwa al-Jāmiʿ al-ṣaḥīḥ.* Edited by ʿAbd al-Wahhāb ʿAbd al-Laṭīf and ʿAbd al-Raḥmān Muḥammad ʿUthmān. 5 vols. (Medina: al-Maktabah al-Salafīyah, 1965).

Tomlins, Christopher. "Framing the Field of Law's Disciplinary Encounters: A Historical Narrative." *Law & Society Review* 34:4 (2000): 911–72.

"Historicism and materiality in legal theory." In *Law, theory and history: new essays on a neglected dialogue.* Edited by Maksymilian Del Mar and Michael Lobban. (Oxford: Hart Publishing, 2016).

"How Autonomous Is Law?" *Annual Review of Law and Social Science* 3:1 (2007): 45–68.

"What is left of the law and society paradigm after critique? Revisiting Gordon's 'Critical Legal Histories'." *Law & Social Inquiry* 37:1 (2012): 155–66.

Tottoli, Roberto. "Origin and use of the term Isrāʾīliyyāt in Muslim literature." *Arabica* 46:2 (1999): 193–210.

Toy, Crawford H. "The Semitic conception of absolute law." In *Orientalische Studien Theodor Nöldeke zum siebzigsten Geburtstag (2. März 1906) gewidmet von Freunden und Schülern und in Ihrem Auftrag herausgegeben von Carl Bezold. Mit dem Bildnis Th. Nöldeke's, einer Tafel und zwölf Abbildungen.* Edited by Carl Bezold. (Gieszen: A. Töpelmann, 1906), 797–804.

Trimingham, John Spencer. *Christianity among the Arabs in pre-Islamic times.* (London: Longman Group Limited, 1979).

Tsafrir, Nurit. *The history of an Islamic school of law: the early spread of Hanafism.* Harvard Series in Islamic Law, 3. (Cambridge, MA: Islamic Legal Studies Program, Harvard Law School, 2004).

Tucker, Aviezer. *Our Knowledge of the Past.* (Cambridge: Cambridge Unviersity Press, 2004).

Turner, Bryan S. *Marx and the end of Orientalism.* (London: George Allen & Unwin Ltd, 1978).

Twining, William. *General jurisprudence: understanding law from a global perspective.* Law in context. (Cambridge: Cambridge University Press, 2009).

"Normative and legal pluralism: a global perspective." *Duke Journal of Comparative & International Law* 20:3 (2010): 473–518.

Ustarūshanī, Muḥammad ibn Maḥmūd (d. 1234/5; Samarqand). *Aḥkām al-ṣighār.* (Beirut: Dār al-Kutub al-ʿIlmīyah, 1997).

Vagelpohl, Uwe. *Aristotle's Rhetoric in the East: the Syriac and Arabic translation and commentary tradition.* Islamic philosophy, theology and science, vol. LXXVI. (Leiden; Boston, MA: Brill, 2008).

Valverde, Mariana. "Between a rock and a hard place: legal studies beyond both disciplinarity and interdisciplinarity." *Critical Analysis of Law* 1:1 (2014): 51–62.

van Berkel, Maaike. "Reconstructing archival practices in Abbasid Baghdad." *Journal of Abbasid Studies* 1:1 (2014): 7–22.

Vansina, Jan. *Oral tradition: a study in historical methodology*. Translated by H. M. Wright. (Chicago, IL: Aldine Pub. Co., 1965).

VerSteeg, Russ. *Early Mesopotamian law*. (Durham, NC: Carolina Academic Press, 2000).

Vesey-FitzGerald, Seymour Gonne. "The future of oriental legal studies: an inaugural lecture delivered at University College London on February 4th, 1948." London, 1948.

"Nature and sources of the sharī'a." In *Origin and development of Islamic law*. Edited by Majid Khadduri and Herbert J. Liebesny. (Washington, DC: Middle East Institute, 1955), 85–112.

Vikør, Knut S. "The origins of the sharia." In *The Ashgate research companion to Islamic law*. Edited by Rudolph Peters and P. J. Bearman. (Farnham, Surrey: Ashgate, 2014), 13–26.

Wafā, Muḥammad. *Aḥkām al-naskh fī al-sharī'ah al-islāmīyah*. (Cairo: M. Wafa, 1984).

al-Wāḥidī, Abū al-Ḥasan 'Alī (d. 1075/6; Nishapur) and Hibat Allāh Ibn Salāmah (d. 1019). *Asbāb al-nuzūl*. (Egypt: Maṭba'at Hindīyah, 1897).

al-Wāqidī, Muḥammad ibn 'Umar (d. 822; Medina/Iraq). *Kitāb al-maghāzī*. Edited by Marsden Jones. (Beirut: 'Ālam al-Kutub, 2006).

Wasserstrom, Steven M. *Between Muslim and Jew: the problem of symbiosis under early Islam*. (Princeton, NJ: Princeton University Press, 1995).

Weber, Max. *Economy and society: an outline of interpretive sociology*. (Berkeley, CA: University of California Press, 1978).

Wegner, Judith Romney. "Islamic and Talmudic jurisprudence: the four roots of Islamic law and their Talmudic counterparts." *The American Journal of Legal History* 26:1 (1982): 25–71.

"The status of women in Jewish and Islamic marriage and divorce law." *Harvard Women's Law Journal* 5 (1982): 1–33.

Weitz, Lev E. "Syriac Christians in the medieval Islamic world: law, family, and society," PhD dissertation, Princeton University, 2013.

Westbrook, Raymond. *Old Babylonian marriage law*. Archiv für Orientforschung, Beiheft 23. (Horn, Austria: F. Berger, 1988).

Westbrook, Raymond and Gary Beckman. *A history of ancient Near Eastern law*. (Leiden; Boston, MA: Brill, 2003).

Westreich, Avishalom. "Compelling a divorce? Early Talmudic roots of coercion in a case of moredet." Working Papers of the Agunah Research Unit (May 2008).

"History, dogmatics and hermeneutics: the divorce clause in Palestinian Ketubbot and the Geonic compulsion of divorce." Working Papers of the Agunah Research Unit (March 2009).

"*Umdena* as a ground for marriage annulment: between mistaken transaction (*kiddushei ta'ut*) and terminative condition." *Jewish Law Association Studies* 20 (June 10, 2010): 330–52.

Westreich, Elimelech. "The rise and decline of the law of the rebellious wife in medieval Jewish law." In *Jewish Law Association studies, XII (Zutphen conference)*. Edited by Hillel Gamoran. (Binghamton, NY: Global Publications, State University of New York at Binghamton, 2002), 207–18.

White, Hayden. *Metahistory: the historical imagination in nineteenth-century Europe*. (Baltimore, MD: Johns Hopkins University Press, 1975).

Wilson, M. Brett. "The failure of nomenclature: the concept of 'orthodoxy' in the study of Islam." *Comparative Islamic Studies* 3:2 (2007): 169–94.

Wimpfheimer, Barry S. *Narrating the law: a poetics of talmudic legal stories*. (Philadelphia, PA: University of Pennsylvania Press, 2011).

Yadin, Yigael, Hannah Cotton, Andrew Gross, and Hevrah la-hakirat Erets-Yisrael. *The documents from the Bar Kokhba period in the cave of letters: Hebrew, Aramaic, and Nabatean-Aramaic Papyri*. Judean Desert Series. 2 vols. (Jerusalem: Israel Exploration Society: Hebrew University of Jerusalem: Shrine of the Book, 2002).

Yosef, Koby. "Between al-Zuhrī (d. 124/742) and Qatāda (d. 118/736): two early treatises on abrogation in the Qur'ān." *Jerusalem Studies in Arabic and Islam* 42:1 (2015): 73–128.

Young, Walter. "Stoning and hand-amputation: the pre-Islamic origins of the *ḥadd* penalties for *zinā* and *sariqa*," Master's thesis, McGill University, 2005.

Zafer, Hamza M. *The ummah: Quranic and early Muslim communalism*. (University of Pennsylvania Press, forthcoming).

al-Zamakhsharī, Maḥmūd ibn 'Umar (d. 1144; Khwārazm). *al-Kashshāf 'an ḥaqā'iq al-tanzīl wa-'uyūn al-aqāwīl fī wujūh al-ta'wīl*. Edited by 'Alī ibn Muḥammad al-Sayyid al-Sharīf Jurjānī, Aḥmad ibn Muḥammad Ibn al-Munayyir, and al-Ḥamawī Muḥibb al-Dīn Muḥammad ibn Abī Bakr. 4 vols. (Cairo: al-Bābī al-Ḥalabī, 1966).

al-Zayla'ī al-Ḥanafī, 'Uthmān ibn 'Alī (d. 1342/3), 'Abd Allāh ibn Aḥmad al-Nasafī (d. 1310; Iraq), and Aḥmad ibn Muḥammad Shalabī (d. 1612/13). *Tabyīn al-ḥaqā'iq; sharḥ kanz al-daqā'iq*. Edited by Aḥmad 'Azzū 'Ināyah. 7 vols. (Beirut: Dār al-Kutub al-'Ilmīyah, 2000).

Zuḥaylī, Muḥammad Muṣṭafá. *Tārīkh al-qaḍā' fī al-islām*. (Damascus; Beirut: Dār al-Fikr, 1995).

al-Zuhrī, Muḥammad ibn Muslim (d. 742; Syria). *al-Maghāzī al-nabawīyah*. Edited by Suhayl Zakkār. (Damascus: Dār al-Fikr, 1981).

Index

'Abbāsid, 151, 153
Abbott, N., 99
'Abd Allāh ibn Umar, 48, 59, 60, 63–4, 65, 71, 81, 174
Abraham, 81, 110, 111, 112–13, 114–16, 117, 118, 123–4, 128; and bodily ritual symbolizing the covenant of, 133–4; and monotheism, 114, 116, 117; and the role in building the Ka'bah in Mecca, 115; self-circumcision at the age of eighty, 117
Abrahamic, 114, 124, 127; circumcision, 120; commands, 115, 127, 134; community, 116, 117, 124; covenant, 134, 204; precedents, 122, 127, 200; traditions, 203; verses, 114–15, 117, 118
Abrahamic monotheism, 114, 117; and circumcision, 119; associated with circumcision, 118; defined as Islam, 124; in Arabia, 114; rejection of polytheism, 124
Abrahamic practices, 122–3, 124, 134, 199; emulating, 122; interlinked, 120; interpreted, 118; quintessential, 105
abrogation (*naskh*), 61–2, 67, 75
Abū al-Jald Jīlān, 115, 118
Abū 'Azzah al-Jumaḥī, 65, 75
Abū Bakr, 48, 59, 63–4, 71, 81, 149
Abū Ḥanīfah, 65, 68–9, 126, 149, 151
Abū Qatādah, 115, 117
Abū Yūsuf, 68, 150–1
Aḥkām al-qur'ān, 63, 115
Aḥkām al-ṣighār, 130
'Ā'ishah, 125
Alfasi (Isaac ben Jacob Alfasi ha-Cohen), 160
'Alī ibn Abī Ṭālib, 52, 59, 126, 131, 132
Andalusia, 107, 115
anti-semitic, 90, 104
Arabia, 40, 52, 54, 57, 59, 109–10, 114–15, 116, 117, 119; and doctrine of sources, 109; and surviving papyri, 9, 24–5, 26–7; customs, 134, 148; documentary sources and archives, 26; papyrology dominated by Western scholars, 26; pre-Islamic, 109–10, 119; seventh-century, 44, 76, 114
Arab(s), 89, 90, 94–5, 102, 107, 109–10, 112, 114, 125; and learning, 155; Christians, 79, 110, 112, 126, 130; circumcision, 15, 105–6, 107, 108–18, 119–20, 121–34, 135, 200; Jews, 91, 92, 107–8, 111, 112, 113–14, 118, 120, 129–30; late antique, 95; monotheists, 15, 81, 120, 122; Muslims, 78, 107, 149, 182; pagan, 48, 109; pre-Islamic, 122, 128
archival practice, 29, 38
archive(s), 26, 29, 34, 38; institutional, 29; maintained oral, 29; non-institutional, 29; oral-written, 39
Aryan law, 87, 88, 92, 93
Aryan/Semitic, 89, 91, 99; countering Renan's binary, 91; hybrid, 89; myth in religious studies, 92
Aryans, 86–7, 89, 90, 93, 99, 106
Asad, Talal, 13, 97
Asbāb al-nuzūl, 62
al-Askarī, Imām Ḥasan, 129
al-Awzā'ī, 151, 152
'Aṭā' bin Abī Rabāḥ, 59
Azami, M. M., 99

Babylonia, 172; divorce practices, 167; rabbinic Judaism, 95, 159
Babylonian Talmud, 110, 111, 122, 130, 143, 158, 168, 170, 185
Badr, battle of, 49–50, 52, 54–5, 57–8, 63, 64, 65, 71, 75; executions, 75, 78; precedents for prisoner executions, 75; prisoners, 48–50, 63, 71, 75, 81
Baghdad, 85, 156, 161
al-Bāqir, 'Alī, 130,
battlefield(s), 44, 46–7, 49, 57, 64
battle(s), 45, 46–8, 49, 50–2, 53, 54, 55, 56, 57–8, 76–7; historical, 47; identifiable, 58; Muslim, 50, 57; of Ḥunayn, 51–2, 55, 58; of the Trench, 51, 76–7, 82; Prophetic, 51, *see also* Badr

Beirut, 158
Bell, Catherine M., 120, 135
ben Hillel, Mordechai, 161
Berkey, Jonathan P., 134
Bevir, Mark, 3, 16
Bible, 81, 110, 118, 204. *see also* Hebrew Bible
Bloch, Marc, 4, 89, 90
borrowing, 17, 86–7, 89, 90, 91, 96–7, 101, 104–5, 106–7, 193; implications, 140; paradigm, 91, 97, 107; processes, 119
Boyarin, Daniel, 112
breach of contract, 18, 167, 169, 193
Byzantine Empire, 51, 80, 94, 131, 148, 158, 190, 194
Byzantine law, 89
Byzantine protection, 51

Christ, *see* Jesus
Christianity, 11, 15, 87, 102, 112; and the new covenant with God, 113; Eastern, 11; Pauline, 113; Western, 11, 187–8
Christian(s), 81, 102, 107–8, 112–14, 115, 116, 118, 119–20, 123, 127–8; Arabs, 110; articulations of bodily rituals, 113; baptism, 113, 116, 120; conversion, 131; differentiation, 108; intertextuality, 6; law, 11; practices, 109; ritual of immersion, 116; teachings on divorce, 187; texts, 109, 110, 113, 134; theologians, 110; traditions, 113
circumcision, 15, 105–6, 107, 108–18, 119–20, 121–34, 135, 200; Abrahamic, 120; Arabian, 109; articulating as a legal command, 124; associated with Abrahamic practices, 122, 123; attempts to ban, 114; blood, 122, 132; bolstered by jurists as an obligatory practice based on Abrahamic precedent, 200; categorized as a recommended practice, 126–7; classified, 126; classified by late antique Muslims as recommended but not obligatory, 126, 200; covenant-based, 135; female, 122, 125, 133–4; history of, 108, 122; identified, 115; identified as one of the Abrahamic obligations, 115; practice of, 110, 119, 120, 129, 135; ritual of, 104, 108, 111, 112, 113, 130, 134, 135; symbolic, 130–1, 132; timing of, 111, 128; viewed, 15, 113, 117, 126
classical period, 25, 137–8, 141, 203
Common Era (meaning of the term), 19, 109
community, 2, 50, 73, 81, 112, 113, 115, 149, 167, 179; Abrahamic, 116, 117, 124; ethnic, 149; gnostic, 110; late antique Muslim, 47, 48, 51, 71, 79, 81, 96; legal, 102, 103, 164, 167, 187; Near Eastern, 40; pre-Islamic, 40; religious, 196; teacher's, 149; tribal, 53
Companions, 28, 48, 49, 57, 59, 70, 81, 125, 148, 151
comparative philology, 12, 17, 86, 90, 91, 93, 98, 100, 104
comparison, 10–11, 14; Ritual Comparisons 106–7; Legal Comparisons 163–207
contextualism, 6
contextualization, 11, 188, 196; geographic, 8; historical, 6–7; intellectual, 10; temporal, 7
contract(s), 167, 169, 193; Aramaic marriage, 166; labor, 193; marriage, 166, 167; socio-political, 79
conversion, 119, 124, 131, 132–3, 137, 183–4; Christian, 131; forced, 132; genuine, 133; Jewish, 130; process, 126, 130–1, 132
Coope, Jessica A., 123
Corpus Juris Civilis, 191
Coulson, Noel J., 88
court(s), 44, 137, 150, 157, 167, 169, 183, 184, 192, 194; bureaucratized, 153; formalized, 150; local, 148, 158, 182, 194; official, 2, 191
covenant, 110, 112, 113, 118, 133
critical historical jurisprudence, 1, 11, 14
Crone, Patricia, 23, 26, 85, 88, 94, 138
customary practice(s), 1, 17, 81, 104, 105, 107, 109, 189, 193, 198; assimilation of shared, 101, 105; being Muslim entailed adapting regional, 15, 105, 114; pre-Islamic, 128; regional (including Arabian monotheism, Judaism, and Christianity), 15; shaping areas of law (taxation, family, property, criminal), 148

divorce, 164–9, 170–6, 177–80, 181–2, 183–4, 185–6, 187, 188–93, 194–5, 196; courts, 175; demanded by non-Jewish women, 183, 192; documents, 178; grounds for, 178; initiating, 166, 168, 169, 178, 181, 189, 191, 194, 195; no-fault, 180; options, 15, 163, 195; practices, 163, 164, 177–8, 185, 191; settlement, 166, 174–5, 176–9, 190, 191–2, 195; unilateral, 181; wife-initiated, 164
divorce decree(s), 167–8, 169, 171, 184, 186, 190, 192; delivered notarized, 194; granting of, 186; husband's, 165; judicial, 184
documentary sources, 9, 24, 26–8, 32, 34
dower, *see mahr*
Dutton, Yasin, 23, 138

Eastern Christianity, 11
Eastern legal practices, 172
Egypt, 9, 25, 28, 62, 109, 129, 149, 156
El Cheikh, Nadia Maria, 119
Encyclopaedia of Islam, 87
Epiphanes, Antiochus, 111
essentialism, 3, 21

essentialist, 5, 6, 23, 43
executions, 48–9, 50, 52, 53, 64, 65–6, 67, 72, 75–6; of prisoners of war, 46, 59, 61, 62, 71, 81, 83; opposition to, 65; permissibility of, 75, 78; prohibition of, 44, 48, 53, 82, 200; recommended by ʿUmar ibn al-Khaṭṭāb, 48, 50, 52, 59, 73
exegesis, 61–2, 70, 82, 117; exegesis and historiography, 61, 74, 119, 124, 151, 198; exegetical materials, 119; medieval exegetes 40, 45, 53, 55, 56, 66, 116, 119; prophetic precedents and exegesis 203

fault divorce, 193
female circumcision, 122, 125, 133–4
Ferguson, Heather, 131
fiṭrah (natural predisposition), 116–17, 120–1, 124
Fonrobert, Charlotte, 133
formative period, 137–8, 141
Fowden, Garth, 9
Frantz-Murphy, Gladys, 27, 101

genealogy, 112; ritual genealogy 108–9
genealogical, 3, 142, 147
Genizah evidence, 168, 172
Gentile courts, 181, 182, 186, 188
Geonic communities, 185
Geonic decree, 41, 169, 170–2, 180–3, 185–8; classification of, 180; divorce practices, 169; of coercing the husband to divorce his wife, 171; related to wife-initiated divorce, 18
Geonic practices, 171, 180, 193; and the twelve-month waiting period for a divorce to be granted, 184; of coercing husbands to divorce "recalcitrant" wives, 168; Rabbeinu Tam rejects the Geonic decree of coercing the husband to divorce his wife, 171
Geonic rabbis, 168, 183, 184, 185
Geonic texts, 184, 185
Geonim, 131, 168, 169, 182, 183, 185–6, 188
God, 54, 63, 71, 80, 92, 110, 113, 115, 116, 118
Goitein, Shelomo Dov, 23
Goldziher, Ignaz, 87, 91, 106
Gordon, Robert W., 139, 141
Greco-Romans, 97, 111; culture, 95; society, 111
Greco-Roman Egyptians, 122
Greek(s), 26, 101, 190
grooming, 120, 121–2, 123, 133, 134

ḥadīth (plural, *aḥadīth*), *see* tradition-report(s)
Hallaq, Wael B., 23, 36, 138
Hammurabi Code, 91–2
Ḥanafī judges, 153
Ḥanafī jurists, 68, 150–1
Ḥanafī legal school, 67, 82, 144, 152, 154
Ḥanbalī jurists, 67, 144, 152, 154; Ibn Qayyim al-Jawzīyah, 106, 124, 127; Ibn Qudāmah, 75; Ibn Taymiyyah, 69
Ḥanbalī legal school, 144, 152–3, 154
ḥanīfiyyah (monotheism), 114, 117
al-Ḥārith, al-Naḍr bin, 49, 64, 65–6, 67, 72, 75
al-Ḥasan al-Baṣrī, 59, 60, 129, 131, 132
Hasan, A., 99
Hebrew Bible, 109, 110
Heirbaut, Dirk, 2
heterodoxy, 6, 8, 15, 17; late antique, 137, 203; legal 164, 200, 204
historiography, 1, 3, 26, 30–1, 32, 74, 82, 83, 142, 145–6; conventional, 4; defined, 21; evolutionary, 203; late antique Muslim, 50; oriented, 4, 103, 106, 137, 138, 203; "origins" methodologies frame, 41, 85, 89; post-Enlightenment, 139; transformed through law, 15
Hodgson, Marshall, 8, 103
Hoyland, Robert G., 94
Ḥunayn, battle of, 51–2, 55, 58
hybrid law, 15, 94–5, 96, 100

Ibn ʿAbbās, 53–6, 58, 63, 65, 66, 114–17, 118, 123, 132–3
Ibn Abī Shaybah, 40, 125
Ibn ʿAffān, ʿUthmān, 59
Ibn ʿAlī al-Bāqir, Imām Muḥammad, 130
Ibn ʿAlī al-Jaṣṣāṣ, Aḥmad, 115
Ibn Ḥanbal, Aḥmad, 127, 129, 152
Ibn Isḥāq, 48, 49
Ibn Jaʿfar, Imām Musá, 128
Ibn Mundhir al-Naysābūrī, 130
Ibn Qayyim, al-Jawzīyah, 106, 124, 127, 130, 132, 133
Ibn Qudāmah, 75, 78
Ibn Rushd, 71–2, 74
Ibn Taymiyyah, 69
Ibn Yaqṭīn, ʿAlī, 128
Ibrāhīm al-Nakhaʿī, 60, 116, 126, 132, 149
identity, 13, 17, 87, 96, 98, 99, 100, 133, 142, 147
identity politics, 13, 96
ijtihād fī al-madhhab, 144, 157
Imāmī Shīʿī, 128; and Ḥanafī, 82; jurisprudence, 62; school, 44
Iran, 72, 87, 152
Iraq, 40, 59, 68, 69, 70, 85–6, 115, 126, 152, 186; schools of legal thought, 158; sphere of influence, 156, 161
Islam, 8–9, 89, 90, 94–6, 98–9, 102, 103, 120, 131, 132; centuries of, 152; discrediting of, 99; meaning, 116; orthodox Sunnī, 143; scholarship stresses "Semitic origins" in Jewish law, 89

Islamic (*cont.*)
Islamic, 17, 22, 41, 84, 162; archives, 26, 31; chronology of wife-initiated divorce, 172, 179, 194; circumcision, 105, 106, 120, 122, 125, 127, 128, 133, 135; courts, 180, 181–3, 184, 185–6; divorce laws and practices, 164, 174; educational institutions, 156; empires, 9, 44, 80, 119, 137, 142, 151; exceptionalism, 16; exegetical materials, 119; genres, 108; historical sources, 28, 37, 39, 40, 42, 51; historiographical traditions, 20, 24, 26, 28, 39, 77, 83, 103, 139; history, 7–8, 24–5, 29, 31, 36, 42, 47, 74, 104, 108; hybridity, 104; "influences," 182, 187; international law, 197; orthodoxy, 5, 142; practice of circumcision, 107, 120; purity codes, 107; ritual of circumcision, 120; scripture, 17, 114, 124, 127; societies, 2, 100, 101, 104, 124–5, 130, 137, 140; texts, 35, 80, 106, 119; traditions, 5, 12, 80, 81, 84, 96, 165; warfare, 48
Islamic jurisprudence, 1, 10, 12, 88–9, 104, 198, 199, 200, 201; dated, 23; methodology, 156; origins in Iraq, 85; orthodox, 37, 70, 145; rulings on prisoners of war, 204; texts, 68; traditions, 74
Islamic law, 1–5, 10, 11–14, 21–4, 83–9, 93–4, 102–3, 137–8, 201–3; and changes in women's access, 165; and Christian law, 11; and Jewish law, 10, 11, 103, 142–3, 157, 205; and paternity tests, 87; and precursor to legal systems in Near East, 84; and Semitic origins, 88; articulated by Goldziher, 91; authority of, 144; beginnings of, 1, 7, 22, 43, 84, 101, 147–8; birth or parentage of, 23, 86; classical, 138, 161; culture, 102; education, 152, 155; enacting of, 197; "essence" of, 6; essentialism of, 21; "formative" period of, 138; genealogies of, 1; heresy constructed over time, 144; historiography, 4, 7, 10, 15, 139, 140, 141, 143, 144, 204–5; history, 3–4, 9, 11–12, 14–15, 17–18, 22, 147–8, 204; identifying of, 88; identity of, 145; in comparison to modern Western law, 10; in relation to Jewish law and to Islamicate legal culture, 197; institutions, 97; literature, 77, 151, 158–9, 160; opinions on prisoner execution, 82, 153; "origins" determined by dating Islamic legal sources, 21; origins of, 26, 28; orthodoxy of, 4, 6, 144, 154, 161, 200–1; practices of, 17, 150, 205; precedent for, 77; pre-modern, 206; reasoning of, 67, 74, 159; recycling processes, 199, 201; relationship to other legal systems, 85; scholars, 36; scholarship, 140; schools, 137, 152, 159; sources of, 21; studies, 4, 6, 12, 18, 22, 23, 41, 136, 139, 146; syncretism, 198; systems of, 10–11, 17, 92, 98, 101, 103–4, 158, 162–4, 196, 205; teachers and administrators, 155; texts, 41, 160, 191, 193; traditions, 73, 83, 84, 101–2, 144, 147, 192, 203
Islamic literature, 107, 134
Islamic monotheism, 108
Islamic movement, 2, 5, 29, 105, 203
Islamic sources, 16, 30–1, 32–3, 34, 35, 36, 38, 39–40, 98, 99; altered, 34; for historiographical purposes, 34; original, 203; orthodox, 84
Islamic states, 15, 25, 119
Islamic studies, 13, 16, 18–19, 29–30, 31, 33, 104, 137–8, 145, 146; contemporary, 39, 98; conventional, 19; scholars and scholarships, 23–4, 100, 145
Islamicate, 8–9, 10, 15, 17–18, 103, 157–8, 193–4, 197, 203–5; culture, 82, 195; defined, 103; law, 104; legal history, 157; pastiche, 17; periodization, 17, 157, 162, 194, 204–5; practiced, 196; shared, 204; society, 95, 100, 143, 203; world, 103, 117, 143, 158, 160, 164, 184
Islamwissenschaft, 91
isnād (chain of transmission), 36–7
Israelites, 50, 112, 113, 118

Ja'far al-Ṣādiq, 128, 131
al-Jald Jīlān, Abū, 115, 118
Jerusalem, 109, 157
Jesus, 81, 112, 113
Jewish, 10–11, 14–15, 17–18, 101, 103–4, 106, 111–12, 144–5, 157–8, 162–3; adulterers, 77; adulteresses, 197; and Christian practices, 109; and Christian sources, 109; and Christian texts, 109, 134; and customary practices, 198; and Islamic divorce laws, 164; and Islamic jurisprudence, 143; and Islamic law, 15, 17, 83, 88, 164, 205; and Islamic legal historiography, 196; and Islamic legal literature, 158; and Islamic legal systems, 11, 17, 103–4, 158, 162–4, 196, 205; and Islamic legal texts, 191, 193; and Islamic purity laws, 107; and Muslim communities, 158; and Muslim jurists, 159, 196; and Muslim women divorcing, 163; Arab tribes, 76, 78–9; Christians, 79, 112, 126, 130; circumcision, 106, 112, 120, 128, 129, 204; communities, 143, 170, 172, 183; conversion, 130; courts, 186; divorce practices in antiquity, 189; genealogy, 112; heritage, 115; husbands, 183, 186, 192; jurisprudence, 17, 159; jurists, 159, 161, 193; origins, 88, 107; orthodox, 164, 179–80, 182, 186, 203; rabbinic, 92; sects, 143, 195; traditions, 10, 119, 129, 165, 185; uncircumcised, 112; wives, 181, 186

Jewish law, 10, 11, 14, 15, 88–9, 103–4, 188, 197, 205–6; and the "influence" on Islamic law, 106; code of, 172; independence of, 157; story of, 143
Jewish practices, 81, 105, 106, 110, 122, 129, 130, 180
Jewish women, 165–6, 168, 183, 186, 187; access to divorce, 172; divorcing their husbands, 181, 184; non-rabbinic, 165
Jews, 91, 92, 107–8, 111, 112, 113–14, 118, 120, 129–30; and Muslims practice rituals, 107; assimilating Christians and Muslims, 105
Jokisch, Benjamin, 85, 88, 97, 98
Jordan, River, 113
Joshua, 113
Judaic, 41, 165, 179; and Islamic legal texts dating from the third through fourteenth centuries, 41; and Islamic purity codes, 107; chronology, 165, 172, 194
Judaism, 11, 15, 89, 107, 108, 111, 114, 120
judges, 2, 44, 148, 150, 153, 155, 158, 189, 195–6, 202; appointment of, 137, 153, 154; Ḥanafī, 153; professional, 2; provincial, 153; salaries of, 154; Umayyad, 150
al-Jumaḥī, Abū ʿAzzah, 72
jurisprudence, 1–2, 16, 61, 80, 82, 139, 152, 201; historical, 11, 14; Islamic, 1, 10, 12, 88–9, 104, 198, 199, 200, 201; Jewish, 17, 159; Muslim, 88; orthodox, 140; Roman, 86
jurists, 60–1, 67–8, 69–70, 73–5, 78, 82–3, 148–50, 151, 154–5, 198; antecedent, 159; dissenting, 74–5; influential, 149; predecessor, 155, 159, 160; rabbinic, 159–60, 166, 172

Kadijustiz, 10
Khan, Geoffrey, 27
al-Khaṭṭāb, ʿUmar ibn, 48, 50, 52, 59, 73
khitān, *see* circumcision
khulʿ divorces, 173, 175–7, 179. *see also* wife-initiated divorce
Kueny, Kathryn, 121, 123
Kufa legal school, 149, 151
Kūfah, 46, 60, 116, 126, 132
Kufan scholars, 65

languages, 1, 74, 93, 203
late antique, 15, 83, 100, 108, 122–3, 124, 126, 134, 200; and the medieval era, 48, 61, 100, 136, 163, 196, 198, 207; and medieval exegetes, 40, 45, 53, 55, 56, 66, 116, 119; Arabia, 1, 79, 114, 175; circumcision, 108; communities, 131; divorce, 190, 193; documentary sources, 28; era, 80, 111, 165, 203; exegesis, 61–2, 70, 82, 117; historiography, 45; Islamic law, 58; jurists, 44, 46, 58–9, 60–1, 63, 65, 70, 75, 79, 82; Muslim historians, 82; Muslim jurists, 40, 45, 58, 60, 80, 141, 199; Muslim scholars, 28, 58, 121, 128, 132; predecessors, 62, 63, 72, 79, 119, 134, 200
late antiquity, 6, 7–8, 28–9, 33–4, 62, 133, 136–7, 163, 165–6, 192–3; pagans, 108; women, 194; world of, 94
Latour, Bruno, 145
al-Layth Ibn Saʿd, 129
legal customs, 103, 105
legal historiography, 2, 4, 14, 41, 142, 203, 205
legal methodology, 81
legal practices, 96, 182, 186
legal scholarship, contemporary Islamic, 141
legal school(s), 67–8, 137, 138, 149–50, 151, 152–5, 156–7; consolidation of, 40, 150, 153; doctrinal, 200; generated consolidated, 150; orthodox Islamic, 8, 44, 127, 140, 152, 157, 200, 204; professional, 136, 151; state-endorsed, 154. *see also madhhab*
legal science, Islamic, 86
legal studies, contemporary Islamic, 13
legal texts, abridged Islamic, 156, 161
legal theory, orthodox Islamic, 47
legal tradition(s), 1, 2–3, 12, 18, 93, 103, 105, 196, 198; continuing and maintaining, 144; fused by Muslim jurists, 101; Jewish and Islamic, 102, 144, 203; non-Islamic, 3, 15, 198; perpetuated and renewed, 1; pre-Islamic Arabian, 101; shared, 101
Letter to the Galatians, 112
Lévi-Strauss, Claude, 14, 103

madhhab (legal schools) or *madhāhib* (legal schools), 136, 144, 149, 151, 157
maghāzī, 16, 28, 40, 77, 141
Maghen, Ze'ev, 89, 107
mahr (dower), 166–8, 169, 171, 173–6, 177–9, 182, 190–1, 200
Maimonides, 107, 160, 171, 184
Maine, J. S., 139
male circumcision, 17, 105–6, 107, 108–9, 118, 127, 129, 133–4; legitimated, 104; practiced, 126
Mālik ibn Anas, 151
Mālikī jurists, 69, 71, 127
Mālikī legal school, 67, 127, 129, 144, 152, 154
Mamluk courts, 157
marriage, 166, 167, 189, 191, 192, 195; and divorce, 191, 192, 195; contracts, 166, 167; of Muslim women, 165; process of, 190; temporary, 192
masānīd, 16, 141
matn (text), 36–7, 38
Mavroudi, Maria, 20
Māwardī, 70–2, 74

Mecca, 1, 48, 49, 50, 52, 59, 85, 115, 148, 149
medieval era, 8, 61–2, 67–8, 132, 136–7, 191, 192–3, 194–5, 200
medieval Muslim historians, 8, 38–9, 161
medieval Muslim jurists, 67, 70, 82–3, 130, 133, 134, 136, 199–201, 203
medieval Muslim scholars, 39, 78, 79–80, 83, 108
Medina, 16–17, 51, 76, 79, 127, 128–9, 130, 148, 149, 151
Mesopotamia, 9, 109–10
Mishnah, 111, 158
Mongol, 156, 161
monographs, Islamic, 124
monotheism(s), 102, 108, 116, 117, 118, 123, 128
monotheistic faith, 117, 118
Mosaic law, 91, 124
Moses, 81, 170
mosques, 149, 152
Motzki, Harald, 23, 36, 99
Muhammadan jurisprudence, 22, 138
Muḥaqqiq al-Ḥillī, Jaʿfar ibn al-Ḥasan, 69n134
Mujāhid (Mujāhid ibn Jabr), 40, 54–5, 56, 57, 62, 63–4, 66, 115–16, 117
Müller, David H., 91
Muqātil (Muqātil ibn Sulaymān al-Balkhī), 55, 56, 57, 62, 66, 115, 116, 117, 123, 149
muṣannafāt, 16, 28, 40, 117, 141, 175
Muslim circumcision, 124, 129
Muslim jurists, 17–18, 77, 81, 151, 154, 156, 157, 159–60, 176–8; female circumcision, 133; for Jewish litigants, 186; late antique, 136; orthodox, 61; professional, 67
Muslim women, 163, 172, 179, 194
Muslims, 48, 54, 103, 104–5, 107–8, 127–8, 129, 133, 134–5, 183–4; and the army, 48, 50–1, 55, 76; and Islamic courts, 181; and Jewish jurists, 159, 161, 193; and Jewish practices, 129; and Jewish subjects, 196; believing, 100; communities, 1, 2, 63, 64, 76, 114, 147, 148, 158, 163; discouraged from circumcising on the seventh day after birth, 129; food restrictions, 123; generations of, 1, 50, 148; historians, 33, 47; identity of, 17, 105, 123, 128; orthodox, 94, 143; ritual acts, 133; ritualized, 120; scholars, 17, 45, 72, 108, 109, 122, 125, 129, 133, 151; traditional, 144; uncircumcised, 132–3

al-Naḥḥās, 62, 63, 65–6
narratives, 30, 32, 35, 47, 48, 50, 52, 110, 125, 176; biblical, 119; historical sources, 24, 25, 27–9, 31, 33, 35, 38; historical texts, 27; juristic, 144; oral, 100; orthodox, 142, 143, 145, 157, 164, 179; scholarly, 145, 157
al-Nāsikh wa-al-mansūkh (the abrogated and abrogating), 62
naskh, *see* abrogation
al-Nawawī, 69
Near East, 6, 9, 11
Nessana, 190
no-fault divorce options, 179–80
Nöldeke, Theodor, 87
non-Arabs, 95–6, 119
non-Jews, 114
non-Muslims, 9, 46, 99, 103, 203

Olender, Maurice, 90
oral sources, 32, 34, 35
Orientalism, 13
"original" Islam, 24, 38
"origins," 4, 21–3, 41, 84–5, 86–7, 88–90, 93–4, 95–8, 100, 138–9
orthodox elites, 143, 144
orthodox jurisprudence, 140
orthodox jurists, 44, 83, 141, 192
orthodox legal historiographies, 142
orthodox legal opinions, 62
orthodox narrative assumptions, 196
orthodoxy: Islamic, 5, 142; rabbinic, 184, 188

Palestine, 111
Palestinian divorce practices, 167
Palestinian Talmud, 160, 170, 188
papyri, 9, 25, 190
Paul (apostle), 112–13, 126
Pauline Christianity, 113
periodization, 7, 8, 17–18, 137–8, 142, 147–8, 157–8, 162–3, 203, 204
positivism, 23, 30, 90
postfoundationalism, 15–16
practices, 45–6, 96–7, 106, 120–3, 128–9, 134–5, 148–9, 161–3, 179–80, 189–91; late antique Muslim, 125; non-Islamic, 104; pre-Islamic, 96, 104; prevalent Eastern, 172
prisoner execution(s), 46, 50, 60, 68, 71, 72, 74–5, 78, 81, 82; advocated by a pre-Islamic legal norm, 80; and majority opinion during the medieval period permitted, 44; deep-rooted customary practice legitimating, 71, 81; normativity of, 78, 81; opposed, 68; permissibility of, 52, 70; permitted, 60–1, 67, 75; permitting, 45, 54; prohibited, 58–60, 82; prohibition of, 45, 60, 61, 64, 72; sanctioning of, 83
prisoner(s), 47, 48, 49–52, 55, 57–8, 60, 65, 66, 69, 73; combatant, 52; enslaving, 57; executing of, 53, 70, 71, 75; legitimated, 67; non-Arab unbelieving, 69; non-polytheist, 59; polytheist, 59; ransoming of, 53, 80

prisoners of war, *see* war prisoners
professionalization, 8, 18, 144, 148, 154, 155, 177, 191, 201, 204
Prophet Muḥammad, 19, 55, 72, 131, 148, 173, 197, 198; acts relating to treatment of prisoners, 72; and circumcision, 125; and Companions, 58, 60, 79, 148; command and practice, 50; death, 23, 37, 45, 47, 58; lifetime of, 37, 45, 52, 53; practice of protecting prisoners, 53; preaching in Mecca, 1; rejection of execution, 48; solicitation of advice from Companions, 63
Prophetic acts, 71–2, 199
Prophetic era, 16, 40, 61, 125
Prophetic precedents, 65–6, 67, 71, 74, 176, 179, 198–9; and exegesis, 203; and Qurʾānic verses, 200; connected, 198
purity, 17, 107, 113, 115, 120, 121, 122–3, 127, 134–5

Qaraite, 143, 158–9, 184
al-Qayrawānī, 69
Qurʾān, 55–6, 57, 58, 61–2, 63, 69–70, 71–2, 73–4, 114–16; fragments, 24; in Arabia and Iraq, 119; teachers, 148
Qurʾānic evidence, 132; acceptance and modification of Mosaic law, 124; authority of, 73; exegesis and historiography, 61, 74, 119, 124, 151, 198; removed from corpus, 62; rulings, 115; studies of, 118; verses of, 40, 45, 46, 58, 62, 70–1, 114, 118, 199, 200
Qurʾānic verses, 40, 45, 46, 58, 62, 70–1, 114, 118, 199, 200
Quraysh, 48, 50–1
Qurayẓah (Jewish clan), 64, 66–7, 75–6, 78, 79; incident, 66, 75, 78, 79, 82; trial, 77
al-Qurṭubī, 63–4, 65, 66, 81

rabbinic Judaism, 5–6, 143, 184, 195; emphasis on circumcision blood, 122; jurisprudence on divorce, 166; law, 10; orthodoxy, 184, 188; traditions, 81
al-Rāfiʿī, 72–3, 74
ransom divorce, 168, 190, 193
ransoming, 53, 54, 59–60, 63–4, 65–6, 69, 70–1, 72, 73, 75
ransoms, 50, 51–2, 54, 55, 57, 63, 64, 69–70, 71, 72
Rashi, 170
recalcitrant wife (*moredet* or *nāshizah*), 167, 169, 172, 173–4, 176–7, 183, 192
recycling, legal, 198, 199
religion, 9, 13, 90, 93, 98, 99, 103, 104, 108, 196
religious law, 89, 93, 98, 104, 207
Renan, Ernest, 90
Rishonim, 143, 170, 171, 180, 186
ritual, 105, 106–8, 120, 121, 122, 128, 133, 134
ritual law(s), 15, 97, 105, 106, 107, 205
Robinson, Chase F., 13, 29
Roman jurisprudence, 86
Roman law, 80, 87–8, 91, 93, 97, 103, 158
Rouland, Norbert, 139

Saʿīd bin Jubayr al-Ṣanʿānī, 59, 65, 75, 116
al-Sarakhsī, 74–5, 78
Sasanian, 14, 79, 148, 194; cultures, 94; law, 89; regions, 94
Schacht, Joseph, 22–3, 85–6, 87–8, 96, 97–8, 106, 138, 140
Schoeler, Gregor, 31
scholars, 34–6, 38, 39, 88, 89, 91, 92, 93–4, 98–9, 155; bibliographic, 36; critical, 99; modern, 11, 36, 37, 38–9, 95, 107; non-Western, 13; rabbinic, 143; Western, 13, 26, 92, 100
scholarship, 4, 12, 13, 18–19, 41, 85, 86–7, 93, 145–6, 206; academic, 206; animate, 87; contemporary, 37, 94, 98; conventional, 21, 24, 119, 140, 205; literary, 35; orthodox, 145; orthoprax, 146; revisionist, 94; unorthodox, 146
schools, 23, 132, 152–3, 154, 155, 157, 195; orthodox Sunnī, 70, 136; professional, 60. *see also* legal school(s)
secular, 10, 30, 93, 99, 206
secular law, 10, 98, 207
secularism, 11, 98, 207
Semites, 87, 90–1, 92, 93, 99, 104
The Semitic Conception of Absolute Law, 92
Semitic language in traditional comparative philology, 203
Semitic law, 91, 92–3, 98
Semitic origins, 89
Semitic societies, 92
Sezgin, F., 99
al-Shāfiʿī, 37, 67, 77, 127, 141, 144, 149, 151, 152, 154
Shāfiʿī jurists, 69, 70, 72
Shāfiʿī legal school, 67, 144, 152, 154
Shaybānī, 68
Sherira ben Ḥanina Goan, 186
Shīʿī, *see* Imāmī Shīʿī
sīrah (biography), 16, 28, 40, 141
Siyar Shaybānī, 68
source criticism, 19, 21, 23–4, 28, 30, 35, 36, 38
Spiegel, Gabrielle, 6, 35
subaltern, 39, 100
subalternize, 39, 98
Successors, 28, 40, 59, 62, 125, 144, 148
Sunnī legal schools, 67, 82, 137, 144, 147, 151, 152, 154, 157, 192; Ḥanafī, 67, 82, 137, 144, 147, 151, 152, 192; Ḥanbalī, 67, 144, 152, 154; Mālikī, 67, 144, 152, 154; Shāfiʿī, 67, 144, 152, 154

Sunnīs, 62, 67, 136, 138, 154, 156
Syria, 69, 75, 106, 113, 124, 127, 129, 152
Syriac Christian traditions, 101
Syriac philosophers, 109

al-Ṭabarī, 62–3, 64, 65, 66, 74–5, 115–16, 117, 118, 119; claims that Islamic version of Christian baptism is circumcision, 116; expounds an instruction to tie the bonds of a prisoner of war tightly lest he escape and cause harm, 64; mentions circumcision as a monotheistic obligation, 115; refers to Ḥasan al-Baṣrī's prohibition of prisoner executions, 60; refers to the imprisonment of Qurayẓah for breaking their truce agreement, 66; *Tafsīr*, 74
tafsīr (exegesis), *see* exegesis
Talmud, *see Babylonian Talmud*; and *Palestinian Talmud*
Talmudic practice, 171, 180, 182
Tam, Rabbeinu, 171, 187
temporary marriages, 192
Tertullian, 112–13
textual criticism, 12, 35–6, 38, 84, 98, 203. *see also* source criticism
al-Thawrī, Sufyān, 46, 60, 116
Tomlins, Christopher, xi
Toy, Crawford, 87, 92
tradition(s), 1, 20, 37, 40, 45, 59, 82, 84, 99, 117; Arabian Abrahamic, 198; biblical, 81; fusing pre-Islamic, 17; historical, 149, 193; oral, 40, 172; talmudic, 185; Western scholarly, 88
tradition-report(s), 28, 36, 39, 48, 57, 58–9, 63, 64, 70, 73, 75, 81, 98, 102, 114–18, 121–2, 124–6, 129, 131, 132, 146, 148, 159, 197, 202
Tunisia, 69, 112

ʿUbayd Allāh, 149
Uḥud, 50, 65, 72, 75
Umar ibn ʿAbd al-ʿAzīz, 60
Umar ibn ʿAbd Allāh, 48, 59, 63–4, 65, 71, 81, 174
Umayyad Empire, 25, 149; appointment of judges, 150; council of judges, 150; courts, 150
Ur-Recht (original Aryan law), 92, 93
Ustarūshanī, 130

Vansina, Jan, 35
Vesey-Fitzgerald, Seymour Gonne, 88, 92

Wahb ibn Munabbih, 130
al-Wāhidī, 63
al-Walīd, Khālid ibn, 52
war prisoners, 44, 53–5, 58, 59–60, 63, 64–5, 68–9, 74, 77–8, 200; enslaving of, 69; executing of, 16, 45, 53, 64, 67, 70, 71–2, 74; freeing of, 54, 57, 60; legal status of, 73, 80; treatment of, 15, 16, 43, 45, 52, 53, 61, 82, 201
Wasserstrom, Steven M., 101
Weberian myth, 10
Wegner, Judith Romney, 89
West, definition of, 13
Western Christianity, 11, 187–8
Western legal history, 92
Western legal practices, 172
Western rabbinic authorities, 172, 181, 184
Western Rishonim, 172, 186–8
Westreich, Avishalom, 187
White, Hayden, 147
wife-initiated divorce, 18, 162, 165, 174–6, 178, 179, 182–3, 188, 199, 200
wives, 171–2, 187, 189–90
wives, recalcitrant, 168–9, 170–1, 172, 180, 185, 192, *see* recalcitrant wife

Yemen, 40, 125, 130

Zoroastrian Arab tribes, 114
Zoroastrian(s), 95, 101, 102, 103, 107, 119, 132, 182